Beauty Matters

STUDIES OF THE WEATHERHEAD EAST ASIAN INSTITUTE,
COLUMBIA UNIVERSITY

STUDIES OF THE WEATHERHEAD EAST ASIAN INSTITUTE
COLUMBIA UNIVERSITY

The Studies of the Weatherhead East Asian Institute of Columbia University were inaugurated in 1962 to bring to a wider public the results of significant new research on modern and contemporary East Asia.

For a complete list of titles, see page 281.

BEAUTY MATTERS

Modern Japanese Literature and the
Question of Aesthetics, 1890–1930

ANRI YASUDA

COLUMBIA UNIVERSITY PRESS NEW YORK

Columbia University Press wishes to express its appreciation for assistance given by the Wm. Theodore de Bary Fund in the publication of this book.

Columbia University Press
Publishers Since 1893
New York   Chichester, West Sussex
cup.columbia.edu
Copyright © 2024 Columbia University Press
All rights reserved

Library of Congress Cataloging-in-Publication Data
Names: Yasuda, Anri, author.
Title: Beauty matters : modern Japanese literature and the question of aesthetics, 1890–1930 / Anri Yasuda.
Description: New York : Columbia University Press, [2024] | Series: Studies of the Weatherhead East Asian Institute, Columbia University | Includes bibliographical references and index.
Identifiers: LCCN 2023038842 (print) | LCCN 2023038843 (ebook) | ISBN 9780231210621 (hardback) | ISBN 9780231210638 (trade paperback) | ISBN 9780231558518 (adobe pdf)
Subjects: LCSH: Aesthetics in literature. | Art and literature—Japan. | Shirakaba School. | Japanese literature—20th century—History and criticism.
Classification: LCC PL721.A27 Y27 2024 (print) | LCC PL721.A27 (ebook) | DDC 895.609/004—dc23/eng/20231012
LC record available at https://lccn.loc.gov/2023038842
LC ebook record available at https://lccn.loc.gov/2023038843

Cover design: Chang Jae Lee
Cover image: Odilon Redon. *Bouddha dans sa jeunesse* (1905). Oil on canvas. The National Museum of Modern Art, Kyoto

For Chad, Yuzu, Beni, Stan

There is no answer that would convince someone who would ask such questions as "Why imitate something?" or "Why tell a story as if it were true when obviously the facts are otherwise and it just distorts reality?" Artworks fall helplessly mute before the question "What's it for?" and before the reproach that they are actually pointless. If, for instance, one responded that fictive narration can touch more deeply on the essence of historical reality than can factual reportage, a possible reply would be that precisely this is a matter of theory, and that theory has no need of fiction. This manifestation of the enigmaticalness of art as incomprehension in the face of questions of putatively grand principle is familiar in the broader context of the bluff inherent in the question as to the meaning of life.

—Theodor Adorno, *Aesthetic Theory*

Contents

Acknowledgments xi

A Note on Sources and Translations xv

ONE Modern Japanese Literature and Aesthetics 1

TWO Natsume Sōseki's Quest for "A Feeling of Beauty" 35

THREE Mori Ogai and the "Inner Flame" of Beauty 83

FOUR Mushanokōji Saneatsu and the Early Shirakaba's Artistic Cosmopolitanism 134

FIVE Akutagawa Ryūnosuke's Literary Anxieties and the "Power to Remake" 177

Epilogue: Why Aesthetics? 230

Notes 237

Bibliography 261

Index 271

Acknowledgments

THIS BOOK IS the product of years of reading, thinking, writing, and revising; these intellectual peregrinations were made possible by the many people and institutions I acknowledge here in gratitude. The seeds of my project were planted during my graduate studies at Columbia University where I met a cohort of delightful peers and extraordinary scholars. My dissertation advisors Tomi Suzuki and Paul Anderer patiently helped me to shape my interests and questions into viable research topics, and to begin to envision how my investigations could culminate in the form of a book. I view them both as role models for the critical insights and personal grace they have shared with me. Tomi Suzuki has continued to give me guidance beyond my years in New York, and I could not have finished this book without her ongoing mentorship and encouragement. At the University of Southern California, David Bialock and others I worked with as a Provost's Postdoctoral Scholar in the Humanities provided me with perspectives that inspired some of the arguments in this book. The faculty at The George Washington University, especially Young-Key Kim-Renaud and Shoko Hamano, were a source of kindness and support as I further developed my project and began my career as a teacher. My stays at Waseda University in Tokyo as a graduate student and later as an Exchange Scholar were fruitful, and Toeda Hirokazu graciously hosted me there on both occasions. The Japan Foundation sponsored me on a

ACKNOWLEDGMENTS

Japanese Studies Fellowship during my time as an Exchange Scholar at Waseda.

At the University of Virginia, my colleagues and mentors in my immediate department and beyond, especially Gus Heldt and Sylvia Chong, have shown me genuine care and goodwill as I brought my book to completion. I am lucky to find myself in such a vibrant and giving intellectual community. UVA's College of Arts and Sciences granted me a Sesquicentennial Research Leave that enabled me to complete my manuscript revisions. The publication of this book is supported by a grant from the Weatherhead East Asian Institute; UVA's Arts, Humanities, and Social Sciences Research Support Grant; and UVA's East Asia Center's Faculty Development Grant and Publication Grant.

Some portions of this manuscript have appeared elsewhere in print. Parts of chapter 3 were published in "The Multivalent Muses in Mori Ogai's Fictions" in the *Routledge Companion to Literature and Art* (Routledge, forthcoming in 2024). Parts of chapter 5 were published in "'Nagasaki' in Akutagawa Ryūnosuke's Taishō-era Literary Imagination" in *Shadows of Nagasaki: Trauma, Religion, and Memory After the Atomic Bombing* (Fordham University Press, 2023); and in "Endeavors of Representation: Visual Art and the Literature of Akutagawa Ryūnosuke," in *Japanese Language and Literature* 56, no. 20, October 2016.

The production of this book also entailed the efforts of various individuals at each stage. Ross Yelsey helped shepherd my project at the Weatherhead East Asia Institute. Haruo Shirane advised me on the publishing process. Christine Dunbar and Leslie Kriesel at Columbia University Press, and my copyeditor Mary Bagg, guided my manuscript to its finalized form. The anonymous readers for CUP made comments and suggestions that helped me to clarify and better organize my ideas. Over the years, my research benefited greatly from the assistance of wise and capable librarians.

And of course, I want to express my love and gratitude for my friends and family who were there for me throughout this endeavor. My time-tested friends AB, UC, SC, LG, JK, PL, PCL, SM, KS, RS, and AV have shared with me their empathy and verve. My mother, father, sisters, and my extended family in Japan, the United States, and elsewhere have offered me incredible patience and understanding. C's brilliance, humor, cooking skills, and love have buoyed and sustained me and our family unit; though you have done so with a smile, you have sacrificed so much so that I could

ACKNOWLEDGMENTS

complete this project. Y, B, and S, I am astounded by all the beauty and wonder you show me each day.

I sincerely thank everyone mentioned here and numerous others not listed.

And I acknowledge that the faults of this book are entirely my own.

A Note on Sources and Translations

THROUGHOUT THIS BOOK I have used an in-text parenthetical citation (including the abbreviated name, plus the volume and page numbers) for works included in the following four primary sources. I also include this list for reference at the start of the bibliography.

ARZ *Akutagawa Ryūnosuke zenshū*, 24 vols. Tokyo: Iwanami shoten, 1995–1998.
MSZ *Mushanokōji Saneatsu zenshū*, 18 vols. Tokyo: Shōgakkan, 1987–1991.
OZ   *Ogai zenshū*, 38 vols. Tokyo: Iwanami shoten, 1971–1975.
SZ   *Teihon Sōseki zenshū*, 28 vols. Tokyo: Iwanami shoten, 2016–2020.

All translations from Meiji (1868–1912) and Taishō (1912–1926) Japanese texts are mine except in cases where I quote from a published English translation. I quote from published English translations of works from this period only if the original text extensively uses classical Japanese syntax, vocabulary, and locutions, and I determined it best to rely on the established accuracy of the extant translations. For those works, I give the translated title as published and the citation for the English translation in an endnote. In such cases, I also give the citation of the Japanese original either in the body of the text if the quote is drawn from one of the four main primary sources listed above, or in the endnote if it is from a different source. For contemporary Japanese critical works that have entered Anglophone discourse in translated form, I quote from and cite their English translations.

Beauty Matters

ONE

Modern Japanese Literature and Aesthetics

BEAUTY MATTERS EXAMINES Japanese writers of the late Meiji (1868–1912) and Taishō (1912–1926) eras who devised an understanding of literature as a distinctive conceptual register, one that encompasses aesthetic ideals and longings fueled primarily by affect, as well as rational responses to worldly circumstances. In other words, their awareness of literature as art was as central to their creative ethos as their belief in writing's ability to critically engage with extraliterary realities. The authors I study in this book include Natsume Sōseki (1867–1916), Mori Ogai (1862–1922), Mushanokōji Saneatsu (1885–1976) and his peers at the *Shirakaba* (White birch) coterie magazine (1910–1923), and Akutagawa Ryūnosuke (1892–1927).

Referring to literature's unique epistemic breadth, in addition to the range of topics and perspectives that modern literary writing could take up as its content, Akutagawa declares in an essay collection titled *Bungei-teki na, Amari ni bungei-teki na* (Literary, all too literary, 1927): "I write novels because among all the arts, novels are the most capacious and I can throw anything and everything into them" (*ARZ* 15: 154).[1] But throughout *Bungei-teki na*—which I analyze at greater length in a later chapter—Akutagawa discloses how his faith in "literary" discourse's conceptual capaciousness was also undercut by his anxieties about literature's "all too" self-reflexive and artistic quality that keeps it ultimately apart from its subject matter, powerless to effect a measurable, real-world impact. The basic contours of this dilemma shaped each writer I analyze in this book: the duality of literature as a simultaneously aesthetic and critical endeavor served as a key theme in their literary explorations. Akutagawa's comment about how he chooses to write novels from "among all the arts" also expresses another crucial notion shared by these writers. They were keenly aware that literary writing is but one artistic avenue among multiple others, and they believed in an overarching notion of art that includes work across various mediums.

An Alternate Lens

Assessing Meiji- and Taishō-period literary figures through their views on art and beauty goes against the tendency of modern Japanese literary histories to be organized in terms of how writers have—or have not—positioned themselves in relation to their surrounding social and ideological contexts. As John Whittier Treat, citing the postwar Japanese critic Nakamura Mitsuo, has observed: "One problem plaguing Japanese literary historiography has been the belief that Japan's modern literature is radically *estranged* from context, and therefore, its history from contextualism."[2] Indeed, much extant scholarship shows an emphasis on Naturalism—deemed by Donald Keene, for instance, as "the mainstream of modern Japanese literature"—and its legacies of a particular brand of realism based on narrowly subjective perspectives.[3] In choosing as my subjects the canonically iconic figures of Sōseki, Ogai, Mushanokōji, and Akutagawa I do not imply that their inquiries into the aesthetic dimensions of literature formed a united and elite belletristic lineage that defied this discursively dominant current. Rather, I focus on what their diverse writings more actively underscore, especially when read alongside each other: that serious meditations on beauty entail reflections about one's navigation of the world as it apparently is alongside one's imaginations of how it could otherwise be, and that such lines of thought often exceed the insularity that purportedly dominated the literary episteme of late Meiji and Taishō Japan. Their texts demonstrate that thinking about beauty and art could illuminate other structures of meaning and feeling, and other positions and perspectives, that resonated broadly in modern Japanese society. I believe that works by all modern authors, regardless of how they have been previously categorized, can also be fruitfully interpreted through the lens of their aesthetic consciousness and put in dialogue with each other. After all, as literary practitioners, writers of all creeds and styles operate under the basic principle that literature is a specifically aesthetic mode of writing. Refuting Naturalism is not the goal of this book. It is, instead, to provide context for, and to clarify the aims and queries of, my own study that I review the received literary historical narratives.

Influential accounts of modern Japanese literary history have located its beginnings in the wake of the People's Rights Movement in the 1870s, when those who were sidelined from political participation established literature as a new arena of thought and activity independent from that of policy and governance.[4] It has been observed that literature came to represent a sanctuary for those like Kitamura Tōkoku (1868–1894) who had aspired to contributing to the political order of the Meiji era but turned to writing essays and poetry inspired by Western Romanticism as he became disillusioned with the consolidation of the new Japanese regime.[5] Tsubouchi Shōyō's (1859–1935) treatise *Shōsetsu shinzui* (*The Essence of the Novel*, 1885–1886), which stated that modern novelists should aim to "depict as they are (*ari no mama ni mosha*)" the "psychology (*shinri*)"[6] of their characters in order to "reveal what is hidden, define what is indistinct" about human nature,[7] is often credited for declaring the aims of the new literary enterprise for a young generation disaffected from public affairs.[8] Shōyō argued that modern novels should depict the complexities of imperfect human thoughts and feelings, and he castigated traditional narratives that attempt to impart moralistic lessons to readers via unrealistically idealized characters. Atsuko Ueda, who points out that *Shōsetsu shinzui* was retroactively granted its originary position in standard Japanese literary historical discourse by later critics, states that "literature came into being as an ontologically independent category" through the "defocalization of 'political' discourse."[9] Writings based on personal views and topics pointedly indifferent to broader social issues flourished over the ensuing decades.

Karatani Kōjin famously analyzed the turn to depicting psychic interiority in late Meiji Japanese literature by considering the formal conventions in Western landscape paintings, premised as they were on a fixed internal agent perceiving the external world.[10] Karatani suggests that Japanese people in the Meiji period came to grasp the perspectival basis of a discrete "self" through the representational practices of Western landscape paintings, and once audiences recognized this concept, its historicity became undiscernible as though the "self" been there all along as a naturally present subject. The result was that the Japanese Naturalist writers from the first decade of the twentieth century who chronicled the unglamorous details of their own quotidian lives—including their often banal or base thoughts—became celebrated for the apparently truthful expression of their inner selves. Tomi Suzuki notes that it was in the subsequent Taishō period when such works became labeled "I-novels" (*watakushi shōsetsu*) by commentators and journalists.[11] Suzuki explains that these pundits designed a "metanarrative"[12] of a cohesive univocal self as the central actor of modern Japanese novels and society, and they retrospectively formulated a literary genealogy that seemed to evince not the production but the a priori existence of such a subjectivity. The various texts that became classed as I-novels, whether older texts identified as such by later consensus or newer ones produced in awareness of this classification, generally narrate the private matters of the main character—presumed to be a direct facsimile of the story's actual author—and use a plain *genbun itchi* (aligning the oral and the written) linguistic style that gives the illusion of unmediated access to this character's innermost thoughts and feelings. Over time the I-novel came to be widely thought of as "the most salient and unique form of modern Japanese literature,"[13] the standard against which all other Japanese literary forms are produced and consumed.

But the limitations of this literary mode were already being noticed as critics were still attempting to codify and propagate it. Writing in 1919, Akutagawa Ryūnosuke summarized the Japanese literary world as follows:

> It is widely known that the Naturalists placed their literary ideals on the sole word of "Truth" (*shin*). The critical essay "Genjitsu bakuro no hiai" (The pathos of exposing reality, 1908) by Hasegawa Tenkei, who had been eminent at the time, eloquently attests to this. But like the saying "things change when cornered," as Tayama Katai's dominance over the literary establishment became an event of the past, a group of writers dissatisfied with the Naturalists' "Truth" let fly an opposing banner that took "Beauty" (*bi*) as its key word. This was the so-called Aestheticism (*yuibi shugi*) group, centered around Nagai Kafū following his return from abroad, that gained the support of the age. Most works by this group feature shades of hedonism or devilish decadence, or at least freely sporadic bursts of colorfulness. . . . Over time, in reaction to this, another new movement began to occur in a corner of the literary world. Interestingly, they

have anti-Naturalist traces too, but simultaneously, the group dedicates itself to "Virtue" (*zen*) and does not bow to the worship of "Beauty"; so things were such that within the great wave of anti-Naturalism, there arose two waves in opposite directions. Needless to say, the leader of this group was Mushanokōji Saneatsu. (*ARZ* 5: 179–180)[14]

Akutagawa's grasp of the varied terrain of mid-Taishō literature is notable especially since he was describing it in media res as a participant. After an overview of the decadent Aestheticist and idealist Shirakaba groups that arose in reaction to Naturalism's sincere if often dour realism, Akutagawa situates himself with what he calls the "New Technical Finesse" (*shin gikō-ha*) or "New Realism" (*shin genjitsu-ha*) group. He describes it as an amalgam of aspects of the two anti-Naturalist groups' respective pursuits of aesthetic virtuosity and humanistic virtues, as well as the realist spirit of the Naturalists (*ARZ* 5: 181). He explains that he and his peers attempted "to balance the concepts of 'Truth,' 'Beauty,' and 'Virtue' that have in turns reigned over the world of Japanese letters," and that "they feel more or less that human beings cannot rest if lacking any one of these elements. Hence, while their works cannot be said to be more serious than those of the earlier writers, it would not be an overstatement to say that they contain a richer quality" (*ARZ* 5: 181–182). That this new wave of writers had seen fit to blend what they deemed Naturalist and anti-Naturalist elements implies that they had regarded the category of Naturalism itself as an admixture of independent components. They rejected some of its characteristics, such as the endorsement of an unadorned vernacular writing style and the limitation of the narrative scope to the author's personal experiences, seeking a greater creative range in their own fictions. Yet they were inspired by the Naturalists' efforts to describe actual human lives and perspectives.

Akutagawa goes on to point out how the hedonistic Aesthetes for whom the portrayal of pleasure and beauty was the paramount aim of literature, and the Naturalists who aimed for honest confessions of their quotidian realities including their carnal appetites, in fact shared worldviews based in the physical realm. He also observes that despite the lofty idealism that had separated them from the materialist inclinations of the Naturalists, the Shirakaba writers shared with the Naturalists a flat writing style that emphasized authorial transparency and downplayed the mediating qualities of language as a narrative medium. For Akutagawa and his literary associates, the dynamic between what was called Naturalism and the various types of self-professed anti-Naturalist writings that followed was not a zero-sum contest between realism and artistic flair, or between a commitment to individual subjectivity and the depiction of wider sociocultural and ideological contexts. They instead understood it as a muddled mix of endlessly reconfigurable oppositions.

Of course Akutagawa and his peers were not the first modern Japanese writers to break away from the parameters of Naturalism or anti-Naturalism. Mori Ogai and Natsume Sōseki, whose respective styles belonged to no particular literary school, and who are often esteemed as the two most significant authors of the Meiji period, seem to present obvious examples. Yet even they were not entirely exempted from the critical benchmarks of Naturalism during their own lifetimes and in later evaluations.[15] As Takada Mizuho assesses them, "Ogai and Sōseki both embarked on their literary paths prior to the establishment of Naturalism, from a point removed from it, and they ended their careers without joining with Naturalism. So it is more correct to call their positions non-Naturalist than anti-Naturalist. We should understand their reactions against Naturalism—and they were, in this regard, anti-Naturalist—as reflective of how the Naturalists were, in fact, anti-Ogai and anti-Sōseki because of their fundamentally non-Naturalist stances."[16] That Ogai and Sōseki had supported the careers of younger writers who more actively identified themselves as opposed to Naturalism further complicates how these labels were applied to them. For example, Nagai Kafū (1879–1959), who headed the *Mita bungaku* magazine (first iteration, 1910–1925) and was named by Akutagawa as leading the decadent Aestheticism movement, and Kinoshita Mokutarō (1885–1945), who headed the *Subaru* magazine (1909–1913) and helped found the *Pan no kai* (1908–1913) salon for Aestheticist writers and artists, had both been Ogai acolytes, while the idealistic Shirakaba writers had regarded Sōseki as their spiritual mentor.

The hegemony of a literary critical framework based on the apparatus of a sui generis literary self was not just a Meiji- and Taishō-period phenomenon. To take one particularly influential case, the postwar intellectual historian Maruyama Masao reinforced the notoriety of the I-novel and its premises as the dominant force of Japanese modernity. His essay "Nikutai bungaku kara nikutai seiji made" (From carnal literature to carnal politics, 1949) posits the I-novel as representative of not just modern Japanese literature, but of a collective national psychic condition. Looking back at Japanese literature's trajectory over the previous half century, Maruyama writes:

> Despite its name, realism is just one "creative" (*sōsaku*) method, and realism is not just the unadorned depiction of the objects of our sensible perception. It is when reality appears not just directly, but as "mediated reality" (*baikai sareta genjitsu*) through the active involvement of the human psyche, that it can be called a "work" of fiction. So the psyche's power to synthesize becomes the decisive factor. However, in a place like Japan, where the psyche is not differentiated and independent from sensory nature ... the psyche's power to synthesize is weak, and fiction lacks an internal cohesion so that as a result, it is dragged about by random and disparate sensory experiences. Because readers for their part are unable to enjoy fiction as fiction, scandals sometimes arise from investigations into the [real-life] models behind fictional works. Ultimately, a sense of uncertainty about "invented matters" continues to overflow.[17]

Maruyama argues that the propensity to accept all phenomena at face value had led to Japanese people's inability to appreciate literature as a realm that could be acted on and "invented" by individual volition and effort. This literalist tendency, he suggests, also resulted in the prewar Japanese populace's political passivity that led to the nation's descent into totalitarianism. Writers' "power to synthesize" literary worlds, and readers' ability to "enjoy fiction as fiction" are theorized as essential for a properly democratic citizenry. In the essay "Fūzoku shōsesturon" (Theory on the novel of public manners, 1950), Nakamura Mitsuo too argues that with their self-centered perspectives, Japan's early twentieth-century I-novels had failed to depict the broader social dynamics against which protagonists could develop themselves as full-fledged individuals.[18] Echoing his prewar essay "Watakushi shōsestsu ni tsuite" (On I-novels, 1935), Nakamura laments the insufficient delineation of the "I" that anchored them. By assigning it the status of a problematic norm that had for too long directed a less enlightened era, and as such must be overcome in the project of national reconstruction, these critics equated the supposedly stable "I" subject driving the "I-novel discourse" with Japanese subjectivity itself, and the insular perspectives associated with Naturalism with the lack of a properly socialized, externally oriented sensibility.

Similar notions have also influenced Anglophone scholarship on modern Japanese literature and art. Notably, the modernist achievements of the 1920s and 1930s have been interpreted by researchers as explicitly or implicitly anti-Naturalist reactions to Naturalist norms. William J. Tyler, for one, calls the Japanese modernist writers of this period stylistically anti-Naturalist in that unlike their contemporaries who had insisted on the transparency of their language, they were "interested in the mediating effect that art exercises in recasting lived experience into narrative. Prose mediates experience, and the writer's task is to construct, shape, and manipulate his or her presentation of reality."[19] Many scholars have noted how the late Taishō and early Shōwa modernists were also iconoclasts beyond matters of style. Literary historians have identified the heterogenous perspectives and experimental linguistic forms that emerged in the novels of this time, viewing them as evidence of the writers' wish to transcend old literary confines and engage with the ideological fluctuations attendant to the intensification of imperialist nationalism and commercial mass culture, which colored all areas of life in Japan, especially in its growing cities.[20] These diverse accounts tend to suggest that modern Japanese literature before the advent of what might be called "high modernism" had been restricted to the private realm of the *literary* per se, whereas later writings more fully addressed the flux of modern life and thus redefined the parameters of literature.

For instance, Seiji Lippit writes: "The formalist negation of interiority, which I trace through various writers and different contexts, provides a framework for analyzing modernist writings as a whole." He observes: "The concept of interiority can be seen as defining the parameters of an individual as well as a national subjectivity, and it links the formalist resistance against the language of *genbun itchi* to a broader representation of modern culture. The formalist externalization of the literary text as a material writing irreducible to any interiorized consciousness is translated in modernist writings into a focus on heterogenous urban topographies."[21] Brian Hurley also notes that it had come to seem to interwar Japanese writers and thinkers that "language and narrative, memory and perception, all seemed to have fractured under the strain of the discontinuities borne by the destabilizing experience of 'modern life.'"[22] Such analyses suggest that a bounded, continuous notion of literary subjectivity had prevailed until later writers deemed it insufficient as the basis of modern experiences and targeted it for rupturing.

I do not contest the insights revealed in such excellent studies, especially regarding how heightened uncertainty concerning the ability of previous artistic practices to depict the volatility of modern existence catalyzed the flowering of theoretical and stylistic innovations in Japan, as elsewhere, in the 1920s onward. But I do want to guard against conferring a logical stability and monolithic solidity to Meiji and Taishō comprehensions and formal representations of modernity that the ensuing generations creatively sought to refute. I argue instead that in these earlier periods too, there were major writers already aware of the porousness between "literature" and "nonliterary" contexts. And I propose that this was in fact an inalienable, formative tension for these writers. I aim in this book to uncover how Natsume Sōseki, Mori Ōgai, the Shirakaba cohort, and Akutagawa Ryūnosuke had envisioned this fluctuating dynamic. I do so less by evaluating how they actively adhered to or deviated from the tenets of subjective interiority that had allegedly defined the literary episteme of their era, and I emphasize instead how they navigated the aesthetic resonances of literature. To some extent, of course, these writers grappled with the paramount modern literary theme of a self as delineated against others. In the following chapters I analyze how each author attempted to triangulate their judgments of beauty as the expression of an intrinsic subjectivity, as well as a conduit for communing with others who shared their aesthetic sentiments.

The Question of Aesthetics

Some context is necessary to explain how I use the term "aesthetics" in this book, for in casual usage it can be a nebulous signifier that covers much ground. And in philosophical discussions, aesthetic judgment has been regarded as a perennially challenging topic because of what amounts to a logical disconnect inherent in its workings. As many thinkers have outlined, assessments of beauty are divorced from any interest beyond beauty itself; they have no empirical standards and are ultimately a matter of subjective taste. Yet they operate on the presumption of universality. They therefore remain distinct from conventional reason. In the words of

Immanuel Kant: "The judgment of taste, with its attendant consciousness of detachment from all interest must involve a claim to validity for everyone, and must do so apart from a universality directed to objects, i.e., there must be coupled with it a claim to subjective universality."[23] The ambiguity of claiming an incontrovertible worth for what is effectively a personal feeling often stymied the writers in this study as they attempted to balance their felt aesthetic convictions and their critically reasoned expositions. Beyond the individual level too, the paradox of "subjective universality" complicated the writers' regard for Japanese sensibilities as culture-specific and rooted in history, yet also attuned to the supposedly universal principles of the worldwide modernity they felt themselves to be a part of.

Throughout this study, I refer to aesthetics as the gamut of affectively led responses of individuals toward things and phenomena they deem beautiful which thus stand in a disinterested yet somehow compelling relation to them, compounded with their understanding that such judgments of beauty are subjectively universal. Steve Odin summarizes this calculus in terms of "artistic detachment" in his study of Japanese and Western philosophy and literature. He finds that in Western philosophy since Kant's *Critique of Judgement* (1790):

> Under such designations as "artistic detachment," "aesthetic contemplation," "psychic distance," "dehumanized art," "intransitive attention," "tranquil recollection," "alienation effect," "resignation," "stasis," "will-less-ness," "isolation," "framing," "equilibrium," "synaesthesis," "objectification," "symbolization," and "letting-be," the Kantian idea of beauty grounded in a disinterested attitude has come to occupy a central place in modern aesthetic theory.... A detachment theory of art and beauty grounded upon the disinterested attitude is to be found, for example, in Shaftesbury, Moritz, Kant, Goethe, Schiller, Schopenhauer, Heidegger, Bergson, Ortega y Gasset, Wordsworth, Bullough, Stolnitz, I. A. Richards, Ingarden, Polanyi, Santayana, C. I. Lewis, Prall, Münsterberg, Langer, Beardsley, and other aestheticians—to mention just a few of the preeminent thinkers in this tradition.[24]

As for the Japanese side, he outlines: "Traditional aesthetic ideals in the Japanese canons of taste—such as *aware* (melancholy beauty), *miyabi* (gracefulness), *yūgen* (profound mystery), *ma* (negative space), *wabi* (rustic beauty), *sabi* (simplicity), *fūryū* (windblown elegance), *iki* (chic), and *shibumi* (elegant restraint)—all contain an element of detached resignation. The detached contemplation of beauty as a means to enlightenment was central in the Japanese Buddhist religio-aesthetic tradition of *geidō*: the *tao* (or way) of art."[25]

As this précis shows, in Japanese and Euro-American cultures alike, aesthetic experiences have long been understood to occur on a plane apart from physiological needs, pragmatic interests, or moral imperatives. Odin explicates this model of contemplative distancing through reference to Eastern and Western philosophical theories and works of literary fiction. But he attends more to encounters with beauty that are characterized by emotional dispassion than how, in the words of one Kant scholar, "the relation involved [between an observer and an aesthetic object] is not a neutral one, as in a standard cognitive judgment, but one that engages our entire subjective being as rational and sensitive creatures in a way that is both active and passive.... In an aesthetic respect we thus enjoy a special kind of disinterested interest in the object in so far as it affects us in a certain way."[26] "Disinterested interest" supposes that judgments of beauty carry an unavoidable affective charge regardless of the extent to which we strive to maintain impartiality toward the object under consideration. Beauty might be considered an element toward which people cannot be truly indifferent, a quality that moves us "in a certain way" whether we plan to act on these intuitive evaluations or not. The many literary examples ahead—and I conjecture that for most of us, episodes from our own lives—show that in aesthetic experiences, the function of one's judgments in response to the things or people we deem beautiful is more consequential than the consciously neutral nature of such judgments. That is, even if what beauty incites in the beholder is nothing so crassly direct as a move to possess the object of beauty, it stokes, as Elaine Scarry puts it, a "willingness continually to revise one's own location in order to place oneself in the path of beauty."[27] It becomes a matter of actively managing aesthetic assessments of, and potential orientations toward, the beautiful thing or person in question. The writers in this study recognized this and knew that beauty has the power to impact how one navigates reality. They believed in literature's ability to activate aesthetic affects in readers that might then, in some way, influence their observable future actions. They saw literature, and the arts at large, as operating in the liminal space between the subjective and objective, and the ineffable and the effable.

In contrast, the focus on the hard minutiae of individual experiences seen in Naturalism and its offshoots leaves out the more fluid, expansive potentials of the aesthetic sentiments stirred by literature. This positivist orientation[28] was already manifest in Shōyō's *Shōsetsu shinzui*, the aforementioned essay lauded for declaring literature an autonomous, worthwhile enterprise in modern Japanese culture and for establishing the discursive insistence that individual subjectivity serve as its proper grounds. Shōyō announces that "as art in itself has no practical use, one expects its 'aims' (*mokuteki*) to be only to give enjoyment to the heart and eye (*shinmoku wo tanoshimashimete*), and to achieve a sublime beauty (*myōshin*)."[29] This shows Shōyō's expectation that literary portrayals would please readers and strike them as beautiful, and also signals an indifference to uncovering the workings of this cognitive process. There are no explanations as to why or how we are moved by artistic representations of the world—let alone in the psychologically realist modes Shōyo endorses—although the allusion to "the heart and eye" gestures at a link between sensory stimuli and affective responses. Furthermore, the invocation of "sublime beauty" valorizes an abstract, absolute ideal that is not contingent on observable local and temporal variables. Setting as art's highest goal a disconnect from the evolutions of style and taste suggests that literature should refrain from attempting to engage with the ever-changing contexts surrounding individual interiority, its sole proper domain.

Shōyō also proffers that "the novel reveals what is hidden, defines what is indistinct, and brings together all man's innumerable passions" so that the reader is led to "reflect (*hansei*)"[30] on human nature, but he does not expound on the intended outcome of such reflections. The implication is that such instances of contemplation are self-evidently desirable for their own sake. He declares: "To arouse in the beholder by its sublime beauty emotions so profound that his spirit seems involuntarily (*shirazu shirazu*) to soar is [art's] proper objective, and that is what makes it art. To beget nobility by its elegance and integrity, by the excellence of its concepts, so that man's nature is bettered in the process, is an incidental effect and not its true aim."[31] The crucial point is that the "soaring" of emotions itself, rather than any socially useful moral or intellectual "betterment" that might ensue, is championed as the express role of art.

Although beauty is posited as the desired goal of art and literature, just stating that an experience of beauty results from human encounters with art and literature marks an endpoint in Shōyō's exposition. While tacitly acknowledging beauty's adjacency to the grandeur of the sublime, he does not attempt a more substantive explication of such ideals that transcend the sphere of private consciousness. Aesthetic concerns occupy a vague position in Shōyō's literary doctrine. He conjectures that beauty is experienced at the individual psychic level in the form of "soaring emotions," but his conspicuous lack of commentary on this process—or on beauty's metaphysical implications, or on beauty's capacity to inspire its beholders to take external actions—indicates a hesitance about claiming beauty as a topic for full appraisal. Perhaps he recognized that in seeming to belong solidly to neither the subjective interiority that he claims as literature's true precincts nor to the extraliterary realms beyond the self's immediate awareness, the subject of beauty threatened the distinctions between "inside" and "outside" that gird his conceptual system.

A binary view of literature—as committed to the nuances of the internal affective experiences of an individual *or* to social and material concerns external to the self—was not unique to modern Japan. The recent rise of "postcritical" scholarship has found that for the past half century or more, North American and European literary and cultural studies have been dominated by a drive to uncover a text's connections to external sociohistorical conditions. As Elizabeth S. Anker and Rita Felski describe it, across a range of scholarly disciplines in the humanities, "criticism" became the dominant conceptual stance in the latter twentieth century. Criticism in this specific sense is marked by "a diagnostic quality" and "the belief that such scrutiny will bring problems to light that can be deciphered by an authoritative interpreter."[32] Psychoanalysis, Foucauldian New Historicism, Marxism, and ideologically backed efforts such as by feminists and advocates of various minority groups are named as examples of the impulse to view literary forms as mirrors of underlying sociopolitical realities for intellectual excavation and analysis. But with the spread of deconstructivist thought in the 1970s and 1980s, these interpretive approaches were "accused of imposing false unities and hierarchical structures onto literature," and skepticism turned to the very practices of language and reading.[33]

Anker and Felski state that the critical gaze has since become even more aimed at itself, giving rise to metacritiques about the role and purpose of critical endeavors. Citing Bruno Latour's words that criticism may have undermined itself and "run out of steam," they declare that a "postcritical" turn is now underway in some sectors of academe.[34] Indeed, we have seen in recent decades a resurgence of research into topics that were previously bypassed in the scholastic treatment of literary texts primarily as expedient pathways to uncovering sociopolitical issues, such as the phenomenology, affective responses, and neural biology that shape human encounters with literature and art. The number of academic studies published on the aesthetic dimensions of literature continues to grow.[35] Anker and Felski suggest that critique's "shift away from suspicion may conceivably inspire a more nuanced vision of how political change comes about."[36] In this new vein, by curbing some of its mandate to transform the social world through exposing the stamp of ideology in literary and cultural texts, critique could begin to examine the more organic ways in which literary and cultural works circulate in public life. I believe this means that giving credence to the aesthetic dimensions of literature need not result in a retreat into myopic decadence, and could instead affirm more productive possibilities for literature's social impact that consider its affective properties.

The Japanese writers of a century ago that I examine in the following chapters contended with questions and hopes strikingly similar to the ones confronting contemporary Western scholars: Is the beauty, and not just the practically applicable insights, of literature worthy of critical interrogations, and why? How does literature influence our ways of interfacing with the extraliterary world? I hazard that Sōseki, Ogai, the Shirakaba writers, and Akutagawa would have agreed with Felski's declaration that "the false picture created by such dichotomies . . . is at issue: the belief that the 'social' aspects of literature (for virtually everyone concedes it has some social aspects) can be peeled away from its 'purely literary' ones. No more separate spheres!"[37]

Multiple Mediums and the Overarching Notion of Art

In their attempts to articulate modern literature's unique properties, the subjects of this book were especially inspired by the discourses of the visual arts that were also undergoing major transformations spurred on by the influx of Western artworks and theories in the late nineteenth to early twentieth centuries. Many Japanese writers in this period were interested in the pictorial arts. Pairings between Western-style imagery (*yōga*) and works of literature written in new modes can be spotted in as early as Nagahara Shisui's illustrations for Tsubouchi Shōyō's novel *Tōsei shosei katagi* (The character of contemporary students, 1885–1886) (figure 1.1), a work through which Shōyō tried to embody the psychological realism that he described as the essence of literary modernity in *Shōsetsu shinzui*.[38] Collaborations between *yōga* artists and writers flourished. Images by pioneering *yōga* painters like Asai Chū and Koyama Shōtarō were featured in the *Shin shōsetsu* magazine (second incarnation, 1896–1925) from its earliest issues. In 1900, the poet Yosano Tekkan (a pseudonym used by Yosano Hiroshi, 1873–1935) founded the *Myōjō* magazine. It gained prominence as a meeting ground—not only for writers of Romantic sensibilities like Tekkan, his wife Akiko, Kitahara Hakushū, and Kinoshita Mokutarō, but also for

FIGURE 1.1 Nagahara Shisui, illustration from Tsubouchi Shōyō's novel *Tōsei shosei katagi* (Portraits of Contemporary Students, August 1885, published by Banseidō) National Diet Library Digital Collection

yōga painters like Kuroda Seiki and Kume Keiichirō known for their Impressionistic styles, as well as for Fujishima Takeji and Ichijō Narumi, who were heavily influenced by the Pre-Raphaelite and Art Nouveau styles. For these turn-of-the century Japanese writers and painters, of prime concern was how, and what it meant, to represent anything amid major changes in sociocultural norms and artistic practices. Sōseki, Ogai, the Shirakaba writers, and Akutagawa focused this abundant creative energy to confirm the characteristics unique to their chosen artistic medium of modern Japanese literary language: What could literature signify that visual images could not? Or conversely, were visual images—in their lack of words—a purer distillation of the ineffable essence of art?

The notion of ekphrasis is useful for judging how writers handled different artistic mediums in their quest to identify what made literature special, and also what literature shared with the other arts. As a rhetorical concept, ekphrasis, from the Greek *ek* (out) and *phrasein* (to speak), designates the verbal description or evocation of an artwork or artistic processes in another medium, most often in the visual arts. Theories of ekphrasis have a long history. In Western culture they can be traced back to the Roman poet Horace's coinage of the notion *ut pictura poesis* (as is painting, so is poetry) as articulated in his *Ars Poetica* (ca. 20–10 BCE),[39] and in Asian traditions to the Song Chinese notion, attributed to the painter Su Shih (1037–1101), that there is "poetry in painting and painting in poetry."[40] At the heart of ekphrasis is the idea that both the literary and visual arts strive to invoke aesthetic sentiments, but that they are not interchangeable. Theorists on the subject have pointed out that ekphrastic writings take the fact of interartistic incommensurability as their starting point, and that aesthetic questions pertaining to both are contemplated in the tensions revealed between images and text. As Stephen Cheeke writes:

> Almost all theorists of ekphrasis emphasize the paragonal aspect of the mode, or "the struggle for dominance between image and word." But what, we might ask, are they struggling over? In what sense, in what activity, do they wish to dominate, out-do, or eclipse each other? At the heart of this lies a philosophical question that goes back to Plato: the problem of representation.... If every thing or object in the world is already a copy of an ideal and unchanging form or essence beyond the world (every bed is merely a single copy of a template of

"the bed"), then every artistic representation of that object will constitute a copy of a copy. It follows that a verbal description of a work of art produces a copy of a copy of a copy.... At such a remove from the ideal Platonic form or essence, verbal description seems a poor substitute, a meagre thing hovering somewhere at the back of a queue to shake hands with "reality." And painting seems to be ahead of poetry in this queue. Painting is a "natural sign" and therefore closer to the object-to-be-represented than the arbitrary or non-natural sign system of language.[41]

We can posit that Japanese writers of the late Meiji and Taishō periods could also not have been unaware that language seemed to lag behind visual images in the pursuit of lifelike representations, especially given the rise of the mediums of photography and oil painting. Photography had been introduced to Japan by the mid-nineteenth century, and albeit in a limited capacity, the visual realism achieved by European oil paintings had been known in Japan through imported books and artifacts even during the Edo period when foreign contact had been strictly regulated. In 1861, the Gagaku-kyoku (Office of Western Painting) was established as a department within the Edo shogunate's Bansho Shirabe Dokoro (Institute for Western Studies), which was opened in 1855, two years after the arrival of the US commodore Matthew Perry's steamships in Uraga Bay. The stated aim of this institution had not been to expand new horizons of artistic development. Rather, the ability to create accurate visual representations was considered a practical skill needed for mapmaking, drafting, and other areas of modern naval defense.[42] From the 1860s onward, pioneering oil painters like Takahashi Yuichi (1828–1894), who had studied at the Bansho Shirabe Dokoro, and others like Goseda Hōryū (1827–1892), came into first-hand contact with Western paintings and photographs at the port hub of Yokohama. Some enterprising individuals like Shima Kakoku painted portraits based on photographs and photographed models posed like painted figures.[43] Such overlaps between painting and photography show that an appreciation of realist painting as a distinctive genre of artistic expression—as a discipline with aims beyond the accurate rendering of surface appearances—was still inchoate.

An iconic intersection between the two mediums of painting and photography in this period is the portraiture of the Meiji emperor (1852–1912).[44] In 1872, Uchida Kuichi took the first photograph of the then nineteen-year-old monarch in formal Japanese court dress, followed by another image of him, in 1873, wearing Western military attire. In 1879 Takahashi Yuichi was commissioned by the Genrōin (the Meiji Senate) to create a life-sized oil portrait of the emperor. Takahashi's painting was based on a smaller painting executed in 1878 by the Italian painter Giuseppe Ugolini in Milan, which had been based on Uchida's 1873 photograph. Takahashi's portrait is thought to be the first likeness of the emperor to have been shown to the Japanese public. And after the promulgation of the Imperial Rescript on Education in 1890, another photograph of the monarch was disseminated to all schools in the nation. This image—which became revered as the embodiment of the emperor's living divinity and a potent visual symbol of imperial Japanese unity—was not a direct photograph of the emperor, but a photograph of a portrait that the Italian artist Edoardo Chiossone had painted in 1888. By this point, the realist capacities of Western painting seem to have become accepted as on par with that of photography. The insight that even photographs are not an entirely neutral record and that photography is an independent art would become central to the rise of the Pictorial style in photography, which utilized techniques such as soft focus and pigment printing unique to the medium, in the first decades of the twentieth century.[45]

Kinoshita Naoyuki explains that in less official capacities, the general Japanese public had initially encountered Western-style paintings as optical curiosities to ogle for their strange realism.[46] As early as 1874, before the advent of museums, galleries, or art schools, Japan's first generation of Western-style painters displayed their work in "oil painting teahouses" (*abura-e jaya*). In stark contrast to the solemn and silent air of today's art museums, these establishments followed the lowbrow, carnivalesque traditions of the spectacle exhibit (*mise-mono*), complete with a raconteur who provided a spirited narrative to accompany the scenes and figures on display. Also popular in this period were paintings of battlefield scenes, as well as large-scale dioramas, panoramas, and peep-box devices showing foreign landscapes and architectural sites. These attractions were marketed as resources for informing viewers about current events and the wider world. In a period when the concept of the fine arts was still nascent, the realism of Japan's first Western-style paintings seems to have been broadly perceived as a means for entertainment and education, not for aesthetic contemplation.

Kanbayashi Tsunemichi claims that naming the nation's first institution dedicated to the teaching and research of Western art as the Kōbu Bijutsu Gakkō (Technical Arts School) when it opened in 1876 underscores how the skills required for realist visual representations were still regarded as a type of utilitarian technology in the first decade of the Meiji era.[47] Scholars like Omuka Toshiharu have shown that the processes by which the notion of "art" came to gain currency in Japan were gradual.[48] Omuka writes: "Roughly speaking, alongside the shift from the Chinese model of *shoga* (ink paintings and calligraphy) to the Western model of *bijutsu* (art), the objects of viewership and the venues for this (from *shoga* meetings and connoisseurship events to public exhibitions) changed as well as—of course—the position of the artist. Viewing audiences themselves were also thus reconfigured and had to be reestablished or nurtured in order to modernize."[49] My study suggests that late Meiji- and Taishō-period literary writers' involvement with the visual arts, and their investment in the notion of an overarching concept of "art" spanning various mediums, played a part in advancing this sprawling, circuitous shift in cultural cognizance.

Though at times prurient, the public interest in the capability of Western oil paintings to achieve a hitherto unmatched level of visual mimesis likely served as an incentive for late Meiji writers to search beyond realism in their quest to establish modern literature's ability to compete against the visual arts in representational prowess. Japanese literature's turn toward psychic interiority can be read in light of these comparisons; even *Shōsetsu shinzui* bears the imprint of interartistic contemplation. Early in the treatise, Shōyō refers to Ernest Fenollosa (1853–1908), an American lecturer at Tokyo Imperial University. Fenollosa became an influential defender of the traditions of the Japanese visual arts against the threat of their being overshadowed by the spread of Western art. In his famous 1882 lecture titled "Bijutsu shinsetsu" (A theory on the truth of art), he argued that the aim of art is the expression of truth and beauty through manifesting the essential idea of the object being depicted—not the mechanical imitation of the object's outer appearances—and that Japanese art was better suited for this task than Western art.[50] Along with his Japanese supporter Okakura Tenshin (a pseudonym used by Okakura Kakuzō, 1863–1913), Fenollosa is known for propagating the modern notion of *bijutsu* (fine art) in Japan and for coining the classifications of Western-style *yōga* paintings versus Japanese-style *nihonga* paintings.

In the opening paragraphs of the first segment of *Shōsetsu shinzui*, Shōyō paraphrases the statement "it is clearly a thing's beauty that makes it art," from Fenollosa's "Bijutsu shinsetsu," and follows it with his own claim: "to arouse in the beholder by its sublime beauty emotions so profound that his spirit seems involuntarily to soar—that is its proper objective, and that is what makes it art."[51] Shōyō then delivers his central point that novels, as art, should produce an affective impact on readers via the portrayal of their characters' human psychologies rather than give readers direct moralistic prescriptions via the depiction of unrealistic inventions. He then muses: "The ancients, in speaking of a poem as a verbal picture, were lauding the ability of poetry to open our eyes to the details of those things not easily seen or painted—and nothing in the world is harder to capture on canvas than man's passions. A superficial portrayal of joy, anger, love, malice, grief, fear, or greed presents no particular difficulty, but it is more than a painter can do to plumb their depths."[52] Apparently relying on Fenollosa's Hegelian notion of core Platonic ideas that lie beneath surface phenomena, Shōyō suggests that the medium of literary language is more suitable than visual images for signifying the deeper, more meaningful essences of human nature.

In the following chapters I evaluate how each writer strove to distill the particular qualities of literature as an artistic medium through stories that feature visual artists as main characters, or give ekphrastic descriptions of works of visual art. In evoking visual artworks by means of linguistic descriptions, the writers sought to test and organize the linkages and the differences between the two art forms. Such stories also reveal the writers' aesthetic visions as extending beyond exclusively literary-linguistic terrain. One effect of this sense of artistic inclusivity was that it fostered for some the expectation that the beauty of visual artworks, no matter their origins, could be "read" and enjoyed at an intuitive level without the mediation of contextual knowledge. This implied that even a foreign artwork could be appreciated without a dedicated effort to learn the stylistic conventions and the historical backgrounds that gave rise to it. In chapter 4, about Mushanokōji Saneatsu and his peers at the *Shirakaba* coterie magazine, I examine more closely this hardy strain of aesthetic cosmopolitanism and the sociocultural climate that fostered it.

MODERN JAPANESE LITERATURE AND AESTHETICS

For all their varying attitudes about the specificity or fungibility of an artwork's medium or its cultural foundations, the subjects of this book shared the assumption that writers and visual artists—as well as their audiences—are motivated by a core aesthetic will. They were invested in philosophical questions as to what makes something a work of art, and how people recognize and take pleasure from artworks as such, in addition to pragmatic questions about the empirically observable impacts and goals of artistic pursuits at the personal and societal levels. To address their concerns, it is thus helpful to consult theories that attempt to define art along both metaphysical and functional lines. For example, in *Aesthetic Theory* (1970), Theodor Adorno writes:

> Art, however, is social not only because of its mode of production, in which the dialectic of the forces and relations of production is concentrated, nor simply because of the social derivation of its thematic material. Much more importantly, art becomes social by its opposition to society, and it occupies this position only as autonomous art. By crystallizing in itself as something unique to itself, rather than complying with existing social norms and qualifying as "socially useful," it criticizes society by merely existing, for which puritans of all stripes condemn it.[53]

Adorno acknowledges that artworks are produced through social processes and take social conditions as their material, but he contends that they are defined as art by eschewing any "socially useful" functions. Following Kant, he posits aesthetics as independent from the dictates of reason and social conventions. But he states that art carries social meaning in that the unsocial presence of artworks pushes audiences to ponder the possibility of alternatives to current social conditions, and to envision how the world might be otherwise configured. It follows then, that "[modern] art has become the ideological complement of a world not at peace," and it would "amount to the sacrifice of its freedom were new art to return to peace and order, to affirmative replication and harmony."[54] Adorno recognizes a diagnostic element in modern art's apparent apartness from society, but he does not explicitly task art with exhorting people to bring about "peace and order." He concludes that, paradoxically, it is because of its apartness from society that art has the special ability to shed a clarifying light on it.

Adorno further proposes that art can foster critical interventions in the world because its central "truth content" requires not just affective surrender but intellectual interpretation. He explains:

> The truth content of artworks is the objective solution of the enigma posed by each and every one. By demanding its solution, the enigma points to its truth content. It can only be achieved by philosophical reflection. This alone is the justification of aesthetics. Although no artworks can be reduced to rationalistic determinations, as is the case with what art judges, each artwork through the neediness implicit in its enigmaticalness nevertheless turns toward interpretive reason. No message is to be squeezed out of Hamlet; this in no way impinges on its truth content.... Artworks, especially those of the highest dignity, await their interpretation. The claim that there is nothing to interpret in them, that they simply exist, would erase the demarcation line between art and non-art.[55]

Whether this means that aesthetic experiences are ultimately subsumed by rational reflections—or that reason can approach an absolute truth content that transcends it—that any "solution" or answer as to how artworks captivate their audiences is offered at all infuses a vitality to inquiries that proceed under this model. By declaring a line between art and "nonart" that is determinable by reflective reason, Adorno suggests a critically substantive path into determining how people process artworks and aesthetic experiences. I discuss in chapter 2 how Sōseki's literary treatise *Bungakuron* (*Theory of Literature*, 1907) presents an analogous attempt to systemically draw the borders between literary thought and scientific reason.[56]

Still, Adorno's proposition of the "truth content" of an artwork involves an elusive chimera. He declares that it amounts to more than a social commentary or message intended by the artist, or a timeless mystical essence that remains external to the artwork itself. In Adorno's words: "Just how little the truth content converges with the subjective idea, with the intention of the artist, is evident to the most rudimentary consideration. There are artworks in which the artist brought out clearly and simply what he wanted, and the result, nothing more than an indication of what the artist wanted to say, is thereby reduced to an enciphered allegory. The work dies as soon as philologists have pumped out of it what the artist pumped in, a tautological game whose schema is true also of many musical analyses."[57]

According to this schema, appreciating an artwork is not solely about deducing its allegorical lessons, or mechanically deciphering the correspondences between representations and their real-world models. The full meaning of an artwork is experienced as the sum of the intellectual and affective responses to the artwork's formal qualities, its subject matter, and the sociohistorical contexts in which it is created and assessed. In that such an ineluctable truth content is a dense and cumulative effect that obtains beyond the artist's conscious intentions, the artist's work might be understood as a matter of channeling it as well as generating it.

This is a cursory and partial view of a complex thought system, but my goal is not to forcibly graft Adorno's aesthetic theories unto the literary oeuvres of Meiji and Taishō period Japanese authors. I suggest, in a broader sense, that the subjects of my study intuitively determined that there does exist some productive kernel of meaning—akin to "truth" in Adorno's parlance—that their critical activities as writers and readers could hope to consciously aspire toward, even as they accepted that literature is an artistic undertaking and aesthetics operate on a register qualitatively apart from rationally discernible logic. The result was that these writers perceived their intellectual interpretations of literature's relation to the social and material conditions around them, and their personal aesthetic-affective responses to literature, as a rich dialectic.

Worth noting too is that Sōseki, Ogai, Mushanokōji, and Akutagawa were not just theorists who sought to demystify aesthetic sentiments and critically articulate their causes and effects. They were also literary artists who tried to invoke the pleasures of beauty and artistic truth content in their own stories and essays. They serve as rejoinders to what an English-language translator of Adorno's *Aesthetic Theory* aptly calls the "generally recognized failing of aesthetics—its externality to its object—that Barnett Newmann once did the world the favor of putting in a nutshell when he famously quipped, speaking of himself as a painter, that 'aesthetics is for me like what ornithology must be like for the birds.'"[58]

Adorno's quote in the epigraph of this book captures the fraught nature of the conceptual crossing required between aesthetic experiences themselves and the nonaesthetic work of explicating them. When he writes that artworks—and metonymically, the artists who create them—"fall helplessly mute" before demands that they logically explain and justify art, we take this not as the hesitation of uncertainty but rather as a frustrated silence reflecting the resigned knowledge that nothing can be said to enlighten those who do not already comprehend what is at stake. Adorno likens such questions about art's meaning to the disingenuous "bluff" inherent in questions about the meaning of life. That is, if we sincerely grasp the type and scope of the thing being asked, we cannot actually expect a concrete, logical answer that would suffice. Similarly, art cannot be adequately explained through exclusively nonartistic means; it would require being at least provisionally inside of artistic understanding to meaningfully ask and answer such questions. The modern Japanese writers who debated their way through aesthetic inquiries were thus remarkable for also having been artists who at their best operated squarely within art's "engimaticalness." They were, to extend Newmann's analogy, both birds and ornithologists.

Japanese Modernity

The uneasy relationship between art and its place in, or beyond, worldly matters can be thought of as a hallmark of modern literature at large. As the mid-twentieth century British literary critic Frank Kermode observed: "The special fate of the novel, considered as a genre, is to be always dying; and the main reason for this is that the most intelligent novelists and readers are always conscious of the gap, consisting of absurdity, that grows between the world as it seems to be and the world proposed in novels."[59] The contradictory condition of modern literature is that it is understood as fictional and aesthetic, but it is also expected to deliver meaningful knowledge about the human condition and the world we live in. This double bind stokes cries of alarm among the cognoscenti about the decline of literature's artistic quality and its slipping cultural significance. It also steers discussions at the wider societal level about the "good" of literature and other disciplines that belong under the broad tent of the humanities, especially as the costs of higher education rise, and universities are pressed to justify the pursuit of disciplines that do not deliver immediately practical results. Late nineteenth- to early twentieth-century Japan, where rapid sociocultural and political changes occasioned an especially explicit and intense questioning about the premises and aims of "literature," "art," and "modernity," makes for an apt context in which to think through these ever-pressing themes. The writers of Meiji- and Taishō-period Japan who attempted to promote literature for rather than despite its aesthetic dimensions faced pushback from those who, like some present-day skeptics of literary studies, expected tangible benefits from reading and writing fictional stories. I return briefly in the epilogue to the issue of literature's shifting location within the wider terrain of knowledge.

But the cultural climate of Japan in the late Meiji and Taishō eras was also markedly different from that of Japan or anywhere else in today's globally interconnected commercial-and-cultural world of late-stage capitalism. Despite the deep cross-cultural awareness often attributed to them (especially in the cases of Sōseki and Ogai), and their reputations for progressive cosmopolitanism (especially in the cases of the Shirakaba writers, and Akutagawa), the subjects of this book maintained a constant understanding of themselves as Japanese as they consumed foreign texts and visual images. This meant that their enthusiasm for other cultures was buoyed by the belief that Japan was already, or at least well on track to becoming, as materially and culturally advanced as its Euro-American rivals. This confidence was also tempered by their acknowledgment of Japan's position as a late, non-Western arrival to the imperial world order. Mass cultural conceptions of Japanese-ness were evolving throughout the Meiji and Taishō periods, and each writer's search for his identity as a Japanese individual was conducted against rapidly changing sociohistorical circumstances.

To review, Western incursion had been a definitive factor for the post-Tokugawa administration inaugurated under the Meiji emperor in 1868. The Meiji oligarchs quickly realized and promoted the practical need to learn about Western technologies, ideas, and institutions in order for Japan to survive in the newly international age. With the development of a popular press and the circulation of translated books by authors such as John Stuart Mill and Jean-Jacques Rousseau, as well as works by home-grown intellectuals like Fukuzawa Yukichi, Enlightenment ideals of personal freedoms and social progress spread. Over the following decades, as the nation industrialized, admiration for Western ideas clashed against antiforeign sentiment among a Japanese populace that was more educated than ever before. Even after the establishment of a political system that limited active political participation to a small, elite segment of the population—which, as we saw earlier, had apparently served as the basis for the depoliticization of the emergent discourse of modern Japanese literature—the nationalistic energies stoked by the People's Rights Movement ran high in public culture, and they were channeled into state-backed efforts to unify and fortify the nation.

Domestic and international dynamics were especially bound to each other in the question of territorial boundaries, the affirmation of which was directly linked to sentiments of national cohesion and to policy decisions about strategic development. Early in its founding, the new Meiji government therefore sought to lay down a boundary to the north of Hokkaido. Despite the logistical commitment of resources and the assumption of responsibility for its defense and administration, Akira Iriye assesses that "for reasons of prestige" Japan laid claim to the Kuril Islands chain.[60] In 1875, a treaty affirming this arrangement was concluded between Russia and Japan; among the Japanese populace it met with popular acclaim since "it was the first significant settlement with a Western power in which Japan had been treated like an equal and had not been forced to make humiliating concessions."[61] Japan also sought to redefine its relations with Korea, which during the Tokugawa regime had maintained a tributary bond with China and a secondary arrangement with Japan's Tsushima domain. Using the same sort of gun-boat diplomacy exercised by the Perry expedition in Japan nary two decades earlier, in 1876 Meiji representatives forced the Korean kingdom to sign a treaty that granted treaty ports and consular rights. The Japanese public celebrated this as evidence of the nation's growing international prestige. Then in 1879, following protracted negotiations with China, Japan also formalized its claims over the Okinawa Islands, which during the Tokugawa period had a tributary relationship with the Satsuma domain and the Qing court. As the Meiji state consolidated its rule at home with the promulgation of the Meiji Constitution in 1889 and the inauguration of elected party politics with the first Diet in 1890, it was spurred on by an expansionist sentiment. Japan's victory in the Sino-Japanese War (1894–1895), and the Russo-Japanese War (1904–1905) gained it control over Taiwan, the southern half of Sakhalin Island, and most of Russia's former rights in Manchuria. And in 1910, Japan officially annexed Korea after declaring it a protectorate in 1905.

Japan's position in world geopolitics thus shifted dramatically during the Meiji era, by the end of which it had become a fully entrenched player in the imperial struggle for influence in Asia. But many could not deny the nagging awareness that these developments had been "externally motivated" (*gaihatsu-teki*), as Natsume Sōseki famously articulated in 1911 (*SZ* 16: 448).[62] Over the course of the nation's transformation, at turns with resentment and with admiration, most Japanese people came to regard the imperial Western nations and their values as representing the inevitable path of progress. Yet the voices that questioned this trajectory and pondered the possibility of more organically Japanese modes of historical development became louder following the so-called Great Treason Incident of 1910 when the government executed socialist activists for an unsubstantiated plot to assassinate the emperor. The incident—which I revisit in chapter 3 about Mori Ōgai, who had served as an unofficial advisor for the legal defense in the case against the socialists—catalyzed Japanese intellectuals of multiple orientations to soberly reflect on the ideological directions of their nation and the seeming deficiency of political consciousness on the part of the citizenry.

To the Euro-American gaze, Japan's swift rise in the international arena presented something of a conundrum. As Grace Lavery argues, Japan was seen as an "Other Empire" that did not conform to the Orientalist frameworks through which Westerners had been accustomed to viewing the lands they were colonizing.[63] Citing Victorian comments about the "exquisite" beauty of things Japanese, Lavery observes that "by the 1870s, Japan appeared to have outstripped Western cultures in its production of objects universally recognizable as beautiful. According to some of the strongest formulations of that position, Japan had not merely approached but already attained the position of universal aesthetic legibility—a development that threatened Euro-American power."[64] That is to say, even before the Meiji regime had cemented its control of domestic politics and developed an industrialized economy, and before the nation attained a position of prominence in world affairs through its imperialist actions, "Japan" represented for certain Western connoisseurs an artistic realm that incited delight alongside a degree of discomfort. Christopher Reed also states: "Japan's marginality to the eighteenth-century Orientalism undergirding the Victorians' confident worldview allowed Japanism, its novelty untapped, to figure so centrally in a second wave of Orientalism, which upended Victorian self-confidence through challenges to fundamental Western ideas about the nature of representation, truth, and civilization itself."[65]

As Lavery tells it, there was more to this Western sense of unease than the cognitive dissonance between Japan's status as a contender in the imperial race for control over territory, resources, and influence, and the perceived inscrutability of its culture that produced disarmingly charming objects. Appreciating the beauty of things Japanese seemed at first to assuage the uneasiness inherent in the notion of the "subjective universal" surmised in Kant's aesthetic thought: "When we call something beautiful, the pleasure we feel is expected of everyone else, just as if it were to be regarded as a property of the object.... But beauty is nothing by itself, without relation to the feeling of the subject."[66] The subject/object slippage that occurs in apprehensions of beauty—the obfuscation of whether a sense of beauty is generated by the viewing subject, or inherent in the viewed object, which I have previously discussed as the logical aporia inherent in aesthetics—allows for the illusion that what is a solitary and subjective aesthetic experience is in fact owing to the presence of universally detectable qualities. But through interpretations of Japanese-inspired Western cultural productions from the late nineteenth century into the present, Lavery demonstrates the limits of such a fantasized sense of subjective universality; in her words, Western depictions of Japan tend to be "stories in which people *believe* that they can experience a 'common feeling' with another human being through an aesthetic medium, and find that belief cruelly rebuffed."[67] Although failed connections obviously also occur between people of the same culture, cross-cultural misunderstandings shine a particularly harsh light on the possibility that the relativity of tastes and affective orientations is predetermined at a mass structural level surpassing individuality, indicating the constructed nature of what are generally assumed to be primary human essences.

My readings of the Meiji and Taishō authors' views of Western cultures echo the basic structure of this paradigm. After all, Japanese people of this era generally approached Western literatures and artworks with the hopeful assumption that they would be able to commune with these works through some shared element of humanity, and then be able to productively incorporate the lessons they gained into their own lives. And in the texts I analyze—as in so many others in the modern Japanese literary corpus—literary protagonists found these expectations diffused as they kept sensing their inability to fully adopt worldviews rooted in Western Enlightenment values founded on a central notion of the individual self. This resulted in varying degrees of anxiety or resignation. Crucially though, the Victorian-era aesthetes' celebration of Japanese art as seeming to affirm a universalist order of beauty that would negate one's melancholic sense of finitude functioned on the presumption that Japan was an "eccentric" place, "a uniquely—but somehow inconsequentially—modern empire."[68] "Japan" tended to be regarded as pleasantly minor by Europeans and Americans because of its pronounced alterity to Western cultural and ethnic norms, and this resulted in its general image as a realm to be accessed aesthetically rather than via more consequential confrontations of a mercantile or military nature. In contrast, the Japanese thinkers of this era did not perceive Europe and America as minor or "eccentric" since the West and its logics, including its cultural codes, were understood as the defining center of the imperial, capitalistic universe. "The West" functioned as a symbolic construct in this conception.

As a result, from the late nineteenth into the early twentieth centuries, Japanese intellectuals' study of Western art and literature was seen within broader cultural conversations not merely as a decadent retreat into an aesthetic sanctuary away from pressing local social and political matters that demanded their attentions, but as a valuable entry into Western mindsets that were widely accepted as advantageous to master. This belief was manifest in the first two decades of the twentieth century through the popularity of the "self-cultivation" (*kyōyō shugi*) ethos that encouraged elite Japanese youths to achieve an elevated, humanitarian sensibility of cosmopolitan tastes and knowledge through the study of Western literature and art. In his best-selling essay collection *Santarō no nikki* (Santarō's diary, 1914–1918), Abe Jirō, who was celebrated as a representative of this trend, stated: "Those that have a just sympathy for, and a wide knowledge and deep understanding of, the thought and lives of the people of the past and present encounter at every turn thought and lives that resemble, and even surpass, those of themselves. Thus, they do not proudly parade about their cheap individuality.... How am I to create a new life by rejecting the thought and lives of Plato, Saint Paul, Saint Augustin, Saint Francis, Spinoza, Kant, Goethe, Schopenhauer, Nietzsche, Rodin?"[69] Abe argues that there is a timeless knowledge to be found in great books of the past, and that his readers would be able to better develop their full potential as human beings through studying these works rather than through unmediated experiences alone. Crucially, the "people of the past and present" from whose writings he recommends that his young Japanese audience cull wisdom about how to live are all Europeans. Besides Abe, writers such as Watsuji Tetsurō and Kurata Hyakuzō were also seen as key figures in this intellectual movement, but there was no unified group that self-identified as the "self-cultivation school" at the time, for this was a categorization defined by postwar scholars.[70] Among others, the writers featured in this study—especially Mushanokōji Saneatsu and his Shirakaba peers in their reverent fervor for Western visual art—too have been seen as proponents of the literary and artistic cosmopolitanism endorsed in the name of "self-cultivation."

However we retroactively delineate it, there is agreement that "self-cultivation" in the sense that Abe and his peers had formulated it had passed its heyday by the tail end of the Taishō period. As Abe himself recalls, by around 1923 he had heard that among the younger generation, "the term *kyōyō* had grown moldy and had no power to pull at people's hearts anymore."[71] By the end of the 1920s, socialist perspectives pervaded the cultural climate in Japan, and the aesthetic universalism exemplified by *Santarō no nikki* and the *Shirakaba* magazine was coming to be dismissed as naïve, bourgeois decadence. Famously, the Marxist critic Miyamoto Kenji described the suicide of Akutagawa Ryūnosuke in 1927 as symbolic of the ultimate "defeat" of a politically effete aestheticism.[72] Although Akutagawa's work shows a tendency for idealism and a sprawling knowledge of Western art and literature, I show in chapter 5 that he had also been attuned to the ideological conditions of his specifically Japanese milieu, and he had been more self-conscious of his own status as a bourgeois writer than Miyamoto suggested.

Overall, my analyses underscore how the authors I have selected calibrated their optimism about the universal significance of art with an awareness of modern Japanese literature's distinctive characteristics as an artistic medium, and Japan's evolving position in the global geopolitical and artistic-cultural world orders. Their views were also guided by their parallax understanding of literature-qua-aesthetic as attuned to the sphere of subjective sentiments, as well as to vaster horizons beyond the self in terms of how beauty might inspire individuals to function in the wider world, and how beauty might lead to a communion with some transcendental spiritual plane. Throughout, my intention is to affirm how writers navigated these multilayered themes and queries, rather than to definitively taxonomize how they charted these intersections.

Chapter Outlines

Each subsequent chapter in this book focuses on an author—or a group of authors in chapter 4—who sought to broaden the conceptual and stylistic horizons of modern Japanese literature through their commitment to aesthetics and beauty as topics of sustained investigation. For these writers, literature represented a space that could supersede the insular perspectives that—according to prevalent historiographical accounts—had shaped the orthodoxies of their eras. And in doing so, literature served them as a platform for new ways of picturing themselves and the world around them. These writers did not present themselves as members of a joint endeavor despite their often-complementary logics, and I focus on each writer's literary-philosophical developments as an arc with its own contexts and cohesions.

Natsume Sōseki is the subject of chapter 2. I begin with a reading of *Bungakuron*, the 1907 treatise in which the author attempted to clarify the goals and meaning of literature through the objective terminology of modern scientific logic. This effort, doomed and quixotic in retrospect, led Sōseki in his subsequent writings to emphasize the prominence of literature's aesthetic elements that elide such quantified approaches. *Kusamakura* (1906) and *Sanshirō* (1908) can be seen as test cases for his commitment to literary aesthetics. Both novels depict male protagonists who view the enigmatic heroines they are attracted to through the vocabulary and techniques of visual arts as they struggle to balance a dispassionate admiration for their muses' beauty with their budding emotions. My interpretations of these texts draw on Sōseki's reliance on the artistic method of *shasei* (sketching from life) that he learned from the haikai poet Masaoka Shiki (1867–1902), who in turn was influenced by the visual artistic discourse of *yōga*, or Western-style painting, which aligned with European concepts, materials, and techniques. I also consider Sōseki's knowledge of scientific advancements and his awareness of changing conditions in Japanese society. My readings reveal that Sōseki's attempts to define literature were shaped by twin concerns for the artistic pursuit of beauty and a critical awareness of the contemporary world around him, a posture that is shared and developed by the other writers selected for this study.

In chapter 3, I evaluate how, perhaps reflecting the bifurcation in his own life as a medical doctor by day and literary writer by night, Mori Ogai's earliest essays and fictions were driven by the adamance that literature be guided by aesthetic concerns while raw, empirical depictions of nature remain the province of science rather than art. His early German-trilogy stories illustrate this binary view well. Ogai supported his literary stances with his knowledge of German idealist philosophies, from which he eventually veered away as he came to accept the blurring of the borders between art and lived experiences. His later writings, particularly those featuring painters in quotidian situations, show the concessions he made and the aesthetic beliefs he retained. The vast scope of Ogai's eclectic thought is especially remarkable in that we can trace its full flowering within the literary sphere. To wit, rather than further aligning himself with the discipline of philosophy that attracted him ever since his student days, or with the field of art criticism that he had remained engaged with throughout his career, or with the policy-oriented arena of statecraft he witnessed in his career as an elite bureaucrat and doctor in the Japanese Army, Ogai chose to explore his metaphysical, artistic, and ethical questions primarily as a literary writer.

Chapter 4 opens with an overview of the failed 1911 effort led by Mori Ogai to form an association of writers from the four leading non-Naturalist literary magazines of the day and the negative reactions of the aristocratic writers based at *Shirakaba* (1910–1923) magazine, who espoused individual connections with transcendentally humanistic artistic values unmediated by local Japanese associations. Through the early stories published in their coterie magazine, I examine the Shirakaba writers' goal of realizing their full personal potentials as human beings and literary artists along universalistic standards, even as it meant overlooking the plight of disadvantaged people in their immediate Japanese society. They couched the optimistic pursuit of their best selves in ethical terms, and their unapologetic spiritual and artistic ideals separated them from the Naturalists' somber realism, although the primacy of the individual subject was a feature of both groups. The Shirakaba writers' attraction to Western visual art, especially the paintings of the Post-Impressionists, further heightened their cosmopolitan aspirations. But my readings of their stories and essays also emphasize how the Shirakaba members' seemingly blithe conjunction of self, humanity, and art were also enmeshed in selectively intentional dismissals of the social and material elements of modern Japan that they hoped to surpass; a current of pragmatic realism had underpinned their celebrated idealism. Mushanokōji Saneatsu, the spokesman of the group, is the main subject of this chapter, which also includes analyses of texts by other key members of the coterie such as Shiga Naoya (1883–1971). I have decided against examining in this book the anti-Naturalism of the so-called decadent Aesthetes (*yuibi-ha*)—a group that, according to Akutagawa's aforementioned 1919 overview of the Japanese literary world, had produced works such as Ueda Bin's "Uzumaki" ("Whirlpool," 1910), Suzuki Miekichi's "Kotori no su" (Bird's nest, 1910), and Tanizaki Jun'ichirō's "Shisei" (Tattoo, 1910) (*ARZ* 5: 180)—although many literary histories acknowledge them as a corollary to the Shirakaba group's anti-Naturalist idealism. This is because their artistic philosophy to elevate the expression of beauty above all else does not fit with this study's focus on writers who had seen literature as committed to the pursuit of aesthetics *and* to the critical acknowledgment of extratextual realities.

Akutagawa Ryūnosuke is the subject of chapter 5. To quote from his 1919 essay again, he had identified himself as part of the "New Realism" (*shin genjitsu-ha*) or "New Technical Finesse" (*shin gikō-ha*) group that drew on the anti-Naturalist Aesthetes' pursuit of aesthetic experiences, the anti-Naturalist Shirakaba writers' humanistic idealism, and the Naturalists' realism, to create literary works of "a richer quality" than those of their predecessors (*ARZ* 5: 181–182). Despite the confidence displayed in this early-career self-assessment, throughout his life Akutagawa remained conflicted about literature's relation to the world. He reveled in literature's dual capacity to engage with modern realities and to transcend them via artistic imaginations, but he also lamented literature's ontological apartness from its subject matter qua art. For example, Akutagawa remained ambivalent about embracing a free-floating, universalist perspective despite his popular image as a representative of the Taishō period's spirit of cosmopolitan erudition. His fictions drew expertly from a broad range of literary texts across cultures and time periods. But he also offered somber assessments on the epistemic upheavals and the possibility of failed understandings that accompany occasions of cross-cultural contact. I close the chapter with a consideration of the idea of "poetic spirit" that Akutagawa arrives upon as the essence of literature shortly before his suicide. It speaks to a mode of abstract thought that verges on the logically impossible.

Throughout this book, Japanese names are given in the Japanese order with the surname first. Sōseki and Ogai are usually referred to by their pen names rather than their surnames. When referring to Sōseki, Ogai, Mushanokōji and the other members of the Shirakaba group, and Akutagawa, I use he/his pronouns. It had not been my original intention to write exclusively about male writers from elite backgrounds, but I realize in retrospect that in tracing the formation of a modern literary thought in terms of a dialectic between aesthetics and more concrete worldly concerns, I had delineated a group of socially privileged individuals who could conceive of the issue in this way. By definition, an appeal to the intangible precincts of aesthetics—unquantifiable judgments of taste that are subjectively experienced but claim self-evident value—implies a mindset that can look beyond material and political exigencies. In other words, although the freedom of aesthetic imaginations is what makes literature accessible to all, to contemplate questions of beauty on par with questions of ethics and actions requires an initial sense of social enfranchisement unavailable to those in more precarious positions. It was because the writers in my study were highly educated men of relative economic means in a patriarchal society, and because they perceived themselves as participants in the critical currents of their environments, that they could begin to envision what else lay beyond matters pertaining to their immediate welfare. So while the maleness of these writers was intended as a less overt issue in this study of their literary formations than their Japanese-ness, it nonetheless serves as a fundamental premise for the creative and ideological choices they made. And in the following chapters, I do consider the authors' gendered perspectives and self-images, particularly when I analyze how they depicted the dynamics between male artists and their female muses, a dynamic that appears frequently in their stories. It could perhaps also be said that the writers' recognition of the power of aesthetics as a vital foil to the dominant regimes of analytical reason implied their fundamental willingness to question the social status quo, and that this tendency disposed them toward more progressive views of gender than was prevalent in their milieus. But I will reserve this topic for future investigations.

TWO

Natsume Sōseki's Quest for "A Feeling of Beauty"

NATSUME SŌSEKI DESCRIBED *Kusamakura* (1907) as a "haiku-novel" concerned with depicting select scenes of intense beauty rather than a "conventional" novel that gives a sustained, informative account of a subject across time.[1] Indeed, there is little in the way of plot as its first-person narrator, an unnamed painter from Tokyo, enjoys an extended stay at a rural hot spring resort in the mountains where he indulges in meandering conversations with a mysterious, beautiful woman named Nami. But it would be inaccurate to claim that nothing happens in the story, and that the world of the story remains beautifully frozen. Details about Nami's complex background and persona begin to emerge. The narrator makes an active decision to end his hiatus and return to the city by the conclusion of the novel. He also manages to resolve the artist's block he had been suffering from. *Kusamakura* thus suggests a willingness on Sōseki's part to rethink the premise of an artist's serene separation from the flux of the world around him, a notion based on the so-called *shasei* (sketching from life) philosophy that he had upheld since beginning his literary career under the influence of Masaoka Shiki's *haikai* poetics. In the novel *Sanshirō* (1908) Sōseki further dismantles this stance of artistic reserve, and he signals a readiness to engage more fully with the complexities of modern life via his literature. I begin this chapter with an analysis of Sōseki's earlier idealization of literature as a realm of beauty set apart from the stress and strife of human society by assessing his *shasei*-inspired views and his attempts to define literary thought against scientific thought in his *Bungakuron* (*Theory of Literature*, 1907) treatise.² I then present close readings of *Kusamakura* and *Sanshirō*, both of which feature male characters who attempt with mixed results to interpret their female love interests through perspectives gleaned from the visual arts. I highlight how the theme of beauty had figured centrally in Sōseki's early literary thought, and particularly how his comparison of the inherent properties of the literary medium versus the pictorial one shaped his conceptual trajectories.

The "Unhappy" World

Sōseki's stay in England from 1900 to 1902 as a government-sponsored scholar of English literature and language had been notoriously miserable. It was not just as a result of his meager pecuniary circumstances that these were "two of the unhappiest (*fuyukai*) years of my life" (*SZ* 14: 12), as he later put it. He felt himself an utter outsider in England. Upon his arrival, the fast pace of the sprawling city unnerved and disoriented him, as he recalled later in the short story "Rondon tō" ("Tower of London," 1905): "Thinking I might be swept away in a human wave when I went outside, and fearing that a steam train might come crashing into my room when I went home, I had peace of mind neither day nor night.... The steam trains, carriages, electric railways and cable railways that crisscross like a spider's legs the wide city of London were unable to provide me with any convenience whatsoever. When I arrived at a crossroad I had no choice but to open up the map and decide, while being pushed back by passersby, in which direction to turn my feet" (*SZ* 2: 3).³

He also keenly felt his racial otherness, as he disclosed in letters to his friend Masaoka Shiki, a *haikai* poet. Shiki shared Sōseki's messages from abroad with the wider public under the title "Rondon shōsoku" ("Letter from London," 1901) in *Hototogisu*, a magazine that he ran with his poetry students. One segment in Sōseki's missive reads: "When I was in Japan I knew I was not particularly white but regarded myself as being close to a regular human color, but in this country I have finally realized that I am three leagues away from a human color—a yellow person who saunters among the crowds going to watch plays and shows.... Two or three days ago I was invited out somewhere and set off in my silk hat and frock-coat only for two men who seemed like workmen to pass by saying, 'A handsome Jap.' I do not know whether I should be flattered or offended" (*SZ* 12: 14).[4]

And in a letter sent from London to his father-in-law, Nakane Shigekazu, Sōseki expressed his shock and dismay at the social inequities he saw around him:

> The failure of civilization in Europe today is clearly because of the extreme gap between the rich and the poor. I lament that the inequality causes many who could be productive (*jinzai*) to starve or freeze to death, or to end up without any education. . . . If we tend toward the same conditions in Japan (and I believe we are presently tending toward them) it will be very important to develop the literacy and intelligence of our laborers. Although I believe that Karl Marx's theories have some faults, even as pure hypotheticals, it is quite natural that such teachings should appear in a world like our present one. (*SZ* 22: 273)[5]

This cumulative sense of deracination contributed to Sōseki's crisis of conscience regarding his professional path as a Japanese scholar of English literature, and the meaning of studying literature at all. This catalyzed him to embark upon an ambitious project to describe the nature of literature in scientific, hence universal, terms. He developed as a result the mathematical notation "F+f" to explain literature as "a compound of cognitive factor F ('large F'), and the emotional factor ('small f')" (*SZ* 14: 27).[6] Although he judged that "it remains an unfinished work—and it cannot but remain incomplete" (*SZ* 14: 12),[7] in May 1907 he published the fruits of his research in the sprawling treatise titled *Bungakuron*. By this time, Sōseki was installed in a prestigious position as a professor at Tokyo Imperial University, and the *Bungakuron* was based on his lecture notes for the course he taught there on English literature. In its oft-cited preface, Sōseki explains how he came to question the fundamental premises of "literature" because he was confounded by his perception of the contrast between the works of classical Chinese literature he had grown up reading and remained fond of, and the works of English literature he had elected to study as an adult but felt estranged from.[8] He muses: "For my sense of like and dislike between the two to be so widely divergent despite my having roughly equal scholarly abilities must mean that the two were of utterly different natures. In other words, what is called 'literature' in the realm of the Chinese classics and what is called 'literature' in English must belong to different categories and cannot be subsumed under a single definition" (*SZ* 14: 8).⁹ During this formative time, Sōseki had been as invested in identifying the elements that accounted for the divergent ideals of each type of literature, as much as the qualities that obtained universally across the Asian and English contexts. Assorted notes he took while in London survive today as the *Bungakuron nōto* (Bungakuron notes). In it, he wonders: "Given Japan's current state, what must a literature that helps Japan's progress be like, as compared to the West?"¹⁰

The tendency to compare Asian culture and society to that of Europe, and the assumption that all pursuits should assist in the nation's collective progress, seem to fit the Meiji era's general optimism about Japan's future prospects on the world stage. But Sōseki had in fact been quite ambivalent about his country's trajectory. As Michael K. Bourdaghs points out, Sōseki was critical of the new regimes of property and wealth emerging with the growth of industrial capitalism, and "in his literary writings he again and again relativized the increasingly dominant position of that form [of society organized around private ownership] by probing its lacunae and by situating it in relation to other possible models."¹¹ Money troubles and inheritance struggles abound in Sōseki's novels. And even before he began writing fiction, he had been aware of the toll that class differences imposed on human relations. Tellingly, in his epistle to Shiki from London, he wrote: "Sometimes I find myself hating England and desiring quickly to return to Japan. But then again, when I reflect on the state of Japanese society, I feel it to be pitifully unpromising. Japanese gentlemen (*shinshi*) are, I fear, extremely lacking when it comes to their moral, physical, and artistic education. How nonchalant and self-satisfied our gentlemen are! How foppish they are! How inane they are! How satisfied they are with modern Japan, and how they continue to lead the ordinary populace to the brink of degeneracy!" (*SZ* 12: 3–4).¹²

Sōseki's dissatisfactions with modern life were rooted not in his judgments about Western civilization and an elegiac longing for traditional Asian values, but rather in his negative view of all humanity as prone to selfishness and disregard for others that, if left unchecked, would lead to the disenfranchisement of socially vulnerable individuals by those with greater means. He knew that Japanese "gentlemen" were as susceptible to corruption and arrogance as their English counterparts. In the *Bungakuron* he admits that leaving England did not resolve the sense of unpleasantness he suffered there, and that "the three and a half years following [his] return to Japan were also an unhappy (*fuyukai*) three and a half years" (*SZ* 14: 13).¹³ It is impossible to pinpoint the exact roots of his dark outlooks although his unstable upbringing, during which he was shuttled between the households of various family members and purportedly neglected at times, lends itself to retrospective conjectures. In any event, by the time Sōseki was a young man, his worldview was plagued by a sense of malaise. As a student he had disclosed in a letter to Shiki: "Recently, I've come to dislike for some reason this world of transient human concerns (*ukiyo*). No matter how I evaluate and reevaluate it, I just can't stand it. But I lack enough courage to commit suicide. Maybe this is because there is still a bit of humanity left in me" (*SZ* 22: 22).¹⁴ In another letter, he called himself a "misanthropic pessimist after all" (*yahari ensei shugi nari*) (*SZ* 22:48).¹⁵ Living in England did not cause Sōseki's skepticism about human nature, but seemed to confirm it.

Perhaps Sōseki's existentially grim assessments of the *ukiyo* drew him to Shiki's *haikai* ideals, especially regarding Shiki's advocation of a placid, artistic remove from the fluctuations of the surrounding world. As early as 1891, Sōseki had declared to Shiki that he too had "awakened to the way of *haikai*" (*haidō hosshin*) (*SZ* 22: 33).¹⁶ But their artistic bond was not cemented until 1895, when Shiki went to recuperate from his tuberculosis symptoms in Matsuyama, the city where Sōseki began his first full-time teaching job. During this time Shiki developed the basis of his subsequent poetic theories and styles, and Sōseki dedicated himself to composing haiku under his friend's tutelage. Shiki also left a major imprint on Sōseki's later endeavors as a novelist; Sōseki even published his debut novel *Wagahai wa neko de aru* (I am a cat, 1905) initially as installments in the *Hototogisu* magazine, whose members he kept in touch with after Shiki's passing. The work narrates the goings on of an English teacher, his scholarly friends, and his family members through the perspective of his nameless cat, a sardonic and bemused observer of human affairs. It was a commercial and critical success. When it was published as a standalone novel in 1906 Sōseki added a preface dedicating it to Shiki, underscoring the ties between them.

Shiki articulated his literary views in the *Nippon* newspaper in 1898:

> In general, the distinct charm of poetry (*uta*) comes from its position beyond the ethical judgments of good and evil. It comes from looking down on the swirling detritus of the common world from above the clouds. Whereas ethics is

on the side of recommending virtue and punishing evil, poetry does not say whether something is good or bad. It only quietly shows the merry things and peaceful places that exist. Whereas the people of the world may chase after fame and fortune, suffer from carnal appetites, and run like maniacs around tiny plots of land [that comprise their spheres of activity], the poet alone looks on from a remove, frolicking with the flowers and breathing in the pure air of the unlimited expanse of the natural world.[17]

This statement calls for the narrative perspective's lofty reserve from quotidian affairs and its clearsighted apprehension of reality that would become central to Shiki's signature aesthetic concept of *shasei* (sketching from life). His acolytes would continue to debate the notion after his death. For Sōseki, the tension between an artistic apartness from his subject matter and a focused attention to it looms especially large throughout his early literary thought and fictions, as he gradually developed his own inimitable views about literature's role in the modern world and its ability to make things seem a little less *fuyukai*.

Aimless Elegance

Shiki received inspiration for his *shasei* approach to writing from realist *yōga* painters like Nakamura Fusetsu (1866–1943) and Asai Chū (1856–1907), so it is not surprising that visuality became a prominent characteristic in Shiki's, and later in Sōseki's, literary imaginations. *Shasei* was a translation for the Western visual artistic concept of sketching, and Fusetsu explained the concept in an essay from August 1894 for the *Nippon* newspaper where he and Shiki both worked: "*Shasei* aims to portray real scenes, but what is the fun in portraying real scenes lacking picturesque appeal? A complete painting is produced only with the technical capabilities of sketching from life (*shasei jutsu*), and the discovery of picture-worthy scenes."[18] Shiki adapted this painterly method to the composition of haiku by identifying it as a two-step process: first, the discovery and observation of depiction-worthy elements of nature through a discerning aesthetic sensibility and, second, the faithful recording of his impressions through language. The essay "Meiji 29 nen no haiku-kai" (The haiku world of 1896) shows the extent to which Shiki conceived of paintings and poems as parallel art forms rooted in targeted observation followed by realistic presentation. Shiki praises poems that "make a clear impression," and claims that reading such works affects readers in "virtually the same way as seeing realistic paintings (*shasei-teki kaiga*)."[19] To illustrate this concept, he cites several haiku by his disciple Kawahigashi Hekigotō, beginning with the simple and evocative: "Akai tsubaki / shiroi tsubaki to / ochini keri." (A red camellia flower, and a white camellia flower, have fallen together.) The camellia is unique in that it sheds whole blossoms at a time rather than individual petals, and Hekigotō's verse captures the dramatic beauty of two fully formed flowers of contrasting shades that have dropped beside each other. As Shiki elaborates: "The poem does not tell us about associated questions, such as how profusely the camellia shrubs grow and what shapes they form, or whether the scene takes place in a garden or on a mountain road. Rather than being disappointed that we lack this information, we are satisfied in feeling as though there is a red camellia flower and a white camellia flower before our eyes."[20] In other words, a haiku and a realistic painting of the same subject are believed to evoke the same vividly *visual* and focused image of that subject for the reader and the viewer, devoid of a larger narrative context.

Shiki also acknowledges the differences between the artistic mediums. He writes: "Given a text as short as a haiku, it is extremely difficult to include the elements of both time and space. Thus, the need to choose one of the two elements arises. [With the limited length of a haiku] it is not possible to depict temporality. Inevitably, we see the depiction of space win out. Therefore, even though haiku belongs to the temporal medium of literature, it strives to approach the spatial medium of paintings."[21] Shiki judges that haiku is like a painting in its ability to effectively depict the intensity of a brief moment condensed into the targeted frame of the artist's vision, and it is unlike a novel, which can follow the unfolding of events over a greater but not indefinite duration. Sōseki reaches similar conclusions about temporal selectivity as a key feature of literature in his 1907 *Bungakuron* treatise in which, to recap, he attempts to summarize literature through the equation F+f, with cognitive factor (F) accompanied by an emotional factor (f). In addition to defining literary aesthetic thought as distinct from scientific thought because of the presence of affect, Sōseki also describes how the dimension of time defines each type of cognition. Whereas scientists must dispassionately observe the causal sequence of events that cumulatively comprise reality and not linger too much on any one segment of this chain, Sōseki finds: "The literary author has the right to take this endless chain of events and cut it at will, and exhibit it as if it is eternal. He has the privilege of taking some part of human affairs and the natural world ruled by this ceaseless, endless development, cleave it at a point of his choosing, and exhibiting a cross-section (*danmen*) divorced from time. Problems as grasped by a painter or sculptor are from the start characterized by such a cross-section divorced from 'time'" (SZ 14: 225).[22] The implication is that like visual artists, writers too should select what they judge to be the most appealing "cross-sections" of time to depict based on their affective attachments ("f"). The determination of what to focus their authorial gaze on requires them to ascertain what they feel an affective pull toward, or in other words, what they find beautiful.

The late Enlightenment philosopher Gotthold Ephraim Lessing's (1729–1781) famous idea—that the "sister arts" of painting and poetry are respectively suited for depicting the qualities of spatiality and temporality—provides a basis for the theories of Shiki and Sōseki. Lessing's ideas had influenced Ernest Fenollosa, the American educator and art impresario who, as an instructor at Tokyo Imperial University, taught Tsubouchi Shōyō and many others in the first generation of Japanese scholars to study Western cultures and literatures.[23] It therefore seems that by Shiki and Sōseki's time, the "sister arts" concept had become a conceptual staple in literary cogitations. And, as I discuss further on, the narrator of *Kusamakura* explicitly refers to Lessing's insights as he ponders his artistic beliefs as a painter.

Shiki brought the notion of *shasei* beyond the realm of haiku by considering how prose, with no restrictions on length or style as compared to the tightly controlled form of haiku, too could be composed in the *shasei* style. In the essay "Joji bun" (Narrative prose, 1900), he intones: "When one sees scenery or a human event that strikes one as interesting (*omoshiroshi*), and he converts this into writing in order to have his readers feel the same sense of interest, one should not use fancy language or add exaggerations. He should just faithfully portray things and occurrences as they are and as they appear (*tada ari no mama mitaru mama*)."[24] Although the call to depict things "as they are" echoes Tsubouchi Shōyō's appeals for unvarnished realism in *Shōsetsu shinzui* (1885–1886), in contrast to Shōyō, Shiki emphasizes the necessity of curating literary content. His goal is not to convey his perspectives in their uncensored entirety but only the segments that are "interesting." Shiki clarifies that *shasei* "requires some discarding and selecting [of phenomena.] Discarding and selecting means keeping the interesting bits and discarding the boring bits, not necessarily keeping major events and discarding smaller ones, or keeping longer-lasting events and discarding shorter-lived ones."²⁵ This choice is ultimately left to the writer's aesthetic judgments.

Sōseki stated his own take on *shasei* in the essay "Shasei bun," presented in the *Yomiuri* newspaper in January 1907, by which point he had already published his debut novel and a collection of short stories: "Adults understand children. However, we should not presume to fully become children. When portraying the emotional reactions of a child, we must remain strongly objective. What I mean by objectivity here is the attitude of depicting *the child* instead of depicting *the self*. . . . *Shasei bun* writers employ the same technique in describing their own emotions" (*SZ* 16: 54). The imperiousness of the analogy of an adult watching over a child is mitigated by the requirement that writers maintain the same attitude of detachment even when examining themselves. According to this methodology, no one is exempt from the radically neutral gaze of the *shasei* writer; the impartial perspective of the feline narrator of *Wagahai wa neko de aru* embodies this ethos. Sōseki warned that the suppression of subjectivity meant that oftentimes, the resulting work would be devoid of a clear storyline since to impose one would require an overt act of authorial intervention. He muses: "Readers of regular novels will find this lacking. There is no sense of tension. There is no sustained sense of storyline to supplement the vagueness. But [*shasei bun* writers] will say the following. What is plot? There are no storylines in the real world" (*SZ* 16: 55). Sōseki underscores the differences between the "regular" longitudinal novel and the notion of a plotless *shasei* writing by identifying the latter as distinctively "Eastern" (*tōyō-teki*) and derived from haiku, noting that "among the works touted as masterpieces of the West, there are no works composed in this stance to be found" (*SZ* 16: 56). In articulating the differences between the two types of writing, the essay does not declare one to be superior to the other.

The preface that Sōseki wrote for the story collection *Keitō* (1907) by Takahama Kyoshi (1874–1959), another literary disciple of Shiki, further examines the emotional disinterest that *shasei* seems to at once endorse with its insistence on neutral observation and to resist with its stipulations that writers only take up topics that are "interesting" to them. Here, Sōseki reframes the issue in terms of stories that show *yoyū* (leisure, or psychological ease) versus those that seem to occur in an unusual state of *hijō* (emergency). He observes that "in both individual and national histories, there occur major life-or-death incidents arising from one's relationships with others (whether in terms of profit and loss, ethics, or any other numerous sorts of issues.) In such a state, the individual or nation in question becomes entirely consumed by that incident" (*SZ* 16: 152).[26] Sōseki then compares stories that depict dramatic life-or-death events to those that depict more languid states of being in which one can maintain emotional calm and thus appreciate beauty and pleasure. He suggests that the latter condition is not only more elegant than the agitation of the former, but also truer to human experiences, since most people do not live in perpetual states of emergency: "To make tea from flower blossoms is leisurely. To joke is also leisurely. To paint, sculpt, and draw is leisurely. Fishing, songs, theater, summer vacations to cool locales, and therapeutic hot-springs are all leisurely. As long as the Russo-Japanese War is not endless, and the world does not overflow with the likes of John Gabriel Borkman [the highly emotional main character of the Henrik Ibsen play], there is leisure everywhere" (*SZ* 16: 154). Sōseki reasons that since most of life takes place in the quiet moments beyond the sort of disruptive, life-changing situations that befall individuals only rarely, it is more realistic for writers to focus on the unremarkable stretches of time when subjects have enough "leisure" to entertain thoughts and engage in actions that do not immediately further the denouement of some all-consuming incident.

Sōseki praises Kyoshi's stories as exemplifying this type of patient observation of quotidian life. He calls Kyoshi a master of digression because his characters do not follow a straightforward progress from their points of departure to their destinations. Instead, they wander about delighting in the details of their surroundings, sometimes entirely abandoning their original missions. Sōseki observes:

> In literary writing, there exists a certain "sense of meandering about" (*teikai shumi*). This is a term that I invented for expediency's sake, so other people cannot be expected to understand it, but briefly put, it points to the way in which one zeroes in on a given subject, calls forth one's own imaginations or ideas in association with the subject, examines the subject from left and from right, finding it difficult to move on from the subject.... But as the name indicates,

writings of this strain have a tendency to remain as long as possible in one spot [in order to gaze at the subject] so it could be said that there is a tendency for the story to make little progress. In other words, it is a tendency that only those with *yoyū* can undertake. (*SZ* 16: 156)

These assessments about the graceful aimlessness of *shasei*-style writings also appear to address Sōseki's own works thus far, particularly his so-called haiku-novel *Kusamakura* published the previous year, in September 1906. They also cohere with Sōseki's apparent goals in his first short story collection, titled *Yōkyo shū* (A collection of floating visions: *yō* = to hover or float around, *kyo* = artificial construction, imagination; *shū* = collection) published in May 1906. The seven stories in the collection each describe a fantastical or surreal mood that, to varying degrees, obfuscates the main events they purport to narrate.

For example, "Rondon tō" ("Tower of London") opens as the narrator discloses his angst and discomfort at being a foreigner newly arrived in the big city. He explains that he had to walk about with a map through the crowded streets, and that he did not use any modes of public transportation because they were too overwhelming for him. But contrary to what readers aware of Sōseki's background might expect, the author's private miseries do not become the focus of the story. Instead, the narrator's beleaguered state of mind as he navigates the frenzy of modern London serves as a foil to the grave stillness of the Tower of London once he manages to reach it. As he begins his tour, he is awestruck by the site's historical significance: "The history of the Tower of London is a distillation of the history of England. The Tower of London is what is revealed when the curtain veiling the mysterious thing called the past tears itself in two, and it reflects a ghostly light over the twentieth century. The Tower of London is the all-burying current of time flowing backward, and fragments of olden times flowing into the present age" (*SZ* 2: 4).[27] The narrator sees the ancient structure as a place where all time is compressed into an ever-stretching present or, in the parlance of Sōseki's *Bungakuron*, a special zone where the visitor might access multiple significant "cross-sections" of time without being subject to its usual linear flow. Over the course of his perambulations across the Tower grounds, the narrator witnesses dreamlike scenes featuring various tragic figures from English history who had spent time incarcerated there before their deaths, such as Archbishop Thomas Cranmer (1489–1556) who led the

English Reformation, Edward V (1470–1483) and his brother the Duke of York (1473–1483) as young boys captured by their uncle who took power as Richard III, and Lady Jane Grey (1537–1554) deposed by her half-sister Mary I. In Shiki's terminology, we could say that these personages and the events they were involved in were the most "interesting" and attractive to the narrator among the countless others he could have chosen from.

Whether he had actually witnessed visions of real scenes from the Tower of London's long and storied past is unclear to the narrator, who upon returning to his lodgings tells his English landlady about what he just experienced. She teases him for his grand claims, which makes him resolve to never speak of the events or to visit the historical site again, apparently to preserve his private, beautiful reveries. The veracity of the narrator's visions becomes further irrelevant in the coda of the story in which Sōseki speaks from his own perspective as the writer of the story, separate from its narrator. He reveals that he had fabricated the entire account. He lists the literary and visual artworks that had been the source material for his imaginations, namely Shakespeare's play *Richard III* (ca. 1592–94); William Harrison Ainsworth's novel *Tower of London* (1840); and Paul Delaroche's paintings *Edward V and the Duke of York in the Tower* (1831) and *The Execution of Lady Jane Grey* (1833). Yet this authorial debunking does not undermine the reader's enjoyment of the preceding story; by revealing the labors that went into its creation Sōseki seems to affirm that the dreamy mood of the story is its main and sole point, since none of the events it narrates had "actually" taken place. Joseph A. Murphy has analyzed how the disjointed impressions that make up the body of "Rondon tō" in fact illustrate the model of human consciousness that Sōseki proposes in *Bungakuron*, wherein a subject's attention shifts from one intense focal point to the next in a successive waveform movement.[28] This scientific interpretation supports how the story indeed functions as a work of *yōkyo* in that it emphasizes only the imagined scenes most compelling to the writer. The result is that the work remains suspended (*yō*) as a blatantly fashioned (*kyo*) literary space, without the hindrance of less interesting narrative interludes or the progression of an active plotline, or a regard for the story's veracity.

The same spirit of stylized, aimless elegance suffuses the other works in *Yōkyo shū*. For instance, "Maboroshi no tate" (The phantom shield, 1905) and "Kairo kō" (Tale of human suffering, 1905) are based on Arthurian legends and written in an ornate, *kanbun*-based language that emphasizes the beauty of the faraway worlds they depict.[29] Both feature seemingly supernatural elements, like magical mirrors and shields, and are primarily love stories between chivalrous knights and beautiful ladies. In "Maboroshi no tate" in particular, the plot becomes obscure toward the end of the story as the hero William slips into a series of dreamlike visions. Sōseki acknowledges the hazy and meandering quality of his writings, and in *Wagahai wa neko de aru* he pokes fun of his own story "Ichiya" ("One Night," 1905), which was also included in the *Yōkyo shū* anthology.[30] In a conversation about poetry and literature, one of the characters remarks: "The other day, a friend of mine named Sōseki wrote a short story called 'Ichiya' but everyone found it vague and confusing, and no one could grasp its message. So I met with him to ask him seriously about the main point (*shu'i*) of the story, to which he replied that he knows nothing of such matters and would not engage with my question" (SZ 1: 261).

Although the characters used to write the name "Sōseki" in the story are different from those he uses in his own pen name, Sōseki clearly alludes to himself with this assessment. Alan Turney, who translated *Kusamakura* as well as "Ichiya," cites Sōseki's acolytes Morita Sōhei and Komiya Toyotaka in stating that "when Sōseki's 'Ichiya' appeared in the *Chūō kōron* in September 1905, it was generally considered to be incomprehensible."[31] "Ichiya" recounts a free-flowing conversation among two men and a woman who appear to be sharing a room together at an inn one evening. Readers never learn the nature of the characters' relationship to each other, and their discussion jumps erratically from one topic to the next. They all remain unnamed throughout the story. According to Turney, the story "has no point, if by 'point' one means plot or didactic significance. It is a picture in words and, as such, is mainly an attempt at creating an atmosphere by means of objective description."[32] It is in this regard that Turney describes the work as a precursor to *Kusamakura*, going so far as to call the outspoken, alluring woman in the story the prototype for Nami, the heroine of the later novel.

"Ichiya" and *Kusamakura* are also similar in that their characters weigh the psychic turbulence that comes from falling in love, and the alternative of preserving an emotional distance from other people by regarding them as beautiful pictures without delving into their complicated depths. One of the men in "Ichiya" rhetorically quips, "I can appreciate the beautiful women that Utamaro paints. Isn't there some way of bringing pictures to life?" (SZ 2: 134).³³ And toward the end of their evening, the following exchange occurs among the trio:

> "Would I make a picture, too?" she asked.
>
> She firmly adjusted the neckband of her *yukata*; the pattern of the robe was not very clear, but it seemed to be a dense covering of arrowroot leaves on a white ground. As she did so, the sinews at the back of her neck stood out in bold relief as if carved from warm marble, winning the hearts of the men.
>
> "Don't move! Don't move! You're a masterpiece just as you are," said one of them.
>
> "If you move, you'll destroy the picture," warned the other. (SZ 2: 140)³⁴

If the scene ended here with the beautiful woman frozen just so in her pose, it would seem to simply affirm the *shasei* edict for viewers to keep a precise distance from their subjects so as to be close enough to be able to observe and enjoy their delectable details but far enough away to avoid emotional entanglements. But the scene continues, and the woman in the "picture" breaks the reverie:

> "It's hard work being a picture," said the woman. Not caring apparently whether or not she seemed pleasing to the men's eyes, she lifted her right hand from her lap and flung it behind her, letting her body keel over at an angle. Her long black hair gleamed in the light and could be heard brushing against the new straw matting.
>
> "God! A thing of joy lasts but a moment," said the man with the beard, tapping himself lightly on the knee. (SZ 2: 140)³⁵

By having the woman refuse to become the passive object of the men's pleasurable viewing, Sōseki acknowledges the limits of subjecting living people to the *shasei* gaze, since no one can or will conform indefinitely to the image their beholders have constructed of them. But after her retort, the woman is also described in a way that makes her seem more beautiful than ever, and the placid, leisurely charm of the narrative continues undisturbed. The woman is not angry and the men are not upset. Nothing seems to have shifted in their group dynamic. The woman's resistance to being made into a picture is subsumed by the picturesqueness of the scene. Soon after, the story ends as abruptly as it started when the three characters decide to go to sleep.

As in "Rondon tō," Sōseki interjects his authorial voice as a coda to the story, but this time, he stresses rather than rescinds the supposed veracity of the foregoing narrative: "How did they come to meet? I don't know. What were their social statuses, backgrounds, and personalities? I don't know that, either. No connecting thread developed from their words and actions, did you say? That can't be helped because what I have been describing is real life, not fiction. Why did all three of them go to bed at the same time? Because they all felt tired at the same time" (*SZ* 2: 142).[36] This claim of realism is clearly implausible and hyperbolic: To start with, from whose viewpoint could the author have been witnessing the events in the closed room? But Sōseki's proclaimed commitment to impassively observing his characters without attempting to judge and interpret their basic motives attests to the *shasei* philosophy underlying the story.

Kusamakura diverges from "Ichiya" in that its main character eventually begins to move away from the attitude of aesthetic detachment that *shasei* is based on. And while the novel takes place deep in the mountains at a rural inn, the world of *Kusamakura* is more linked to greater society than the single, isolated room that "Ichiya" remains suspended in. The social conventions of class and gender hierarchies permeate *Kusamakura*, whereas in the earlier story the two men and the one woman are devoid of context and abstracted to just their poetic bantering. When the woman plays at being a picture and then rejects the role, she seems to be making a statement about how patriarchal social norms objectify her and womenkind in general. Yet her two male companions hardly react to her words and actions, and the trio's easy camaraderie remains unchanged. Also, though such an arrangement would have been rare for members of opposite gender lacking familial ties in Meiji era Japan, the three characters seem accustomed to sleeping in the same room, and they drift off to a seemingly comfortable slumber together. They seem to exist in their own aesthetic dimension set apart from the world, embodying the platonic *shasei* ideal.

The "Realm of the Unhuman": *Kusamakura*

At one point in "Ichiya," the characters address the escapist comforts offered by beauty.

"If you can't go somewhere beautiful in dreams, where can you?" The woman answered. Her expression implied that this was a sordid world.

"Has the world grown old and sordid?" he asked.

"It has," she said, fanning her beautiful skin with the white silk fan. (SZ 2: 133)[37]

Kusamakura opens with a similar sentiment: "To work according to reason alone leads to conflict with others. But if you surrender yourself to emotions, you will be swept away. To get your way by force is uncomfortably constricting. However you put it, it is difficult to live in the human world" (SZ 3: 3). With these memorable lines, *Kusamakura*'s first-person narrator, an unnamed *yōga* painter from Tokyo, sets off on a peripatetic sojourn in the mountains of Kumamoto; *kusamakura* (grass [for one's] pillow) is a classical Japanese poetic term signifying travel. The narrator's mission is to get away from the everyday stresses of living in society and to experience the "realm of unhuman sentiment" (*hininjō no tenchi*) where he believes that poetic beauty abounds (SZ 3: 11). He ends up at a hot spring resort called Nakoi where he befriends Nami, the young proprietress of the establishment. The bulk of the novel comprises the painter's serene conversations with Nami and his quiet descriptions of her, along with his lofty digressions about the nature of art. In a commentary about the work titled "Yo ga *Kusamakura*" (My *Kusamakura*, 1906) written shortly after the novel's publication, Sōseki states that his aim in writing the work had been purely aesthetic: "My aim is only for a kind of feeling—a feeling of beauty—to remain in the mind of the reader. I have no other special objective than this. Hence, there is no storyline or development of events" (SZ 25: 230).[38] He calls *Kusamakura* a "haiku-novel" that intended to challenge the goals and conventions of novel writing (SZ 25: 231). Sōseki explains that "it is fine for novels, in the usual sense, to evoke life truths, but simultaneously I think there should also exist novels that aim to give comfort [through their beauty]."

The aim of the painter's trip is comfort and pleasure, rather than the pursuit of deep and difficult truths. He is explicit about not wanting to become embroiled in any emotional complications or social obligations, declaring: "I intend to regard everyone I meet on this trip aloofly as though from an elevated and distant position, so that the forces of human sentiments do not occur between us. If I do so, no matter how the other person behaves they cannot breach my heart, and it would be like standing in front of a painting, watching the figures therein run about here and there" (*SZ* 3: 13). This stance mirrors the notion that aesthetic experiences are based on the viewer's disinterest toward their object, a position that dates back to Kant's *Critique of Judgement* (1790), perhaps the ur-text of modern Western aesthetic philosophy. Kant explains:

> All one wants to know is whether the mere representation of the object is to my liking, no matter how indifferent I may be to the existence of the object of this representation. It is quite plain that in order to say that the object is *beautiful*, and to show that I have taste, everything turns on what I make of this representation within myself, and not on any factor which makes me dependent on the existence of the object. Everyone must allow that a judgement on the beautiful which is tinged with the slightest interest, is very partial and not a pure judgement of taste. One must not be in the least prepossessed in favour of the existence of the thing, but must preserve complete indifference in this respect, in order to play the part of judge in matters of taste.[39]

That is, in judgments of beauty, one feels pleasure in perceiving an object without the wish that it gratify any further desire. To that end, whether the object even exists is irrelevant, for it is only the object's *"representation within myself"* [my emphasis] that matters. *Kusamakura*'s narrator resolves to view everyone through precisely this sort of detached gaze.

But, returning to my discussion from chapter 1, aesthetic judgments encompass the dilemma of the "subjective universal." To reiterate Kant's words, "the judgement of taste, with its attendant consciousness of detachment from all interest, must involve a claim to validity for everyone, and must do so apart from a universality directed to objects, i.e., there must be coupled with it a claim to subjective universality."[40] In other words, "everyone" is expected to *subjectively* judge a thing's beauty in the same way, although there are no *objectively* measurable qualities that make a thing beautiful. So if multiple individuals were to subjectively deem the same object beautiful, this would imply that everyone involved had—most likely through conditioning—developed the same aesthetic standards. In raising the hypothetical figure of "an Iroquois *sachem* who said that nothing in Paris pleased him better than the eating-houses" as an example of someone who lacks the proper sense of disinterestedness required for aesthetic experiences,[41] Kant himself, perhaps unwittingly, seems to allude that his notions of "universality" and "everyone" pertain only to those who abide by the European Enlightenment worldviews he takes as the norm. Conversely, this accommodates the possibility of other cultural paradigms with their own aesthetic sensibilities. The caveat remains though, that even among those who share a cultural context, no two people feel exactly the same subjective sentiments, aesthetic or otherwise.

Let us now return to *Kusamakura*'s narrator. He professes admiration for classical Chinese poetry and its worldviews, which he explicitly juxtaposes against modern culture's increasingly Western values. That is, he situates his aesthetic ideals in a specifically Asian tradition. He marvels that "elegant worlds are constructed using only the twenty characters of the poem. The virtues of these worlds are not the same as what novels like *Hototogisu* or *Konjiki yasha* offer" (*SZ* 3:10). He contrasts the beauty of the spare, antiquarian *kanshi* poems to Tokutomi Roka's *Hototogisu* (The cuckoo, 1898–1899) and Ozaki Kōyō's *Konjiki yasha* (Golden demon, 1897–1902), both of which are melodramatic novels that proved immensely popular with Meiji-period readers. As Komori Yōichi points out, these works represent the pressures attendant to life in modernizing Japan.[42] In *Hototogisu*, the heroine contracts tuberculosis and her marriage is broken up by her mother-in-law, who fiercely protects the new aristocratic standing conferred onto her family by the Meiji emperor. The heroine of *Konjiki yasha* is enticed to leave her fiancé for a richer man, and the jilted lover becomes a cold-hearted money lender. The dizzying pursuit of status and money depicted in these novels may offer readers entertainment but they also reveal the pressures of a liberal society and the emotional toll they take on individuals. The resoluteness with which *Kusamakura*'s protagonist vows to harden himself against his sentiments during his getaway suggests that perhaps some personal heartache he experienced in his stressful urban environment had catalyzed the trip to Nakoi, but this is left unspecified. He just laments: "Suffering, anger, agitation, and tears are inevitable when living in human society. I too have endured this for thirty years and am tired of it" (*SZ* 3: 9). What we know is that he seeks respite from his life in Tokyo by turning to the classical Asian tropes of a poetic retreat in a natural setting.

With a touch of drama, the narrator projects his personal need for a spiritual hiatus as a matter of urgency for the Japanese nation at large. After observing that "in Western poems, human affairs are their foundation so even so-called pure poetry does not escape this realm" (SZ 3: 9), he states that classical Chinese poems give access to an alternative realm of "unhuman" calm (SZ 3: 11). Citing the fourth-century poet Tao Yuanming as an example, the painter exults that when reading classical Eastern works of poetry, "one can feel aloof and free from worldly things, rinsed clean of the sweat of self-gain and loss" (SZ 3: 10). He then turns to a wider cultural critique, explaining why the Asian classics are especially relevant in the modern era: "They offer a blessing that is like a deep sleep of total oblivion after being exhausted by steamships, trains, rights, duties, ethics, and manners. If such sleep is necessary in the twentieth century, the poetics of transcendence too is important. Unfortunately, people who compose poems today, and those who read them, are all enamored of Westerners so they do not bother to float a jaunty raft on the waters to take a ride down to the poetic realm of peach blossoms (tōgen)" (SZ 3: 10).[43]

The sojourn in the mountains of Kumamoto was meant to provide the painter not only an escape from the turmoil of his personal life in Tokyo, but also a reprieve from the general overstimulation and emotional uncertainties that suffused late Meiji Japan. As Jonathan Crary has observed, sleep offers modern people "a periodic release from individuation—a nightly unraveling of the loosely woven tangle of the shallow subjectivities one inhabits and manages by day. In the depersonalization of slumber, the sleeper inhabits a world in common, a shared enactment of withdrawal from the calamitous nullity and waste of 24/7 praxis."[44] In that the individual is the prime unit of liberal societies, and the race to advance one's standing therein is a constant driver of its members, the serene selflessness of sleep could be seen as a temporary break from the existing social order. Focusing on the modern Japanese cultural context, Kin'ya Tsuruta identifies *Kusamakura* as expressing a widespread literary longing for a sense of sanctuary, which he calls the *mukōgawa* (other side), and thus conjectures:

> In the largest sense, *mukōgawa* is a by-product of Japan's rapid modernization, for among other things, modernization forced on the Japanese the complex problem of individuation, one of the components of modernity by which the people of Japan have been simultaneously attracted and repelled. The novels of *mukōgawa* give expression to that side of the modern Japanese character which feels ill at ease with the relentless drive for individuation. As such, *mukōgawa*

represents a brief moratorium, an evening at the lukewarm *onsen* (hot springs), away from the steady push for modernization.[45]

This notion too draws a separation between the pressures of modern life and the appeal of a timeless rest.

Significantly, both Crary and Tsuruta deem the sanctuary offered by sleep, or a trip to a *mukōgawa* space, as inherently limited. Sleepers expect to wake and return to their workaday routines, and *mukōgawa* visitors are aware that they cannot stay indefinitely. In this way, Nakoi serves as a sanctuary that is porous and transitional. The hybridity of this setting echoes *Kusamakura*'s mixed status as a "haiku-novel" aiming to provide its readers comfort through expressions of poetic beauty that eschew the advancement of a novelistic plot. This notion reveals Sōseki's continued dedication to the insights he gained from Masaoka Shiki, who considered a haiku with its compact form to be more like a painting that conveys the intensity of a single slice of time than like a novel that depicts events over a longer duration. It is fitting then, that *Kusamakura*'s protagonist is a painter dedicated to what he knows to be the evanescence of moments of beauty. He is actively motivated to get away from the imperatives to action in his daily life and to focus, if temporarily, on his aesthetic meditations. The Nakoi resort exists diegetically as a liminal space between the pressures of modern life and a full release from it, and metadiegetically as an experimental literary realm between the forward momentum of plot-driven novels and the spatially sprawling stasis of paintings.

The painter holds an eclectic view of his own artistic practices. He suffers from a creative block, and as he analyzes this dilemma from a wry remove worthy of a *shasei bun* writer, it occurs to him that he should try his hand at another artistic medium if he cannot paint. He muses:

> It seems that the realm I am urgently trying to present is unlikely to be realized through poetry. Time may exist in my psychological state of joy, but this state contains no events that develop through time. My joy is not produced by one thing's departure, a second thing's arrival, and then the disappearance of this second thing leading to a third thing's birth. Rather, I rejoice in staying motionless inside a single moment. As long as I stay motionless in a single spot, when I try to translate the experience into common language there is no need to arrange the material I use in a temporal framework. As with a picture, I should

be able to compose a poem just by arranging my objects in space. But the question is what scene I should bring into the poem to depict this vast and essential feeling. Once I manage to capture this sense, my poem should succeed even if it doesn't follow [Gotthold Ephraim] Lessing's theories. (SZ 3:78)

The painter assesses that his emotions do not arise singly and successively. Instead, intense emotions seem to him to exist outside the flow of time as individual moments and that were he to adhere to Lessing's edict about language's linearity as opposed to visual art's spatiality, he would be unable to accurately express his profound emotional experiences through poetry. Although he does not yet know what form it would take, the painter is confident that a spatial poem is possible.

Kusamakura itself achieves its expansive effect by presenting scenes of striking visual beauty and flashes of philosophical inspiration with little in the way of causal connections linking them. No single central event unfolds over the arc of the novel, and it is often difficult to ascertain the passage of time between episodes. The various scenes coalesce in a collage-like manner. This visual effect is enhanced by detailed descriptions of the artworks that decorate the picturesque inn, including an ink painting of a crane by the seventeenth-century artist Itō Jakuchū and calligraphy by the eighteenth-century Buddhist monk Kōsen Shōton (SZ 3: 29–30). In fact, the *nihonga* painter Matsuoka Eikyū was inspired to create, along with twenty-six of his peers, the *Kusamakura emaki* (1926)—an opulent three-volume *emaki* (picture scroll) series depicting twenty-eight passages from the novel—which attests to the artistic, self-contained charm of the discrete vignettes that each amplify the fictional world they cumulatively create.[46] As Sadoya Shigenobu states: "Of all of Sōseki's works, *Kusamakura* is most deserving of being called a 'fine arts novel' (*bijutsu shōsetsu*) or a 'painter's novel' (*ekaki shōsetsui*)."[47] Its use of formal innovations to overcome the characteristics conventionally assigned to novelistic narratives can be viewed as strikingly modernist. Steve Odin even proclaims: "Insofar as *Grass Pillow* is a plotless novel with a discontinuous storyline and no development of events, it is a precursor of the *nouveau roman* or 'new novel' of postmodernist literature. For Sōseki's *Grass Pillow*, as for the decentered novels of James Joyce, the purpose is not to tell a story but to record epiphanies of beauty."[48] The classical Chinese poetic elegance that Sōseki evokes throughout *Kusamakura* and the modernist experimentation of writers like

Joyce both offer literary paradigms that diverge from the expectation for modern novels to chart their central characters' progressions over time.

Kusamakura's protagonist himself declares the virtues of a nonlinear, planar approach to literature. In one scene, Nami enters the painter's room where he had been reading. He tells her, "I'm not studying. I just open my book on the desk like this, and am randomly reading whatever passage it happens to open to" (*SZ* 3: 106). He draws a distinction between studying as a dutiful exercise of reason and reading for leisure. Teasingly, but with what apparent sincerity, he tries to explain to Nami the extreme aesthetic detachment that makes him wary of committing himself to any one story as a reader: "I am a painter so I have no need to read a novel from start to finish. But whatever section of it I happen to read is enjoyable to me. I also enjoy talking with you, so much so that I would like to talk with you every day while I am here. I would even be glad to fall in love with you. That would make things even more interesting. But despite how smitten I become, there is no need for us to marry. If we accept the need for people in love to get married, there would have to be a need to read novels from start to finish" (*SZ* 3: 109).

In comparing nonlinear reading and nonmarital love the protagonist intends to relativize the conventions of both longitudinal reading and matrimony that lead to predetermined outcomes, and to instead shift the emphasis to cherishing the beauty of each chance textual or romantic encounter. He claims that he is not against love but just questions the societal standardization of it as a prelude to matrimony. Of course his argument is not purely theoretical; although he reveals his attraction to Nami, he implies that whatever might transpire between them would be transitory. In a characteristically roundabout way, he informs Nami that in the amalgam of disjointed scenes that make up his life she could only be a charming player, not the leading lady, because he refuses to prioritize any one subject across time. The painter's words could be read as a compliment to Nami's picturesque charms or an insult displaying his lack of any desire for a deeper, long-term commitment to her. Without missing a beat Nami remarks cuttingly, "So painters fall in love in an inhumane (*funinjō*) manner," to which he replies calmly, "It's not inhumane. I fall in love in an unhuman (*hininjō*) manner. I read novels in an unhuman manner too, so the plot is meaningless to me" (*SZ* 3: 109). He indicates that he is not "inhumane" in that he is not apathetic to human feelings, but that in his moments of leisure he wants to preserve his own emotional distance from such entanglements. Reading a novel out of order would ensure that he not become too entrenched in any one storyline or character. Readers might interpret this logic of narrative discontinuity as Sōseki's thesis for *Kusamakura*, and a harbinger for the narrator's eventual resolve to leave the rustic charms of Nakoi and return to his work as a modern *yōga* painter in the metropole of Tokyo. He seems aware that he is starting to become too invested in Nami, and that nothing can stay static even during his resolutely placid hiatus.

Indeed, although not much transpires within the diegetic timeframe of the novel, it is not accurate to say that no cohesive story is developed throughout *Kusamakura*. For one, we gradually come to see Nami's depth as an individual. The painter arrives at Nakoi forearmed with gossip about her, which he had picked up at a local teahouse: her parents had made her marry a local wealthy man despite her wishes to wed someone else, and, after her husband lost his fortune, she left him to return to her natal home at Nakoi. Nami is viewed by the townspeople as both notorious and tragic for this. People still recall the sight of her as a beautiful bride descending the mountain on horseback on her way to her unhappy wedding. Through his subsequent interactions with the villagers, the painter also learns that Nami is rumored to have gone insane because of her outspoken ways and brash mannerisms, although a Buddhist monk that she has been studying with describes her as enlightened. At the end of the novel when the narrator and Nami go to the train depot to send off her young nephew Kyūichi, who is deploying for the Russo-Japanese War, we witness two instances that further reveal the complexity of her character: first, her overtly stoic words to Kyūichi—"You'll lose your honor if you come back alive" (SZ 3: 162)—and second, her unguarded expression of *aware* (pitying compassion) (SZ 3:171) as she catches sight of her former husband, who is also aboard the train carrying the throngs of soldiers-to-be to their port of departure. She is caught between her veneer of controlled coldness and the force of her inner emotions. The narrator had been unable to paint her previously despite his fascination with her, but upon seeing the look of genuine compassion cross her face, he at last feels ready: "With this moment, the painting in my heart was completed" (SZ 3: 171). The novel concludes at this point, before he begins the actual painting.

Since readers are not privy to the mental picture the narrator claims to have completed in his heart, the final image we have of Nami is a composite of fleeting and conflicting impressions accumulated over the preceding chapters rather than a single grand pinnacle that they had been building toward. The artist had previously felt that despite her physical beauty, Nami lacked some crucial element that would have made her a truly compelling muse. In an earlier passage he had lamented: "Not a bit of compassion is visible in Nami's expressions. This is why it feels as though something is lacking. When a sudden shock causes the sentiment of pitying compassion to flash across her brow, my painting will be complete. Except—I don't know when I will be able to see this. Her face is usually brimming with a faintly mocking smile, or her brows are furrowed in an expression of anxiety belying her constant drive to win against others" (SZ 3: 123). That this passage so neatly presages the painter's resolve to paint Nami at the end of the novel suggests that for all its celebrated meandering qualities, *Kusamakura* does have a cohesive throughline. And it is not just Nami who lets down her emotional guard, for the narrator too begins to open himself up to the "human sentiments" (*ninjō*) he had sworn to deny. The story of Nami's evolution—from her past as a powerless girl married against her wishes, to her present as a proud, solitary woman stuck in social limbo in an insular community—as well as the story of the Tokyoite painter's journey of artistic and emotional affirmation in the remote calm of Kumamoto, can be said to have made progress, muddying Sōseki's claims about *Kusamakura*'s "unhuman" aesthetics and its lack of a plot. Despite the claim he makes in the commentary "Yo ga *Kusamakura*" that the novel was intended only to evoke a "feeling of beauty" in his readers, the novel harbors a more nuanced examination of the dynamics between profound experiences of beauty and prosaic human events.

A Return to Emotions

This ambivalence is in fact evident from the start of the work. For example, before the painter arrives at Nakoi, he traverses a rough mountain path while trying to keep his thoughts elevated on his artistic theories. But the strain of the hike and the worsening rain soon intrude upon his meditations. At first, he tries to distance himself from his plight by seeing the charm of the situation. Rainy scenes were popular among Edo-period artists, such as Katsushika Hokusai who painted eleven such works and

Utagawa Hiroshige who painted forty-eight, as well as among haiku poets like Matsuo Bashō and Yosano Buson;[49] he likely attempted to picture himself in the scenic world shown in such works. Yet his priority soon becomes the practical one of finding shelter from the elements: "If I think of my increasingly sodden appearance in the hazy ink-washed world streaked with multiple slants of silver as that of someone else, the scene can become a poem and be sung as a haiku. It is only once I forget my physical self and take up a purely objective perspective that I attain a beautiful harmony with the natural scenery as someone in a picture. However, the rain was miserable and the moment I noticed the exhaustion in my legs, I was no longer a figure in a poem or painting" (SZ 3: 14). The narrator cuts a sympathetic though comical figure to readers because of the marked gap between his physical discomfort and his futile attempts at maintaining his artistic thoughts.

Grimly, the painter marches on until he finds a teahouse to rest in. As he regains his bearings, the old woman who waits on him recommends that he make his way to the inn at the hot springs at Nakoi. That she reminds him of a character from a Noh play evinces how intent he is on perceiving everyone he encounters through an artistic lens. She informs him that before her marriage, Nami, the daughter of the inn's proprietor, had to choose between two suitors much like the Nagara maiden, the heroine of a long-ago local legend who drowned herself in a pond to escape her predicament. The painter is ecstatic: "How wonderfully unexpected that I would come to such a remote place, and hear from such a poetic old woman this elegant tale in such elegant language!" (SZ 3:25). But he tunes her out when she starts to discuss how Nami ended up leaving her husband and returning to her natal home. He intuits that hearing about Nami's marital difficulties and her current unglamorous situation would undermine his fantasies about her as a mysterious beauty languishing in a picturesque natural setting.

The painter keeps Nami mentally ensconced in the realm of art by associating her with a well-known artwork. Before meeting her, when he first hears the old lady at the teahouse speak about how beautiful Nami had been on her wedding day, he arbitrarily decides that she must resemble the British Pre-Raphaelite artist John Everett Millais's painting *Ophelia* (1852) (figure 2.1). Sōseki had visited many museums during his time in London—the Tate Gallery, the National Gallery, and the Victoria and Albert Gallery,

FIGURE 2.1 John Everett Millais, *Ophelia* (1851–1852). Oil on canvas. Tate Britain Museum

among others—and he often references the fin de siècle art that he saw abroad in his literary writings.[50] Even after he comes to know Nami he keeps associating her with the image of the drowning girl from Shakespeare's *Hamlet*. The painter's juxtaposition of the British Millais's ethereal, macabre image with the vivid Japanese woman he befriends supports his efforts to keep his feelings for her in check. Kin'ya Tsuruta posits: "Beauty should not be something that deprives the painter of his control and that threatens him, as is the case with Nami. By placing her in the pond, for generations the grave of beauties such as the maiden of Nagara, he can observe her as an aesthetic object without being threatened by her life force, a force which constantly startles him."[51] In other words, the painter tries to circumvent his attraction to Nami by seeing her as an image without depth, as a picture of an attractive woman rendered serene and powerless in her watery grave. The link between Nami and *Ophelia* in his mind are further strengthened when one day, while contemplating the pond where the Nagara maiden is said to have perished according to local lore, he spies Nami perilously posed above a large rock towering over the surface of the water.

The painter springs to his feet "without thinking" (SZ 3: 129) but she runs away. It is unclear whether in that moment, the painter had been shaken from his artistic reveries and had seen Nami as a troubled—potentially suicidal—woman in need of help, rather than an alluringly dark muse to be observed with dispassion.

This tenuous double image mounts over the course of his stay at Nakoi. Throughout, the artist appreciates Nami's beauty but is unwilling to be seduced or shaken by it. He remains unmoved even when she displays disturbing behavior, which range from editing the poems in his notebook without his permission to casually suggesting that she might drown herself and that he should paint a picture of her corpse floating on the water. Among the most memorable of such unsettling episodes occurs when the narrator is enjoying a leisurely night-time soak in the hot spring thinking about Millais's *Ophelia* painting when from among the shadows and the haze of the steam, Nami appears in the nude. They exchange no words, and the narrator, ever unperturbed, observes her while mulling over art historical discourses about depictions of the human body, his thoughts moving from ancient Greek sculptures, medieval Buddhist paintings, and modern trends in nude paintings. He watches the naked Nami through the hot steam as though she too were a painted image: "What's more, her appearance was not brazenly exposed like a conventional nude thrust in front of my eyes. It only hinted coyly at her full beauty, amid an air of spirituality that transforms everything into an object of *yūgen*.[52] Like a mythical creature evoked by the dashes of an ink painting depicting a few of its scales, her appearance was endowed with an atmosphere, warmth, and otherworldliness worthy of artistic contemplation" (SZ 3: 92). This conspicuously flowery commentary overrides any discomfort or desire from arising on his part, and he—perhaps with some conscious effort—is able to admire her purely for her form.

The dreamy, contemplative mood is broken when Nami, with a sharp laugh, abruptly exits the bath and leaves the narrator dazed. It is as though Nami is knowingly goading the "unhuman" aesthetic gaze that he has been fostering, testing its limits. She is too intelligent to be unaware that any power she holds over the wealthy visitor from Tokyo is due to her beauty. The painter has presumably come to Nakoi to take respite from the socioeconomic or personal responsibilities that would weigh on a man of the leisurely class who can afford such an open-ended vacation. He mentions prior itinerant journeys to other parts of the country, and he even tells the woman at the teahouse that it is not his first time in this region although he does not elaborate on the circumstances of his previous visit. Clearly, he is not eager to establish ties anywhere. Both he and Nami know that were they to enter into a deeper relationship, it might entail consequences exceeding their purely aesthetic interest in each other.

After an unspecified amount of days or weeks have passed in this tenuously artistic seclusion, the painter comes to ponder his standing as a professional artist and as a "member of society" (*shakai no kōmin*) (SZ 3: 147). He begins to consider ending his experiment of living according to "unhuman" aesthetics and rejoining the world of humanity. When he accompanies Nami and her nephew to the train station in the novel's final chapter, his ambivalence about the "real" world resurface in a visceral manner. The train embodies for him the evils of modern civilization that he had hoped to escape by coming to Nakoi:

> I was finally dragged out into the real world. By the real world, I mean places where one can encounter trains. There is nothing that symbolizes the twentieth century as much as the steam train. It rolls along noisily with hundreds of people stuffed into each box. There is no mercy. The people in the boxes move at the same speed, stop at the same stations, and are uniformly doused by its steam. People say they take the train, but I say they are loaded aboard. People say they go places by train, but I say they are transported by train. Nothing disregards individuality as much as trains. After using all means to develop individuality, civilization tries to suppress it using all means. . . .
>
> Every time I see a train roar by with no regard for its surroundings, carrying passengers like so much cargo, I mentally compare the people stuffed onboard with the steel cars utterly indifferent to their individual natures and I think—This is dangerous, quite dangerous. This is dangerous unless one is careful. The stench of this danger permeates modern civilization. The train, blindly hurtling toward darkness, is a prime example of this danger. (SZ 3:167–168)

As we have observed throughout the novel, for our narrator, the realm of timeless aesthetics represents the antithesis of what he perceives as the soul-crushing teleology of modern technological progress.

This impassioned invective against the superhuman scale and industrial impersonality of trains also finds expression in *Bungakuron*, published the following year. Building on his tenet that literary thought is characterized by the lens of emotion and subjectivity whereas scientific thought aims for pure objectivity, Sōseki alludes to the work of the English Romantic painter J. M. W. Turner (1775–1851) to illuminate these differences. Turner's impressionistic, almost abstract, painting of a train impresses him and he writes: "[Turner's] image of a train speeding through a rainstorm is rendered so dark and vast, it is as if the train were running on the surface of the water itself. Given that this type of ocean and this type of land . . . are not to be found in the natural world yet possess sufficient literary truth, and respond to demands above the demands of nature—that is to say, that we recognize here a firm and indomitable life force—we would have to say that in his paintings is to be found not scientific truth but a pure literary truth" (SZ 14: 259).[53]

Consistent with the principle of F+f, which states that anything can serve as literary content (F) as long as it is accompanied by emotion (f), Sōseki considers how Turner takes up the locomotive, a symbol of technological triumph in the nineteenth century, as an artistic subject (figure 2.2). He indicates that breaking with attempts at objective realism, Turner renders the train according to his own aesthetic and emotional sensibilities (f) and focuses on its majestic beauty, while ignoring its technological workings and societal function. But in *Kusamakura*'s final scene, confronted with the train's blatant purpose of efficiently transporting his fellow civilians so that they might fight and possibly die for the sake of the expanding nation-state, Sōseki's narrator is unable to remain so aloof. He cannot maintain a cool, "unhuman" impartiality and see the train as just a thing of beauty. This perspectival disruption, in turn, leads up to the artistic breakthrough he achieves upon witnessing Nami's look of compassion at the novel's conclusion.

Kusamakura ends when the painter feels ready to paint his muse because he can finally see past her external beauty and behaviors, and into the deeper well of her emotions. Up to this point, although he refers to himself as a painter (*ekaki*), he has not completed a single painting during his time at Nakoi. But if his intention all along had been to perfect his artistically "unhuman" mindset, the lack of a resulting physical painting is perhaps beside the point, and we can measure his gains in other ways. During his stay at the mountain inn he composes many verses of haiku and lines of Sinitic poetry as he dwells on his aesthetic theories. He proudly affirms that he has made tremendous philosophical strides since coming to Nakoi declaring, "I am a first-rate painter. Though Michelangelo surpasses me in

FIGURE 2.2 J. M. W. Turner, *Rain, Steam, and Speed—The Great Western Railway* (1844). Oil on canvas. This is presumably the work Sōseki writes about.
The National Gallery, London

technique and Raffaello is more skillful, my persona (*jinkaku*) as an artist marches as an equal to the giants of the past and present, and I do not see any point in which I am lacking" (*SZ* 3: 144). Is this false bravado or sincerely meant? Regardless, the story ends with the verbal allusion to, if not a fully descriptive evocation of, the narrator's mental image of Nami's portrait before he executes it on canvas. The appeal to the elusive element of an artistic "persona" suggests that the essence of art surpasses the specificities of medium, a conclusion that underscores *Kusamakura*'s status as a "haiku-novel" suspended between image and narrative.

Readers are not told whether the painter's attitude of "unhuman" aesthetic restraint will thaw further once he completes his painting of Nami. We do know that his real challenges will come after he goes back to Tokyo and resumes his usual life as a professional artist, in which he must create paintings and interact with others on a regular basis. Neither his portrait-to-come of Nami nor the time covered by the novel are the climax in this larger implied story. Our protagonist has just begun to broach the looming question of how to be an artist and appreciate beauty while actively living in human society—which in modernity has become both increasingly focused on individuality, as well as impersonal in the systemic pursuit of collective progress. In this regard, the narrator's references to a mix of Eastern and Western artworks and poetry throughout the novel indicate more than a naïve idealism about the transcendental beauty of the arts. He had originally blamed Western influences for the strife and stress of Japanese society's modernization, and as the reason why he sought to escape his usual urban life. But the aesthetic sanctuary he establishes at Nakoi is not exclusively Eastern, as we can see from his repeated references to Pre-Raphaelite artworks and European artists. For all his laments about Western values, his own imagination is shot through with imported referents.

And in the final scene at the train station, the narrator realizes that the realm of art represented by Nakoi is literally connected to the world beyond it. This includes Tokyo where his own life is based, as well as the wider world outside Japan. Nami's nephew and her estranged husband, along with the countless other young Japanese men boarding the train that day, are being sent to Manchuria where they would fight the Russians completing the Trans-Siberian Railroad; for the narrator, seeing Nami's emotional expression at their departure, world events lose their distant, abstract nature and become palpably real. According to Lessing's paradigm that he had cited earlier, his chosen profession as a practitioner of the spatially oriented visual arts could be seen as representing his desire to step out of the inexorable evolutions of sociohistorical temporalities. But we could also posit that at the end of the novel, the narrator's reversion to the medium of painting implies a reinvigorated willingness to engage with the shared expanse upon which all beings coexist.

Sanshirō: An Awakening

There are many overlaps between *Kusamakura* and *Sanshirō*, most obviously in that each novel examines a male protagonist whose emotional equilibrium is threatened by an attractive woman whom he tries to keep at a distance by viewing her through the dispassionate filter of artistic discourse.[54] Sōseki wrote the following synopsis in an advertisement for *Sanshirō*: "Sanshirō, a graduate of a rural college who enters a university in Tokyo, is exposed to a new atmosphere. He begins to move in various ways through contact with his colleagues, his mentors, and young women. All I have to do is release these people into this atmosphere. I think they will then go about as they please, and drama will arise on its own" (*SZ* 26: 252).[55] Echoing his earlier theories on *shasei*, Sōseki purports to situate himself as merely an observer of the drama that his characters create among themselves. As with the unnamed painter in *Kusamakura*, Sanshirō at first embodies this passive attitude. He is a self-described country bumpkin, and he constantly struggles to keep up with the fast pace of the people and things around him. As a student at Tokyo Imperial University he is clearly a member of the intellectual elite but he has yet to experience love or loss in any real way, and he projects an open innocence to his new friends and to readers.

To recall, Sōseki had eschewed imposing a storyline in *Kusamakura*, his "haiku-novel," because its ostensible goal had been to solely evoke "a feeling of beauty." *Sanshirō*'s free-floating narrative, and its eponymous character who diffidently ponders the events that befall him, also defy the teleological impetuses of a standard plot-driven novel. In Karatani Kōjin's words, "The poetic taste (*hai-mi*) of *Sanshirō* arises from the 'unhuman' (*hininjō*) quality of its writing style which regards from a distance—as though viewing natural scenery—the frustrations and dilemmas that its characters may inherently be suffering."[56] The novel, with its neutrally detached narrative perspective and emotionally unexpressive protagonist, is similar to *Kusamakura* in that both refrain from directly depicting the emotional turmoil of its characters. Also, both contain little externally observable plot. But if *Kusamakura* explored literature and aesthetics as a temporary means of escaping from and coping with the various pressures of modern life, *Sanshirō* marks a shift. By the time he wrote this work, Sōseki had joined the *Asahi* newspaper in a full-time capacity after leaving his teaching position at Tokyo Imperial University. Reflecting Sōseki's own move away from the ivory tower, *Sanshirō* focuses on a young man from rural Kumamoto who learns to navigate life in the vibrant metropolis of Tokyo. It shows a more active interest in considering the meanings and potentials of art and literature in the new social climate of late Meiji Tokyo than *Kusamakura*, which had featured a protagonist who retreats to a rural mountain resort to search for a specifically classical mode of poetic beauty. The novel's serialization in the *Asahi* accentuates the theme of integrating aesthetic contemplation with worldly events.

Sanshirō has been viewed by some scholars as a bildungsroman.[57] Though his first experiences as a young adult living away from home culminate in heartbreak when his love interest Mineko becomes engaged to another man, the hero of the novel makes incremental progress toward the goal of adult masculinity. Still, such growth comes about via his emotional reactions toward others, rather than through the soul-searching or the experiences he creates via his own agency. This is emphasized by the calm tone and incisive judgments of the narrative voice that exists apart from Sanshirō's inner monologue, although their points of view mostly overlap. This independent voice carries the story forward with sophisticated insights that elide the often hapless and naïve main character. For example, as Ishihara Chiaki has also pointed out, the following early lines of the novel diverge from the perspectives of Sanshirō, a country boy marveling at the face pace of the city[58]: "Sanshirō did not yet notice the energy of the world of ideas that sprawled behind student life. Meiji thought was repeating three hundred years' worth of Western history in the span of forty years" (*SZ* 5: 40). Whereas in *Kusamakura* Sōseki depicted observations and expressed theoretical ideas through the consciously intellectual protagonist's own point of view, in *Sanshirō* he maintains an authorial autonomy from its protagonist.

Differences in how *Kusamakura* and *Sanshirō* depict the relationship between the visual arts and literature also indicate a shift. Although the earlier novel concludes just before the unnamed painter realizes his portrait of Nami, it implies that he has finally gained enough understanding of her inner spirit that his painting of her would be a definitive culmination of their time together. His pontifications suggest the belief that a painting could capture a subject in a select moment of intense beauty and emotion, free from a prose narrative's laborious commitment to a chain of events that includes that climactic instance. And during his hiatus at Nakoi, the protagonist conducts himself in a conspicuously "unhuman" mode; he regards everyone as though they were paintings until he decides to resume his "real" life in Tokyo with his artistic powers, and perhaps his emotional availability, restored. In sum, painting and literature represent related but ultimately different modes of cognition in *Kusamakura*, with painting apparently privy to a clarity and intensity that eludes the verbal arts. In contrast, Sanshirō ends up continuously unnerved rather than comforted whenever he attempts to envision Mineko as a visual artwork. He first sees her from a distance, and she strikes him as a beautiful image. He stares, confident in his position of safety as a unilateral spectator until she squarely returns his gaze: "He was firmly aware of the moment her dark eyes shifted their focus toward him. In that instance, the impression of colors vanished, and he was met with something ineffable.... He became frightened" (*SZ* 5: 302). Mineko is not, he begins to realize, a passive object for his viewing pleasure.

Sanshirō's heavy emphasis on the visual arts has been studied in connection with the numerous references to specific painters and painting styles that pepper the characters' thoughts and conversations,[59] as well as the pictorial dynamics of Sanshirō's gaze.[60] These analyses show that Sanshirō's allusions to the discourse of painting, especially in his attempts to understand and assess Mineko, are rooted in his desire to order his churning feelings and assert his sense of agency amid the dizzying interpersonal dynamics and dense urban environment he is learning to navigate. The protagonist of *Kusamakura* had adopted a similar technique to keep his attraction to Nami in check by associating her with Millais's *Ophelia*. But for Sanshirō, his attempts to contain the lively and mysterious Mineko within pictorial idioms are mostly in vain. To take one instance, Sanshirō compares Mineko to a portrait by Jean Baptiste Grezue (1725–1805) (figure 2.3) and describes her unsettlingly seductive charms as "voluptuous"—using the English term he had heard in an art history lecture—before he realizes that there is in fact no physical resemblance between her and the women in the eighteenth-century French academic paintings (*SZ* 5: 369). Also, throughout the novel, the beautiful Mineko has been posing as a model for the painter Haraguchi. At the story's conclusion, Sanshirō finds the completed painting inadequate to match what has, by that point, become his rich mental portrait of her. In pitting the visual and narrative mediums against each other in *Sanshirō*, Sōseki seems to suggest that literature, more so than painting, is uniquely capable of capturing the shifting energies and complex sentiments of modern experiences.

FIGURE 2.3 Jean Baptiste Greuze, *Girl with Doves* (1799–1800). Oil on mahogany panel. Sōseki does not specify which Greuze portraits Sanshirō had in mind. This is one of Greuze's depictions of a young, "voluptuous" woman.
The Wallace Collection

From early on, Mineko is presented as an attractive and vivacious woman with her own sense of agency easily outpacing Sanshirō's efforts to enclose her within his gaze. Although her educational background is not specified, Mineko's English abilities imply that she seems to have attended at least a women's secondary school (*kōtō jogakkō*), still an unusual accomplishment in this period. She represents a newly emergent category of educated young women capable of intellectually holding their own among male peers, although social opportunities beyond marriage were in short supply for them.[61] As Shiozaki Fumio puts it, society expected such women to "indefinitely maintain a posture of 'waiting' until the day a spouse of suitable social position and educational level appeared."[62] Not having seen enough of the world yet, Sanshirō wears his social and material privileges lightly, but he grasps that it is not impossible that Mineko might consider him, a twenty-three-year-old university student of comfortable if not extravagant means, as a potential suitor. Yet she exercises her hold over him with her beauty, keeping her words and actions flirtatious but noncommittal.

In fact, the prospect of intimacy of any kind with a woman fills Sanshirō with trepidation. He can be seen as an easy mark for seduction, as is underscored in an incident that occurs at the beginning of his story. Given the charged symbolism of the train as a vehicle of modern progress, as we previously saw in *Kusamakura* and *Bungakuron*, it is fitting that Sanshirō's coming-of-age story begins on his train journey from Kumamoto to Tokyo, where he will start his first semester at Tokyo Imperial University. The trip is long and he stops for the night in Nagoya, where a young woman he had encountered earlier on the train, also traveling alone, asks for his assistance in finding a suitable inn. He is too confused and timid to decline her request, and he does not protest when the innkeeper, believing them to be a married couple, places them in a single room with a shared futon. He spends an uncomfortable night trying to ignore the strange woman's advances, and upon parting the next morning, she tells him: "You are quite the coward, aren't you?" (*SZ* 5: 282). He is shaken by this encounter because it confirms that even if he did not yet identify as such, he is now socially perceived as an adult male empowered to make his own choices and to determine his own path in the world. His awkwardness indicates to readers, and perhaps to himself too, that his new status puts him in an oddly vulnerable position.

But this episode could also be read through the lens of Sanshirō's nascent understanding of his own budding potency, and his less than innocent attention to the woman from the train. The opening scene of the novel reveals that he had been eyeing her quite openly before they arrived at Nagoya, noting her "very dark" complexion and deeming her a "Kyūshū-colored woman" (SZ 5: 273). The objectifying tone of these appraisals, particularly the implication that he views her as an extension of his home territory because of her color, suggests his sense of entitlement to her. On many occasions he could have stopped conversing with the woman or have asked the innkeeper for separate rooms. Although it is undeniable that the woman had asked for his help, and that Sanshirō had panicked when they ended up in the same bed, he may have been at least partly complicit in the turn of events that produced this extraordinary situation. The episode could be seen as a preview of how Sanshirō's future attempts to appraise people as visual images and thus gain mastery over them will fail.

Back on the train, he fumes to himself: "How could there be such women in the world? How could women be so calm and unbothered like that? Was she uneducated? Bold? Or was she just naïve? He had no way of knowing because he had not tried to go as far as he could have. He should have dared to go ahead with it. But he had been afraid. It shocked him when she called him a coward upon their parting. He felt as though the shortcomings of his twenty-three years had been abruptly revealed" (SZ 5: 283–284). Although he begins by denigrating the woman for her oddly brazen behavior—betraying an underlying condescension toward femininity, the imprint of the patriarchal values that he had apparently been raised with in his rural community—he eventually turns his criticisms toward himself. The recognition of his strait-laced passivity implies that although he could not yet admit it, some part of him had in fact wanted to be seduced by the woman from the train and to experience the unknown.

But as a young man from the provinces going to the capital to mingle with his peers from the nation's elite, Sanshirō is the epitome of the Meiji ideal of *risshin shusse* (rising up and advancing in the world.) To deviate even for a night from this rational, goal-oriented trajectory would have been unthinkable, so more than anything it seems to be fear that he feels when recalling his night in Nagoya. By opening *Sanshirō* with a scene in which the transient woman calls the protagonist a coward because he is doggedly committed to staying on the rails of predictable respectability, Sōseki in effect also critiques the conventional linearity of most novels. Such a beginning prepares readers for the possibility that the novel might stray from this expected pattern. The mysterious stranger's incisive analysis of his cowardice sets in motion the story of Sanshirō's awakening to his agency and the wider world of ideas, emotions, and experiences that he might reach for, as well as Sōseki's exploration of a new kind of literary writing capable of such ambitious forays.

The "Great Darkness"

Sanshirō begins conversing with the man sitting across from him as the train speeds toward its destination. The man, Hirota, is an English instructor at the college affiliated with Sanshirō's university, and a part of the group of friends that he would later fall in with. Hirota's shabby outfit initially leads Sanshirō to judge him as a low-ranking teacher: "Seen against the great future that awaited him, the man seems somehow inconsequential. He must already be forty, and unlikely to advance any further in the future" (SZ 5: 285). The narrative subtly mocks the protagonist's youthful arrogance, but Hirota soon reveals a type of philosophical wisdom that Sanshirō had never encountered before. As the two men enjoy the peaches that Hirota buys from a vendor at Toyohashi station, the older man remarks: "Our hands naturally reach out toward the things we like, you know. It can't be helped. A pig doesn't have hands, so instead, his snout will reach out. It seems that if you tie a pig down so that he can't move and then place a feast in front of him, the tip of his snout will gradually grow until it reaches the food. There is nothing as terrifying as desire" (SZ 5: 288). Sanshirō laughs, but readers can assume that these words resonate with him after the previous evening, when he had brushed up against his unconscious desires and had almost given in to them. Hirota then describes what is considered today as a bit of lore handed down to illustrate Leonardo da Vinci's scientific methodology: his experiment of injecting arsenic into the trunk of his peach tree, which resulted in the death of a person who plucked and ate the poisoned fruit from it. Hirota intones: "Dangerous. It's very dangerous unless you're careful" (SZ 5: 288–289). This macabre comment seems arbitrary to the conversation, but if Hirota is evoking Leonardo as a symbol of the High Renaissance affirmation of empirical reasoning above all, he may be obliquely advising his new young friend about the importance of guarding his core values amid the ruthlessly efficient and competitive atmosphere of late Meiji modernity that awaits him in Tokyo.

Hirota shocks Sanshirō even more with his views about Japan's place in the modern world order. Catching Sanshirō admiring a handsome Western couple at Hamamatsu station, Hirota says: "We Japanese are pathetic compared to them. Even if we beat the Russians and become a 'first-class nation,' it's no good as long as we have these same sad faces and remain so physically meager. Even our new buildings and gardens—they are what you would expect from faces like ours" (SZ 5: 291). But even more shocking than Hirota's offhand comment on racial inferiority that echoes the remarks Sōseki had made during his period in London, or the way he downplays the nation's victory in the Russo-Japanese War (1904–1905), is his pessimism about Japan's future. He baldly predicts that "Japan will perish" (SZ 5: 292). This presages Sōseki's later, albeit more tempered, criticisms of Japanese modernity, such as the speech "Gendai Nihon no kaika" (The civilization of modern Japan, 1911) in which he proclaimed the nation's progress falsely hollow because of its *gaihatsu-teki* (outwardly instigated) as opposed to *naihatsu-teki* (internally and organically driven) nature (SZ 16: 430).[63] In conservative Kumamoto, Sanshirō had never met anyone who dared to question the directions of the imperial Japanese state. Hirota tells him that "Tokyo is bigger than Kumamoto. And Japan is bigger than Tokyo.... The inside of your head is even bigger than Japan" (SZ 5: 292). These words make Sanshirō realize that he has embarked upon a new phase of his life in which he will have to think for himself, and that more broadly speaking, it is also a pivotal moment in Japanese history when the future is open with multiple possibilities.

But despite his apparent wisdom, Sanshirō learns that Hirota never publishes anything to share his knowledge with the world and to claim his place in society as an intellectual. Sanshirō's classmate Yojirō, who lives with Hirota as his protégé and assistant, has nicknamed him "The Great Darkness" (*idai na kurayami*) because he emits no light despite his impressive erudition and original ideas. Hirota is an idealistic philosopher who is pathetically out of touch with material and social realities. He has never been married but has concluded that having a wife would not be agreeable. He has also decided that Japan is inferior to the Western countries although he has never traveled abroad, and he has only seen foreign lands through photographs. Yojirō assesses that Hirota's "mind is more developed than the actual world" (SZ 5: 359). He claims that Hirota is helpless about practical affairs and depends on him to organize basic quotidian affairs regarding meals and lodging.

When a post for a Japanese professor of English studies opens up at the University, Yojirō concocts a plan to place Hirota in the running by publishing an anonymous article about his untapped genius in a student magazine. The ploy backfires spectacularly. The university hires another professor, and some even suspect Sanshirō of having written the article at Hirota's behest. Sōseki makes a sly reference to himself in explaining that the new instructor is "an excellent scholar who had recently been studying abroad under government orders" (SZ 5: 561). It was well known that Sōseki had landed his teaching post at the Tokyo Imperial University following his government-sponsored stay in England. This joke also links the novel to the extra-textual social climate of the late Meiji period when there was a push to bring in new Japanese instructors to replace the foreign professors hired by institutions of higher learning when they first opened in earlier decades. Furthermore, by thus stressing that the neurotic Hirota is not a direct stand-in for Sōseki himself in the autobiographical Naturalist mode, he underscores the novel's status as a deliberately constructed work of fiction.

When Sanshirō visits the older man after this debacle, Hirota is in surprisingly good spirits. He is not disappointed about losing the chance to research and teach English literature at the prestigious university, and he is content to go on teaching English language classes at the preparatory college. This Zen-like calm suggests Hirota's noble indifference to worldly concerns. But the absent-minded scholar also cuts a poignant, solitary figure against the rapid pace of modern society. In a previous scene, Sanshirō spies Hirota walking on campus and is struck by how out of place his mentor looks among the bustling crowds:

> The cold street was teeming with the vitality of young men. In the midst of this he spotted the long shadow of Professor Hirota in his gray tweed overcoat. Among the young ranks he had wandered into, his stride marked him as an anachronism. Compared to the pace of the others around him, his stride looked much more sluggish. The Professor's shadow vanished through the College's gate. Inside, a large pine tree blocked the front entrance with its branches

spread out like a colossus's umbrella. By the time Sanshirō passed the gate, the Professor's shadow was already gone. All he could see before him now were the pine tree and the clock tower over it. This clock was always out of kilter, or it wasn't running at all. (SZ 5: 567)[64]

Hirota's expansive knowledge of English literature and Western cultures imbue him, on the one hand, with intellectual sophistication. But his asceticism and lack of individual drive put him at odds with the spirit of the Meiji period in which young men of talent could make their name in the new social orders being established. Hirota is out of synch with his surroundings like the stopped clock in the college square. The description of the "sluggish" pace of his unhurried gait evokes Sōseki's earlier espousal of a "leisurely" mode of writing rooted in a timeless and classical poetics. In Hirota's case, however, the effect is one of isolation and pathos rather than of elegance.

But Hirota is not immune to the passage of time. Even if he does not seem to be forging an active path toward the future, a wellspring of unresolved emotions still connects him to his past. Hirota tells Sanshirō about a dream in which he saw a girl he had met as a young student. He makes a point of telling Sanshirō that their encounter had been in 1889, the year of the Meiji constitution's promulgation. Though less than twenty years ago, the implication is that it had felt like an entirely different era. Hirota recounts his strange dream:

> She had the same face, the same clothing, the same hairstyle, and of course, the same mole from before. She was thus twelve or thirteen, just as I saw her twenty years ago. "You haven't changed at all," I said, and she replied, "You've aged quite a bit!" I then asked her, "Why haven't you changed?" and she said, "I stay like this because the year I had this face, the month I wore these clothes, and the day I had my hair like this was my favorite time." "When was that?" I asked her. "It was when we met twenty years ago," she said. I wondered to myself, "Then why have I aged like this?" She told me, "It's because you wanted to keep going past that moment, moving toward ever more beauty." I said to her, "You are a painting," and she said, "You are a poem." (SZ 5: 577–578)

Sanshirō hesitantly asks Hirota whether it was because he could still not let go of this girl's memory that he had never married, and after a pause Hirota answers in the affirmative. Sanshirō is moved by what he interprets as his friend's romantic dedication to his first love. But Hirota explains that some people simply do not believe in the institution of marriage, and he offers up the hypothetical situation of a young man whose mother tells him in her dying moments that his biological father is not the man he had been led to believe as such his entire life. Hirota is obviously speaking about his own experiences despite framing the account as fictive. This enables us as readers, and of course Sanshirō, to conclude that the trauma of learning about his mother's secret betrayal had made Hirota unable to trust the prospect of marital love, and that he came to idolize the girl he had met just prior to his great disillusionment.

Yet Hirota's dream also reveals that his emotional development had not stopped in his boyhood. In the dream, whereas the girl is frozen in time like a "painting," he has continued to age like a "poem," "moving toward ever more beauty." This analogy acknowledges that we cannot remain static as long as we go on living, and that there will be more beautiful encounters as long as we remain open to them. And despite the emotional guardedness he has cultivated, the years between the shocking discovery of his parentage and the present have not been barren for Hirota, for through books and artworks he has been gaining new ideas and cultivating his affective sensibilities as though in preparation for the day he resumes a fuller engagement with humanity. He has also been forging connections with friends who admire him, like Yojirō and Sanshirō. The invocation of poetry as a temporally evolving medium and painting as a fixed one harkens back to Lessing's *Laocoon*, which Sōseki refers to in *Kusamakura*, *Bungakuron*, and elsewhere. In the emotionally charged context of Hirota's dream the comparison seems to favor literature as the vibrant medium affirming life energies, casting painting as the medium of stillness and stagnation. But the scene could also be understood as a gesture toward a new mode of synthesis between the two mediums. Instead of a "haiku-novel" that sacrifices the progression of plot for the sake of expressing an image of perfection, by having Hirota and the long-ago girl unite in this dream space, *Sanshirō* points to the possibility of novels that can more fully accommodate both beauty and change.

Sanshirō shows Sōseki reassessing the capacities of the literary and visual artistic mediums. Watching as Mineko poses for the painter Haraguchi in his studio one day, Sanshirō asks: "Could the expression of the model's eyes always remain unchanged when you paint them like this, day after day?" (*SZ* 5: 548). Haraguchi answers: "They certainly change, of course. And it's not just the model who changes. The painter's mood changes every day too, so there really ought to be multiple portraits when you're done, but that is unacceptable. It's strange but in the end, I produce one rather coherent painting." In stating that a painting is in fact a concentration of many moments, Haraguchi complicates Sōseki's previous interartistic views, which held that a painting conveys a particular moment chosen from among others. To recall, *Kusamakura* concludes when after much time with Nami, the narrator experiences a singular epiphany when he feels he has finally spied her true humanity. But in the final scene of *Sanshirō*, the titular character undergoes no such transformative experience when sees Haraguchi's completed portrait of Mineko. Although Yojirō guilelessly exclaims that it is "wonderfully (*sutekini*) painted and big" (*SZ* 5: 606), the painting did not seem to Sanshirō to capture the subtle expressions and emotions that Mineko had shown him throughout their time together. At each meeting he had seen more of her complex character, and despite its surface beauty Haraguchi's image falls short of Sanshirō's diffuse impressions of her external beauty and inner humanity.

The "Romantic Naturalist"

In *Bungakuron*, Sōseki set forth his view that science (F) is qualitatively different from literature (F+f) in being free of subjective affect. Sōseki also revisits the dynamics between the literary and scientific modes of thought in *Sanshirō*. Nonomiya Sōhachi, a physicist at the university who becomes another mentor for Sanshirō, plays a key part in this regard. However, the seemingly unemotional scientist Nonomiya ends up no more desirable as a role model than the solipsistic language and literature scholar Hirota.

It is Sanshirō's mother who urges him to visit Nonomiya, a distant relative from Kumamoto. Sanshirō finds himself challenged by the older man's unfamiliar intellectual territory despite their familial link. During their first meeting, Nonomiya's underground laboratory strikes Sanshirō as strange and otherworldly, cluttered with ominous looking machinery; the physicist is researching the pressure exerted by a beam of light. The topic shocks Sanshirō. He cannot grasp the kind of pressure a beam of light could have, and what purpose such a pressure might serve. Nonomiya kindly demonstrates his scientific equipment while Sanshirō politely keeps his confusion to himself. As he had done with Hirota, Sanshirō judges the older man's plain clothing and is not impressed. He muses that "perhaps Nonomiya planned to never have contact with the real world" (SZ 5: 299). At an intellectual level, however, Sanshirō admires Nonomiya's devotion to his work and wonders whether he too should "lead a life like this, removed from the living world." But Sanshirō's instinctive alarm at such isolation gives way to the opposite assessment: "It seems that he needed the real world" (SZ 5: 300).

The care with which Sōseki describes Nonomiya's experiment shows that his awareness of the natural sciences—which had shaped his radical questioning of "literature" as a scholar—had not been limited to an abstract respect for the rigors of the empirical method. As a student in preparatory college, Sōseki had evinced a talent for math and the sciences, and his peers had expected that he would pursue his higher studies in those fields.[65] It has been pointed out that in London, his friendship with the chemist Ikeda Kikunae, a fellow Japanese expat, was pivotal in Sōseki's overcoming his increasing frustrations with his literary studies.[66] Sōseki also often conversed about innovations in the field of modern physics, such as relativity theory and atomic theory, with the physicist Terada (1878–1935), who became a literary disciple.[67] The knowledge that Sōseki gleaned from Terada finds expression in *Sanshirō* when Nonomiya refers to James Clerk Maxwell, the Scottish founder of electromagnetic theory, and the Russian physicist Pyotr Lebedev. Drawing on an essay by Terada, Koyama Keita has traced Sōseki's description of Nonomiya's work to an experiment conducted by the American physicists Ernest Fox Nichols and Gordon Ferrie Hull in 1903, the results of which were published in the American journal *Physical Review* and the German journal *Annalen der Physik*.[68] The field of physics made great strides in the early twentieth century because of scientists who built on each other's discoveries, and Nonomiya is depicted as a participant in this discourse that transcended national and cultural differences. From London, Sōseki had written to Terada that "if one is to be a scholar, one must pursue a *cosmopolitan* field.[69] . . . Even in England, English literature cannot hope to hold its head high [in this regard]" (SZ 22: 236–237).[70] In contrast to his conflicted feelings about studying English literature, particularly as a Japanese scholar, Sōseki expresses envy for what he perceives to be the egalitarian and universally meaningful field of the sciences.

Mizumura Minae analyzes Nonomiya as Hirota's "polar opposite" in this aspect.[71]

Nonetheless, like the reticent English-literature scholar Hirota, Nonomiya the physicist holds reality at arm's length, engaging with it only on selective terms. At a dinner party, Hirota points out to Nonomiya: "To test the pressure of light, it is not enough to just open our eyes and observe nature.... It doesn't seem that 'the pressure of light' is printed on nature's menu. Isn't that why we use artificial devices like crystal threads, vacuums, and mica, and contrive to make the pressure visible to the eyes of physicists? So physicists are not Naturalists.... To place the light and the thing that receives the light in a spatial relationship that is not found in the normal natural world is indeed a Romantic thing to do" (SZ 5: 512). Hirota deems physicists who intentionally set up experiments to test for nonobvious natural laws as closer to Romantic literary writers who intentionally craft stories than to Naturalist writers who ostensibly just record their unadorned observations. But such a framing of literary Naturalism begs the question of whether any writing can be completely objective since the choice of narrative focus already implies a subjective interest at work, a theme that we saw in the formation of Sōseki's aesthetic thought. Another guest at the party proposes the hybrid term "Romantic Naturalist" (*romanteki shizen-ha*) to describe physicists' approaches to their experiments (SZ 5: 513), a term that might be applied to Sōseki's own writings as well.

Sōseki therefore draws a connection between the aesthetic and scientific modes of thought here, although he had previously posited them as fundamentally distinct from each other. To wit, *Kusamakura*'s protagonist had sought to escape the rational spaces of modern urban life by retreating to his poetically rural sanctuary. In *Sanshirō* too, Hirota's early remarks about the dangers symbolized by Leonardo's experiment with the poisoned peach tree seems to warn against the dehumanizing possibilities inherent in modernity's ongoing quest for reason, productivity, and technological progress. In contrast, Sōseki's later writings expand upon the view that artistic pursuits and scientific advancement share similarities, as he does in this passage from the speech "Dōraku to shokugyō" (Leisure and occupation, 1911)[72]:

> Philosophers and scientists only study domains that are far removed from the real lives of people in society, so they cannot gain widespread popularity even if they tried. It is also very rare that the attitudes and other personal attributes of

such researchers could affect whether their philosophical or scientific ideas gain currency in broader society. Seeing this type of eccentric holed up in the laboratory working from morning to night, or locked in the study lost in deep thought indifferent to all other matters, I cannot help but think of how selfish this kind of work is. Artists too are like this. (SZ 16: 428)

Sōseki then assesses his own work as driven by a personal desire to write, not by the desire to please his readers. Komori Yōichi suggests that when read alongside the speech "Gendai Nihon no kaika" (1911), which he delivered days later, Sōseki appears to advocate for both scientific and literary labors that are conducted for their own sakes, rather than for the external aims of efficiency or profit; the later essay stresses the need for an "organically driven" (*naihatsu-teki*) progress rather than just an "outwardly instigated" (*gaihatsu-teki*) one, and endorses the pursuit of "active" (*sekkyoku-teki*) innovations rather than just the "preservation of energy" (*katsuryoku setsuyku*) and "convenience" (*riben-sa*).[73]

As with Hirota and his posture of philosophical detachment, Nonomiya appears to Sanshirō as a model of this sort of intellectual purity. But even though Nonomiya's seeming disconnect from the conditions of his quotidian life is symptomatic of his admirable focus on his research, it also indicates a certain precarity. Given how little we are told about other facets of his persona, it is difficult to determine whether Nonomiya has the humanistic capacity to prevent his scientific work from being put toward uses that might create short-term gains but deleterious results later, such as the production of weapons of mass destruction or irreversible environmental damage. In the late Meiji period, which saw Japan's rise as an imperial and industrial force, such concerns about the uses of technology could not have been far from Sōseki's mind.

Nonomiya's passivity vis à vis the immediate world is manifest most concretely in his effeteness as Mineko's suitor. It is impossible to determine whether Mineko—who ends up marrying another man entirely—had truly loved Sanshirō or Nonomiya. But it is clear that there had been some kind of bond budding between Mineko and Nonomiya before Sanshirō's arrival in Tokyo. For instance, at the beginning of the novel Sanshirō accompanies Nonomiya on a walk and they stop at a shop where Nonomiya buys a woman's hair ribbon. Several days after, Sanshirō sees Mineko wearing an identical item. In another scene, Yojirō makes a teasing allusion to the prospect of Nonomiya's moving in with Mineko. Sanshirō also recognizes her handwriting on an envelope that Nonomiya had been carrying. But it seems that the two eventually have a falling out, and Mineko bitterly complains to Sanshirō about "someone who likes to avoid responsibility" (SZ 5: 416). Mineko, however, graciously remarks in a later conversation: "Someone like Sōhachi [Nonomiya] is beyond our understanding. He is so far above us, thinking grand thoughts" (SZ 5: 456). While Sanshirō's growing feelings for Mineko constitute the main vein of the novel, the evolving drama between Nonomiya and Mineko forms a parallel story. Sanshirō—and the readers who cheer for his romantic fruition—might intuit that Mineko had been interested in Nonomiya romantically, but disappointed by his dedication to his research and his coolness toward everything else, she is ready to move on with someone more emotionally available.

Mineko and Nonomiya's strained relationship becomes most noticeable when Mineko invites Sanshirō to an art exhibit. Spotting Nonomiya in the crowd, she makes a show of whispering something to Sanshirō before they approach him together. Her actions seem to have their intended effect. Nonomiya pointedly remarks to Sanshirō, "What a strange companion you've brought!" to which Mineko brazenly replies, "We're well matched, aren't we?" (SZ 5: 500). Sanshirō senses the tension between them and suspects she had used him to foment Nonomiya's jealousy, so he privately confronts her. To her credit, Mineko does not deny that she had intended to manipulate Nonomiya's feelings with her charade. She only claims that she had not been toying with Sanshirō. As though out of respect for the unexpected directness with which he expressed his annoyance at her flippant behavior, which in turn reflected the seriousness of his feelings for her, she admits to him: "For some reason, I just wanted to do it. But I didn't mean any disrespect to Nonomiya" (SZ 5: 506). This honest confession of her conflicted feelings shows Sanshirō that in this moment she sees him as an emotional peer, and that she feels a closeness with him that she could not experience with Nonomiya. Although she would elude him too by abruptly becoming engaged to another man soon after, it can be said that Sanshirō is able to achieve a real emotional intimacy with Mineko in this instance and that through this, he undergoes a certain coming of age. We presume that in the future, he would be more in touch with his own desires and agency in the world and that, unlike Hirota or Nonomiya thus far, he would be able to attain love. Sōseki leaves his readers with hope that Sanshirō—and perhaps, literary writing more generally—would evolve beyond the dispassionate aesthetic remove from the world as embodied by Hirota, and the bloodlessly objective approach to it as embodied by Nonomiya.

Sanshirō has been regarded as a turning point in Sōseki's oeuvre after which the more socially oriented themes of individualism in modernity and the ethical dilemmas of coexisting with others became central themes in his writings, and his novels began to unfold along clearer storylines that advance an examination of these core issues.[74] Ebii Eiji, for one, states: "We can probably be forgiven for saying that Sōseki became worthy of being called a serious author of modern realism after *Sanshirō*."[75] In the latter phase of his career, he also delivered a series of public lectures that directly addressed the state of modern Japanese society, including his aforementioned "Dōraku to shokugyō" and "Gendai Nihon no kaika" speeches. But Sōseki also continued to write shorter pieces that focused on the expression of subtle, subjective impressions, such as in *Eijitsu shōhin* (Short pieces from long days, 1909) and *Garasudo no naka* (Within the glass doors, 1915). And even as his later novels feature less overt references to works of visual art, and discussions comparing literature to the visual arts, they too were not devoid of visually arresting poetic images with symbolic power.

For example, *Sorekara* (1909), the novel he wrote after *Sanshirō*, opens with the striking sight of a fallen camellia blossom by the bedside of the protagonist Daisuke (SZ 6). Waking from sleep, Daisuke contemplates the dropped flower as he feels the steady beating of his pulse. As the headlines of the morning paper enter his vision signaling the exigencies of ongoing world events, he brings the blossom up to his face to feel its softness before putting it down to begin his day. The still and quiet contemplation of the beautiful camellia plays no diegetic role in the story to follow but it fortifies Daisuke for the hard encounters with social and economic realities that await him. Through this image of the flower, particularly one so closely associated with the *haikai* poetics of Masaoka Shiki, Sōseki seems to attest to the presence of beauty in what could be a harsh or banal world. I revisit *Sorekara* in chapter 4 when I consider how the young and eager writers of the Shirakaba group received its messages. But for Sōseki's part, it might be said that as he shifted his literary focus away from characters looking out at the world from the controlled confines of their subjectivities, and as he began to explore how they might engage more critically with the wider world, he did not lose sight of literature's capacity to also offer comfort and pleasure through the evocation of beauty.

THREE

Mori Ogai and the "Inner Flame" of Beauty

IN AN ESSAY he wrote in 1917, after more than a quarter of a century as a figure in the public eye, Mori Ogai reflects on his long career as a man of letters and as a high-ranking doctor in the Japanese Army.[1] His tone is humble and frank:

> I served in an official capacity by studying medicine. But I have never risen to social attention as a medical doctor....
>
> It is in my career as a man of letters that I gained some social renown.... As for novels, I have attempted to craft several dozen short works for practice, but I gave up when I got to the daunting incline of a longer work. As for plays too, I managed to complete a few one-act works as practice, but I idly looked on at the unscalable heights of plays longer than three acts. As for philosophy, I was a doctor and confounded by the lack of an overarching unity (*tōitsu*) spanning the natural sciences, so I sought provisional refuge in Hartmann's philosophy of the Unconscious. Perhaps a faint reminiscence of the Neo-Confucian principles I had heard as a child remained at the pit of my soul, and drew me toward Schopenhauer's school of thought. However, I did not come to the point of making public proclamations as a philosopher. (OZ 26: 543)

Ogai's self-evaluations may strike the contemporary reader as overly self-deprecating, for we know that in his medical career he had by this point reached the rank of surgeon general in the Japanese military, and as a writer he continues to be esteemed as "one of the giants in modern Japanese literature and intellectual history."[2] Less clear is how to evaluate his comments about his lack of standing as a philosopher. For example, Ogai did not develop or expound upon a particular paradigm of thought, and his formal academic training had been in medicine. As Ogai himself disclosed, his first calling was in the natural sciences. From there he began to consider the prospect of a metadiscursive logic by which to situate one branch of knowledge against the others, and he was then drawn to the works of Eduard von Hartmann (1842–1906) and others who attempted to offer such comprehensive conceptual systems. Also, rather than in the context of purely theoretical discussions, Ogai introduced Western philosophers' ideas to the Japanese public over the course of topical discussions or debates against other literary writers and cultural critics. He produced numerous translations of German philosophical texts, but he refrained from building on these to present a system of his own theories. But his literary oeuvre shows a persistent desire—what we might regard as a distinctively philosophical drive—to order a cohesive conceptual framework that could comprehend the significance and ideals of his various pursuits in relation to each other.

Or perhaps, it might be more accurate to say that Ogai had situated his wide-ranging philosophical investigations about the conditions of knowledge, subjectivity, and aesthetics in the modern era within the literary sphere. His literary career comprises three main creative phases: The initial romantic period is exemplified by his "German trilogy" stories—"Maihime" (The dancing girl, 1890), "Utakata no ki" (A record of froth on the water, 1890), and "Fumizukai" (The courier, 1891).[3] The middle period, when he resumed writing his own fiction, began in 1909 following nearly a two-decade hiatus during which he continued to produce translations and critical essays while advancing his career as a bureaucrat and military doctor. And in the final period he turned to composing historical biographies. I begin this chapter with an examination of the early phase when Ogai endorsed a demarcation between an artistic idealism informed by European art and culture, and a critical, pragmatic engagement with lived conditions in imperial Japanese society; this binarism mirrors his attempts to keep his burgeoning literary and medical careers separate. I then trace how, in the middle phase of his literary trajectory, Ogai gained a more nuanced willingness to investigate the potential for a literature and art that can be created and appreciated amid modern Japanese social and political conditions. During each of these stages it was often through discussing the visual arts that Ogai explored how the aesthetic and critical modes of cognition stand in relation to each other. My aim is not to provide a comprehensive account of Ogai's vast oeuvre, but to focus on nodal texts that especially reveal the range of his inquiries and underscore his belief in literature's capacity to draw on overlapping artistic, social, and intellectual discourses.

First Forays

Ogai entered the arena of public discourse in Japan with "Shōsetsuron: cfr. Rudolph von Gottschall" (Theory on the novel: cfr. Rudolph von Gottschall),[4] an essay of literary criticism published in the *Yomiuri* newspaper in January 1889, shortly after his homecoming from Germany where he had spent 1884 to 1888 studying medicine as an attaché with the Japanese Army. The essay garnered little attention when it first appeared because its main argument laments the rise of Naturalist literature in France as represented by the author Emile Zola (1840–1902), a phenomenon yet unknown in Japan at the time. The full-blown rise of Japanese Naturalism as defined by the arrival on the literary scene of writers like Tayama Katai (1872–1930) and Kunikida Doppo (1871–1908) would occur more than a decade later. Kobori Kei'ichirō suggests that Ogai had been motivated to warn against Naturalism after reading Tsubouchi Shōyō's literary treatise *Shōsetsu shinzui* (1885–1886), which called for authors to depict their characters with psychological realism.[5] We cannot entirely dispel the impression, however, that Ogai had, in Kobori's words, been "emptily waving around his sword" against threats that were yet to emerge.[6] In any case, the essay helped articulate key tenets of Ogai's budding views on the qualitative divide between literary-aesthetic descriptions and scientific writing, and the author's role in establishing this difference.

Scholars have shown that "Shōsetsuron" is essentially a summary of a chapter in the book *Literarische Todtenklänge und Lebensfragen* (On death and life in literature, 1885) by the now largely obscure German literary critic Rudolf von Gottschall (1823–1909).[7] Ogai begins the essay by outlining the broad turn toward scientific reason in modern Western thought, and then situates Zola's novels as a literary manifestation of this shift:

Claude Bernard states that today's knowledge is based on observation and experimentation. When we meet with things in our midst which cannot be changed by human power, we observe them, and when we meet with things in our midst which we can affect, we experiment with them. In medicine when we seek to know the true workings of the human body, we supplement our observations with the methods of experimentation....

Heeding these words, Zola directly employed them in his novels. In his works, Zola analyzed and dissected his characters. (*OZ* 22: 1)[8]

Ogai then claims that readers find themselves unable to dismiss Zola's literary characters as mere experiments, citing the liveliness that Zola could not help imbuing them with despite his attempts to adhere to a cold and detached objectivity.[9] Zola's character Nana, Ogai suggests, exceeded scientific depiction because of her beauty and vivacity: "The vital, living flesh of the naked prostitute Nana posing in a myriad ways in front of her mirror cannot be seen in the same light as the corpse of a criminal at an autopsy with its pallid, cold skin." Ogai concludes the essay by distinguishing between straightforward scientific descriptions and literary artistry achieved through the writer's intentions and techniques: "To treat as Zola does the results of analysis and dissection as a novel is not appropriate.... While in medicine, gaining truth is sufficient, writers should not be satisfied with just this.... Truth is a good ingredient for writers. Yet, the actual method of adapting and using this should only be through the power of imagination" (*OZ* 22: 2). But Ogai does not describe what he deems to be a sufficient amount of artistic intervention needed to convert empirical observations into literature.

The "Ra-Kochō" (Naked Kochō) incident that erupted in the same month as the publication of Ogai's "Shōsetsuron" essay led him to further consider the divide between artistic representations and lived experiences. An illustration accompanying Yamada Bimyō's historical story "Kochō" (Butterfly) in the January 1889 edition of *Kokumin no tomo* magazine stoked a public uproar (figure 3.1). The work was written in a vernacular style except for the dialogue, which used an ornate and old-fashioned language to enhance the periodicity of the story set during the Gempei wars of the twelfth century. The illustrator, Watanabe Seitei, was a celebrated *nihonga* painter whose works had won awards at two world's fairs, the 1878 Paris Exposition and the 1883 Colonial Exposition, Amsterdam. But neither the

FIGURE 3.1 Seitei Watanabe, illustration from Yamada Bimyō's story "Kochō" (Butterfly) in *Kokumin no tomo* 37 (1889).

elegance of the text accompanying it, nor the gilded status of its artist, prevented the broad disapproval that met Seitei's image of Kochō, an aristocratic lady-in-waiting, depicted nude after washing ashore following a sea battle in which she was thrown overboard from a ship. In fact, the narrative context of the illustration seemed to increase its shock factor, and the novelist Ozaki Kōyō wrote in the *Garakuta bunko* magazine about his dismay that a lady of nobility should be depicted in such a shameful state.[10] Other critics concentrated more on the fact of a nude image appearing in a national publication at all. For instance, although it went unpublished at the time, the writer Futabatei Shimei commented that "the naked body is ugly to the human gaze" and unfit to be published.[11]

The debate threw into relief the conflicted attitudes of Japanese intellectuals toward Western-inspired artistic innovations, and Ogai, eager to publicize his expertise in European cultural mores, entered the fray. He defended the controversial illustration in a spirited editorial titled "Hadaka de yukeya" (Go naked) published in the Yomiuri newspaper on January 12, 1889. His garrulous, low-vernacular tone was reminiscent of the Tokugawa-period writings enjoying a resurgence of popularity at the time as a reaction against Western literary influences.[12] To indicate that he was not merely repeating European theories, Ogai commented: "It would be a problem if this argument, which has continued for a thousand or two thousand years in the West erupts here too. . . . There is no use arguing if we think that a prostitute working at a storefront in Western clothing is classy, but a lady at her bath is vulgar. . . . Don't mind the experts. Just go naked, Poesie! (*Hadaka de yukeya, Poesie!*)" (*OZ* 38: 117).

Nakayama Akihiko, for one, assesses that Meiji Japanese reactions to Watanabe's illustration showed an attitude of "hyperrealism" "that does not consider how a painting's representational quality equals its ability to stand in for its subject," and he argues that Ogai's reaction too shows this tendency.[13] But while critics objected to the "Kochō" illustration out of the assumption that the very state of nudity is shameful without analyzing the context of its depiction—and though Ogai's commentary too references states of dress and nudity in various social settings rather than in artistic ones—his last cry for "Poesie" and not for actual Japanese women to go naked shows that his interest lies in the *representation* of nudity in art rather than life. His rallying call to Poesie implies the view that human corporeality could be depicted without vulgarity in the right aesthetic circumstances. As we will see, the notion of an artistic register apart from quotidian existence—Poesie, as he calls it here—continued to impact Ogai's views throughout his career.

Ogai's interest in the discourses of painting, hinted at in the Naked Kochō editorial, found fuller and more direct expression in the art commentaries he began to write at around this time. The first of these was a review of the Meiji Bijutsu-kai's (Meiji Art Group's) first exhibit, which he cowrote with Harada Naojirō (1863–1899), a Japanese painter he had befriended in Munich. Scholars have noted how Ogai's bond with Harada helped shape his artistic tastes and his interest in the visual arts.[14] Like the literary sphere, the art world too was undergoing a period of reorganization and institutionalization, and Ogai allied himself with the Meiji Bijutsu-kai to which his friend belonged. The group was established in May 1889 as the first official Western painting organization in Japan, and it counted among its prominent members *yōga* painters like Asai Chū, politicians like Hara Takashi, bureaucrats like Izawa Shūji, and academics like Toyama Masakazu (1848–1900). The members were united in the cause to promote the Western arts in Japan amid the rise of nationalist sentiments fanned by the American academic Ernest Fenollosa and his patron Okakura Tenshin, who claimed the superiority of classical Japanese ink paintings over Western oil paintings. Okakura spearheaded the establishment of the Tokyo Bijutsu Gakkō (Tokyo Art School), which aimed to foster the Japanese arts and thus included no departments for teaching the Western arts, when it opened in February 1889. The new institution replaced the Kōbu Bijutsu Gakkō (Technical Arts School), which had been established in 1876 with departments in Western painting, sculpture, and architecture, each headed by foreigners under limited-term contracts. The school closed in 1883 under the wave of popular nationalist sentiments that surged in reaction to what many perceived as the Meiji state's extreme emphasis on Westernization.[15]

Ogai and Harada cowrote the essay "Abura-e manhyō" (A free-wheeling review of oil-paintings), which was published in the November 1889 edition of the *Shigarami zōshi* magazine.[16] It shows Ogai's eagerness to endorse *yōga*—and by extension Western learning—although he remained measured in his approaches. He writes:

> Many of today's Japanese artists realize that there is a certain appeal to the paintings unique to our country, and we question whether they have not

forgotten that there are also large advantages to Western pictorial methods, or blindly believe the remarks of one or two foreigners who flatter [the Japanese] by raising the shortcomings of Western paintings and praising the strengths of Eastern paintings. Alas, it is not that we Japanese do not know the elegance of our traditional paintings.... And we also know about the comments of some Europeans like Brinkman, who said, "In order for the Japanese arts to continue being beloved by the Europeans, we must by all means protect their purity and import their special elements so that they will not be ruined." But we know that in order to further elevate the sentiment of beauty (*bisō*) among the people of our country, we need to [also] take in the Western arts.[17] (OZ 22: 83)

Ogai decries what he perceived to be the condescending gaze of Europeans attracted to the Japanese arts purely for their quaint exoticism, and he warns his countrymen against being flattered by such questionable forms of praise. He believes the solution is for the Japanese to actively learn from Western culture instead of disengaging from it. He then refers to a public debate he had engaged in during his time in Munich with Edmund Naumann (1850–1929), a geologist who had spent from 1875 to 1885 in Japan as a Meiji-government-sponsored advisor. In response to Naumann's condescending and incorrect remarks about Japanese culture presented in the prestigious *Algemeine Zeitung* newspaper on June 26 and 29, 1886, Ogai penned a sharply worded essay correcting the respected German scholar. This essay, and a follow-up he composed in response to Naumann's reply, were published in January 1887 in the *Algemeine Zeitung* as well, a remarkable feat for a young foreign student.[18] Through his personal encounters with both the richness of European culture and the frustratingly Orientalist attitudes of some Europeans, Ogai emerged cautious about the Japanese internalization of biased Western views on Japan.

But despite its open-minded call for artistic progress and eclecticism, "Abura-e manhyō" revealed little about Ogai's artistic standards. In Mikiko Hirayama's words, the comments were "brief and simplistic. The coauthors paid close attention to the technical aspects such as brushwork and proportion, but their criticism was permeated with ambiguous words such as 'good,' 'vague,' 'uninteresting,' 'tasteful,' and 'inspirational.'"[19] A similar lack of clarity is noticeable in "Shigarami zōshi no honryō wo ronzu" (On the main aims of the *Shigarami zōshi*, October 1889), the inaugural statement Ogai wrote for the coterie magazine that served as his literary base until its closure in 1894. He starts the essay with a broad assessment of the previous generation's approaches to Western culture: "When Western scholarship first entered the East, its products were introduced but not its spirit. [The Japanese] came to know of Western learning in terms of rules and laws, engineering and military methods, and they came to know of Westerners as a clever people but not as a people of special morality, let alone of elegance" (OZ 22: 27). Ogai contends that Japan has since evolved, and that people were now welcoming Western plays and dramas alongside technological innovations. But, he cautions, this bred a state of "chaos in which the elements of aesthetic judgment (*shinbi-teki bunshi*) from our country, China, and the West fly about haphazardly" as multiple types of literature proliferate. Ogai declares that the mission of the *Shigarami zōshi* was to fix this state of affairs by adopting a "gaze of aesthetic judgment in critically evaluating (*hyōron*) the writings of the world" (OZ 22: 29). Although he does not offer prescriptive details in the essay, Ogai presents an optimistic expectation that universal literary-aesthetic criteria could be delineated by Japanese writers.

"Maihime": A World of Beauty

"Maihime" (The dancing girl), Ogai's debut work of fiction, provides clearer clues about the literary directions he had favored at this time. Notably, it underscores his perception of a stark dichotomy between the aesthetic and the rational modes of thought, reflecting Rudolf von Gottschall's theories that he referenced in his earlier "Shōsetsuron" essay. The story is written in an elegant *gabun*-style language that employs classical grammar mixed with Western vocabulary and turns of phrase that cumulatively heighten the romantic otherworldliness of Berlin where its events take place. The essay "Genbun ron" (Theory on speech and writing, April 1890) reveals Ogai's linguistic views at the time.[20] He was in favor of preserving traditional syntactical features against the rising *genbun itchi* (aligining the oral and the written) language-reform movement, and to make his point he paraphrases the Japanese language scholar Mozume Takami (1847–1928):

> It is not necessarily the case that [the classical poetic tropes of] snow, moon, and flowers are bad or that elegance is bad, but when we try to compose a work about such themes, we naturally look to the examples of past poets, or come to

study their verse patterns. We then become unable to write what we truly think, and we end up looking for words before concepts, only starting to think after we have our words, triggering a habit of sequential reversal.... In order to stem this habit, for a year, whenever I composed writing, even in older language or any other linguistic register, I assiduously used *genbun itchi* to avoid the entry of old meanings from old sentences. I then rewrote these sentences in older language. (OZ 22:146)

Mozume and Ogai shared a conception of literary writing not as the direct transcription of one's thoughts, but a distillation of them through an intentional choice of words and phrases. In short, Ogai was not against the aims of *genbun itchi* to voice one's sincere, heartfelt thoughts, but he wanted to maintain awareness of the mediated nature of verbal articulation especially in composing a literary text, a consciously aesthetic act. The epistolary form of "Maihime" reflects Ogai's self-reflexive consciousness about the act of writing.

Because "Maihime" continues to be examined from a variety of angles by scholars in Japan and beyond, I offer here only a brief summary, as it retraces information no doubt familiar to many.[21] The story is presented as a first-person journal entry by Ota Toyotarō, a young Japanese man on a steamer ship making his way back to Japan after a number of years spent in Berlin. He reflects on his relationship with "Erisu" (Ellis), the poor German dancing girl he had fallen in love with. With the help of his stalwart friend Aizawa, Toyotarō eventually leaves Ellis and returns to Japan to advance his career. The story's ambiguous ending expresses Toyotarō's awareness that he has made a reasonable decision, as well as his regrets about having been unable to buck societal expectations to follow his heart and stay with his lover.

Toyotarō's initial status as an ambitious, government-funded student matches that of Ogai's situation during his years in Germany. And the romantic relationship that Ogai had established while abroad became well known within a month of his return to Japan, when a German woman named Elise Wiegert arrived in Tokyo to see him, though she was soon convinced by Ogai's alarmed family to return home. Ogai left no direct records of this dramatic incident in his diaries or his correspondences, but this youthful episode has attracted the attention of scholars who continue to search for details about Elise's involvement with her Japanese paramour and her later life.[22] It is clear that "Maihime" was at least partly based on

Ogai's own experiences, but the story may also have been inspired by his friend Harada Naojirō, the son of an aristocratic politician who himself had spent time in Germany in his youth and admired European culture. Harada, an aspiring painter, was encouraged to pursue his artistic ideals during his time abroad rather than adhere to the rigid course of a bureaucratic career, as was Ogai's case. Harada's travel expenses were paid for with family funds, and he was not obliged to report on his progress to any institutional authorities. Ogai seems to have admired such freedom, and he described his artist friend as "unattached and unselfish" (*kattan muyoku*) (OZ 25: 132) and "much loved by his teachers and peers for being such a pure person (*shizen ji*)" (OZ 25: 131).[23]

But Harada's circumstances were more complex than an initial glance suggested. He married at eighteen and already had a child by the time he left for his studies in Germany at the age of twenty-one, following the advice of the pioneering Western-style painter Takahashi Yuichi. Takahashi expected that the new Tokyo Art School—the planned replacement for the shuttered Tokyo Technical Arts School—would need Japanese instructors trained in Western artistic techniques. Ogai thinks that Harada had been too modest to bring up his personal life, and thus reluctant to tell his new acquaintances in Germany about his familial status.[24] Harada eventually ended up romantically involved with Marie, a waitress at a café frequented by art students. There is a single, passing mention of Marie being pregnant with Harada's child in Ogai's diary (OZ 35: 154) but no further information as to what happened later to her or the child after Harada's return to Japan in 1887.[25]

Niizeki Kimiko proposes that in "Maihime," Ogai had aligned himself not with the protagonist Toyotarō but with the supporting character Aizawa Kenkichi, since he had introduced Harada to Hamao Arata, a visiting government official who hired Harada to serve as a translator and guide while touring the art academies of Germany.[26] Ernest Fenollosa and Okakura Tenshin had initiated a study of the European art academies as a part of their preparatory research for the new Tokyo Art School. Hamao, a member of the Ministry of Education and Culture (the Monbu-shō) who was already in Europe on other bureaucratic business, was among those contacted for this mission. It was in this capacity that he enlisted Harada's services. Unlike Ogai's protagonist Toyotarō, Harada was unable to parlay his short-term assignment into a job placement in Japan. When the Tokyo Art

School finally opened in 1889 after years of groundwork by Tenshin and Fenollosa, it focused on teaching traditional Japanese styles and techniques. It did not include a Western arts curriculum and therefore had no openings for Harada, who had expected a position there upon his return to Japan. Despite clear dissimilarities between Harada's and Toyotarō's circumstances, Niizeki argues that in "Maihime," Ogai expresses his conflicted feelings about having led his friend to hope for an opportunity that did not materialize and, however indirectly, had caused him to leave the artistic freedoms of Germany and a pregnant mistress to return to his homeland where the infrastructures for supporting his style of artistic expression did not yet exist. This interpretation is further supported by how Ogai later wrote under the pen name Aizawa Kenkichi in response to criticisms of the story.

There are no guarantees that identifying the real-life counterparts to a work of fiction by examining biographical parallels will unlock the work's "true" meanings.[27] But what is evident throughout the story is that Toyotarō is caught between his private artistic passions and cautious, social reason. In an early scene when he first arrives in Berlin, Toyotarō exclaims, "What luminosity arrests my eyes! What colors tempt my heart!" (OZ 1: 427). He admires the proud officers and attractive girls on the streets, then shifts his gaze upward to the high buildings and the spray of water fountains against the clear sky, and farther down the vista toward the Brandenburg Gate and the statue of the goddess on top of the Victory Tower. This method of first establishing tone and a color palette, then focusing on subjects in the foreground, and lastly confirming the more distant elements, mimics an ekphrastic description of an artist painting a scene. Toyotarō's gaze is already actively engaged with the landscape of Berlin. Therefore, when he states that "in my heart was a vow not to be moved by the transience of beautiful sights under any circumstances, and I always blocked out the external stimuli that assaulted me" (OZ 1: 428), it rings falsely hollow. He cannot claim apathy toward a scene that he has made his own.

Ogai continues to highlight the tensions between the young man's wide-eyed penchant for beauty, and his attempts to stem these tendencies so that he might concentrate on his studies. Toyotarō had embarked on his studies with the intent of becoming a serious legal scholar, but he begins to lose his former drive and passion. "I used to diligently answer even the most arcane queries about the law but from this point onward, in the correspondences I sent to the magistrate [to whom I reported], I argued that one should not be bound by the specific details of laws. I declared that once one grasped the essential spirit of the law, complicated matters would become clear" (OZ 1: 428). The restless Toyotarō soon finds refuge in love. The defiant solitude with which he fortifies himself against the Japanese peers who mock his depression gives way when he sees Ellis crying alone in a shadowy side street: "Surprised by my footsteps she turned to me, and her visage was such that I cannot describe it without the words of a poet. Her pure blue eyes were questioning and contained an element of sadness. They were half shaded by her long, wet eyelashes. How did just one look from her penetrate to the depths of my cautious soul?" (OZ 1: 430). It is beauty that inspires him—one doubts whether Toyotarō would have been as moved by a less pretty face—and offers him a refuge from the drab world of law and rules. The narrative's subsequent descriptions of the dim, warren-like apartment that Ellis shares with her mother dramatizes Toyotarō's slippage into a dreamy realm apart from the well-lit streets of modern Berlin and the orderly logic of his legal studies.

Toyotarō's personal history helps readers better comprehend his dramatic rebellion against his previously obedient existence. He was raised by his mother following his father's early death and became a scholastic overachiever out of a desire to meet his mother's hopes for his success. But once out of her reach in Germany, he comes to question this maternal pressure. Toyotarō grieves when the notice of her death uncannily arrives in the same batch of mail as a final letter from her. This coincides with the loss of his official government sponsorship when his supervisors learn of his relationship with Ellis. In this orphaned state, unmoored from family and nation, Toyotarō moves in with Ellis and withdraws fully, if temporarily, into his romantic and creative idylls. His turn away from his studies and social obligations inspires him to read and write freely about a range of current events and developments in European culture as a freelance correspondent for a Japanese newspaper. Somewhat paradoxically, he begins to feel a renewed engagement with sociopolitical and intellectual developments in the wider world.

In spite of their happiness, the beginning of the end of Toyotarō's relationship with Ellis arrives once he learns about her pregnancy. It is while Toyotarō is apparently vacillating about how to confront this visceral development that his friend Aizawa introduces him to translation work for a visiting Japanese official. Toyotarō shares his plight with Aizawa, who offers him harsh advice: "How long could a man of education and talent lead an aimless existence out of sentimental attachment to one girl? ... Even if she is sincerely committed to you, and your passions are deep, this is a love based not on the mutual understanding of each other's natures but on a customary sort of practice. Be firm and end things with her" (OZ 1: 439). The months pass and, impressed with his work, the visiting Japanese official offers Toyotarō a permanent job in Japan. Overwhelmed by the dramatic turn of events, Toyotarō becomes ill and falls into a coma just when he must finally decide between a family life with Ellis in Berlin or a bureaucratic career in his homeland. During his incapacitation Aizawa arranges for Toyotarō's separation from Ellis and his return to Japan. Upon his recovery, Toyotarō does not fight the events set in motion for him.

Toyotarō's failure to analyze, even in retrospect, the blank period of unconsciousness that marked the conclusion of his dreamy hiatus with Ellis echoes the famous Freudian proposition about "the navel" of the dream:

> There is often a passage in even the most thoroughly interpreted dream which has to be left obscure; this is because we become aware during the work of interpretation that at that point there is a tangle of dream-thoughts which cannot be unraveled and which moreover adds nothing to the content of the dream. This is the dream's navel, the spot where it reaches down into the unknown. The dream thoughts to which we are led by interpretation cannot, from the nature of things, have any definite endings; they are bound to branch out in every direction into the intricate network of our world of thought. It is at some point where this meshwork is particularly close that the dream-wish grows up, like a mushroom out of its mycelium.[28]

Jacques Derrida summarizes this opaque crux of the dream as "a night, an absolute unknown that is originarily, congenitally bound or tied (but also in itself unbound because ab-solute) to the essence and to the birth of the dream.... What forever exceeds the analysis of a dream is indeed a knot that cannot be untied, a thread that, even if cut, like an umbilical cord, nonetheless remains forever knotted, right on the body, at the place of the navel."[29] In "Maihime," Toyotarō instinctively seems to know that his coma cannot be untangled because it is a primal aporia that had spawned both his attachment to Ellis and her beauty, as well as his passive decision to let

Aizawa steer his future back onto the path of conventional Japanese responsibilities and obligations. Within the scheme of this story, the dream's "navel" is a locus of conflicting desires that cannot be reconciled in waking life. Aesthetic affect—subjectively felt and enjoyed for its own sake—and pragmatic logic, which strategically steers social advancement, are depicted as incompatible forces.

Evolving Aesthetics: Hartmann and Harada

When "Maihime" debuted it garnered praise for its romantic air and evocative language,[30] as well as criticism for the seeming inconsistency between Toyotarō's tender feelings for Ellis and his decision to abandon her and their unborn child.[31] In the postwar twentieth century, Toyotarō's poignant account was upheld as an exemplar of "a literature about 'modern subjectivity'" ('*kindai-teki jiga' no bungaku*) and the work, arguably Ogai's most famous today, is a staple of high school literature textbooks.[32] But it is also necessary to situate the story as an early work written when Ogai was still building his intellectual foundations. Sharp divisions between the precincts of beauty and rationality also characterize the second story in Ogai's German trilogy, "Utakata no ki" (A record of froth on the water), about a young Japanese painter studying abroad at the Academy of Munich, clearly based on Harada Naojirō.[33] Like Toyotarō in "Maihime," the protagonist of "Utakata no ki" almost ends up being led astray into a hazy realm of beauty and romance by a devastatingly attractive woman, but at the story's end he manages to recover his bearings by breaking away from her. His relationship with his muse, for all its emotional intensity, ultimately proves as transient as froth. Though it was published in August 1890, some evidence suggests that the story had been written prior to "Maihime."[34] In any event, both stories trace the drama of individuals caught between a private realm of beauty and emotion, and a public sphere of reason and progress. In his third German trilogy story, "Fumizukai," Ogai signals a new shift toward considering how to bridge, rather than maintain, this binary view. His "Future of Japanese Painting" debate with Toyama Masakazu can be seen as a key catalyst for this transition.

The Meiji Bijutsu-kai group was scheduled to hold its second exhibit in spring 1890. But the proposed dates overlapped with the third Naikoku kangyō hakurankai (Domestic Industrial Exposition), so the Meiji Bijutsu-kai members instead entered their paintings in this government-sponsored event.[35] There was tension from the start, because under Okakura Tenshin's direction there were no *yōga* specialists among the judges in the exhibit's fine arts division.[36] The Meiji Bijutsu-kai thus sent Harada Naojirō and another *yōga* painter, Matsuoka Hisashi, to join the judges' panel. The showcase, which featured both *nihonga* and *yōga* works, prompted the poet and Tokyo Imperial University literature professor Toyama Masakazu to deliver a three-hour lecture on the theme "Nihon kaiga no mirai" (The future of Japanese painting) at a gathering of the Meiji Bijutsu-kai group on April 27, 1890. A full transcript of the talk was printed in the *Tokyo Asahi* newspaper over the following two weeks.[37]

Toyama's argument, which instigated Ogai's vociferous protest, begins by suggesting that more so than their divergent representational methods, a deeper issue facing both *yōga* and *nihonga* painters is the selection of appropriate subjects for their artworks. Toyama states that contemporary Japanese painters are solely preoccupied with the outer appearances of their artistic creations with little emotional investment in their subject matter: "Only when a painter has some element of faith should he endeavor to paint. Only when there is something he is moved by should he endeavor to paint. Only with *inspiration* should he endeavor to paint."[38] Referring to the works displayed in the Domestic Industrial Exposition as examples to illustrate his points, he complains that present-day paintings, in both the *yōga* and *nihonga* styles, are tired reiterations of classical tropes.

Special ire is reserved for Harada's *Kiryū Kannon* (Kannon on a dragon, 1890) (figure 3.2). Toyama criticizes the 3-meter by 2-meter image, wondering: "Did [Harada] want to paint the Kannon goddess on a dragon without believing in Kannon or dragons?"[39] He also mockingly implies that the Kannon's lifelike appearance is not befitting a figure of religious veneration: "[It] makes one question whether this is an image of a female circus performer lit by torchlight."[40] He suggests that the problem lies in the choice of subject matter, and that in the secular modern era, theological themes are no longer appropriate. Instead of religious paintings, he argues that painters should endeavor to create "*shisō-ga*" (conceptual paintings) that "incorporate a mix of concepts" by portraying scenes from real life.[41] In closing, Toyama proffers several examples of themes for paintings that are jarring for their bizarre specificity. For example, he suggests a scene featuring a

FIGURE 3.2 Naojirō Harada, *Kiryū kannon* (Kannon Goddess on a Dragon, 1890).
Oil on canvas.
The National Museum of Modern Art, Tokyo

rickshaw driver who arrives out of breath at Omori station, carrying two foreign customers, when he suddenly faints and expires with his hand still outstretched to collect his fare. His customers coldly depart as his aged father looks on in "dazed despair" at the death of his son.[42] Toyama also envisions a scene of an impoverished family of three atop the Ryōgoku Bridge lit by a midwinter night's moon, the father about to throw his infant into the river while his older son tries desperately to stop him.

Ogai objected to Toyama's lecture over the course of three essays, none of which managed to elicit a response from the older scholar. The first of these, "Toyama Masakazu shi no garon wo bakusu" (Attacking Mr. Toyama Masakazu's theory on paintings) was published in the *Shigaramai zōshi* on May 25, less than two weeks after the serialization of Toyama's lecture in the *Tokyo Asahi* newspaper ended. Ogai's essay, even longer than Toyama's, was marked by his querulous tone and references to the aesthetic philosopher Eduard von Hartmann's terminology. This was the first time Ogai had fully applied Hartmann's ideas to his own arguments,[43] and Ogai's expanded conceptual vocabulary conveys a sense of his intellectual confidence. Ogai first claims that while Western oil paintings and Japanese ink paintings are fundamentally different from each other, there are other art mediums in the West, such as watercolors and pastels, that are closer to Japanese painting styles and would make for better points of comparison (*OZ* 22: 176). Next, he attacks the main body of Toyama's argument by stating that the problem plaguing the arts in Japan is not the painters' poor choices of subject matter; in his estimation, the more pressing issue is how the subjects of the artist's inner imagination manifest in external form through his "technical skills (*gijutsu*)" (*OZ* 22: 177). He contends that without this intentional confluence, a painting would be unsuccessful regardless of its theme. Using Hartmann's theoretical language, Ogai then alleges that Toyama's ideals for a contemporary "conceptual painting" refer to an "individualistic notion (*kosō*)" [glossed in German as *individualismus*] of its subject (*OZ* 22: 180).[44]

He also accuses Toyama of conflating artistic imagination with actual religious faith (*OZ* 22: 183). Responding to Toyama's snide remark that Harada's Kannon goddess resembles a circus performer, Ogai scoffs that just as theaters audiences do not expect an actor playing the role of a thief to hold real feelings of avarice, it is unreasonable to expect a painter to harbor feelings of true devotion when depicting a Buddhist deity (*OZ* 22: 195).

Again employing Hartmann's terms, Ogai states that there is a qualitative difference between "provisional, aesthetic sentiments" (*shinbi-teki kari kan*) and "actual sentiments" (*jikkan*). He compares *Kiryū Kannon* to a painting of the Madonna by Gabriel von Max (1840–1915), Harada's former painting mentor in Munich.[45] Ogai praises both works for their ability to transcend their religious themes and stimulate viewers' aesthetic imaginations by evoking their own distinctive "microcosmic understandings" (*shō tenchi shisō*).

In Hartmann's hierarchy, "generic notions" (*ruisō*) based on imagined generalities were the lowest type of aesthetic imagination. Those were followed by "individualistic notions" (*kosō*) based on the contemplation of specific subjects, with "microcosmic understandings" (*shōtenchi shisō*), or transcendental principles evoked through the artistic depiction of individual subjects, as the highest ideal. This aesthetic system is outlined in Hartmann's *Zweiter systemaischer Theil: Philosophie des Schönen* (The second part of the system: The philosophy of the beautiful), the latter of his two-part study, *Aesthetik* (1886–1887). As Ogai summarizes it, Hartmann's ideas "overcame the aesthetic systems of abstract idealism, and attempted to foster an aesthetic system of realism and the actualization of ideals [in artworks]" (OZ 23: 6).[46] Ogai reflects: "I used to depend on Gottschall's poetics to analyze the criticisms of the people of the era by drawing a dichotomy between reality and ideals, but that was a long time ago" (OZ 23: 5). Though the dismissal of his relatively recent reliance on Rudolf von Gottschall's ideas as belonging to the distant past might strike readers as youthful hubris, this statement highlights Ogai's conscious switch from a binary separation "between reality and ideals," to a more holistic view. Ogai's sustained commitment to Hartmann's theories can be seen in his references to the philosopher in multiple critical essays, as well as his translation of the opening sections of *Philosophie des Schönen* as "Shinbi ron" (Theory on aesthetic judgments) in the *Shigarami zōshi* magazine from 1892 to 1893. In 1899, he and the art historian Omura Seigai would also publish the stand-alone volume *Shinbi kōryō* (Code of aesthetic judgments), which provides a condensed introduction to Hartmann's philosophies.[47]

The young Ogai's defense of Harada's painting using Hartmann's ideas therefore seems to have been motivated by more than simple loyalty to his friend. That is, *Kiryū Kannnon* presented an opportunity for Ogai to affirm and articulate his own budding artistic ideals. The scholar Haga Tōru's eloquent description captures well the mix of realism and fantasy that had drawn Ogai to the painting:

> The grotesqueness of the mythical beast bathed in flames twisting downward through dark clouds running diagonally across the sky; the faint eroticism of the goddess who leans back lightly with her face and garments illuminated by the glow of the flames; the flowing mass of clouds that covers the sky behind her as black as soot, billowing with a storm; the barely visible dawn sky lit up by the morning sun and the ink-colored sea and mountains sunken far below—looking over *Kiryū Kannon* once again, its subject, motifs, composition, and colors, might it not be assessed as a painting in the vein of the German Romantic school instead of as a Meiji Japanese oil painting of a Buddhist or religious image?[48]

From as early as "Shōsetsuron" (January 1889), his debut work of criticism that had critiqued Emile Zola and French Naturalism, Ogai had maintained suspicions about the use of blatant realism in creative works. But his favorable comparison of Harada to Gabriel von Max shows that Ogai's artistic tastes did not simply favor the flair of the fantastic. Although his *Kannon* painting was more dramatic than any photorealist portrait, it is anecdotally known that Harada had employed Yamamoto Take, the wife of a live-in staff member at Ogai's father's hospital, as his model.[49] Max's romanticism too was tinged with what one art historian describes as "the intellectual ferment of a 'scientific age' that sought truth in scientific method and in emerging disciplines such as experimental parapsychology."[50]

Max, among the most celebrated artists in fin-de-siècle Munich, was known for his theatrical renderings of biblical tales and literary works such as *Faust*, the simultaneously forensic and sensual attention to the details constituting his subjects, and attraction to the occult conditions between life and death. His distinctive style garnered both praise and censure for their "mesmeric spell" and "want of naturalism."[51] For example, *The Anatomist* (1869) (figure 3.3), which was much discussed upon its debut at the First International Art Exhibition (1 Internationale Kunstaustellung) in Munich[52] embodies his signature blend of empiricism and mysticism. Rendered in the dark colors that characterized the academism style of the latter half of the nineteenth century, a somber physician whose balding forehead gleams in the shadows contemplates the pale corpse of a young girl lying supine across the foreground of the image. The clinical pragmatism, conjured by a

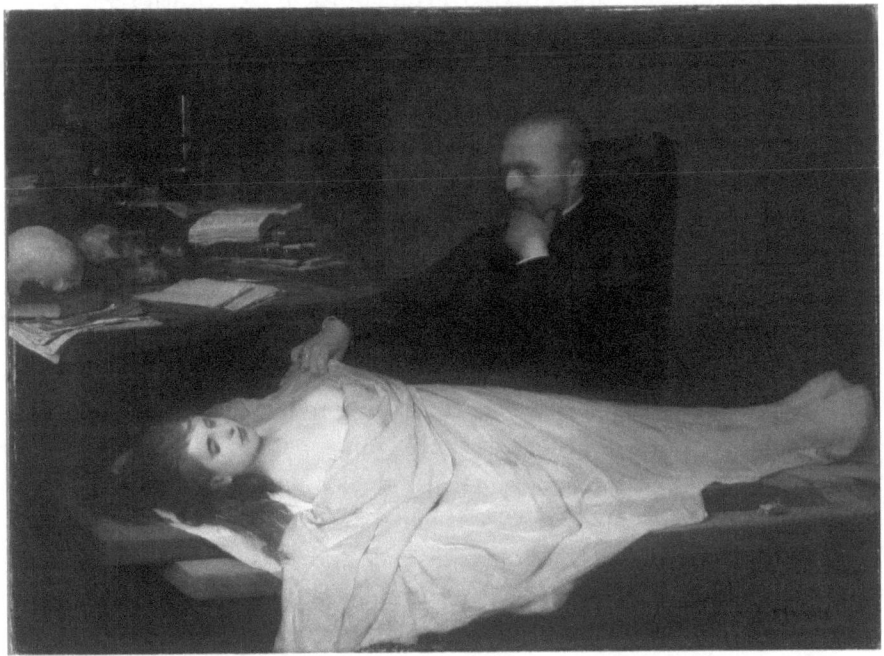

FIGURE 3.3 Gabriel Cornelius von Max, *The Anatomist* (1869). Oil on canvas. Neue Pinakothek

desk scattered with what appear to be medical books and two skulls in the background, contrasts against the somnambulant radiance of the dead girl's delicate features and unblemished skin. As we have seen, the juxtaposition of a lifeless corpse to be dissected by a physician and a young girl full of vitality was a central image in Ogai's "Shōsetsu-ron" essay; it is conceivable that Max's *Anatomist* inspired this imagery.

For Ogai, Harada and his mentor Max represented a synthesis of empirical observation and aesthetic invention. The painter Kuroda Seiki recalls Harada telling him that "to take a sketch from life (*shasei*) and declare it, as is, as a painting is not a true painting."[53] This echoes Ogai's own remarks from "Shōsetsuron" that "truth is a good ingredient for writers. Yet, the actual method of adapting and using this should only be through the power of the imagination" (OZ 22: 2). Deploying Hartmann's ideas in defense of Harada's painting against Toyama's critiques enabled Ogai to begin considering such an artistic process in more detail.

"Fumizukai" and Further Philosophical Explorations

"Fumizukai" (The courier, 1891), the third and last of the German trilogy stories, continues in the otherworldly, romantic vein of Ogai's two earlier German stories but includes the seeds of his later trajectories as well. In elegant *gabun*-style prose, the narrator, a Japanese military officer named Kobayashi, recounts his curious experiences with an aristocratic German girl named Ida whom he met at her family's castle in Deuben during his tour abroad with the Saxon Army. Ida was engaged to marry Meerheim, a military officer she did not love. To extricate herself from the impending union, she had Kobayashi convey a secret epistle to her well-connected aunt in the royal court at Dresden, requesting to be summoned there as a lady-in-waiting. Ida is described as striking in appearance, tall and slender with a pale complexion, black hair, and eloquent eyes, but not—Ogai stresses—as conventionally pretty as her sisters (OZ 2: 33). This marks her as different from the heroines of "Maihime" and "Utakata no ki," who had been characters defined by their external beauty and the disorienting effect it had on their respective admirers. In contrast, Ida is more connected to her surrounding realities, able to assess her own social position and then devise a practical plan of action for herself.

Ogai presents Ida as an active creator and afficionado of artistic pleasure rather than a passive figure of beauty to be admired by others. But to Kobayashi she initially appears reserved and cold in comparison to her more extroverted sisters. Only when she plays the piano for her guests at the request of her fiancé Meerheim does Kobayashi gain a glimpse of her hidden passionate nature. Ogai employs his skill at ekphrasis to describe her piano playing, which expresses the inner dilemmas that she cannot speak out loud in the context of her conservative, patriarchal family:

> Her fingers calmly struck the piano's keys, producing golden reverberations. As the piece picked up, a delicate flush appeared over her gaze. When her playing was as gentle as the clinking of a trail of crystal prayer beads, it became so quiet that it was as if the Mulde River had ceased to flow. When suddenly, the music rang with urgency like the clashing of swords and spears, it was raucous enough to startle the roving spirits of olden times and to disrupt the centuries-long slumbering dreams of the castle's ancestors. It seemed that the girl's emotions, which she normally kept locked in her narrow breast since she lacked the means

to express them in words, was pouring forth from her thin fingertips. It felt as if the castle were floating on the waves of her music, and we were all drifting along, bobbing and sinking in turn. As the piece reached its peak, the various spirits of the strings inside the piano quit their individual laments of endless curses and their cries rang out in unison. (OZ 2: 34)

But the sound of a flute accompanying her playing throws Ida into confusion. Distraught, she abruptly quits her performance. Later, Meerheim explains to Kobayashi that when she was younger, Ida had interceded on behalf of an orphaned boy on the family's estate by pleading with her parents to have a doctor fix his harelip. She also arranged for him to be taken in as a shepherd on their property. Now a young man, the shepherd is deeply in love with Ida and he watches her from afar. Whenever he hears her playing the piano inside the castle, he stands beneath the window to accompany her with his flute. Kobayashi, who had been moved by Ida's music, is so stirred by this story that he has a dream of her that night.

In the dream, a nightmare of sorts, he sees Ida astride a horse that has a human head with a harelip. Her countenance then turns into a stone sphinx's head with pupil-less eyes, while the horse turns into a lion resting with its front paws together. In Freudian fashion, the dream of Ida's union with the shepherd boy—unthinkably scandalous in reality—expresses the narrator's instinctive understanding of her suppressed feelings and desire for agency. This time, it is not through music but visual imagery that Kobayashi perceives Ida's inner nature. For her part, Ida too intuits Kobayashi as a kindred spirit untethered to the social stratifications that rule her existence.

The following day, although she had barely spoken to him earlier, Ida volunteers to show Kobayashi the view from the pyramid overlook on the castle's grounds before he departs for the next stop on his troop's military tour. There, atop the exotic decorative structure "that seems to have been built after the pyramids of Egypt" (OZ 3: 31), "separated from the world below" (OZ 3: 39), she asks him to secretly convey a letter to her aunt in Dresden because she has no other confidential means of communicating with her. Egypt is far from the lived realities of Ida and Kobayshi, and the stylized, aesthetic space of the garden serves as a neutral place—a kind of dreamscape—where they might temporarily escape from their German milieu. She does not know that Kobayashi has already faintly begun to suspect that she did not care for her fiancé, let alone that he had "seen" her connect instead with the shepherd she had pitied. Whether she recognized him as an ally based on his outsider status as a foreign visitor or because he appreciated her music the night before, she states: "I have a favor to ask of you since I feel like I know you" (OZ 3: 40). Kobayashi feels "drawn to her by a strange attraction that was neither lurid curiosity (*iyashiki monozuki*) nor lust (*ironaru kokoro*), but such that she appeared in my dreams and occupied my waking thoughts. The plains of Saxony that we gazed at below us was indeed beautiful but no match for the lush groves and deep pools that must have existed in this girl's heart" (OZ 3: 39). His appreciation of her beauty is purely platonic, yet he feels that she seemed particularly beautiful as she spoke with him. He quickly agrees to her request without question and carries out his secretive task as her messenger at his troop's stop in Dresden.

In the last scene of the novel, Kobayashi visits Dresden again months later to attend a ball at the royal castle, and he sees Ida there in her new post as a member of the court retinue. She offers to show him a display of Oriental porcelainware, and in a deserted hall they manage a hurried private conversation as the other guests enjoy the bustle of the party in the main ballroom. The gallery is filled with imported objects of beauty, a temporary sanctuary from German society much like the faux-Egyptian pyramid at the castle where Ida had entrusted Kobayashi with her fateful letter. In this secluded space, surrounded by colorful vases removed from everyday use, she tells him how with his help she had managed to appeal to her aunt and circumvent her pending marriage to Meerheim while preserving social appearances. She begins by telling him that she had read books by European travelers who scornfully remarked that in Japan, there are marriages arranged by parents and that many Japanese couples do not know true love. Evincing a wry cosmopolitanism, Ida says that the same could be said for Europe. She then declares:

> Even though I was born an aristocrat, I am also a person. I have come to see lineage and bloodlines as meaningless customs, and have no use for them in my heart. It would have been shameful for me, as a woman of high birth, to throw myself into a vulgar love affair. But couldn't someone support my attempts to step outside of these oppressive customs?
>
> In Catholic countries there are people who become nuns, but this is not possible in Protestant Saxony. So it occurred to me: the royal palace, which like the

Catholic church understands rituals but not human compassion, would become my tomb. (OZ 2: 45–46)

This is much more, quantitatively and qualitatively, than she had said when she had been an unmarried daughter living in her family's castle. Although she is now "entombed" in a life of respectable service at the court, Ida has managed to retain her autonomy as an individual by refusing a loveless marriage that her family expected of her. But after her confession, she quickly slips back into the ball and returns to her responsibilities as a member of the royal entourage, showing that she still does not have full agency over her actions. Ida cannot dally for long in conversation with Kobayashi despite the spark of allyship between them. Also, perhaps she prefers not to be reminded that in claiming a new station in life, she had left behind the shepherd boy who had loved her loyally from a distance. It is a loss that she cannot afford to face and question. She leaves Kobayashi with her composure and pride intact, and as he too takes his leave, Ida remains preserved in his mind as a poignant, beautiful memory.

It is a crucial detail that both of the two conversations that Ida initiates with Kobayashi had been under artistic pretexts. The first invitation was to survey the scenery from an architectural overlook, and the second was to see a porcelain exhibit. Ida seems to have sensed that beauty can be enjoyed across cultural differences and among strangers, as long as there is a basic shared appreciation of the inherent worth of aesthetic experiences. This echoes the sentiment evoked in Theodor Adorno's observation cited in the epigraph of this book: "Artworks fall helplessly mute before the question 'What's it for?' and before the reproach that they are actually pointless."[54] The implication is that aesthetic affect is self-evident, and irreducible beyond itself. Ida had correctly sensed that even if she and Kobayashi had little else in common, he was equipped with the core faculties for appreciating beauty and art. Through their shared understandings, Ogai suggests that aesthetics is not just a realm of entirely private sentiments. Rather, the story suggests, beauty can also be enjoyed with like-minded others as a source of solace and inspiration amid the ongoing obligations of workaday life.

"Fumizukai" has also been read as a tale of oblique personal disclosure for Ogai. This theory suggests that through Ida's words regarding Meerheim, the man she did not love, Ogai expresses his own feelings about

Toshiko, his first wife whom he divorced shortly after she gave birth to their son Otto.[55] Their marriage had been plagued with allegations that Ogai had only married her at the insistence of his family in the wake of his Berliner paramour Ellis's unexpected visit to Japan. Toshiko was the daughter of a high-ranking naval officer. Their union was meant to shield Ogai's social reputation and burnish it with prestige, but it lasted only about a year. As though to dispel the easily drawn parallels between Ida's revulsion toward her arranged marriage and his own situation, when the story was first published in the *Shincho hyaku shu* anthology, Ogai had arranged for illustrations by Harada Naojirō to depict the Kobayashi character with an unmistakable resemblance to Ogai's visage, and the Aida figure with her face hidden (figure 3.4). Niizeki Kimiko has suggested that by visually aligning himself with Kobayashi rather than Ida, Ogai attempted to save Toshiko from embarrassment by exculpating her from comparisons with the unappealing Meerheim.[56] Whatever the personal motivations for writing the story, in contrast to his two previous works, it is clear that in "Fumizukai" Ogai explores the viability, however hard-won, of maintaining the sanctity of one's personal ideals while remaining within the web of social relations.

Broadening Aesthetic Horizons

Ogai did not compose any new works of fiction until 1909 after he was sent to the battlegrounds of the Sino-Japanese (1894–1895) and Russo-Japanese (1904–1905) Wars and stationed in the provincial city of Kokura (1899–1902) as a doctor for the Japanese Army. Despite the consuming nature of his official duties during this period, he maintained his presence in the Tokyo-based literary world through his critical essays and translation work, including the aforementioned translations of Eduard von Hartmann's philosophical writings. Seemingly reflective of the challenges he had faced in balancing his military-bureaucratic responsibilities with his literary activities, the stories from Ogai's middle period contemplate how the appreciation of beauty can be calibrated within the ever-evolving conditions of everyday life. Unlike the German trilogy stories, which were written in a stylized, traditional *gabun* mode that emphasized the writer's consciously aesthetic intentions, these post-1909 stories use the modern, vernacular-based *genbun itchi* style. According to Yamamoto Masahide's widely cited

FIGURE 3.4 Naojirō Harada, illustration from Mori Ogai's story "Fumizukai" in *Shincho hyaku shu* (January 1891).

study, 78 percent of novels published in Japan in 1905 were using *genbun itchi* language, and by 1908 the rate had reached 100 percent.⁵⁷ In addition to this linguistic turn, many of his middle-period works portray Ogai's everyday life in Japan without aestheticizing it. Although his earlier stories too had been inspired by his own youthful time abroad, as we saw, they created an impression of faraway romanticism rather than of prosaic realism.

The essay "Tsuina" (Exorcising demons, May 1909) displays Ogai's new literary ethos in both form and message.⁵⁸ He was by this time a well-known public intellectual, and the essay discusses his view of literature and philosophy not as a means for fantasy and escapism, but as crucial elements in a full life. Ogai writes in a frank, first-person voice and begins by describing his grueling schedule: "I am exhausted by the time I return home from the office. Other people probably have a drink and then enjoy a merry slumber until the morning. But I dim the lamp and take a nap, preparing to awake in a short while. I wake up at midnight. My head is slightly recovered. I then write until two" (*OZ* 4: 587). Working a full-time job while writing is clearly exhausting, and in the lines that immediately follow, Ogai obliquely explains why he nonetheless continues to pursue literature: "Daytime thoughts are different from nighttime thoughts. There are times when I have a problem in the daytime to which I think I find a neat resolution during the night, but in thinking it over the next day, I discover that it is not a solution at all. There is something rather unreliable about nocturnal thoughts." He seems to imply that as day and night are mutually necessary halves of a single unit of time, so too are the asymmetrical spheres of pragmatic daytime thought and open-ended nighttime dreaming that together constitute human cognition and comprise the polyphonic stuff of literature.

This logic recalls the short essay "Yume" (Dreams, 1889), which Ogai had written for a medical journal shortly after his return to Japan from Germany. In it he states that in dreams, "normally forgotten things resurface unexpectedly in variously changed forms, are expanded upon, turn like images from a magic lantern, and like scenes from a play, time and space flow freely" (*OZ* 29: 285).⁵⁹ Though Sigmund Freud's ideas would not fully enter Japanese discourse until the 1910s, these remarks suggest that Ogai had already been familiar with the basic Freudian notion of the conceptual freedoms supposedly accessed in dream-states.⁶⁰ Many of Ogai's stories—notably, for example, "Hannichi" (Half a day, 1909), *Vita Sexualis* (1909), "Masui" (Anesthesia, 1909), and "Konpira" (1909), and to some extent even

"Fumizukai" (1891) from his German trilogy discussed earlier—present dream sequences and make use of Freudian terminology to describe their characters' mental and emotional conditions. Notably, Ogai's collection of books includes a first-edition copy of Freud's *On Dreams* (1901).[61] His readings of the plays and stories of the Austrian author and psychologist Arthur Schnitzler, a close contemporary of Freud in Vienna, have also been studied.[62] An interest in the potentials of psychology to scientifically illuminate human nature remained a latent thread throughout his oeuvre.

"Tsuina" continues with Ogai musing about his literary beliefs: "By means of my nighttime thoughts, I declare that in novels, it is fine to write about anything in any manner. Is the history of real literary development like the annual Carneval,[63] when a new king is chosen each year and paraded around, and then discarded without a second glance when the festival is over? Who was last year's king? Who is this year's king? Those who want to cry could certainly cry over this, but at the same time, isn't there also something laughable for those who want to laugh?" (*OZ* 4: 588–589). Ogai states his premise that like dreams, literature is an open terrain that allows for all subjects to be depicted in all manners. Fleeting trends mean little in the long view, and "the history of real literary development" unfolds at a more fundamental level. In the analogy of the Carneval, it is not the long-standing institution of the annual rite itself that is questioned, but the public fixation with its constantly changing king. This trope—which evokes Bakhtin's notion of "carnivalesque" literature that can temporarily disrupt dominant social logics—echoes the symbiosis between orderly "daytime" thoughts and more mysterious "nighttime" thoughts that Ogai introduced earlier. It thus serves as a segue into the latter half of the essay, which recounts a memorable evening that Ogai had once spent at a folk-traditional "Tsuina" demon exorcism performance. The shift in topic might at first seem abrupt, but Ogai's appreciation of the enduring age-old ritual provides an effective counterpoint to the disdain he expresses for the ephemeral nature of contemporary literary fads.

Ogai names Japanese Naturalism as a prime example of what he classifies as a passing, meaningless trend in modern literature. He writes that as he headed to an out-of-the-way teahouse for the Tsuina performance, he had felt excitement about his imminent encounter with the unknown. He snidely quips: "This is not because I expected to meet beautiful women there. Today's Naturalist novels show that writers' thoughts are constantly preoccupied with women, but I think this is because those authors are so young. When you approach fifty like me, my sex drive does not occupy the majority of my life" (*OZ* 4: 590). In a self-deprecating but unapologetic nod to his reputation as a notoriously scholarly writer, Ogai ends the essay with notes on how the Japanese demon-exorcism tradition dates back to the medieval era, and how a similar custom exists in Rome. Like the Tsuina rituals that have become ingrained into the fabric of people's lives and psyches over time, he suggests that "real" literature should provide meaningful contributions to the collective welfare of a community instead of— he further alludes—titillating the public with graphic depictions of their characters' often base thoughts and actions in the manner of the Japanese Naturalists. The essay proposes that the ineffable aesthetic sentiments of "nighttime thoughts" are distinct but ultimately inseparable from the critical rationality of the waking hours, and that literature's raison d'être lies in its special ability to encompass both realms.

"Hanako" and the Articulation of Artistic Vision

The visual artist in his encounters with non-artists is a motif that Ogai employs for exploring the viability of aesthetics within more quotidian settings. A particularly notable artist makes an appearance in his story "Hanako" (July 1910).[64] The story features the French sculptor Auguste Rodin (1840–1917), who was gaining wider recognition in Japan at the time. The Japanese had first learned of him through the painter Kume Keiichirō's reports from the 1900 Paris Exposition.[65] Shirai Uzan, an instructor at the Tokyo Art School who was newly returned from France, referenced him in a lecture in 1903.[66] The critic Shimamura Hōgetsu's article about the sculptor in the November 1907 issue of *Waseda bungaku* is credited for introducing his works to the broader Japanese public.[67] Rodin's works inspired young Japanese artists like Takamura Kōtarō (1883–1956) and Ogiwara Rokuzan (1879–1910), who would go on to become influential sculptors. The publication of "Hanako" in 1910 was timely, for the popularity of Rodin among the Japanese cognoscenti would rise even more later that year after the *Shirakaba* literary magazine dedicated its entire November issue to this artist who was boldly proclaimed "Le Connoisseur de l'âme de tout le people" (the connoisseur of the souls of all humanity), an event I analyze in the following chapter.[68]

Ogai's story takes a less overtly adulatory tone. It imagines the French artist's first meeting with Hanako, a Japanese actress who became a model for him. It is told from the perspective of Kubota, a young Japanese medical researcher who volunteers his services as a translator for the occasion because he is a fan of the artist. Rodin had requested this meeting with the Japanese actress after seeing a Cambodian dancing girl who had been brought to Paris. "Struck by a certain beguiling charm in the sinuous movements of her long, thin limbs," he had come to "believe that all races have a beauty and it is up to the beholder to discover it" (OZ 7: 190). Although to present-day perspectives, the fact that the sculptor's admiration for one charming non-Western performer stoked his desire to meet other non-Western performers could suggest an Orientalist fascination with a generalized exoticism, Ogai seems to portray Rodin as having a noble, egalitarian appreciation of beauty as a universal quality. When Rodin speaks briefly with his prospective model—who is quietly and impassively judged by Kubota as "no beauty" (OZ 7: 192)—the artist decides that he wants her to pose nude for him, implying an aesthetic approval of her that escapes Kubota's more typical understandings. Ogai does not describe the sketching session itself. The narrative instead shifts its focus to Kubota, who reads the following passage from Charles Baudelaire's essay "A Philosophy of Toys" (1853) while waiting in the artist's library: "Children handle their toys in play, and after a while they try to break them. They wonder if there is anything behind these things. If it is a moving toy, they come to want to investigate the mechanism of its motions. Children are drawn more to the *Métaphysique* than the *Physique*" (OZ 7: 196).

After the sketching session, Kubota tells Rodin what he had read, and the artist explains his own aesthetic philosophy: "With a human body too, it is not physical form for physical form's sake that it is interesting. Rather, it is as a mirror of the soul. It is the inner flame that is transparent through and above the form that is interesting" (OZ 7: 197). Rodin apparently means to reassure the younger man that his appraisal of Hanako's beauty is rooted in a metaphysical interest about her soul, rather than in any base urges instigated by her physical form. He claims to view Hanako as beautiful because of her "inner flame." Ogai characterizes how, as an artist, Rodin seems attuned to a special aesthetic dimension that elides the conventional eye and mind as represented by the scientist Kubota.

The discussions by Akira Mizuta Lippit concerning Jacques Derrida's notion of "avisuality" could illuminate this suggestion. Lippit raises this idea in relation to the revelatory impact of the modern technologies of psychoanalysis, X-rays, and cinema, all of which gave human beings entry into previously unseen aspects of the physical universe. He explains the concept of "avisuality not as a form of invisibility, in the sense of an absent or negated visibility: not as the antithesis of the visible but as a specific mode of impossible, unimaginable visuality. Presented to vision, there to be seen, the avisual image remains, in a profoundly irreducible manner, unseen. Or rather, it determines an experience of seeing, a sense of the visual without ever offering an image."[69] Similarly, Rodin's aesthetic view of Hanako's "inner flame that is transparent through and above the form" might be understood as a mode of avisuality. Kubota's gaze can be posited then, as the foil of standard, empirical visuality against Rodin's artistic vision.

Lippit suggests that exposing the interior, avisual layers of the human being and configuring them as open spaces can destroy the living unity of the subject. This too might apply in the case of the aesthetic gaze as portrayed in "Hanako." Although Hanako's exterior body is preserved—as in the case of a patient undergoing an X-ray of her inner organs but not in the case of a victim of atomic radiation, to use Lippit's examples—something of her humanity can be said to be effaced throughout the process of the aesthetic exposure of her soul. Indeed, though the story is titled after Hanako, and it recounts her physical appearance in detail, the narrative reveals little of her interiority or history. The central subject of the story is Rodin's gaze, which perceives her as beautiful in a "profoundly irreducible manner."

Hanako was an actual itinerant Japanese actress active in Europe,[70] however. Ogai's choice to base his titular character on a historical rather than invented figure, and to have her interact with his fictional version of Rodin, indicates his understanding that despite her fragmented presentation in his story, she cannot be dismissed as a mere specter of either his or Rodin's artistic imaginations. "Hanako" had been born Ota Hisa in 1868 to a bourgeois family in what is now Gifu Prefecture. She learned Japanese dance and music from an early age. After both her birth family and her adoptive family encountered financial hardships, Hisa joined a troupe of traveling actors. In 1902, at age thirty-three and by then a seasoned performer, Hisa went to Denmark as part of a group of Japanese actors touring Europe. At the time, popular interest in Asia was surging in Europe and America, and Asian stage performers were in high demand. For example Sada Yakko (1871–1946) attracted American audiences with her faux-Japanese performances—she was Japanese but her acting was not in any classic Japanese style. The French performer Cleo de Merode (1875–1966), originally a ballet dancer, gained acclaim with her "Cambodian" dances at the 1900 Paris Exposition when the original Cambodian dance troupe defected.[71] When Ota's group performed in London she was discovered by the American dance innovator and stage producer Loie Fuller, who decided to promote her career. In 1906, Fuller introduced her to Rodin at the Marseilles Colonial Exhibition. He invited Hanako to visit him in Paris so that he could sketch her there. Rodin eventually made fifty-three separate masks of her (figure 3.5). When she moved back to Japan in 1920, she convinced the French government to allow her to bring back two of these pieces, *The Head of Death* and *Meditating Woman*, which are now in the Niigata City Museum.

Ogai's descriptions of Hanako's "short face with a truncated forehead and chin, her exposed neck, and ungloved hands and arms" (OZ 7: 192) were perhaps inspired by the photographic images of her featured in publications during her lifetime, as well as the masks that Rodin had produced of her. Ogai may have wondered how Rodin, a world-class authority on the beauty of human forms, had come to appreciate this petite, unassuming-looking woman as a muse. Ogai's view of his heroine is ambiguous. He alters or invents certain elements about her biography, while preserving the veracity of other elements. For instance, it could have been because the European press presented little of her background or gave false accounts of it that Ogai had assumed Hanako to be significantly younger than she was at the time that she posed for Rodin, although it might have been a strategic choice to render the actually thirty-eight-year-old woman as a seventeen-year-old girl to dramatize the difference in age between Rodin and his muse.[72] More significantly, Ogai portrays Hanako's behavior as wooden and unremarkable. She is affable enough, and "Having become accustomed to Europe, Hanako smiles in a friendly manner" (OZ 7: 193). But her adherence to rote conventions obscures her character's actual thoughts and feelings.

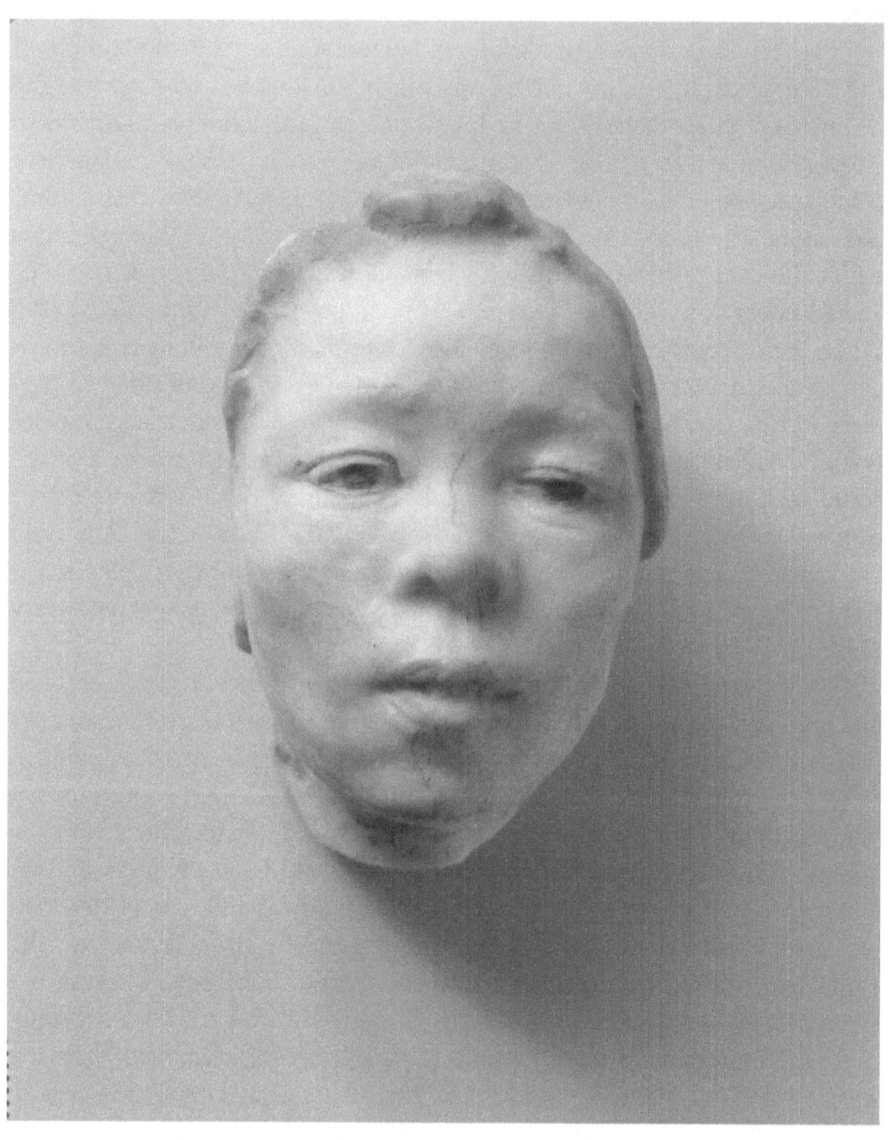

FIGURE 3.5 François Auguste René Rodin, *Hanako* (conceived 1908, executed 1925). Pâte-de-verre (ground glass refired in a mold).
Rodin Museum/Philadelphia Museum of Art

Rodin seems to be pleased at Hanako's diffidence because it does not disrupt his purported view of her soul. Hanako speaks directly to Rodin only when answering his questions about whether she had grown up near the mountains or the sea, and whether she had rowed her own boat as a young girl. Her pithy responses "made images arise in his mind" (OZ 7: 194). That he does not ask her about her impressions of France or anything related to her day-to-day realities suggest his determination to maintain an image of her as an aesthetic object. In contrast, Rodin asks Kubota about his work when they first meet. Of course, Rodin and Hanako's conversation is stilted in large part because it is mediated by Kubota's translations. But even to her compatriot, Hanako does not volunteer any aspect of her personality.

Kubota—apparently invented by Ogai for the story—maintains an attitude of cordial aloofness toward Hanako. Throughout the narrative, his thoughts are mostly consumed by his admiration for Rodin and his hesitance about introducing to his hero what he deems to be Hanako's unremarkable looks as representative of Japanese femininity. When Rodin asks him to inquire if Hanako would be willing to pose nude for him, he attempts to persuade her to please the great artist. "If it were anyone else, there was of course no way that he would arrange for a showing of a female compatriot's nudity. But there was nothing he would refuse Rodin" (OZ 7: 194). Kubota goes beyond his role as an impartial translator and entreats Hanako: "I think you (*omae*) know that the Sensei is an unparalleled sculptor (*chōbutsu-shi*), and he sculpts people's bodies. He would like to ask you something. He is asking if you would oblige him by briefly showing him your naked form. How about it? As you see, the Sensei is an old man, almost seventy years old. And he is clearly a serious man. How about it?" The choice to describe Rodin's occupation using the old-fashioned term *chōbutsu-shi*, which connotes a skilled artisanal carver rather than the more modern term *chōkoku-ka* couched in the discourse of the fine arts, also implies that he doubts her ability to comprehend elevated artistic discourse.[73] Kubota's enumeration of the sculptor's advanced age and trustworthy nature further indicates that he imagines her to fear the older man's vulgar motives. And the young scientist's use of the familiar term *omae* to address Hanako shows that he regards himself as her social superior.

But despite their respective condescension toward Hanako—Rodin in viewing her more as a subject for artistic rendering than as an individual, and Kubota in viewing her as a younger and less sophisticated woman from his native country—Ogai complicates the complicity between the two men by having Kubota read Baudelaire's essay while the artist sketches the girl. Perusing the essay, it would require almost no stretch of imagination for Kubota to envision Rodin, an eminent and older Western artist, "toying" with Hanako, an unknown Japanese girl of seventeen. Baudelaire writes that "children dominate their toys; in other words that their choice is determined by dispositions and desires, vague, if you wish, and by no means formulated, but very real."[74] Kubota is therefore made aware of the power imbalance between players and their toys—or in this case, viewers and their objects. And despite his elite position as a young male scientist working at the prestigious Institut Pasteur in Paris with the backing of the Meiji state, Kubota's forthrightness in disclosing to the older artist what Baudelaire essay he had been reading suggests his awareness of the uneven power dynamics between them, and between Europe and Japan more broadly.

At this point the sculptor intones his aesthetic statement: "With a human body too, it is not physical form for physical form's sake that it is interesting. Rather, it is as a mirror of the soul." He diffuses notions of lurid Orientalist motives coloring his interest in Hanako by shifting their conversation to a philosophical register. Kubota does not respond. But presumably wanting to see how Hanako's metaphysical "soul" has been expressed on paper, he approaches Rodin's sketches. The artist warns him that they are "too rough too tell what's what" (OZ 7:197), and Kubota does not proffer any comments, even of polite praise. Ogai refrains from ekphrastic descriptions of those rough sketches, leaving readers to engage their literary imaginations to envision the images and their model. It is possible that Kubota is impressed with Rodin's work and the philosophy behind it, but it is also likely that he is still thinking about Baudelaire's essay and the elements of her soul that the artist claims to see in Hanako's form. Through Kubota's inability to see how Rodin sees, Ogai seems to conclude that aesthetic appreciation occurs according to its own principles, beyond empirical forms of perception and reason. The story suggests that Ogai is more interested in how artistic vision and more conventional modes of cognition can constructively or at least peaceably coexist than in charting its inscrutable processes.

Mixed Blessings: "Tenchō"

"Tenchō" (Blessings), published in the April 1915 issue of the *Ars* magazine, is another story in which Ogai considers an artist's distinctive orientation to their surrounding world. The protagonist is a struggling art student named M whose painting is denied admission into the official Ministry of Education and Culture exhibit. Ogai actually served as a judge for this annual event from the time of its establishment in 1907 until 1918. The story was inspired by Ogai's friendship with Miya Yoshihei (1893–1971), a young artist who had entered the contest in 1914 with the painting *Tsubaki* (Camellia, 1914) and met Ogai at the time.[75] In the story, M's painting is said to be "executed by tiny dots of intense pigment. On one hand, it appears to be a richly colored fabric, and on the other hand, like light refracted through shattered glass. Studying it, two figures are blurrily visible. From the spread of their hemlines, they must be women" (OZ 16:65). Though it seems to show just one picture, the style of *Tsubaki* (1914) matches this ekphrastic description (figure 3.6).

The story is told from the viewpoint of a narrator, presumably Ogai's fictional stand-in, who had served as a judge on the panel that rejected M's painting. When M asks him why his work did not meet the standards for admission in the show, the narrator states that while he is not authorized to comment on official evaluations, he will explain his own feelings on the matter. Thus begins their strange interview. The narrator starts by asking his guest how he feels when he paints, to which "M made a pained expression. He slowly replied, 'This is difficult. I don't know how to describe it in words'" (OZ 16: 67). The narrator is satisfied with this vague answer because he knows from his own experiences as a writer that the creative process cannot be precisely articulated. He reflects: "I do not paint. But I have 'attempted' to write novels and plays. I too would be at a loss if asked what my feelings were as I wrote them." This shows Ogai's understanding that the interior processes of artistic production eludes precise description, even by those whose creative medium is language.

M nonetheless tries to explain the tortuous efforts he puts into his paintings: "It is as though my head fills up and I am filled with the urge to bring its contents out." Listening to the earnest artist, the narrator deems that M's "psychological state became the internal reason, and the limitations of time and resources the external reason, behind that painting"

FIGURE 3.6 Yoshihei Miya, *Tsubaki* (Camellia, 1914). Oil on canvas. Azumino Municipal Museum of Modern Art, Toyoshina

(*OZ* 16: 68). Clinically analyzing M's dilemma in terms of "psychology" and "time and resources," Ogai departs from defining aesthetic work in the opaque metaphysical terms he had used in "Hanako." But his narrator is still unable to clearly diagnose what makes M's painting artistically lacking in his estimation. Rather than tell M to seek solace in literature or philosophy, the narrator advises the younger man on concrete steps he can take, such as seeking guidance from his professors and peers. From this point onward he stops speaking of M in the third person, and starts addressing him directly in the familiar, second-person voice as "you (*kimi*)," which indicates the intimacy he came to feel for the painter following their initial meeting.

The latter part of the story takes place half a year later when M visits the narrator to show him his new paintings, and to tell him about the tumultuous events in his life over the recent months. M explains that shortly after their last meeting his father had died, making it impossible for his family to keep paying for his art school tuition and support his life in Tokyo. This led him to find part-time employment as a live-in assistant at an art supply store that provided him with tuition fees and boarding. But despite his poverty, M came to find it impossible to paint while holding down a job. He told his employer Takenaka: "Life as a shop clerk from the day before disturbs the paintings of today" (*OZ* 16: 71). Takenaka accepted this and agreed to let him focus on his art, conceding that real artistic work cannot be performed alongside practical work. They settled on an agreement to have M sell art supplies to his classmates during school hours instead of working at the store after class, although eventually, even this proved too distracting. At Takenaka's behest, M reluctantly approached an established artist, W, to ask him for a professional assessment of his future potential as an artist. M stated to the older painter: "I ask not because I want to know for myself, but to reassure Takenaka. I have no doubt about my future success, and don't need anyone to guarantee me" (*OZ* 16: 75). This moved W, and he signed on to give M a small stipend in exchange for light chores and to support him as a mentor. M ends his account by saying that he has since found a small studio where he could at last concentrate on his art. He unveils his new paintings, and the narrator finds that "neither one depicted blurry figures like last year's painting" (*OZ* 16:78). This presents in a literal manner the newfound clarity of M's vision.

But it does not suggest that Ogai has completely abandoned his interest in the spiritual and ineffable dimensions of aesthetic pursuits. The story ends with the narrator telling M that he is lucky to have found such supportive benefactors, and that he is a *"fils de la fortune* (child blessed by the heavens)," to which M just responds "Oh, is that so," with "wide, astonished eyes" (OZ 16: 79). It seems that although he came to accept the harsh reality that money and material matters cannot be ignored even if he decided to dedicate his life to painting, the consummate artist M would always retain a certain disconnect regarding practical concerns. Over the course of the tale, M shows a remarkable amount of frankness in his interactions with others, in some cases making comments that might be perceived as eccentricity or sheer arrogance. For instance, he shows significant boldness in approaching the narrator who, as a member of the judging committee, had rejected his work in an art contest. The narrator, anticipating a barrage of grievances from a disgruntled artist, agrees to speak with M only after noting how "innocent" (*mujaki*) he is, and how "there was no sign of defensiveness in his words" (OZ 16: 67). It is also extraordinary that given his dire straits M could admit to Takenaka, or even to himself, that he was dissatisfied with his part-time work at the art store and needed to be even freer for his painting. Had he been less magnanimous, Takenaka could at this point have terminated his patronage altogether. M's utter lack of pretenses is remarkable.

His brazen attitude toward the older painter W also could have been interpreted as a sign of disrespect. It is fortuitous that M came away from this meeting without offending the established artist, and almost incredible that he managed to gain an understanding mentor and sponsor. Ogai seems to indicate that it is indeed thanks to these multiple "blessings" (*tenchō*) that M could continue his existence as an artist, with his idealism intact. Reflecting on how the story's model Miya Yoshihei ended his long life and career in relative obscurity despite his friendships with other painters from the era who attained greater renown, his biographer Horikiri Masato surmises that this was because for Miya, "painting and interacting with other people was certainly not a means of worldly advancement (*shosei*.) He painted and loved people with sincerity.... It seems that Ogai's "Tenchō" foresaw the entirety of Miya's life."[76]

The story's narrator highly rates M's disarmingly unaffected attitude on both visits. Especially at their second meeting, his affection for the painter is evident in his observation of M as he recounts his recent travails: "You sometimes laugh lightly. Based on the story of what you've gone through, this laugh could have become *ironique* depending on your nature, but it is a laugh thoroughly without malice" (*OZ* 16: 69). This is reminiscent of Ogai's estimations of Harada Naojirō, his painter friend from their youthful days together in Munich, as an "unattached and unselfish" (*kattan muyoku*) (*OZ* 25: 132) man who was "much loved by his teachers and peers for being such a pure person (*shizen ji*)" (*OZ* 25: 131). Ogai interprets M's ignorance about the need for *shosei* as directly linked to the generosity and good will bestowed on him.

But Ogai also seems to present M's aversion to labor in a lightly mocking tone. Even Takenaka, an ally and supporter of the arts, cannot accommodate M's complaints about selling art supplies to his classmates at school, after he had already been excused from working in the art store itself. He dismisses M's proposition to leave a quantity of supplies at the school *atelier* for free use by the other students, and to tally their consumption and collect payments only periodically. This idea had originally come from the older painter W, who had heard about such arrangements in Europe. Takenaka explains to M in clear terms that he cannot be so loose with his inventory: "Maybe such things can be done in the West, but there is no businessman in Japan that can do this" (*OZ* 16: 77). This comment highlights how in their artistic enthusiasm, both W and M tend to overlook the actual ground conditions of life in modern Tokyo. The narrator's use of French words throughout the story to describe M reinforces the painter's sense of dissociation from his surroundings. But the first chore that W assigns M as a symbolic show of his patronage suggests that the young artist's delicate temperament need not be crushed by the drudgery of labor. M is sent to a rose nursery to pick up W's order of fresh flowers. The narrator recounts how "the gardener handed you a basket of roses that have been brought to bloom in the greenhouse. You brought this back to Azabu and got [your stipend of] five yen from W" (*OZ* 16: 78). That M ends up with such "rosy" work delivering flowers to his mentor is befitting of his precious status. Ogai seems to imply that like the carefully grown hot-house roses, a true artist is a rare being requiring protection and cultivation.

The story demonstrates that it is through the support of external logistics that an artist's aesthetic sensibilities and his ability to keep producing beauty are preserved. It was an opportune story to contribute to the inaugural issue of the art magazine *Ars*; perhaps Ogai had meant for it to serve as a reminder to readers of the new magazine that patronage of the arts by conscientious individuals is critical for their existence and development. The story ends on a hopeful note for the arts, with M sobered by his experiences but undeterred from his artistic dedication. Despite the hardships that he now knows this path would entail, he cannot be anything else; he is simply an artist. "Tenchō" suggests that the rare, pure artist can exist in symbiosis with society, but only by having their fundamental otherness recognized and valued by supporters and facilitators. The literary writer, on the other hand, is positioned as an intermediary in this relationship. At once participating in artistic creation and analyzing and articulating the worldly conditions in which creative acts take place, the writer fulfills a unique and necessary role.

In Defense of Artistic and Intellectual Freedoms

From the turn of the twentieth century onward, balancing the autonomy of artistic expression with the maintenance of social order became an especially urgent topic in Japanese cultural discourse at large as the Meiji government intensified its efforts to suppress potential challenges to its authority. In response to the harsh working conditions and price inflation that resulted from rapid industrialization and urbanization in the aftermath of the Sino-Japanese War, organized labor movements and socialist ideas gained traction among an increasingly disgruntled populace. In 1901 Katayama Sen, Kōtoku Shūsui, and their peers had established Japan's first socialist political party, the Shakai Minshu Tō (Socialist Democratic Party). But it was immediately disbanded by the police under the Chian Keisatsu Hō (Public Order and Police Law) established the previous year during the conservative Meiji oligarch Yamagata Aritomo's tenure as prime minister. The central government's anxiety to contain ideological dissent and maintain public order also expressed itself through the ever-more stringent censorship of printed matter by the Naimu-shō (Home Ministry). Many writers expressed their frustrations with the opacity of the standards by which their works were either prohibited from entering, or retroactively removed from, circulation.

The Naturalist writer and critic Hasegawa Tenkei was among those who spoke up. In an essay titled "Bungei'in no setsuritsu wo nozomu" (We wish for the establishment of a literary academy, June 1906) published in the *Taiyō* magazine, he calls for an overhaul of the Meiji state's censorship practices: "Current censorship practices lack fairness. This is not intentional but is a result of [the government censors'] lack of ability to judge literary value.... If a literary academy could gather literary writers of discernment (*kenshiki aru bungakusha*) and have them evaluate the value of published texts, the unfair banning of book sales, and cancellations of dramatic performances and calls that their scripts be rewritten, would not arise."[77] Both socialist and Naturalist writings were censored at unprecedented rates in the first decade of the twentieth century. The writer Satō Haruo recalls that in that period, "our government knew nothing about either Naturalism or socialism and classified both as dangerous philosophies, grouping them roughly together."[78]

Ogai too had a firsthand brush with uncomprehending censors. His semiautobiographical novella *Vita Sexualis* was deemed problematic; the July 1909 issue of *Subaru* magazine, in which the story first appeared, was banned from bookstores a month after publication. The timing was especially awkward because just five days before this official prohibition against his work Ogai had been awarded an honorary doctoral degree in literature by the Tokyo Imperial University. There is speculation that the novella had in fact passed an initial screening, but that the Home Ministry changed its position in reaction to journalistic commentary that the government would not dare to exercise their authority against a figure as widely respected as Ogai.[79] In any event, despite its provocative title the story contained no pornographic scenes, and its ban illuminated the murkiness of how the state enforced its policies.

Vita Sexualis amounts to an oblique meditation on, and critique of, the explicit nature of Naturalist writings rather than an actual example of such a work. The protagonist is a middle-aged philosophy professor named Kanai Shizuka. He embarks on a mission to record the events of his sexual awakening because of what to him seems a disturbing trend in recent Japanese literature. "Every time Kanai read a novel by the Japanese Naturalists, he would see that their characters harbored sexual thoughts at every turn without pause. Critics would, in turn, accept this as a realistic depiction of life. Kanai wondered whether life were indeed like this, and simultaneously, whether he deviated from normal human psychology by being indifferent to sexual urges. Was he born with an abnormal sexual condition that might be called *frigiditas?*" (*OZ* 5: 86). Kanai decides to investigate whether his own carnal urges indeed contained the roots of his identity and the meaning of life as the Naturalist writers and their supporters seemed to believe. Thus, in a spirit of skepticism and scientific inquiry, he begins to write about his sexual development starting with childhood memories in which the adults around him laughingly allude to obscene matters that confuse him. He dutifully narrates how an awareness of human sexuality gradually dawned on him as he matured into a young man, but he stops without describing any of his own experiences: "He did not want to write something having no artistic value.... Real passion cannot exist in sexual urges devoid of love, and he could not help but recognize that something lacking in passion was not suitable for an autobiography" (*OZ* 5: 177). The story ends with the narrator's judgment that there is little a reader might gain from his chronicles. This conclusion pointedly opposes the Naturalists' expectations that valuable truths about human nature would be revealed in the unfiltered confession of one's most intimate thoughts and actions.

As we have seen, Ogai's suspicions about Naturalism have a long history going back to as early as "Shōsetsuron: cfr. Rudolph von Gottschall" (January 1889), the essay with which he made his debut as a literary commentator by criticizing Emile Zola and his popularity in France. His preemptive fears about the trend entering into the Japanese literary sphere eventually came to fruition with the popularity of Naturalist works like Shimazaki Tōson's *Hakai* (1906) and Tayama Katai's *Futon* (1907).[80] Katai's insistence on doing away with rhetorical techniques and focusing exclusively on "blatant depictions" (*rokotsu naru byōsha*) directly conflicted with Ogai's belief that the visual arts and literature should uphold aesthetic ideals even as they stand in inexorable relation to surrounding realities.[81] In a March 1908 letter to the writer Ueda Bin, Ogai complained about the surge in critical tastes favoring the Naturalists: "Criticism by the current literary world is slanted so that it seems there are no other writers besides Kunikida [Doppo] and Tayama [Katai]" (*OZ* 36: 304).

It was not animus, however, that he felt toward the Naturalists. The essay "Yo ga tachiba" (My position, December 1909) provides a pithy overview of his mindset.[82] Ogai starts by observing the prominence of Naturalist writers such as Katai and Tōson. He then muses: "Standing in their shadows, it seems that people think that I am resentful.... [But] I think that I, for my part, am just doing what I like on my own terms. And I am fine with it. I do not mind if I am ranked as better or worse than others" (*OZ* 26: 391–392). From the discussion of his literary preferences, he pivots to his state of mind more broadly. "The best word to express my emotional state would seem to be 'resignation.[83] This is not just in regards to literature. This is how I feel toward all aspects of the world. So when other people think that I am suffering greatly, I am actually serene (*heiki*)" (*OZ* 26: 393). The notion of "resignation" could seem to imply an aesthetic sense of calm indifference not just to literary subjects but to life itself, and a corresponding acceptance of the social status quo. Ogai's fellow writers have described him as a cold-blooded intellectual with few personal investments. For example, the novelist Arishima Takeo, who belonged to the Shirakaba group of writers that I examine in the following chapter, deemed him as "entirely lacking in passion."[84] But Ogai's writings and actions, most notably in the wake of the so-called Great Treason Incident (Taigyaku jiken) of 1910, conflict with his self-professed "resignation" about the state of the world and his reputation for artistic detachment. Rather, they evince his sincere defense of artistic and intellectual freedoms, and they point to his recognition that the autonomy of the arts needs to be actively fostered by members of society.

The Great Treason Incident began in May 1910 when twenty-six socialists, including the writer Kōtoku Shūsui, were arrested in various cities across Japan for an alleged plot to assassinate the emperor. Because the newly tightened Press Laws (Shinbunshi hō) of 1909 forbade the publication of any news that might potentially threaten social stability, the public came to learn of these events only in November of 1910, by which time the defendants' preliminary hearings, held in closed court, had already concluded. Their actual trial began on December 10, 1910. Ogai makes no mention of it in his own diary but a *Mainichi denpō* newspaper reporter recounted sighting him in the state officials' section of the court gallery that day.[85] In historical retrospect, there is consensus that beneath the heavy cloak of secrecy and the general aura of grand scale danger that it hinted at, the government's case against the socialists was weak and would not have held up to public scrutiny.[86] As Hiraide Shū, one of the lawyers for the defense, stated in a 1913 story about the case titled "Gyakuto" (Rebel): "This had been a conspiracy among only four or five suspects. If we are to consider this a conspiracy aimed toward a single goal, it would have perhaps been more appropriate to try these few suspects apart from the rest."[87]

In addition to his work as a lawyer, Hiraide was a writer, and he served as the publisher of the *Subaru* magazine, Ogai's literary base since its founding in January 1909. To prepare for the trial, Hiraide took the advice of his *Subaru* colleague Yosano Tekkan, a Romantic poet and longtime recipient of Ogai's support, and he sought and received close tutoring on socialist thought from Ogai, an expert on Western ideas. The various accounts left behind by the defendants as well as the other lawyers attest that Hiraide effectively used his new knowledge in court to counter the prevalent, hazy notions that socialism was a violent doctrine whose purpose was to destroy the Japanese nation.[88] Ogai's unparalleled knowledge was also considered an asset by the conservative authorities who sought to suppress the spread of harmful imported ideologies. From his terse diary entries we know that he continued to see the politician Yamagata Aritomo and his associates at meetings of the Tokiwa-kai poetry circle throughout this period; Ogai had helped found the group in 1906. We can only imagine the stress he endured in navigating his loyalties to these opposing factions.

Taking a Stand: Stories on Censorship

Because of his connections to both Hiraide and Yamagata, we can surmise that Ogai had known about the Great Treason Incident in its incipient stages before it entered public consciousness in the weeks leading up to the defendants' trial in December 1910. In this period, Ogai wrote the stories "Fuasuchiesu" (Fasces, September 1910), "Chinmoku no tō," (Tower of silence), November 1910), and "Shokudō" (Cafeteria, December 1910), in which he seems to obliquely advise bureaucrats against the dangers of excessive state control over intellectual and artistic discourses, even though he never mentions specific current events in Japan.[89] He also avoids a direct defense of the socialist, anarchist, or Naturalist concepts targeted with growing intensity by the Home Ministry censors. Ogai was not alone in sounding the alarm about errant censorship practices. In March 1910, the Chūō kōron publishing company hosted a symposium on what it termed the Bungei hogo mondai (Issue of protecting the literary arts). The featured speakers—including the philosopher Kaneko Chikusui, the historian and critic Yamaji Aizan, the writer Iwaya Sazanami, and others—castigated the seemingly arbitrary methods of the state's censors.[90] That August, Imamura Yasutarō, the head judge of the Tokyo Court of Appeals, attempted to explain the government's approaches to policing printed matter in an essay titled "Kanken to bungei" (Bureaucrats and the literary arts) in the *Taiyō* magazine. Imamura states, rather tautologically, that each censor must "utilize their intellect to coolly think about the conventional ethical standards and conceptual benchmarks of our society in the present day (*genzai ni okeru waga shakai ippan no dōtoku kan'nen, shisō hyōjun*)," and then use these to judge what is acceptable or not.[91] Ogai uses parody in the story "Fasces" in an apparent attempt to refute Imamura's claims.

The Latin term *fasces* refers to the Roman symbol, consisting of birch rods and an axe bound together with leather thongs, that signifies the power of the law. In the context of the story, it might be seen as a symbol of the tenuous ties between individuals' thoughts and the authority of the state. The first section of the story introduces a judge whose arbitrary standards are questioned by a newspaper reporter. The judge's arrogance is further emphasized in the second section of the story when a literary writer questions him about his techniques. Ogai has the fictional judge repeat Imamura's wording almost verbatim in both exchanges. For example, in response to the writer's question as to how a court official might deduce the parameters of "conventional thought" by which to evaluate the acceptability of a literary work, the judge flippantly replies: "If I think rationally using my brain, standards arise. I use these standards to form my judgments. It's quite an easy thing" (*OZ* 7: 317). Ogai's implied wish to have the relevant authorities delineate objective, concrete benchmarks by which to determine the moral fitness of literary and artistic works is reminiscent of his earlier attempts to use Hartmann's systematic philosophy as the aesthetic guidelines for modern Japanese art and literature. "Fasces" ends on a surreal, absurdist note when a demon appears and lambasts the "spineless writer" (*hero-hero bunshi*) (*OZ* 7: 318) for not adequately defending the rights of intellectuals and artists. He also stridently berates the judge: "You're given power so that you'll carry out justice (*seigi*). Have some respect for learning and the arts!" (*OZ* 7: 319). Ogai assigns culpability not just to the brutish ignorance of the bureaucrats who wield political jurisdiction over intellectual and aesthetic matters that they have no understanding of, but also to the detached idealism of artists who do little to advocate for their rights and beliefs.

"Chinmoku no tō" is set in a context farther removed from ongoing events in Japan, taking as its subject matter the Zoroastrian Parsi people of the Western coast of India. The Parsi are a real and distinctive population who were known to Meiji-period Japanese readers through historical accounts about the region. Such accounts described the group's history of emigration to India in the seventh century to flee religious persecution in their homeland of Iran, and "their wealth and industry which enable them to compete against the Europeans."[92] The story's unnamed Japanese narrator states: "The Parsi youth are taught foreign languages, and they gradually came to read foreign books" (OZ 7: 386). Through such descriptions about the Parsi people's studious and progressive nature, Ogai seems to have intended for the group to serve as an analogy for the Japanese.

The story is told through the perspective of the narrator who is situated in a Western-style hotel lobby in colonial India. From a local newspaper article about the recent mass executions among the Parsi population he learns of individuals who read "dangerous Western books" and spread their new ideas (OZ 7: 388). These events were fabricated by Ogai. The Parsi people had indeed faced persecution during their initial centuries in India, but by the twentieth century they were well established in their new homeland and held positions of social prestige. Despite its distant setting, the story takes on an eerie vividness through the grim descriptions of how the Parsi dead are disposed of through exposure to carrion birds atop the Tower of Silence on Malabar Hill. Excarnation was among the most salient facts described in Meiji- and Taishō-period Japanese accounts about the Parsi population's cultural practices.[93]

Ogai's reasons for concocting such a macabre fiction becomes clear as his narrator reads a newspaper account about the Western books considered "dangerous" by the Parsi censors. They range from Fyodor Dostoevsky's novels, which praise individualism and thus seemed to support anarchism; to August Strindberg's dramas, which challenge class hierarchies; to Oscar Wilde's stories about the basic amorality of human beings. The narrator muses: "From the Parsi perspective, any art today whose value is recognized, and is not absolutely trite, is considered dangerous" (OZ 7: 391). Although Ogai sets the story in a specific historical context far removed from his own, the criticisms expressed in the story seem pointed at the Japanese government's crackdowns on new directions in thought and literary expression as the case against the Great Treason Incident made its way to trial.

In closing, the narrator of "Chinmoku no tō" considers the revolutionary potential of the arts:

> The value of art is that it breaks down traditions. Works that stay within tradition are unremarkable. From the perspective of tradition, all real works of art appear dangerous.
>
> Art delves beyond superficial thoughts and enters into the instinctive urges that lie at their depths. As a painter uses fixed colors in paintings, and a musician uses the chromatic scales, a writer uses sentences to express fleeting impressions with sentences. It is therefore to be expected that art delves into the instinctive urges [that give rise to such impressions]. (OZ 7: 391)

This statement cogently addresses key themes in Ogai's literary aesthetics: "real" art, no matter the medium, is the intentional expression of ideals that exceed the mere surface appearances of phenomena and fulfill the deeper psychological and affective needs of people. It is also no accident that by recognizing art's ability to delve into hidden human "instincts," Ogai appears to recognize the validity of the aims of Naturalism, even though he spurned it as the antithesis of his own literary preferences. Of more pressing concern than the judgment of good or bad artistic taste, Ogai seems to stress, is safeguarding the basic freedom of individuals to pursue new artistic directions. He suggests that intellectual thought must stay open to new ideas or perish: "Academic study tears apart convention in moving forward. Academic study will die if it is made to comply with the moods of one period in one nation" (OZ 7: 392). This alludes to Ogai's well-publicized knowledge of a range of literatures and ideas from the Eastern and Western cultures of the past and present, and his consistent conviction that the pursuit of knowledge in the modern age cannot be confined to any one cultural sphere. The foreign setting of the Tower of Silence in "Chinmoku no tō" underscores this stance of intellectual cosmopolitanism, and contrasts against the opinion of the judge parodied in "Fasces" who had claimed that bureaucratic censors should base their judgments solely on "'current, 'conventional,' and 'Japanese'"[94] standards.

Ogai's dark musings about the "death" of knowledge echo the desperate calls of other intellectuals of the period who more directly urged the intellectual classes to stand up to the government's suppression of political ideas and artistic expressions. Among these is the essay "Onken-naru jiyū shisōka" (Well-behaved freethinkers) by Uozumi Setsuro (1883–1910), published in the *Asahi* newspaper on September 16, 1910. Setsuro writes:

> Thus far, the righteous, self-proclaimed free-thinkers and writers have looked upon the suppression of socialism and anarchism as fires on the opposite shore. Some have tried to claim their positions as entirely other to such dangerous extremisms. They have not noticed, or pretended not to notice, that as free thinkers, their position in the history of civilization puts them in the same position as those [being suppressed]....
>
> The spread of individual rights in the West has deeply rooted reasons. There was a long history. There was an absolute spirit of reform. We have been sliding on the surface [of these ideas], swallowing them whole, prematurely quoting Ibsen and Nietzsche.... I believe it will be fortunate if the recent suppression of free thought has a medicinal effect, and makes the public aware of the need to chew before swallowing."[95]

This assessment, that the current panic over "dangerous thoughts" is due to an incomplete understanding of the imported concepts entering Japanese discourse, summarizes the widespread frustration among progressive thinkers of the Meiji period opposed to the government's far-reaching crackdowns on intellectual exploration. Setsuro stresses that the only antidote is through a reasoned study of the ideas at stake, and Ogai's efforts to share his knowledge with not just individuals wielding institutional power like Yamagata Aritomo and Hiraide Shū through his personal exhortations, but with a wider general audience through his literary output, can be seen as a direct contribution toward this cause.

Ogai squarely acknowledges his double position as a senior agent in the bureaucratic establishments of the state and as a respected don in the literary arts in "Shokudō." Dispensing with the whimsical tone of "Fasces" and the ostensibly faraway setting of "Chinmoku no tō," the story unfolds in the shabby offices of an unnamed Japanese government agency that seems to be involved in the policing of new publications. The story recounts a lunchtime conversation among bureaucrats about the latest spate of censorships and their suspicions about anarchist thought. Their comprehension of the ideas under debate is patchy and vague, evincing Ogai's apparent censure of government officials' lack of study. The main character Kimura, an official with a scholarly bent, tries to correct his peers' misunderstandings despite his reluctance to place himself in a politically suspect position by speaking too much. Ogai features Kimura in two other stories, "Asobi" (Play, August 1910 in *Mita Bungaku*) and "Dengaku tofu" (Miso tofu, September 1912 in *Mitsukoshi*), which focus on his measured, unflappable nature and the calm—or the Zen-like "resignation"—he has reached in balancing his bureaucratic job with his personal literary interests. But in "Shokudō" which takes place entirely in his official workplace, readers detect in Kimura a dilemma arising from his wish to meld his two worlds by trying to enlighten his professional peers about artistic and intellectual developments and his dread at this uphill prospect. After a brief but erudite explanation about anarchist and nihilist thought, he proclaims: "'Oh, I only pay a little bit of attention to the history of literature. World affairs are reflected in literature like a shadow, so I grasp things indirectly.' Kimura's words sounded both modest and defensive" (*OZ* 7: 417). The stance Ogai himself took as a government employee is succinctly conveyed in the cautious, sensible sentiment voiced by Kimura: "I believe in the importance of the freedom of expression, so I lament the too extensive degree to which we prohibit sales [of books deemed dangerous]. Although of course, I admit that there do exist circumstances that make this unavoidable" (*OZ* 7: 418). Through these words, Ogai seems to plead with government officials not to unconditionally suppress artworks and ideas that they do not understand, while reassuring them of his broad support of their mission to maintain social order.

Through the fictions he published in the months leading up to the final verdicts in the Great Treason Incident trial, Ogai thus appears to suggest to his peers and supervisors in government bureaucracy that he could offer his services to clarify misconceptions about imported philosophies and the latest trends in the arts to help them make informed decisions as to their purported influence on Japanese activists. Simultaneously, he seems to signal to proponents of modern Japanese literary and intellectual progress that he believed in their cause. In sum, these stories evince his hope—sustained and honed throughout the various phases of his literary and conceptual development—that a critical understanding of competing value systems and philosophies, a humanistic appreciation for the artistic products they give rise to, and the preservation of the overarching structures of social order, need not be mutually exclusive.

FOUR

Mushanokōji Saneatsu and the Early Shirakaba's Artistic Cosmopolitanism

THE DESIGNATION "SHIRAKABA writers" presents a challenge because the membership of the group shifted over the span of the *Shirakaba* magazine's publication from 1910 to 1923, and individual writers developed their own literary legacies apart from this collective venture. Conventionally speaking, the "Shirakaba group" has come to refer to the many writers who had been based at the publication at some point during its run. Mushanokōji Saneatsu, Shiga Naoya, the Arishima brothers [Arishima Takeo (1878–1923), Arishima Ikuma (1882–1974), and Satomi Ton (1888–1983)], Kishida Ryūsei (1891–1929), Yanagi Muneyoshi (1889–1961), and Nagayo Yoshirō (1888–1961), all from the magazine's earlier period, are among its most well-known members. Its founders were friends who had attended the exclusive Gakushūin Peers School as the children of hereditary aristocracy or industry moguls. Critics—both contemporary to them and in later literary scholarship—have noted that their sense of social and material privilege precluded them from understanding the sociocultural tensions that surrounded them. On the other hand, the group has also been praised for spreading an air of egalitarianism and cosmopolitanism throughout Japanese culture, especially in introducing previously rarified masterworks of Western visual art to popular audiences through their publication. Furthermore, they have been credited with bringing the *genbun-itchi* (aligning speech and writing) linguistic movement to fruition with their un-self-conscious, unpretentious use of language.

MUSHANOKŌJI SANEATSU AND THE EARLY SHIRAKABA

In this chapter I examine the *Shirakaba*'s initial period when its writers began to develop their shared belief in the primacy of individual subjectivity and to establish a sense of aesthetic cosmopolitanism. Despite their seeming oblivion to the challenges that such a stance entailed—championing selfhood while coexisting with others, and navigating cultural differences while espousing a universalist notion of art—the development of their distinctively rosy worldview was in fact based on a selective self-awareness. I demonstrate that to varying degrees, the Shirakaba writers understood that their lofty ideals at times required the willful overlooking of the more immediate social and political circumstances that they found less appealing.

Championing the Self

On January 18, 1911, under the general direction of Mori Ogai, members from four of the late Meiji period's leading non-Naturalist literary magazines—*Subaru* (1909–1913), the first iteration of *Mita bungaku* (1910–1925),[1] the second iteration of *Shin-shichō* (1910–1911),[2] and *Shirakaba* (1910–1923)—convened to discuss a possible joint endeavor. Ogai inaugurated *Subaru* in January 1909 with Romanticist writers, such as Kinoshita Mokutarō and Yosano Tekkan, who looked up to him as a mentor. In May 1910 he also helped launch *Mita bungaku* under the editorship of Nagai Kafū, whom he had nominated to head the literature department at Keiō University. We saw in the previous chapter that although Ogai eventually came to view the artistic realm and quotidian, social concerns as connected rather than separated, he remained consistent in his skepticism about Naturalism, seeing it as a form of blatant realism lacking in aesthetic aspirations. Also, Ogai had been active in expressing, if obliquely through his fictional writings, his concerns about the suppression of press coverage for the case involving the Great Treason Incident, an unsubstantiated socialist plot to assassinate the emperor; the closed trials for the case ended in December 1910, and resulted in the execution of twelve individuals, including the writer Kōtoku Shūsui, and the life imprisonment of twelve others. The meeting of the four magazines' representatives coincided with the day of the alleged criminals' sentencing. Given the increasingly conservative social climate, it seems that Ogai's motivations for proposing a literary alliance was not solely to form a broadly Romanticist faction to oppose Naturalism, but to establish a united front against the erosion of their collective freedoms of artistic expression. Government censorship extended beyond writings on politically dissident thought, and anything suspected of corrupting public morals was a potential target.

But Mushanokōji Saneatsu, the most vocal spokesperson of the *Shirakaba* coterie, recounts that from the start he had questioned working under Ogai's leadership. In a later autobiographical novel written in the third-person voice, he recalls his reaction when Hiraide Shū, a writer at *Subaru* as well as a lawyer who had worked for the defense during the Great Treason trials, first contacted Ogimachi Kinkazu (1881–1960), a member of the *Shirakaba* group, to propose the joint project:

> He and Shiga [Naoya] were nonplussed. They were not satisfied with Naturalism. But at the same time, they were equally dissatisfied with the likes of *Subaru* and *Mita bungaku*. There were many people who were fond of Mr. Ogai, but none among them wanted to have him serve as their head. He and Shiga did not particularly respect Mr. Ogai. While they admitted his intelligence and good taste, they did not take pleasure in his lack of passion and tendency to skip over the heart of the matter no matter what he wrote about. They thought that if it were Mr. Natsume [Sōseki], they would not mind showing him their respect. But they had no intention of respecting anyone else. (MSZ 5: 211)[3]

Shiga Naoya echoes these sentiments in a later autobiographical essay of his own: "I suppose that it is from Mr. Natsume that I can say I received my literary influences.... As for Ogai, his older belletristic writings (*bibun keitō no mono*) did not suit me to begin with, and I still don't feel comfortable with his writings. Honestly, I have barely read him."[4] Mushanokōji and Shiga viewed Ogai as a dispassionate intellectual and a formalist, whereas they viewed Sōseki as a writer of high morals. They were suspicious of the decadent, hedonistic poeticism of *Subaru* and *Mita bungaku* as well as the starkly grim realism of the Naturalists, although as Shiga admits: "We bad-mouthed Naturalism quite a bit but no matter what we say, we have been influenced by it."[5]

Indeed, much of the *Shirakaba* ethos was about unapologetic self-exploration, a tendency owing much to the autobiographical focus of the Naturalists. But there were also significant differences. The *Shirakaba* members saw themselves as iconoclasts in that they rejected the dour despair attendant to Naturalistic presentations of the darker aspects of their psyches. Yet they felt that they were also unlike the other anti-Naturalist writers, the Aesthetes (*tanbi-ha*) and the Decadents (*kyōraku-ha*), who emphasized only the most intensely beautiful and pleasurable elements of their experiences. The *Shirakaba* writers espoused a new mode of individualism that was founded on their commitment to facing and celebrating all aspects of themselves, and to aspiring toward higher spiritual and aesthetic ideals through this pursuit. In Mushanokōji words, "in addition to the world of the spirit," he and his peers "also tried to affirm the world of the flesh because of its beauty" (*MSZ* 5: 215).

At the January 1911 meeting with the other magazines' representatives, Mushanokōji made his dissent known when Hiraide from *Subaru* said that their potential publisher wanted each contributing publication to skip an issue when the collaborative venture was launched so that their respective regular readers would buy the new magazine. Mushanokōji refers to Hiraide as "H" in his account: "In that moment he suddenly said to Shiga as though he could not hold back, 'There is no way that the *Shirakaba* will cease publication.' . . . Shiga agreed as Mr. H asked in an aggressive tone, 'Is there no way?' . . . The meeting then lost momentum, and the matter was derailed" (*MSZ* 5: 212). The non-Naturalist project thus came to a halt before it even launched, and each group of writers continued on its own trajectory. In his diary, Ogai mentions the meeting but not how it ended (*OZ* 35: 512). Mushanokōji, Shiga, and the other members of *Shirakaba* doubled down on their uniquely defiant individualism, which gathered a devoted following among a generation of young, idealistic readers. As the Taishō period progressed, public sentiments shifted from the tense quietude following the so-called Great Treason Incident to the hopeful ethos of "self-cultivation" (*kyōyō*) that called for literary youths to develop their intellects and spirits along universal humanistic values by studying works of Western literature and philosophy. The Shirakaba group soon found themselves wielding greater influence in cultural discourse despite their irreverent, upstart mentality.

The *Shirakaba*'s run, from its founding in 1910 to its closing in 1923, covered a markedly optimistic but volatile stretch of time in modern Japanese history. It saw the dawn of "Taishō democracy," when a system of party politics gained ground. Socialism and feminism gathered momentum and public support during this time. World War I (1914–1919) caused a boom in the Japanese economy that resulted in increased industrialization and higher workers' wages, as well as severe price inflation that crippled the economy for years afterward. This led to a spate of labor movements. Abroad, Japan continued its program of imperialist expansion. Upon the outbreak of World War I the Japanese joined the British side in August 1914, and at the conclusion of the conflict in 1919, they were granted former German territories in China and the Pacific Islands. The global-scale conflagration catalyzed Japanese thinkers of various stripes to consider the uniqueness of the Japanese nation against the global context it was now undeniably entrenched in; among them were the Naturalist writer Iwano Hōmei who founded the *Nihon shugi* (Japan-ism) magazine in 1916, and the philosopher Watsuji Tetsurō, affiliated with the ethos of cosmopolitan "self-cultivation," who turned to traditional Japanese culture and began writing essays like "Nihon bunka ni tsuite" (On Japanese culture) in 1917. Following the war, as a part of the victorious coalition, the Japanese joined the peace negotiations at Versailles where the Western nations confirmed Japan's expanded areas of control but refused to ratify a racial equality clause as part of the covenant for the League of Nations, much to the disappointment of the Japanese public. Yet the *Shirakaba* discussed little of these shifting geopolitical conditions in direct ways. It was instead in its resolute focus on the individual self—and the belief that this self was directly in touch with the broad specter of humanity via an aesthetic consciousness that bypassed engagement with material and political circumstances—that the magazine left its imprint on the Japanese literary world.

The distinctively unvarnished *Shirakaba* voice was directly enabled by the spread of *genbun itchi*-style language. As discussed in previous chapters, the *genbun itchi* campaign had been a movement to rid the written Japanese language of the heavy character usage and archaic structures rooted in the Chinese-derived *kanbun* system, as well as the formalism of the *gikobun* system dating from the Heian period. It strove to replace these dated conventions with a simpler, unified writing style close to modern vernacular Japanese in the Tokyo dialect. Yamamoto Masahide assesses that the Shirakaba writers had been instrumental in popularizing the potentials of the new writing style: "Mushanokōji Saneatsu used everyday language most freely and boldly, freeing writing from the restrictions of archaic styles," and "with the appearance of Shiga Naoya's simple and direct vernacular style, the verbosity and weakness of the *genbun itchi* style was overcome, and the modern vernacular style reached completion."[6] It could be said that their streamlined language gave the *Shirakaba* authors the psychological ease to confront, develop, and articulate their subjectivities in ways that had not been previously possible in older versions of written Japanese, which, in its formal complexities, had called for a greater attention to the conscious labor of writing. Previous writers—including Natsume Sōseki and Mori Ogai in their early stages—experimented with elegant *gabun* linguistic modes to underscore the intentionally artistic nature of their literary works.

Uno Kōji (1891-1961), a writer from the generation following the *Shirakaba* era, explains the revolutionary nature of the Shirakaba style of writing:

> Mushanokōji's novels were more like the essays of an elementary or middle school student, than traditional novels. His protagonists, called "the self" (*jibun*) seemed to be the author himself.... In retrospect, he was the true ancestor of colloquial writing (*kōgo-tai*), a revolutionary, and an innovator in the reduction of Chinese character usage and improvement of *kana* usage. But in the spirit of freestyle writing, rather than consciously striving to create a true colloquial writing, or thinking that he must reduce character usage and that it would be more convenient to use *kana* phonetically, it seemed that what he did according to his whims naturally resulted in these effects.[7]

Indeed, Mushanokōji writes with such a simple straightforwardness that readers receive the impression that the literary work is a guileless reflection of the author's thoughts and impulses. The childish aspect that Uno addresses comes from this apparent psychological naivete as well as its expression through the informal style of the prose. This tendency can be observed from as early as Mushanokōji's first novel, aptly titled *Omedetaki hito* (A naive person, 1910).[8]

The story revolves around the desire of the main character to marry Tsuru, a girl he has spied from afar but does not personally know. In his imagination she is the ideal woman. His repeated proposals—never directed at Tsuru herself but indirectly orchestrated through an intermediary's approach to her guardians—are rejected, however, and the tale concludes with her marrying another man. The drama of love and heartbreak therefore takes place almost entirely in the narrator's mind, rather than in the observable terrain of interpersonal relationships. The protagonist's statements are thus performative in that he creates and apprehends his personal reality through his narrations. So firmly entrenched is the protagonist in his own point of view that even after he learns of Tsuru's marriage, he continues to pine for her, believing that she too must secretly reciprocate his feelings. An apparently seamless continuum between the narrator's psychological states and their linguistic expression occludes external facts and conditions that conflict with them. What lies beyond his subjective perspective is irrelevant to him.

Notably though, Mushanokōji's protagonist seems aware of the selfishness of his obsessions, even as he remains so deeply mired in it. He coolly explains: "I, thirsting for a woman, attained in her an object of desire Thereafter, I came to love her, and I fell in love. I came to think that becoming my wife would mean happiness for Tsuru too" (*MSZ* 1: 80). Throughout the story, Tsuru is presented solely through narrator's desiring perspective rather than as a full-fledged character in her own right. Such a perspective might reflect the aristocratic Shirakaba writers' sense of feudal entitlement. Honda Shūgo assesses: "The Shirakaba school's attitudes toward women is to the extent that it seems an unspoken but most eloquent manifestation of their sense of social superiority."[9] The story is based on Mushanokōji's own failed efforts to court Hiyoshi Taka, a woman with whom he had never even conversed.[10]

We might interpret that by emphasizing the unilateral nature of his character's wanton pining, Mushanokōji had attempted to call into question the socially entrenched conventions of male entitlement. But there is no sense of parody in *Omedetaki hito*'s inevitably unhappy ending. The protagonist remains steadfast in his love for Tsuru not because he fails to realize its problematic intensity, but because he revels in it. At the conclusion of the novel the protagonist muses without irony: "Even if Tsuru were to say, 'I have never, even once, thought of you,' to me that would only be empty words" (*MSZ* 1: 107). This admission that he is attuned exclusively to his own desires, regardless of how his beloved Tsuru feels, is grounded in what he describes as a belief in "the commands of nature, its deeply sacred signs" (*MSZ* 1: 100). The invocation of "nature," as a supreme and self-evident order that the self instinctively obeys, completes a closed circuit of self-affirmation: subjectivity is linked to nature, which is self-evidently beautiful and good. With the ironic nuances operative in the word *omedetaki* (unreservedly joyful; naive) in the title, Mushanokōji acknowledges the sincere joy as well as foolish pathos of the protagonist. He is cast as a figure to be celebrated for his unassailable sense of personal confidence, and to be mocked for his blindness to broader social and communal dynamics. These mixed connotations cannily presage the affection, admiration, scorn, and frustration with which the *Shirakaba* endeavor would be regarded by the Japanese public.

A Self-Aware Selfishness

The mid-century critic Miyoshi Yukio writes that the Shirakaba group had lived in what seems to have been the "good, old times," and "it is difficult to banish feelings akin to jealousy" regarding the egotism of these literary youths from an apparently simpler age.[11] He notes: "It was not just that the young generation who gathered at the *Shirakaba* was lucky enough to be born into an *alten guten Zeiten*.... It should be enough to note the fact that Ishikawa Takuboku's essay "Jidai heisoku no genjō" (Situation of our present bind), was also written in Meiji 43 [1910, the year the *Shirakaba* was established]."[12] In this essay, Takuboku, a poet who worked at the *Asahi* newspaper, lamented the political apathy of the young intellectuals of his generation: "Problems concerning the state only enter our minds when they have bearing on our personal welfares. After it passes, we go back to being strangers."[13] Miyoshi suggests that because of their unique social and material status the Shirakaba writers were able to ignore the mounting political turmoil of their era, which troubled more socially aware youth like Takuboku, and then turn their attentions inward to focus on their private ideals. Mushanokōji himself was not as wealthy as Shiga or the other members of his group, although as a descendant of Heian-era aristocrats he had social privileges that offset his relative lack of means, such as free tuition at the elite Gakushūin Peers School.

Critics contemporary to them had also raised similar objections against the Shirakaba group's sheltered and limited perspectives. Their magazine was mocked widely upon its establishment as the "Bakarashi" (silly, inane),[14] a pun pointing to the endeavor's seeming lack of seriousness. Mushanokōji divulges that he and his peers had resented the attention their magazine gained because of their aristocratic backgrounds: "We felt that people were mocking us, as though they were amused at monkeys pretending to be humans by producing a magazine" (MSZ 15: 544).[15] Yet, he acknowledges, this publicity contributed to brisk sales of their publication. Ikuta Chōkō, a literary critic and the translator of Nietzsche's collected works into Japanese—beginning with *Thus Spake Zarathustra*, which he translated from 1909 to 1911—offered one of the most cutting critiques of the group with the essay "Shizen shugi zen-ha no chōryō" (The free rein of the pre-Naturalists), published in *Shin-shōsetsu* magazine in November 1916. Ikuta writes:

> The so-called Shirakaba group is said to be simple, serious, and honest.
> But in my unapologetically harsh view, their simplicity is not one that has encompassed, digested, and overcome difficulties. It is not the noble simplicity of people who arrive upon it in their dying gasps after being thoroughly exhausted by modern, nineteenth-century difficulties, like Tolstoy and Dostoevsky. Their simplicity is instead the extremely cheap simplicity of little rich boys who have not been exposed to the winds of real life.[16]

Ikuta goes on to claim that because Mushanokōji and his peers had not yet completed the necessary step to celebrating Naturalism by confronting the darker aspects of life, they had "not yet been baptized by [it]." But the very fact that Ikuta felt compelled to pen such a bitter review six years after the *Shirakaba*'s establishment shows its continued public influence. Critics like Watsuji Tetsurō and Akagi Kōhei wrote in defense of the magazine's positive energies, while others like Morita Sōhei and Eguchi Kan questioned its blithe idealism.[17] The debates that sprouted around the Shirakaba group's endeavors and Mushanokōji's use of increasingly grand terms, such as "humanity" (*jinrui*) and "humanism" (*jindō*), in his writings spurred the reexamination of what it meant to hold artistic aspirations that were at odds with actual lived experiences, in many sectors of the Japanese literary world.

One of the earliest and clearest critiques about both the virtues and shortcomings inherent in the Shirakaba movement came from Arishima Takeo, who was a founding member of the coterie through his familial connections and personal friendships. The April 1911 issue of the magazine, which marked its one-year anniversary, included Arishima's review of Mushanokōji's aforementioned first novel *Omedetaki hito*, published two months earlier. Arishima writes in an open-letter form and addresses his younger friend with candor and familiarity: "I cannot help but feel a very acute sensitivity in reading your work.... Reading your work I often feel hesitant and as though I am shrinking back, as though you were taking my hand and plunging it deep into your chest to the red and sticky depths where your heart is, urging me to touch."[18] Through the graphic imagery of this analogy, Arishima compliments Mushanokōji's success in creating a fictional protagonist who bares his faults and feelings with so much raw directness and intensity. But pointing to this same unrestrained and unfiltered use of language that marked Mushanokōji's prose, Arishima also warns: "As your philosophy becomes more refined and develops, the technical skills of your writing too will have to keep up."[19] He further adds: "I understand that right now, you are focused on your own creative activities and cannot be distracted. But surely, you do not intend to stay within this circumscribed territory.... I long for the time when you will smile and through the windows of your fortress, you will take in the wider world."[20] Arishima covers in this letter the central issues that would recur throughout Mushanokōji's literary career: balancing the urgency of self-expression with formal technique and the intentional articulation of beauty, and the ethics of prioritizing personal concerns over wider worldviews.

Mushanokōji published his reply to Arishima in the same issue of *Shirakaba*. He admits that his focus on himself is indeed the source of his artistic inspirations, but instead of apologizing for this limited scope, he defends his choices. He writes: "I cannot bear the pain of worrying about other people's destinies. It is painful to continue my current life unless I act oblivious to the plight of others" (*MSZ* 1: 364).[21] He contrasts this defensive egotism against an earlier phase when he had professed devotion to a Tolstoyan, humanitarian compassion for the dispossessed, and its attendant tenets of self-denial and austerity.[22] Mushanokōji explains that eventually, he will want to expand his horizons and "worry about the destiny of others, but I cannot do this now. This causes me unbearable suffering." Behind this melodramatic statement is a clear-sighted understanding of his present selfish vision. Rather than aspire toward a selfless and noble altruism that seeks to fix the injustices of the wider world, he claims that he chooses to confine himself to the sphere of his own immediate concerns. He retains the possibility, though, that in some undetermined future when he is better positioned to do so, he might emerge to share his enlightenment with others.

An earlier free-form essay from the June 1910 *Shirakaba*, titled "Jibun to tanin" (Myself and others) shows further evidence of Mushanokōji's struggles with the imperatives of self-love and a broader compassion for humanity. He begins stridently, declaring: "I am glad that I am indifferent (*reien*) to others. I am glad that others are indifferent to me. Since I cannot do anything about the fate of another person through loving him, or worrying about him, it is a blessing that I can become indifferent about others" (*MSZ* 1: 317). But he is not satisfied with cutting himself off from human contact altogether. In a rather convoluted fashion he writes: "I do not like disliking others, or to be disliked by others. I would rather have no relations than to dislike, or be disliked by, other people. Yet I do not want to obsessively focus on myself." Given his concerns about being disliked, Mushanokōji is not truly "indifferent" to others. He invokes his ideal state of existence, in which he is neither embroiled in the welfare of others nor resented for his lack of involvement, by using a pictorial analogy. "I would like to be the central figure along with my lover, with my friends as the supporting figures, and those with shared interests as background figures." This is reminiscent of the unnamed painter in Sōseki's *Kusamakura* who had decided to "regard everyone I meet on this trip aloofly as though from an elevated and distant position, so that the forces of human sentiments do not occur. If I do so, no matter how the other person behaves they cannot breach my sentiments, and it would be like standing in front of a painting" (*SZ* 3: 13). Both he and Mushanokōji envision the controlled stillness of a visual image as a means of preserving one's emotional distance from others. Mushanokōji concludes by once again appealing to "nature" as justification for his self-centered perspectives: "I have unconsciously been following the commands of nature in following this path. From now on, I will do so more consciously" (*MSZ* 1: 318). He seems to conclude that rather than adhering to an artificial path of self-denial, a more fundamental cosmic law dictates that he obey his own desires.

The Early Shirakaba

Members in the group besides Mushanokōji were also aware that becoming the "central figure" in any one particular worldview would banish others to the periphery, and they too pondered the ethical implications of this. For example, Shiga Naoya's story "Abashiri made" (As far as Abashiri), published in April 1910 in the inaugural issue of *Shirakaba*, considers the affective and ethical limits of the subjective perspective. The story was originally published in 1908 in an earlier coterie magazine that Shiga and several subsequent *Shirakaba* writers had founded as students at Tokyo Imperial University. The narrator of the story is a young man on a leisurely train trip to visit a friend. As the train departs from Ueno station in Tokyo, an attractive but frazzled woman with an infant and a small cranky boy sit down across the aisle from him. The young man offers the window seat next to him to the petulant boy, and he and the mother begin talking. He learns that the boy has ear and nose problems in addition to chronic headaches, and casually remarks that the boy's bad temper must be a result of these difficulties. The mother replies: "The doctor said that these conditions are because his father would drink so much alcohol. I'm not sure if this explains the nose and ear problems, but I think his bad moods do come from that."[23] The mother's matter-of-fact candor about her seemingly dark domestic circumstances increases when the young man asks her where they are going and she replies: "We are going to Hokkaido. It is supposedly a place called Abashiri, very far and very inconvenient."[24] They fall silent, and the young man observes the woman and her son. He starts to imagine what the child's father must look like, and finds himself thinking of a former, rather unsavory schoolmate named Magaki who had been arrogant and had problems with alcohol. He speculates that the patriarch of the family before him must be a man like Magaki.

He remembers that in his simplicity, Magaki could be rather jovial in some respects, but he thinks: "Such attitudes are often not indicative of one's true nature. Even jovial men could become difficult when faced with failure. They could become mean. They could pick on their weak wives in their unkempt houses, in an attempt to rid themselves of their sadness."[25] The image is an unhappy one, showing Shiga's awareness of the gap between controlled outer appearances and messy private realities. As the train hurtles northward the infant starts to cry, and the little boy continues to pester his mother. When the protagonist prepares to disembark at Utsunomiya, a few hours away from Tokyo, the mother asks him to mail some postcards for her from the station. They part without exchanging names. The young man is tempted to read the postcards before he deposits them in the mailbox at Utsunomiya station, but he refrains from doing so and continues on his own journey.

Though he gleans several grim clues about the circumstances of the young mother's life, Shiga's main character does not involve himself in her drama beyond offering her a few passing courtesies. He imagines with some compassion that the trip ahead of her will be difficult, but he does not veer from his own path to understand her problems and to offer his aid to her. She is beguiling to him, but not enough so to derail his own plans. Admittedly the mother does not tell him explicitly that she is unhappy with her life and that she needs his assistance, and it is possible that perhaps despite her challenges, she is glad to be heading to Hokkaido with her children. Their father figure might in fact be a better man than the long-ago schoolmate that the protagonist arbitrarily imagines him to resemble, regardless of his drinking habits. The young man's restraint from reading the mother's postcard messages shows his acceptance of the perspectival limits he has imposed upon himself; he might be curious about the seemingly tragic woman, but since he cannot and will not take responsibility for her actual situation, he decides it only fair to respect the privacy of her intimate thoughts. Readers are left to imagine the rest of the young fatherless family's long train ride to the northernmost reaches of Japan, and the narrator's subsequent visit with his friend, as two completely separate stories.

Like Mushanokōji's conjuring of a static painting in which he is the main subject surrounded by a select group of kindred figures in a carefully orchestrated sequence, Shiga's story captures its characters in a fleeting exchange in which each remains carefully apart from the other. The motif of strangers converging in the impersonal, anonymous space of a moving train is recurrent in modern Japanese literature—for example, as we saw earlier, Sōseki employs it to dramatic effect in *Sanshirō* when the titular character and a nameless fellow female traveler from his train end up spending an odd night together at a stop in Nagoya. Shiga deploys this charged setting in his story to stress how every individual has their own back-stories and future destinations. The mother's unusual frankness with the protagonist could be explained by her tacit understanding that anything she says to a stranger in the liminal space of a traveling train will not affect either of their respective lives, but perhaps she is nonetheless in want of someone with whom to temporarily share her story. The narrator's attitude can be read as cruelly cold in this case. Yet his refusal to involve himself, even as his sympathy is mildly stirred, allows him to proceed unencumbered. While he lets himself imagine the young mother's hardships, he stops short of identifying with her. The story thus emphasizes how even as individuals coexist in shared spaces, each person is in control of only their own life and can only perceive the world through their own perspectives. The note of poignancy with which Shiga ends the tale indicates his awareness of the compassion that is lost in such a curtailing of one's views. Shiga will develop this theme in his later oeuvre, which explores how each individual might find peace with others and eventually achieve peace with their existence in the world, including in the novel *An'ya kōro* (A dark night's passing, 1921–1937), widely seen as his magnum opus.

The other work of fiction in the inaugural issue of *Shirakaba*, the short story "Yorozu ya" by Ogimachi Kinkazu, is lesser known but involves a similar dynamic. The tale unfolds in retrospect as the narrator, a young man of comfortable means, recalls traveling by himself and staying at a seedy inn called "Yorozu ya" in the rural Kōshū mountains that lie between the Kantō and Kansai regions. He notices two women lodging in the room across the hall from him. They pique his curiosity not because of their beauty—their looks are unimpressive in his estimation—but because they are young and seem to have arrived with almost no luggage. Later that evening he is startled when he hears the old innkeeper ask the two women whether they would mind sharing their room with another guest, a single man. The narrator catches sight of the man's "pasty complexion and crass features."[26] It strikes him as strange that the inn has placed the new lodger with the two women rather than with him, but he says nothing. Through the thin partitions, he overhears the conversation that unfolds in the other room.

The man, apparently a traveling salesman of women's accessories among other items, speaks in ingratiating and familiar tones with the women he has just met. He first tries to sell them some of his wares. They do not seem especially discomfited. The trio continue their bantering well after the narrator has turned off his lamp to go to sleep for the night. In the dark, the narrator listens impassively as the man tells his roommates that he has an interesting book that is "good for seeing at night,"[27] followed by the women's laughter. When they decide to finally go to sleep, the man tells the women that he is sleeping with his robes unfastened and suggests that they too would be more comfortable doing the same. "There is no need to record anything further," the narrator declares at this point. But he does mention that what he overheard gave him "an oppressive feeling (*munagurushisa*) as though in a nightmare," noting that it seemed "as though the smell from the tepid warmth of their flesh, which exposed human frailties in the ugliest way, hovered in the air." The next day the narrator goes to the pier to board a boat to travel down the Fuji River. It is a cold day and he huddles around a fire with the other waiting passengers, a married couple, when the two women from the inn hesitantly approach the pier. The wife of the pair wonders aloud about the women who head toward a different boat, and her husband answers that they must be going to the textile factories around Omiya where they will seek employment. He solemnly remarks: "No matter where they go, they won't be able to get the kind of wages they want."[28] The story ends here with the narrator remaining silent.

As with "Abashiri made," the protagonist of "Yorozu ya" is left to wonder about the lives of the individuals he happens to encounter while in transit. But unlike Shiga, Ogimachi characterizes his narrator as simply unable to imagine the rougher life circumstances of those in lower socioeconomic classes than himself. For instance, he is ignorant of the apparent two-tier pricing system at the inn, where the discount-price lodgers must share their room with strangers even of the opposite sex; he is decisively derisive in his estimation of the itinerant salesman's features as "crass"; and he is oblivious about why two young women might be traveling without luggage until a fellow traveler spells out their motivations. Moreover, the narrator's discomfort with the coarse behavior of the salesman toward the two young women is tinged with distaste, suggesting that he feels morally superior to them. He feels sufficiently removed from all three of them so that it does not occur to him to step in and defend the women. But there are also hints in Ogimachi's narrative about the predations awaiting the young women. That the wife of the couple at the pier who sees them heading toward a boat with no luggage is concerned enough to ask about them points to how conspicuously vulnerable they appear, a fact the narrator never directly articulates. Her husband's remarks about the low wages they would likely earn at a textile factory is also ominous. In "Abashiri made," Shiga does not disclose to readers why his main character decides to close himself off from becoming emotionally invested in the precarious-looking family he meets on the train. It may have been a volitional decision, such as the one made by the unnamed protagonist of Sōseki's *Kusamakura* to uphold an "unhuman" detachment from others so that he can view them aesthetically, or because he knows he does not have the emotional capacity to truly care. But in "Yorozu ya" Ogimachi seems to propose that his protagonist is unable to see beyond his limited frames of reference not because of any ethical calculus, but because he is young, innocent, and sheltered by his class and wealth. Whether this exculpates him touches on a dilemma central to the Shirakaba endeavor: Are those claiming dedication to universal humanism beholden to addressing the social inequities they witness in the context of their own lives? Or can a scrupulously *aesthetic* sense of kinship with the world override such concerns?

Mushanokōji Saneatsu attempts to address these questions in his play *Momoiro no heya* (The rose-colored chamber), published in the February 1911 issue of *Shirakaba*. The work oftentimes reads more like a stylized parable than dramatic fiction because its characters orate their philosophical ideas explicitly instead of expressing them through actions or subtler comments. The writer Akutagawa Ryūnosuke, who would rise to prominence in the generation after the Shirakaba's, noted a "rushed quality" in much of Mushanokōji's writings (*ARZ* 4: 128).[29] The observation suggests that in his eagerness to convey his theories to readers, Mushanokōji does not provide sufficient narrative context in his stories for his characters to voice their ideas in a diegetically plausible, natural, and—most importantly to Akutagawa—*artistic* manner. This critique calls to mind aspects of the theorist Sianne Ngai's notion of how the integration of "ready-made" concepts into a novel can result in a literary version of a "gimmick." As she puts it, gimmicks are "overrated devices that strike us as working too little (labor-saving tricks) but also as working too hard (strained efforts to get our attentions). In each case we refer to the aesthetically suspicious object as a 'contrivance.'"[30] In the case of literature, to call something a "gimmick" is to identify what seems to be the techniques the writer uses against readers' expectations of the labor a writer must invest in order to produce what is conventionally thought of as literary artistic value. Ngai writes that the mode of writing known as the "novel of ideas," in which theoretical or philosophical concepts are imported into the story as independently existing material, can display a "willingness to court the accusation of relying on overly transparent stylistic devices."[31] But the appellation of the "gimmick" might not apply to Mushanokōji's writings because it is unclear whether his intention is to produce literary art at all; his characters are often barely synthesized enough into their invented settings to appear as stylized mouthpieces for his ideas, and his "fictions" can seem more like direct manifestations of his thoughts. Of course, Mushanokōji's overt transparency and lack of apparent style itself might be considered a contrivance.

The main characters of *Momoiro no heya* are the Rose-Colored Woman and her husband, the Young Man, whom she tries to shield from the endless demands of the Gray Masses that he feels compelled to commiserate with. The play opens when the Young Man returns to his warm and comfortable home from a visit to the "outside world." He exclaims: "The coldness out there is unbearable. People are curled up with no coal to burn. They are shrunken. They have gray faces and suspicion in their eyes" (*MSZ* 2: 22). The woman tries to convince him to stay within the happy confines of his abode, but the man hesitates. "It feels rather lonely to be the only one in possession of a rosy heart when everyone else in the world has a gray one. I feel guilty." To make him understand that he need not deny his ideals or renounce his privileged circumstances, the woman tells him a story about an artist's noble, solitary struggles. I quote a long section of the dialogue in order to show Mushanokōji's radically unadorned—perhaps "gimmicky"— use of the vernacular style.

YOUNG MAN: Was this in Japan? Or in a foreign country?
ROSE-COLORED WOMAN: That's irrelevant. Anyhow, in the artist's vicinity, there was no one who appreciated art. But because he didn't have to worry about earning a living, he painted what he wanted to paint, in the manner that pleased him. Everyone said he was ornery, or lazy, or selfish. They said he was not productive. But he continued to paint confidently, although no one would admire his work when he was done. Everyone who saw his work complained. Not one person sympathized with him or understood him.
YOUNG MAN: Oh.
ROSE-COLORED WOMAN: He was so lonely he couldn't stand it. He lived alone. The people in his village were deeply annoyed by him.
YOUNG MAN: Yes, I'm sure he annoyed them,
ROSE-COLORED WOMAN: Yes, they have to work hard for a living while he wakes, sleeps, eats, and paints at whim. And he always seems to lounge around. How oblivious he is to the struggles of others! How arrogant. Everyone thought that he was lazing about in his wealth. However, the artist was not as spineless as you.
YOUNG MAN: (in a mock-angry tone) Don't be stupid.

ROSE-COLORED WOMAN: He would say, "I have work to do that you do not comprehend. To you I might seem a useless, annoying figure. To other people though, I am a fountain of strength, their defender. They are joyous and thankful that I exist." (*MSZ* 2:23)

The Young Man is heartened by the Rose-Colored Woman's belief that an artist's mission cannot be deterred by criticism from the uncomprehending masses. That the woman deems as irrelevant his question of whether the artist in her story lived in Japan or elsewhere points to a striving for universal enlightenment that overlooks local identifications. Mushanokōji's lack of interest in following literary conventions to develop a detailed fictional setting for his story enhances the abstract and deracinated, or theoretical and universal, nature of his musings. Over the course of the play, the Young Man's sense of obligation to socially responsible, quantitative productivity is gradually overcome by his acceptance of a more personal artistic calling as espoused by the Rose-Colored Woman. But just as he reaches this resolution, the Gray People enter his happy home and try to lure him out. Though he wavers, at the end of the play he chases them out and declares: "Fine! Even if everyone becomes my enemy, I am going to protect my autonomous self (*jiga*)! I praise love and beauty. I will dye to a rosy color the hearts of those who identify with me!" (*MSZ* 2:31).

Though the play seems to represent the victory of egotism and artistic vision over social awareness and empathy, the artist in the Rose-Colored Woman's parable and the protagonist himself both claim strength from the belief that their creative work is significant and that others will eventually come to appreciate their lonely struggles. The couple hopes that among the scornful masses, there will be a few that become "joyous and thankful" because of their work. For them, art is not produced merely for private leisure. Or rather, they believe that creating art for themselves—an act they define in an Adorno-esque manner as intrinsically meaningful with no socially purposive agenda, which in a sense renders it a critique of society—contributes to the overall betterment of society. The Young Man is not content to enjoy his private, rose-colored domesticity indefinitely. He aspires to eventually dye the world in his happy hue.

To recall, Mushanokōji had previously aspired to a Tolstoyan compassion for humanity at large, but then chose to channel his desire to serve the world via the less direct path of his work as an artist. In an interview decades later, Mushanokōji stated that contrary to critical speculation,[32] *Momo iro no heya* had not been intended as an ideological statement against the government suppression of political dissenters during and after the so-called Great Treason incident. He reminisces in breezy tones: "At that time, anarchist thought was at its peak and I suppose it's true that I wrote with some notion of that ilk in mind, but that was the extent of it.... I had foremost a feeling of wanting to let myself truly live, and I think I wrote the work to express my fear of losing myself by becoming sucked into a [collective] gyre."[33]

Mushanokōji continued to ponder the link between the individual enterprise of self-expression and the creation of artworks to be shared with others. For example, in an essay published in the *Shirakaba* in March 1911, he stated: "It is for myself that I take up my pen. For any other reason, my pen does not flow. More than for anyone, my work is directly for myself. This is my main characteristic, and also my flaw. It is because of this flaw that I am often misunderstood by people, and that I offend them. However, if my work has any value, it is because of this flaw. Anyone who understands this is the person I seek, a person who will understand my work better than anyone. There are few other writers who write so explicitly for themselves" (*MSZ* 1: 347).[34] The conflicting wishes to write solely for oneself, and to gain an understanding readership, are offered a tacit resolution in the notion that individual ideals can have a communal validity, at least for a discerning and sufficiently enlightened audience focused on shared, universalist principles. This echoes the Kantian notion of subjective universality, which acknowledges how aesthetic sentiments are essentially subjective and not based on objectively quantifiable standards but are also believed to hold interpersonal validity.

The young Shirakaba writers searched for artistic examples that displayed the artist's uncompromising independence, while speaking to a wider sense of humanistic relevance. The current state of literature in Japan seemed lacking to them. Looking back on the early days of the *Shirakaba*'s launch, Shiga Naoya wrote: "We were full of energy and feared no one. Natsume Sōseki was about the only person we respected, and we didn't even look at Ogai, [Shimazaki] Tōson, or [Tokuda] Shūsei. We made no mentor figures, and showed our manuscripts to no one outside our group."[35] Mushanokōji's comments from that time also expressed his dissatisfaction: "It might be because today's Japanese lack energy, but there are few artists, and almost no writers or *yōga* painters, who seem to be pushing progress. Even [Kunikida] Doppo is not satisfying. Tōson neither. I admire that they are acting according to their subjective will, but they have not progressed enough. . . . One must be unapologetic in developing individuality (*kosei*). The masses with no connection to their own individual natures should give way to those who have such a link, and one must keep going forward" (*MSZ* 1: 468).[36] In Mushanokōji's estimation, neither Ogai's theoretical sophistication, nor the Naturalists' unabashed depictions of the unglamorous aspects of their personal lives, sufficed to show how subjective perspectives can hold broader humanistic meanings and universal aesthetic appeal.

Even Natsume Sōseki, whose nuanced, clear-sighted critique of Japan's modern condition had earned him wide renown as a progressive thinker and cultural authority, ultimately did not meet the Shirakaba writers' ideals, although he did come closest. Mushanokōji wrote a review of Sōseki's novel *Sorekara* (1909) in the inaugural issue of *Shirakaba*, beginning with an homage to the author: "Natsume Sōseki is in a true sense like a teacher to me, and the person I respect as the greatest figure in today's literary establishment" (*MSZ* 1: 326). He states admiration for Sōseki's beauty of language and broadness of intellect, and he goes on to praises the older writer's skill in depicting the protagonist's suffering between societal demands and personal desires. Though Mushanokōji admits to liking the open ending of the novel, since it pulls the reader further into the story, he concludes by stating that he "hope[s] to see whether Mr. Sōseki would continue to feel pessimistic toward society or discover a balance between society and the nature of humanity. I believe he will follow the latter path. And at that time, I believe that rather than try to make nature fit society, he will try to make society fit nature. It will be then that he truly becomes a teacher for the people of the nation" (*MSZ* 1: 332). Mushanokōji expresses regret about Sōseki's hesitance to let "human nature" prevail unambiguously against the conventions of "society" in his novel.

The strife between self and others is indeed a central theme of *Sorekara* (*SZ* 6). The novel follows Daisuke, a wealthy young dilettante, as he discovers the courage to follow his heart and seek to marry Michiyo, the wife of a former classmate who has fallen into financial straits. Pursuing her entails defying his powerful father, who wants him to marry a woman from the family of a business ally, and this results in Daisuke's being excommunicated by his family. That Mushanokōji and his fellow aristocratic friends identified with Daisuke and his strife with his status-conscious family—and were inspired by his act of rebellion in the name of true love—is not surprising. But Mushanokōji's reading dismisses Sōseki's critiques of the systemically stratified nature of late Meiji Japan's capitalistic society, which he develops throughout the novel. For example, Daisuke suspects that his own comfortably aimless existence is enabled by the corrupt business practices of his father, and he is tacitly resigned to this fact. And despite their love, Daisuke and Michiyo's future is depicted as uncertain at the end of the story. He has never worked before, and she is in ill health; it is implied that to survive on their own would be difficult, regardless of their love for each other.

The Shirakaba group soon seized upon the visual arts of Post-Impressionism, and a selection of European art from earlier periods, as evincing more direct affirmations of the subjective perspectives that they felt was missing in the Japanese arts and letters. The visually striking colors and unconventional styles of the Post-Impressionists appealed to the young Japanese writers, while their distant European origins seemed to prove that individualism held cross-cultural value. The Shirakaba members became avid collectors of imported art books and prints, and through the pages of the *Shirakaba* magazine in which they featured photographic reproductions of foreign artworks along with essays explaining the ideas that they believed were embodied therein, they transmitted their art-based cosmopolitanism to an eager Japanese readership.

Artistic Cosmopolitanism

The theorist W. J. T. Mitchell, among others, has pointed out that, "the visual arts are 'sign systems' informed by 'conventions,' that paintings, photographs, sculptural objects, and architectural monuments are fraught with 'textuality' and 'discourse.'"[37] In other words, for audiences to engage with works of visual art as such, they need to have already been initiated into the general practices and premises of art appreciation. But as we have reviewed in previous chapters, artistic images are often believed to be experienced at a visceral and subjective level unfiltered through the social medium of language. It has been suggested that the Shirakaba writers' interest in the Western arts arose from the illusion of immediate comprehension evoked by visual artworks, which was also compounded by an awareness of their own scholastic and linguistic limitations. Despite their enthusiasm for gaining knowledge about the world outside of the Japanese cultural contexts familiar to them, a lack of foreign language skills often prevented the Shirakaba members' serious academic study of Western literatures. For these writers, the seemingly intuitive nature of visual experiences was preferable to the belabored acts of reading and studying in other languages. In Honda Shūgo's words: "The *Shirakaba* writers spoke at length and without hesitation about Van Gogh, Rodin, and Rembrandt. And this was widely accepted. If it had been literature, and not art, it can be assumed that things would have gone differently."[38]

Mushanokōji himself would largely have concurred with this assessment. He writes of himself and his peers in their school days:

> [We] began to gradually like paintings. That is to say, [we] looked at photographic reproductions of these in art magazines and books from the West. These triggered [our] imaginations and made [us] think many things, and brought much joy. Looking at images was easier than reading books, and freer. It saved us from having to enslave one's thoughts to the work. It freed one's imagination, thoughts, and souls. Also, no matter how distracted [we] felt, there was time enough to look at images. It was also not unpleasant to be titillated by gently erotic sensations from them. (*MSZ* 5:159)[39]

This frank admission shows that imported art images served not as the basis for diligent study but rather as a platform upon which writers could actively form their own free associations and ideas. The mention of the "erotic sensations" evoked by certain visual images also shows that they saw artworks more as objects to be experienced sensorily rather than interpreted intellectually.

At the Gakushūin Peers School, the Shirakaba members had been careless students for the most part. Because Shiga was held back twice, he came to be in the same class as Mushanokōji, two years his junior. Mushanokōji fondly recalls of his schooldays: "Once we got to know each other better, Shiga too would often say that he was glad he had failed his classes. He was not stupid but was apparently lazy. The topic of failing reminds me too of Arishima Ikuma. He and Shiga had been in the same class, but he dropped out earlier" (*MSZ* 15: 599).[40] These privileged young men seemed to adhere to an outlook of easy exceptionalism whereby they believed they could navigate the global modern age without relying on the mediation of classroom instruction or social institutions. Mushanokōji declared: "We are psychologically and spiritually children of humanity (*jinrui no ko*). We are children of the world to an extent that cannot be felt by people older than us. This is because there are great people in foreign countries, and they provide support and harmony for our spirits" (*MSZ* 1: 395).[41] No amount of learning could replace such raw confidence about connecting with the "great people" of the world.

Cosmopolitanism as a worldview can be defined in moral, political, and sociocultural terms, and there are as many iterations of it as those who claim to practice it. But broadly speaking, one major point of contention has been about the tensions between cosmopolitanism and nationalism, and whether an allegiance to both forms of identification is meaningfully possible.[42] Mushanokōji's brand of cosmopolitanism confounds such inquiries, for while it functions on the suppression of a serious engagement with local Japanese conditions, its adherents also remained noncommittal about the volatile, evolving state of the global world order and the particularities of the various foreign societies therein. And to reiterate, the artistic universalism Mushanokōji proposed rested on the paradoxical status of aesthetic sentiments as subjectively felt and universally valid. When the Shirakaba members declared the beauty of their favorite European artworks, their supporters understood them as expressing not only their personal judgments but also as general statements that everyone whose sensibilities were sufficiently evolved would concur with. The question then, is who exactly they had envisioned as a part of their communal perspective.

The views that Mushanokōji espoused were often at odds with the values of the surrounding mainstream Japanese society. For example, as Maya Mortimer and other scholars have also noted, Mushanokōji's reactions to the death of the Meiji emperor, and the subsequent suicide of his loyal retainer General Nogi Maresuke (1849–1912), evince how detached he felt from the Japanese zeitgeist.[43] Nogi's suicide was a major event in the intellectual life of the nation because it embodied the unresolved tensions between a classically feudal mindset and the individualistic values of modern life. Natsume Sōseki, for example, refers to these historical events in the iconic novel *Kokoro* (1914) about a character paralyzed by the spiritual disconnect felt by Japanese individuals caught between a traditionally collectivist worldview and a modern egocentric one that overlapped at the end of the Meiji period.

Mushanokōji, however, was nonplussed by Nogi's suicide. He wrote an editorial in the *Shirakaba* disparaging Nogi's dramatic death, calling it "unfortunately lacking in humanistic elements (*jinrui-teki na tokoro*)" (*MSZ* 1: 494).[44] He deemed that in contrast, "Van Gogh's suicide has a humanistic element. It has the potential to stir the sympathies of advanced people of each nation." Mushanokōji goes on to criticize the backward state of Japanese culture itself: "Only the perverse rationality of a people fostered in a thought system created by the distortions of nature in a perverse age could allow itself to praise the suicide of General Nogi. The rationality of a people who have awoken to the fundamental life force of humanity through Western thought will not allow for such praise" (*MSZ* 1: 495). Shiga Naoya too wrote in his diary: "When I heard from Fusako that Mr. Nogi has committed suicide, I thought, 'What a fool.' It was the same sort of feeling I would have when a maid does something silly without thinking."[45] Mushanokōji and Shiga were dismissive of the suicide because it seemed to display the general's unthinking dedication to an anachronistic value system and his lack of self-determination. Mushanokōji goes so far as to say that "the fundamental life force of humanity" is to be stimulated in properly rational people by Western sources of inspiration, which reveals how he conflates Western culture with modern reason and humanistic standards based on the sovereignty of the individual. In this conception, he regards the "West" not as a distinctive cultural space with a long history that should be studied to be understood, but as a type of default mindset accessible to all people willing to tune into their inner humanity.

But Mushanokōji did not blindly fetishize the Western nations and denigrate Japan. He was consistently suspicious about the concept of nationhood and the use of force. For example, he published the following aphorism in *Shirakaba* in April 1915:

> Thieves give rise to the police. So the current social order (*gense no seido*) should be grateful to thieves, because it is guarded by the police.
> The same can be said of wars. Wars give rise to soldiers. Nations (*kokka*) should be grateful to wars because they are guarded by soldiers. (*MSZ* 3: 444)[46]

The circuitous analogy situates the enforcement of the authority of nations through biopower; under the Conscript Law established in 1873, Japan's male citizens could be made to participate in military activities, and potentially die as soldiers in allegiance to the nation. The anthropomorphizing of "the current social order" and "nations" accentuates this direct relationality. In another impressionistic piece in the June 1915 issue of the magazine, Mushanokōji portrays the "nation" as a bully coming between individuals and the greater bond of humanity:

> Humanity will scream.
> But the nation will silence this. Or it will intentionally misinterpret this scream in conveying it to the nation's people. Someone said, "Humanity (*jinrui*) seems to be telling individuals (*kojin*) to live." The nation yelled, "Humanity wants individuals to live for the nation and to die for the nation...." The nation glared. The person became afraid and said, "Yes, well, humanity told the citizens of a nation to die for their nation." The nation looked pleased as though he had won his way and said, "Indeed. This is how it must be." (*MSZ* 3: 418)[47]

Here, the nation is presented as controlling its citizens through the fear of force instead of through shared associations of common cultural elements and values, or even shared economic interests. Mushanokōji implies that modern geopolitics, with its divisive emphasis on national might, are to blame for conflicts that are avoidable if only individuals could commune directly with their shared, latent spirit of humanity by tuning into their aesthetic faculties.

That Mushanokōji engaged in these musings with the ongoing World War I in mind becomes more explicit in a later section of the same essay. He writes:

> In this war, the people of Europe are ignoring each other's positive aspects, and they fear they might forget to respect [the nationalisms] they each strove to establish above humanity, and most of all they fear destruction.
> It goes without saying how regrettable it is that although each has the qualities to complement what the other lacks, they fear each other and cannot help but keep killing each other.
> From now on, what steps will humanity (*jinrui*) command us to take in regards to the fighting between the races (*jinshu*), or between nations? We

should wait for its command with anticipation. This is so that we are not dragged down by each other. (*MSZ* 3: 421)[48]

The syntactical construction is odd but the key sentence of this excerpt states that in the current conflagration, the people of Europe are deeply divided and only see negative and irreconcilable differences with their enemies, but on the other hand—due, it is implied, to the suffering wrought by the war—they are also losing their reverence for the nationalist ideals that each group of people had worked hard to promote above a more general concept of humanity. That people might "forget" to accord respect to nationalisms is an awkward concept, but it seems to suggest the superficiality of the divisions imposed by nationality. Yet the use of the term *jinshu* (race) to discuss the people of each nation, although it was likely for the neat parallel it forms against the all-encompassing term *jinrui* (humankind), also connotes an organic distinctiveness to each group. Mushanokōji concludes that what transcends all differences and unites everyone is a fear of destruction, particularly since the world has become so intertwined that the devastation of one state could mean the downfall of the others. The only solution, he proposes, is for the spirit of humanity immanent in all people to provide a moral compass for a common way forward.

Thus it seems that even World War I struck Mushanokōji not as a concrete ideological and humanitarian crisis, but as an abstract horror against "humanity" in general. Throughout his long career he would abstain from explicitly political activity, in keeping with his core views that local or national identifications prevented the realization of humanity's ideals of unity, and he would prefer to contribute as an artist, rather than as an activist, to the betterment of the human condition. But Mushanokōji came close to criticizing the Japanese government when, in the November 1915 issue of the *Shirakaba*, he spoke out against the harsh sentencing of the Han and Aboriginal Taiwanese who had participated in the Ta-pa-ni uprising against Japanese colonial authorities earlier that year.[49] In his shock at the news that the colonial government planned to execute more than eight hundred Taiwanese people, Mushanokōji penned an essay in which he lamented: "I don't mean to only criticize the fact that it is such a large number of people, but I think I'd like to see the faces of those who are fine with sentencing several hundred people to their deaths. Who can believe that the trials for several hundred people could have been completed so quickly?

It seems like there is something that should not have come to pass, something unethical, about this. Perhaps they do not truly see the aborigines as people" (*MSZ* 3: 433).⁵⁰ But Mushanokōji also diffuses his acerbic comments with self-deprecation: "I don't mind if people laugh at how immature my words may sound, or how little I know about politics" (*MSZ* 3: 434). While apparently guileless, these words may also have been strategic in signaling to authority figures that he does not intend to threaten their rule. He stresses that he is chiefly driven by a general sense of humanism rather than any specific political allegiances: "This is a humanitarian (*jindō-jō no*) problem." Nonetheless, he concludes: "Is there no way to save them from the horror of death? If not, is this not shameful for Japan?" This shows that despite his wish to bypass politics in linking the individual with universalistic principles, he recognizes that calls for humanity are indeed connected to political realities. In the following month's *Shirakaba*, Mushanokōji expressed relief that of the more than nine hundred Taiwanese people who had been sentenced to execution, about eight hundred were spared by a decree of clemency from the emperor. He writes that he wishes that more people could have been spared but that it is a consolation to him that many lives were saved. He declares: "There is more I'd like to say, but I will consider this matter closed and intend to say no more on it" (*MSZ* 3: 489).⁵¹

Post-Impressionism

The stance of aligning individuals with universal ideals fueled the Shirakaba group's search for inspiration from artworks from abroad, particularly in the visual arts. The hope was that visual imagery would be especially conducive for bypassing the differences and divisions between Japanese audiences and foreign artists; if Japanese viewers could appreciate the beauty of works by foreign artists it would suggest that they share common sensibilities, and hence enhance the illusion of a higher-order, humanistic objectivity to strive toward. In addition to short stories and essays, every issue of the *Shirakaba* magazine featured photographic reproductions of artworks, often accompanied by essays about the lives of the artists, especially in the earlier years of the publication. A focus on the persona of the artist was a crucial characteristic of the *Shirakaba* that differentiated it from the more specialized art magazines that started to establish themselves from the mid-Taishō period onward.[52] In particular, the *Shirakaba* published intensively on the Post-Impressionists in this manner.

Works by Auguste Rodin, Paul Cezanne, Paul Gauguin, and Vincent van Gogh appeared repeatedly throughout the years so that loyal readers would have developed a visual familiarity with their styles. These images were accompanied by the Japanese writers' essays and poems proclaiming the Western artists as role models in what they saw as the universal endeavor of subjective artistic expression. One stanza of Mushanokōji's poem praising Vincent van Gogh in the July 1911 issue of the magazine reads: "Oh Van Gogh, with your spirit as though burning, every time I think of you, I gain strength" (*MSZ* 1: 379).[53] The poet situates himself on the same spiritual plane as Van Gogh, and it is not even the painter's work that delights him but the painter's fiercely iconic spiritual essence that he claims to perceive therein. In turn, such imagined proximity to foreign artistic heroes served to implicitly allay readers' geopolitical concerns—rather, their concerns about not having greater concerns about geopolitics—by seeming to substantiate an identification with a humanism that, as Mushanokōji obliquely suggested, might eventually solve the strife between nations and other social ills. The Shirakaba group's claims about a core humanity that could transcend the granular specificities of local and national frames of orientation gave its members a plausible ethical justification for not confronting the struggles that take place in actual cross-cultural and cross-linguistic interactions.

A further corollary of forging identifications with artists across differences in cultural and temporal contexts, as well as across artistic mediums, was that the Shirakaba writers could view their Japanese literary productions as working in concert with the Western visual arts. They did not despair that the linguistic medium they used for singing the praises of paintings lacked the power to recreate their vivid visual impressions, or that the paintings they admired were limited in the complexity of the stories they could tell. In not strictly problematizing the parameters of each artistic medium, the early Shirakaba forged a conveniently post-ekphrastic understanding of the relationship between language and image as neither rivals nor helpmates with abilities to depict different dimensions of aesthetic objects and experiences, but interchangeable peers in the all-important endeavor of self-expression.

Though they counted among their members Yanagi Muneyoshi and Kojima Kikuo, who later became professional art historians, and painters like Arishima Ikuma and Kishida Ryūsei, most of the Shirakaba coterie lacked formal knowledge or training in art history or aesthetic theory. Their commentaries on artworks were often prefaced with statements like, "We are, after all, amateurs (*shirōto*), so we expect you to read the following knowing this."[54] And they published purely private asides like, "This edition's print of 'Pere Tanguy' [by Van Gogh] is very popular among our members. All of us love this uncle (*ojisan*) in the painting."[55] The group's popularity with readers lay in their unpretentious and easy intimacy with Western art. But some critics, both in their own time and in later scholarship, have questioned the seemingly haphazard tendencies of the Shirakaba group's artistic understandings.

A protracted debate over the work of the Shirakaba-affiliated painter Yamawaki Shintoku (1886–1952) provided the stage for some of the most incisive of these criticisms. It began innocuously in the June 1911 issue of the *Chūō kōron* magazine when the *Subaru*-based writer Kinoshita Mokutarō reviewed an exhibit that Yamawaki had just held at the Rōkan-dō gallery from April to May.[56] Mokutarō praised the high emotions and idealism evident in Yamawaki's works but deplored his uneven painting methods. He wishes that the artist had been able to harness his affective energies and present these through "the well-comprehended rules of painting" (*yoku rikai sareta kaiga no yakusoku*).[57] Mokutarō compares the raw energies of Yamawaki's works to the predicament of "an angry mute" who cannot adequately articulate his vibrant inner turmoil. Mokutarō, like his mentor Mori Ogai, was a medical doctor, and he practiced dermatology in addition to his literary and critical activities. His opinions imply that, like Ogai, he believed in the importance of technical skills as a necessary means for expressing aesthetic inspiration. He ends his review by calling for the establishment of basic formal standards within Japanese artistic discourse before individual experimentations could take full and meaningful flight. The implication is that for Yamawaki's painting style to properly communicate itself as an intentionally unmethodical "gimmick" for expressing his freedom from prior artistic traditions— recall the discussion of "gimmicks" earlier in this chapter—he needs to have first shown his competence in conventional painting methods.

In the September issue of *Shirakaba*, Yamawaki responded by recounting how his initial pursuit of "realistic depictions" (*shajitsu*) had eventually led him to "destroy the forms of objects" in his pursuit of their essences, and to "enter the realm of the shapeless image."[58] He discovered that "depictions of the objective truths of nature had reached their limit with the early Impressionists. It is only natural that later artists should fall into their interiorities."[59] Yamawaki aligns himself with Post-Impressionism, the Shirakaba group's preferred mode of painting. This was precisely what bothered Mokutarō when he declared in the November 1911 issue of the *Shirakaba*: "In order to also objectively view Japanese culture and gain balance, I would like a Verständnis (understanding) of Manet, a mediator of traditions, rather than of Van Gogh and Cezanne, who are the most modern of modern men."[60] Eduard Manet was a pivotal figure who presaged Western art's shift toward Impressionism and its prioritization of light and color over traditional academism's attention to form and detail; Mokutarō's statement amounts to a pointed objection to Yamawaki's dismissal of the Impressionists in favor of his identification with the historically and conceptually later Post-Impressionists, such as Van Gogh and Paul Cezanne.

In sum, Mokutarō suggests that Yamawaki's "Post-Impressionistic" turn toward interiority was suspect because his comprehension of the preceding stage of Impressionism, which explored the optical perceptions of the external qualities of things, was insufficiently developed. Notably, Mokutarō addresses the whole of "Japanese culture" rather than Yamawaki as a single artist. His interest seems to be in assessing Japanese modernity at large, where—in his estimation—ideas and values from multiple time periods and cultural contexts coexisted without a full comprehension of each element. Yamawaki seems to have incited such a strong response from Mokutarō because he and his artworks appeared to embody this conceptual state of confused hybridity. Mushanokōji—who by then was gaining public notoriety for his beliefs about artistic universalism—soon began writing in defense of Yamawaki as well. The debate among the three men continued into February of the following year with no one conceding to the views of the other. As the art historian Nakamura Giichi assesses: "This debate was significant not only because it revealed the philosophical makeup of the unique author Mushanokōji Saneatsu, but because through the debate, Mushanokōji articulated his self-centered philosophies in an unexpectedly clear manner as though it were a manifesto for the Shirakaba movement. Yet as a debate, it does not seem that there was real critical engagement by the two sides, or any dialectical progress. It seems that each side was simply catalyzed by the other's disagreement, and each side stopped at freely and loudly asserting its opinions."[61]

Mokutarō's critiques were indeed crucial in catalyzing Mushanokōji to describe his artistic ideals. For example, in an epistolary essay in the December 1911 *Shirakaba*, shortly after Moktarō's call for a logical "Verständnis (understanding)" of art, he recounts his emotional reactions to looking at a series of prints with his friend Yanagi Muneysohi, the future art historian:

> Yesterday, seeing the paintings of Cezanne, Gauguin, Van Gogh, and Matisse, Y and I became very excited. I thought it false unless I went this far. I felt I am wandering haphazardly. Once you understand their paintings even a bit, other people's works appear lukewarm. It is a wonder how we can bear this state of things. It is not manly....
>
> When I see recent paintings, I feel the painters' souls touching mine. I then feel a deep strength and joy. The value of such art is not measurable by traditional standards. Nor can it be measured by new ones. These arts give no room for criticism by others. I feel that recent art tries to touch the souls of others without leaving room for criticism. (*MSZ* 1: 403–406)[62]

He articulates here a sense of spiritual communion with the Post-Impressionist artists' expressive works, which leave "no room for criticism by others." Mushanokōji only speaks in subjective terms and does not attempt an ekphrastic description of the images that causes his tide of feelings. There is no mention of the objectively observable elements of the Post-Impressionists' paintings—their use of color, space, line, or modes of abstraction. As it were, it seems that Mushanokōji consumes the images primarily in an affective manner that cannot be rationally explained, even in terms of the sensory pleasures he gains from the interplay of colors, forms, and textures.

Yanagi's essay "Kakumei no gaka" (Revolutionary painters), published the following month in the January 1912 issue of the magazine, provides a further explanation of the Shirakaba group's admiration of the Post-Impressionist painters. Yanagi draws heavily from the British writer Lewis C. Hind's 1911 book *The Post Impressionists*[63] and states:

If we ask what Post Impressionism is, the answer is clear.—If you see within yourself the only realm that should be, and hope to express the overflowing entirety of its existence with seriousness, you are already living in accordance with the spirit of the Post Impressionists. When all phenomena become alive to you, and you perceive yourself in all phenomena, when your entire personhood flows as one with the rhythm of nature's entire existence, what remains is your eternally affirmed life force. It is this affirmation and fulfillment of life that is the force that gives birth to Post Impressionism. When your individuality becomes great, your art must have a transcendental value and meaning.[64]

Though he situates Post-Impressionism in the trajectory of Western art history, Yanagi highlights the movement's ideals of self-affirmation as an inclusive philosophy that his Japanese readers might live by, rather than present it as a rarified style of foreign art. We can already detect the egalitarian approach to art that he would go on to espouse in his later career as a founder and promoter of the Japanese *mingei* (folk craft) movement in the 1920s and 1930s.[65]

With these basic premises laid out, "Kakumei no gaka" goes on to call the nineteenth century a special and pivotal time: "The nineteenth century was a great century. This is because it was a century of great progress. Upon all fronts of culture, the battle flag raised against the classicists changed the path of progress and had the power to change the course of life. In this 'astonishing century,' humankind first tasted the joy of free development by returning to the self. The affirmation of individuality and the freedom to breathe were the most significant products of this age."[66] The use of the term "humankind" shows that Yanagi understood the epochal awakening to individuality as a globally shared phenomenon. He did not need to remind his readers that in Japan too, the nineteenth century saw massive conceptual shifts brought about by the nation's modern interactions with the Western world. He then sets forth Hind's outline of the progress of visual art from Manet onward and summarizes: "Whereas the Impressionist painters directly depicted the impressions they received from nature, they did not know to stop at this passivity, and ultimately had to progress to actively projecting themselves upon nature."[67] Cezanne is called "a personage as pure and certain as his still-lives. Faced with this unwavering personage, all things seem flimsy and weak. Like an immobile mountain range, he grew and expanded his territory in silence, guarding his position in the awareness that in this world only he and nature exist, and he lived a life of peace and strength."[68] And Yanagi writes of Van Gogh: "Everything he painted was active life itself. The clouds he painted dance, the trees he painted burn. When he painted these things, he was always at the heart of this burning nature. He always lived and breathed with his paintings. He never knew how to paint through technique."[69] Yanagi next classifies Gauguin's art as "quiet and kind," and his art as depicting "a pure, primitive nature filtered through [his] gentleness."[70] He lastly describes Matisse's art as "the effect of a psychology that has abolished the relationality between self and other, blending self and phenomenon," summarizing that his "astonishingly simple paintings are the endpoint of the past two thousand years of art history."[71] Yanagi characterizes each artist's temperament carefully and affectionately, as though he were speaking of close friends rather than of distant foreign masters perceived only via their paintings.

To recap, the early Shirakaba members were galvanized by Post-Impressionism, which seemed to meet their demands for an art that celebrated individual perspectives while cohering to a transcendental sense of humanism. The vivid styles of these European paintings seemed to communicate the essences of the artists who created them, and they inspired the Japanese writers on a personal, emotional level to pursue their own artistic endeavors in their Japanese milieus. Post-Impressionism's place in the larger arc of modern Western art's progress was of secondary interest to the writers—as we saw, Yanagi, echoing Hind, describes Matisse as the endpoint of artistic development—and later developments in modern art did not engender the same degree of passion among the group. The magazine did not feature in-depth articles about Picasso and Cubism, Duchamp and Dadaism, or the other subsequent strands of European art more contemporary to them in the 1910s. The early Shirakaba group was captivated by what they collectively referred to as the Post-Impressionistic perspective, discovering in it a timeless aesthetic cosmology that seemed to justify and amplify their own philosophies.

Reaching Beyond Books

The Shirakaba writers' nonacademic ethos and selective tastes certainly bolstered their sense of connection with Western artworks, as did the remote conditions of their contact with the images they wrote about. A few among their number had studied abroad and visited the museums of Europe in person, such as Arishima Ikuma and the painter Umehara Ryūzaburō, who became a contributor to the magazine after Arishima befriended him in Paris.[72] But the other Shirakaba members based their knowledge of Western art history almost entirely on the imported books they purchased with personal funds. As Shiga Naoya describes in an autobiographical novella: "When I ran out of money, I inquired of a used bookseller I knew in Kanda which titles they would purchase for the highest prices. I would then buy these [on credit] at Maruzen or Nakanishiya, and deliver these by carriage to the used bookstore for cash. Maruzen and Nakanishiya would come to my home to collect their credit, so they would give me an unlimited supply of books."[73] Such unlimited access to art books, especially foreign ones, was a privilege not available to most Japanese people of the time. But the publishing industry was expanding and through the proliferation of books and magazines that were more affordable than ever, mass audiences were eagerly gaining access to texts that formerly used to be the province of the elite. Abe Jirō's best-selling essay collection *Santarō no nikki* (Santarō's diary, 1914–1918), based on the author's own diaries from 1911 to 1914, was considered a quintessential text for proponents of the "self-cultivation" mindset of this period, and it reveals a core assumption driving this expanding readership: "With the exception of an extremely fortunate minority, for us to have a 'mentor' is to commune with the inner experiences of a single individual through the written works (*chosaku*) they produce during their lifetime."[74] Under this worldview, books were valued as a reliable and democratic portal for providing intimate access to knowledge and inspiration from "mentors" across time and space.

That images and knowledge of the Western arts were still a rarity for the general public in Japan enhanced the respectful care that the Shirakaba writers accorded to their books, and the eager reception of their reprinted images by their readers. The philosopher Walter Benjamin famously remarked that the aura of artworks is lost in the age of mechanical reproductions, but it might be said that for the Shirakaba members and their fans the reproductions of artworks were also precious. The magazine coterie's involvement in editing each monthly issue and selecting the images to be printed in them enhanced their sense of physical familiarity with the prints. Frank comments in the ongoing communal "Henshū-shitsu ni te"

(Inside the editorial room) column revealed the concerns and logistics that went into choosing the specific images featured in its pages. For example, one commenter notes in the January 1912 issue: "The Gauguin insert is a copy of a print that was in some German art magazine, but the blue color is a bit off. However, the colors in the image in the German magazine too, are also supposedly a bit different from the original. Too bad."[75] In August 1911, another writer explains: "This issue, we took a chance and used a three-color ink process. We worry about how it will turn out. If it turns out well, in the future, we will occasionally use three-color processing. But this is expensive, so it will only be once in a while. Let's hope it goes well."[76] The affection that the Shirakaba group felt toward the photographic reproductions of Western artworks were fostered by their still limited conditions of access. During the course of its publication, the magazine hosted numerous public art exhibitions that featured such prints, alongside a smaller number of original artworks owned by the members, as well as contemporary works by Japanese artists within their circle.

Although the Shirakaba members were thus adept at contemplating European art from afar, they occasionally gained actual contact with the artists. Among the highlights of the magazine's earliest days was when they received a postcard from Paul Klinger (1857–1920), a German symbolist painter and sculptor whose work had been featured in their pages since the inaugural issue. Kojima Kikuo had written an introductory essay about the artist in the December 1910 issue accompanied by a photograph of the artist in his studio, and he sent Klinger a copy of the magazine along with a letter in German expressing admiration of his work. Kojima, who unlike the other Shirakaba members had been a serious student and eventually became an art historian, was fluent in German. In April he received a postcard of thanks from Klinger, and the joyous celebration that this caused among the Shirakaba coterie is described in the May 1911 issue. But this pales in comparison to their exchanges with Auguste Rodin.

We saw in the previous chapter's analysis of Mori Ogai's story "Hanako" (July 1910) that Rodin's work had been steadily gaining recognition among the Japanese cultural cognoscenti during the first decade of the twentieth century. The Shirakaba coterie claim to have been admirers of the French artist since 1905 when Shiga Naoya first discovered a short article about him in a magazine that a friend sent him from America.[77] For several months, the group was involved in planning a special issue of the magazine

FIGURE 4.1 Kunzō Minami, cover of the *Shirakaba*, November 1910 edition dedicated to Auguste Rodin. Print.

dedicated to the sculptor in honor of his upcoming seventieth birthday on November 14, 1910. Arishima Ikuma, who was chosen to represent them because of his French skills, wrote to Rodin to inform him of their intentions, and Rodin replied with a message of thanks dated September 22 along with a signed photograph of himself. This image was featured as a frontispiece in the Rodin issue, which appeared as planned in November 1910 (figures 4.1 and 4.2). The issue included essay contributions from numerous individuals outside of their usual coterie—including the writer and sculptor Takamura Kōtarō, the novelist Nagai Kafū, and Kinoshita Mokutarō, with whom Mushanokōji would become embroiled in the aforementioned debate about Post-Impressionism the following year—and was instrumental in cementing Rodin's popularity among the Japanese public.

Mushanokōji's essay from the issue, "Rodan to jinsei" (Rodin and life), captures the esteem they held him in:

> Rodin is the person who sings his own song with the strongest, most firmly rooted power in modernity. For this, he made many enemies. He also made allies.

Finally, he won against himself, as well as those who raised a ruckus against him. He and those who made noise against him now sing their songs together in his tune. Those who don't have been silenced. The crown of victory fell to him.

He lives in this world as one of its most victorious individuals. . . .

In a word, I worship (*sūhai*) Rodin because I want to let myself (*jiga*) live as well as possible. I don't think there is anyone who has let, and continues to let, his own self live as well as Rodin. (*MSZ* 1: 350)[78]

Mushanokōji seems to project his own experiences as a part of the Shirakaba group, which was mocked at first by the literary establishment, on the French artist who too rose above his critics. Yanagi Muneyoshi further

FIGURE 4.2 Photograph of Auguste Rodin in *Shirakaba* (November 1910). The signature below appears to be that of the photographer, "Henri Mannes." Rodin handwrote a message: "To Mr. Arishima, Cordial greetings from France to Japan. The arts of Japan know how to find the soul of the smallest as well as the grandest things in existence: for example, the sea, the clouds, the forest, the insects, etc. I too follow this school of art. Aug. Rodin." The original French wording and the Japanese translation of the message appear on subsequent pages of the magazine.

conveys a sense of worship in his praise for the sculptor: "As a religious figure, Rodin has finally appeared before us as an authority figure. How we long for and admire such an authority figure, such a personage."[79] In addition to such essays of adulation, the issue also featured Rodin's biography, a bibliography of French books about him, and eighteen photographic prints of his works.

In an editorial in the February 1912 issue of the *Shirakaba*, Mushanokōji describes how he and his peers sent this special issue of their magazine to Rodin along with a pledge to send him some *ukiyo-e* if he would acknowledge their tribute.[80] This promise indicates the young writers' assumption that the French artist might not immediately perceive them as modern kindred spirits, but as inhabitants of an exotic place represented by *ukiyo-e* from a bygone era. That is, in order to increase their chances of hearing back from the older French artist, they seem to have made a strategic decision to emphasize their Japanese heritage even as they reached out to him in a universalist spirit. The months passed and although they did not receive a response, in August 1911, they sent Rodin thirty *ukiyo-e* that they deemed to be of high enough quality to present to their hero. These consisted of twenty prints they purchased, as well as ten prints from among the members' personal collections. Twenty out of the thirty images that the group sent to Rodin have been identified in the artist's holdings,[81] and they include portraits and landscapes by late-eighteenth and mid- to late-nineteenth century artists like Katsushika Hokusai, Kitagwa Utamaro, and Utagawa Hiroshige. In response, the Shirakaba members received a warm letter of thanks from Rodin, who promised to send them three bronzes. When the sculptures finally arrived in December, their excitement was immense. Yanagi Muneyoshi went to Yokohama to claim the bronzes on behalf of the group. Mushanokōji recounts:

> Yanagi called us at five. "It went well, banzai! Where should I bring them?" I said, "Shiga, Kayano, and Hirasawa are here so come over." Yanagi agreed. We waited in excitement for half an hour and Yanagi arrived. We were mad with happiness, saying, "This is great," "They're finally here," "Banzai." We opened the carefully wrapped packages; Yanagi had left the boxes in Yokohama because they wouldn't fit on the train.
>
> We called everyone but most people were unfortunately out. We went to dinner still holding the bronzes. This is because it would have been horrible if they

were stolen, or if there were an earthquake. And also because we wanted to see them. We showed my mother, who was extremely happy. (*MSZ* 5: 210)[82]

Alongside Mushanokōji's essay, the February 1912 issue of the magazine featured Yanagi's account of the event, Rodin's messages to the Shirakaba group and their Japanese translations, and photographs of the three Rodin bronzes (figures 4.3–4.5). The entire episode was significant because it confirmed for themselves, and their readers, that the artistic exemplar they had longed for from a distance did in fact exist with them on the same physical plane. That he seemed to support their artistic mission buoyed their confidence. The successful exchange of not just written letters but also tangible goods—the *ukiyo*-e and the bronze statues—proved to them that the universal space of aesthetics that they accessed through books and paintings was in fact connected to the material space of actions and commerce.[83]

As the *Shirakaba* evolved, the writers each went on to confront for themselves how to connect the realm of their artistic ideals and that of their lived

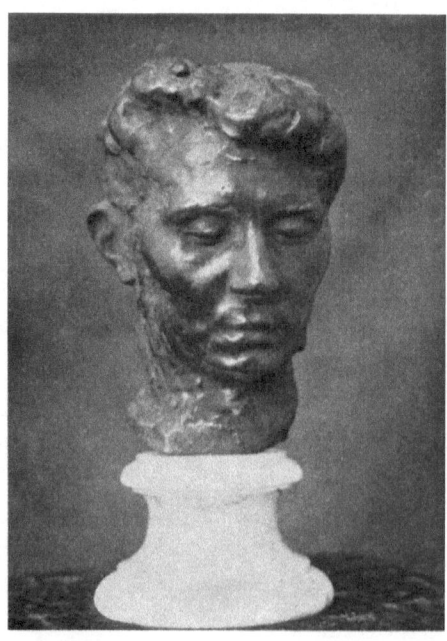

FIGURE 4.3 Photograph of Rodin's *Madame Rodin* (1882) in *Shirakaba* (February 1912). The statue is bronze and in the collection of the Ohara Museum of Art.

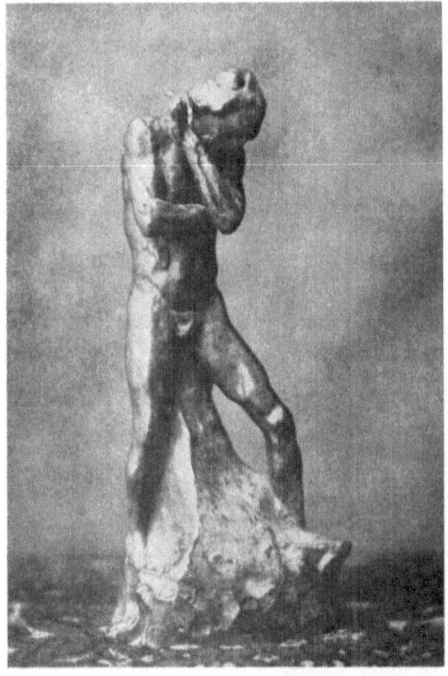

FIGURE 4.4 Photograph of Rodin's *Une Petite Ombre* (Little Shadow, 1885) in *Shirakaba* (February 1912). The statue is bronze and in the collection of the Ohara Museum of Art.

experiences. Mushanokōji would attempt this by founding the Atarashiki Mura (New Village) farming and arts commune, which he officially inaugurated in 1918 on Rodin's birthday, November 14.[84] Mushanokōji hoped that the village would become a new type of society based on love and equality for all, but he was adamant in maintaining a distance from the class warfare and political strife that revolutionary socialism called for. The Russian Revolution of the previous year had made the government warier than ever of the threat of socialist dissent, and Mushanokōji carefully maintained an uneasy but essentially passive attitude toward public authorities. In explaining his vision for the Atarashiki Mura settlement, he wrote in the April 1918 issue of *Shirakaba*: "We do not want to use violence to resist violence. We will harmonize with the current society as much as possible. Rather than engage in a fight that will surely be lost, we will focus diligently on developing our talents" (*MSZ* 4: 13).[85] His political apathy, and blithe expectations that issues

FIGURE 4.5 Photograph of Rodin's *Tête de Gavroche Parisien* (Head of a Parisian Ruffian, 1885) in *Shirakaba* (February 1912). The statue is bronze and in the collection of the Ohara Museum of Art.

of class differences might be overcome through the shared pursuit of artistic activities and humanistic goals, irritated socialist activists. The leftist writer Katō Kazuo summarized such skeptical sentiments about Mushanokōji's mode of utopianism in stating: "The true spirit of universal brotherhood does not consist of breaking apart from the society of reality and can only be fully realized by living within it."[86]

Shirakaba members such as Shiga Naoya, Yanagi Muneyoshi, and Nagayo Yoshirō wrote articles that publicly endorsed their friend's project although they did not become official dues-paying members of the association, let alone join Mushanokōji in the actual village in rural Miyazaki Prefecture. Shiga, for example, published a piece titled "Jibun wa kare wo shin'yō shite iru" (I believe in him) in the July 1918 issue of the newly established *Atarashiki Mura* newsletter.[87] In it he expresses support for the project because of his unshakeable confidence in his longtime friend. Yet his enthusiasm is based on his love of Mushanokōji and not on the new endeavor itself. By this time, Shiga was no longer based in Tokyo, and he had begun to establish his own more realist literary directions. He would continue refining his literary techniques, and eventually become widely recognized by many as a paragon of the modern Japanese novel—Akutagawa Ryūnosuke, the subject of the next chapter, was among his admirers. Shiga remained lifelong friends with Mushanokōji but admitted years later: "I began to feel uncomfortable and moved a bit away from the *Shirakaba* when its humanistic color (*jindō-shugi no iro*) became too intense."[88] His new directions drew from his early roots in the Shirakaba group though. In 1919 one admirer, the writer Hirotsu Kazuo (1891–1968), remarked of Shiga's work: "Whereas a typical realist's attitude toward life and human beings is rational, harsh, and cool, his attitude has a humanistic warmth. It is precisely because of this warmth that his works give me a feeling of pure delight.... No such thing called humanism is remotely visible on the surface of his works. But those who truly savor his works cannot help but feel the humanistic warmth that beats deep within."[89]

In contrast to Shiga, the novelist Arishima Takeo—a founding member of *Shirakaba* who had written the cautiously critical review of Mushanokōji's debut novel *Omedetaki hito* (1910) that proved to prophesy Mushonokōji's subsequent challenges—expressed doubt about his younger friend's vision for the Atarashiki Mura commune. Arishima, whose aristocratic family were hereditary landowners, had become attracted to socialist thought following an extensive period of study in America and Europe. While he praises Mushanokōji for his ambitious plan to create a better world through labor and art, he warns that in reality, "war and peace are freely controlled by a minority called the capitalists. And the lives of the majority are mercilessly victimized as a result."[90] He seems incredulous that Mushanokōji's idyllic and peaceful society could be achieved without a class struggle to overthrow the rule of the elites. Arishima states rather elliptically: "I believe that even if you carry out your plans with much precision and care, it will end in failure. I think it fitting for the plan to end in failure.... I pray that rather than achieve a success that does not suit its goal, this plan, the first of this sort to be executed in Japan, will meet with failure by committing fully to its philosophies."[91] Also, since he had spent time on his family's farmlands in Hokkaido in his youth, and had gone on to attend an agricultural college after graduating from Gakushūin, Arishima had a clear-eyed awareness of the logistical labors awaiting the amateur villagers who intended to cultivate a wild land and live off of its bounty. He did not romanticize farm work. His predictions of doom and the disclaimer that any successful results for the village would be merely superficial flukes understandably angered Mushanokōji. After an exchange of opinions in the *Shirakaba* magazine, the two friends ceased contact with each other until 1921, when Shiga Naoya intervened. By then, Mushanokōji was well acquainted with the material hardships and interpersonal stresses of the communal rural lifestyle he had initially envisioned in rosy colors.

As socialist thought gained momentum in Japanese intellectual and literary circles in the intervening years, Arishima's own philosophies too evolved. He eventually became convinced that a proletarian revolution must be carried out by the working class for itself. He states in his famous 1922 essay "Sengen hitotsu" (One statement) that those outside of the dispossessed "fourth estate" are powerless to aid or hinder such a revolution.[92] Later that same year he turned over ownership of his land holdings in Hokkaido to the peasants who worked there. This dramatic move was motivated by a sober consciousness of class politics, whereas the Atarashiki Mura was based on an adamantly optimistic faith that egalitarian ideals and a love of art would smooth over social tensions.

Arishima and Mushanokōji shared the remarkable determination to attempt to turn their theoretical ideals into material reality. Their later fates were, however, markedly divergent. Arishima committed suicide with his married lover in 1923, and the cooperative farm he founded reverted to private property after World War II. Mushanokōji died in 1976 at the age of ninety-one. According to its webpage, a century after its founding the Atarashiki Mura—which relocated to Saitama Prefecture in 1938—still exists with a few members who host regular events in the village where visitors are welcome.[93] The other members of the Shirakaba too moved on in their respective paths, but their collective ideals of what they had intuited as an inseparable and immediate connection between the self, humanistic ideals, and artistic expression continued to reverberate in the broader landscape of modern Japanese literature and culture.

FIVE

Akutagawa Ryūnosuke's Literary Anxieties and the "Power to Remake"

AKUTAGAWA RYŪNOSUKE COMMITTED to literature as his life's work for the intellectual and aesthetic sustenance it provided, but he remained constantly aware of the asymmetries between literary insights and lived realities. On the one hand, as seen by his high estimation of the Shirakaba writer Shiga Naoya, he believed that writing could make something essential about the author's living persona and their insights known and familiar to readers. Simultaneously, Akutagawa was drawn to literature because it gave him access to perspectives and ideas that far exceeded his own frames of reference and experiences. This tension about literature's ability to evoke both the actual and the imagined not only shaped how he wrote about himself in his semiautobiographical fictions, but it also tempered his views about Japan's cultural modernity, which were quite ambivalent despite his reputation for an optimistic cosmopolitan outlook. Like many of his forebears, Akutagawa often investigated literature's uniqueness as an artistic medium by comparing it to the visual arts, and his understanding of literature was inseparable from his aesthetic philosophies at large. But Akutagawa's views can be distinguished from those of the writers who preceded him—such as Sōseki, who strove to delineate the nascent concept of "literature" using scientific terms, or Ogai, who attempted to systematically map its premises and limits through speculative philosophical systems—because his awareness of "literariness" as a conceptual register, beholden to both aesthetic ideals and critical cognitions of sociohistorical conditions, served as a point of departure for his musings rather than his eventual conclusion.

Writing and Living

Akutagawa Ryūnosuke was among those who had been struck by the radical frankness of Mushanokōji Saneatsu's style of writing. Akutagawa recounts that as students coming of age just as the *Shirakaba* magazine was reaching public renown, he and his peers had been "very pleased that Mushanokōji had opened the windows of the literary establishment to let in some fresh air" (ARZ 4: 128).[1] He explains that "in many of [Mushanokōji's] essays, there was a virile energy like that of a great wind that stoked the fires of idealism within our hearts and made them momentarily flare up." Yet despite his admiration of the older writer's lofty notions, he was not a fan of Mushanokōji's literary creations, which seemed to "display too much of a rushed quality in the anticipation of their completion." Akutagawa points out a strictly "neutral relationship between form and content" in Mushanokōji's works in which ideas appear plainly and starkly without stylistic flourishes. Even as a fledgling writer, Akutagawa had a taste for literary virtuosity and did not admire this artlessness. He valued the formal elements of a literary work as well as its narrative content and philosophical premises, whereas Mushanokōji's priority, as we saw in the previous chapter, was first and foremost the expression of the writer's immediate emotions and perspectives.

Yet Akutagawa greatly respected the work of Shiga Naoya, who had begun his writing career with Mushanokōji as a part of the Shirakaba group. He recounts this admiration in *Bungei-teki na, Amari ni bungei-teki na* (Literary, all too literary), a wide-ranging essay collection published over the course of several installments during 1927 until his suicide in July of that year.[2] In the essay, Akutagawa declares that he considered Shiga "the purest writer among us," and praises him for his "ethical" (*dōtoku-teki*) and "unsullied" (*seiketsu*) stance toward life (ARZ 15: 155). He also admires Shiga's technical mastery of literary realism: "[His] realist entry into minute details is without precedent. Speaking solely on this point, it might be said without exaggeration that he was even more detailed than Tolstoy." Akutagawa concludes that Shiga manages to "pour into this realism a poetic spirit that stands on the basis of Eastern tradition" because of the purity of his personal nature and strong, unclouded values. Crucially though, Akutagawa doubts whether Shiga himself was cognizant of the rare talent he possessed to suffuse his writings with his spirit because writing seemed to come so naturally to him. The conflation of an artist's actual persona with their work, and the transparency of the artistic medium—whether linguistic or visual—had been major premises for the artistic philosophies of the Shirakaba group. On the other hand, writing had always been a painstakingly intentional artistic act for Akutagawa, a fact that weighed heavily on him especially toward the end of his life.

In the same essay Akutagawa muses on trends in modern writing:

> Modern prose seems to have trod the path of "speech-like" writing. As (recent) striking examples of this phenomenon, I want to count the prose of Mushanokōji Saneatsu, Uno Kōji, and Satō Haruo. Shiga Naoya too can be included as an example. But it is also a fact that our "way of talking"—leaving aside the Westerners' "way of talking" for now—is less musical than that of our Chinese neighbors. It is not that I have no desire to "write as I talk." But simultaneously, I also think I want to "talk as I write." As far as I know, Natsume [Sōseki] Sensei was in some aspects an author who truly "spoke as he wrote." (ARZ 15: 160)[3]

Reflecting on the large-scale reshaping of Japanese writing over the previous generations through the *genbun itchi* (aligning speech and writing) language reforms, Akutagawa observes that recent literary language has come to mirror vernacular patterns. For his own part though, he remained committed to the distinctiveness of writing as a linguistic mode deliberately separate from the apparently more spontaneous processes of speech, and he did not see speech as superior to writing as a means of expressing oneself.

The government had instituted the Genbun itchi kai (Council on Genbun itchi) in March 1900, when Akutagawa was eight years old, with the aim of spreading the simplified grammar and syntax of the new writing style through education in public schools. The initiative was shuttered in December 1910, when Akutagawa was eighteen, because the mission was deemed sufficiently complete. The state's linguistic campaigns continued into Akutagawa's adulthood. In December 1924, the Ministry of Education and Culture (the Monbu-shō) announced the Proposal to Amend Kana

Transcription (*Kana-zukai kaitei an*) to further bring writing closer to speech by revising the transcription of words to reflect their phonetic pronunciations. It met with resistance from many writers, and the proposal was eventually aborted.[4] In the March 1925 issue of the *Kaizō* magazine, Akutagawa wrote a scathing critique of the proposal using an ornate belletristic style replete with classical maxims and traditional syntax. "Faced with the single, glittering term of 'simplicity' (*kan*)," he complained, "the Monbu-shō's proposal does not take into consideration the corruption of the Japanese language and ignores the sanctity of reason" (ARZ 12: 118).[5]

Although it was too late to advocate against the streamlined grammatical and syntactical forms of *genbun itchi*, Akutagawa wanted to maintain, to the extent still possible, the markers separating the written and spoken languages by preserving traditional transcription rules. Using the examples of how certain phrases lose their meaning when written as homophones in the newly proposed uniform method, he points out that on a practical level, doing away with the historical methods of transcription would lead to confusion and hinder communication. He then widens his view and argues more generally against the dismantling of writing practices which were organically developed over time. "Looking at its development since the Meiji period, our Japanese writing styles were achieved through the many geniuses who preceded us—in other words, it is constituted by the hard work of great scriveners. Rome was not built in a day. Writing styles too are like this" (ARZ 12: 118–119). Akutagawa names the many literary giants of the previous generations that had contributed to the development of current writing practices, including Natsume Sōseki and Mori Ogai. The prospect of state officials meddling in the accumulated richness of written language clearly unnerved Akutagawa. He goes so far as to lament that "even if this were a joke or something of the sort, this present announcement of the Proposal to Amend Kana Transcription is a joke akin to a bomb scare" (ARZ 12: 119).

That he perceived the linguistic reform plan as such a threat evinces how integral writing had been to Akutagawa's worldviews. For contemporary readers, Akutagawa's hypothetical proposal to "talk as I write" rather than to write as though talking, and his adamance about preserving orthographic particularities, may be suggestive of Jacques Derrida's deconstructivist program of grammatology, which begins by questioning conventional assumptions about the primacy of speech over writing. Derrida famously explained how traditional phonocentrism was based on the premise of the "absolute proximity of voice and being, of voice and the meaning of being, of voice and the ideality of meaning," all of which amount to a metaphysics of presence that he calls logocentrism.[6] By this, Derrida addresses the Western philosophical tradition at large. Gayatri Spivak explains that in grammatological thought, "the name 'writing' is given here to an entire structure of investigation, not merely to 'writing in the narrow sense,' graphic notation on tangible material."[7] It does not refer specifically to literature, which as a material and creative practice, falls between these two senses, but to "writing" in the sense of an overarching conceptual structure within which any attempt at conveying meaning involves a chain of signifiers that never arrives at a fixed essence. But as Spivak also notes: "The usual notion of writing in the narrow sense does contain the elements of the structure of writing in general: the absence of the 'author' and of the 'subject matter,' interpretability, the deployment of a space and a time that is not 'its own.' We 'recognize' all this in writing in the narrow sense and 'repress' it; this allows us to ignore that everything else is also inhibited by the structure of writing in general, that 'the thing itself always escapes.'"

The chasm between the unfettered fluency of literary imaginations and the limitations of lived cognitions, and on a personal level the asymmetries between his confident authorial subjectivity and his faltering certitude about his own identity—the fear of "the thing itself always escaping"—had were perennial themes for Akutagawa. He appreciated these anxieties as fundamental features of literature, or at least of modern literature, rather than as problems that might be overcome with proper technique or perspective. It could be said that Akutagawa fixated on the practices of transcription and style, and he reveled in the sprawling intertextuality of literary texts—their openness to infinite interpretations and referentiality to other texts—because he recognized the conceptual slipperiness of writing. And his love of the visual arts, as evinced throughout his oeuvre, might be attributed in turn to his perception that they appeal to viewers at a nonverbal, seemingly more visceral level. Of course, Akutagawa was not a deconstructivist who aimed to dismantle literature's pretensions at "subjecthood," "self-presence," or the like. He had, however, seen literature as a reserve that enabled him to experiment with such paradigms; it gave him entrée into a web of new texts and subjectivities as a reader and a writer, away from the ontic level of his own experiences. Beginning with his official debut story "Rashōmon" (1915),[8] which was based on tales drawn from the Heian period *Konjaku monogatari* collection, many of Akutagawa's stories derived their inspiration from other texts, showing the degree to which reading had been integral to his processes as a writer. Taking place in a variety of historical periods and cultural settings, these works make oblique as well as overt references to Western, Chinese, and classical Japanese texts and evince the author's wide-ranging erudition. Hori Tatsuo, who had been a younger friend and admirer of the author, described Akutagawa as "a writer who 'made art from [other] artworks,'" and states that: "He ultimately did not have a masterpiece that was original to him."[9]

Akutagawa's suicide has commonly been read in terms of his despair over his inability to connect the gilded world of literature, which allowed him to access the collective insights of writers from all lettered cultures in all time periods, to the vicissitudes of his own life in Japan's rapidly shifting present. Hirotsu Kazuo, a friend of Akutagawa, deemed Akutagawa's death "the embodiment of the suffering of a certain group of writers whose nerves were becoming frayed by the inability to move from under the weight of past cultures."[10] On the other hand, in an essay titled "'Haiboku' no bungaku: Akutagawa Ryūnosuke no bungaku ni tsuite" (The literature of "defeat": On the literature of Akutagawa Ryūnosuke), the Marxist writer Miyamoto Kenji dismissively stated that "in this writer's 'complete world of the intellect,' I have only vaguely felt his delicate neurosis, and cold gaze toward life."[11] He concluded that Akutagawa's downfall proved the limits of the bourgeois insularity that characterized his writings. Both readings cast Akutagawa as an aesthete toppled tragically, or foolishly, when the harshness of reality encroached on his refined idealism. That is, they assume Akutagawa had whole-heartedly conflated the aesthetic exhilarations of reading and writing with life itself, and that upon realizing the gap between the two distinctive spheres of art and reality, he had tumbled into distress. But Akutagawa's writings show that he had harbored an awareness of this divide long before his downfall, and that he had not always regarded the unique ontological status of literature with despair.

As mentioned in chapter 1, Akutagawa had classified his writerly stance as a mix of the Naturalists' realist depictions of "true" phenomena, the Aesthetes' attraction to "beauty" above all else, as well as the Shirakaba writers' affirmation of the innate "virtues" of humanity (*ARZ* 5: 181–182). For him and his peers, literature was an artform that could channel multiple aspects of human experiences, coming close to replicating reality or at least our perceptions of it. He explores this dynamic in the story "Saigō Takamori" (1918).[12] The story is presented as the narrator's retelling of an account he had heard from his acquaintance Homma, a history professor. The narrator is presumed to be Akutagawa himself because he notes meeting with Homma "last winter before moving to Kamakura," and Akutagawa had moved from Tokyo to Kamakura in December 1916. But Akutagawa also attempts to extricate himself from the tale by having Homma announce: "It is up to the listener to determine if this story is true or false" (ARZ 3: 63). These multiple diegetic layers cast uncertainty about the story's veracity, highlighting its theme of literature's oblique relationship to empirical truth and artistic beauty.

The story is set seven or eight years prior to the narrator's retelling. At that time, Homma was completing his graduation thesis on Saigō Takamori (1828–1877), a samurai from the domain of Satsuma. Saigō played an important role in the Meiji Restoration and was regarded as a folk hero for his later rebellion against the centralization of power under the new Meiji government. Homma had just concluded a research visit to Kyoto where Saigō had been posted early in his career as a Satsuma bureaucrat. Homma is on the train headed back to Tokyo when he falls into conversation with an eccentric elderly man in the dining car. Upon learning that Homma is studying history, the old man identifies himself as a fellow historian and he says with a laugh, "Historians are nothing but almanac-makers," quoting the eighteenth-century British poet and critic Samuel Johnson (ARZ 3: 67). The old man becomes garrulous as he nurses his glass of whiskey. He warns Homma to be careful in researching the Seinan War of 1877, in which Saigo had taken his last stand: "There are many false records about that war, and those false records have become enshrined as accurate historical materials. So unless you are very cautious in your treatment of historical materials, you will unknowingly commit errors" (ARZ 3: 69).

Homma eventually grows irritated with the pompous stranger until the old man agrees to share an example of a widely held misconception about the history of the Seinan War. "The thought that this man might be crazy suddenly crossed Homma's mind. But at the same time, having pursued the matter this far, it seemed a shame to simply let this so-called truth slip away" (ARZ 3: 71). In the transitory space of a train car, the young Homma is enticed by the possibility of learning a historical secret from the bizarre but oddly authoritative stranger. He is still not entrenched enough in the discourses of his field to be unable to question its tenets.

The old man then discloses to him that contrary to conventional beliefs, the samurai hero Saigō Takamori had survived the Battle of Shiroyama where he is said to have died and in fact is still alive, decades afterward. Exasperated by the wild claim, Homma patiently recounts the widely held theory that Saigo had died at Shiroyama "in an argument as precise in its deductions, and as decisive and as logically sound, as was usual for him" (ARZ 3: 73). The old man shrugs off the historical documents that Homma names as evidence pointing to Saigō's downfall at Shiroyama, saying that the former samurai was at that moment in an adjacent train car. After being led to a man greatly resembling the famous warrior asleep in his seat, Homma experiences conflicting emotions. "He was at a loss. What should he believe—the historical materials accepted as conventionally accurate, or the aging giant he had just seen?[13] If doubting the former is to doubt his own head, doubting the latter would be to doubt his own eyes" (ARZ 3: 77). Seeing the student's confusion, the old man offers some advice: "Leaving aside for the time being the theory of Saigōs death in battle at Shiroyama, there is no such thing anywhere as historical material that can be sufficient for judgments about historical matters. In recording a fact, everyone naturally writes by selecting details. This cannot be helped because they do this despite their intentions. That is to say, this already means a distancing from objective reality" (ARZ 3: 77).

The old man says that although historical documents agree that on September 24, 1877, Saigō had perished at the Battle of Shiroyama, all that is actually known is that someone believed to be him had died. And now, it is also known that someone who greatly resembles an aged Saigō is asleep in their locomotive. Homma is flummoxed by these arguments until the elderly man tells him that the sleeping man is actually not the famed warrior but just a friend. He then presents his business card to Homma, revealing himself to be a noted historian. Homma is humbled and says: "Professor, you are a skeptic" (ARZ 3: 81). The story concludes with the professor saying: "We know nothing, not even about our own selves, let alone about the life and death of Saigō Takamori. Hence, in writing history, I do not purport to write a history free of fabrication. I am satisfied with writing a beautiful history that seems convincing. When I was young, there was a time I thought about becoming a novelist." (ARZ 3: 81).

AKUTAGAWA RYŪNOSUKE'S LITERARY ANXIETIES

Akutagawa obfuscates the conventional divide between history, with its attempts to determine the truth of past events, and literature, whose concern is to craft "beautiful" stories that merely sound convincing. Through the professor's words Akutagawa implies that all writing is mediated by the writer, but unlike historical writing that ostensibly aims for veracity, literature can aim to create an impression of beauty not contingent on worldly truths. Although the professor first calls historians "almanac makers," referring to their seemingly straightforward task of recording observable facts, he undermines this later by questioning the very possibility of such an objective writing. "We know nothing" for certain but must continue onward, he says. Rather than jadedness about the impossibility of writing anything with certitude, the story ends on a pragmatic, forward-looking note that clears the provisional grounds for future writing.

But Akutagawa's optimism would eventually fade, giving way to his personal and artistic crisis of conscience and subsequent suicide. In 1927, upon learning of Akutagawa's death, his literary hero Shiga Naoya astutely stated: "From start to finish, Akutagawa had doubted his own art."[14] He suggests that Akutagawa had immersed himself so thoroughly in the pursuit of literary virtuosity not because he had sincerely believed that it allowed him to rise above the circumstances of his own life, but because he could not truly be convinced of this. He and Akutagawa had not been close, but the older writer recalls that Akutagawa had visited him in July 1922 and asked him about a period of writer's block that he had undergone earlier in his career. Shiga had been involved in a train accident in 1913, and compounded with the strain of family strife, he did not produce literary work for almost three years following this traumatic incident. Shiga recounts that the younger writer "implied that he too had arrived at a similar situation, and said that he was not the sort of person who could write novels." At that juncture, Akutagawa had not only been at a creative crossroads, but a personal one as well. His health had been poor since his visit to China the previous year in 1921 as a reporter for the *Osaka Mainichi* newspaper, and the unexpectedly complicated aftermath of an extramarital affair was causing him much emotional distress. Especially because he had been mostly sparing in his praise of writers contemporary to him, it is significant that Akutagawa had admired Shiga enough to approach him for advice in his hour of crisis. The older man's suggestion that he "take an extended hiatus from writing and recuperate"

[185]

was of no help to him though, because unlike Shiga who had family wealth, not working was not an option for Akutagawa.

We know from his assessments in *Bungei-teki na, Amari ni bungei-teki na* (1927) that Akutagawa had admired Shiga for the apparently unconscious ease in his writing. In his view, Shiga lived ethically (*dōtoku-teki*) and was naturally able to channel his purity of spirit into his writings; he muses that "the influence of the ethical genius Mushanokōji Saneatsu played no small role in this tendency" (*ARZ* 15: 156). In contrast, he could not help but fret about the distance between the intentional, artistic realm of reading and writing—the world of infinite textuality and new possibilities—and the constant challenges and meanness of everyday living. That Shiga had no useful advice for him must have further convinced Akutagawa of what he apprehended as a major difference in their basic orientations to writing and to living.

The Lives of Artists

Akutagawa had anticipated from early in his career that life as a professional writer would be fraught with stress. "Gesaku zanmai" (A life of Gesaku, 1917), the first story that Akutagawa serialized for a newspaper, already presaged many of the challenges he would face in his later years.[15] The work covers a day in the life of the Edo-period writer Kyokutei Bakin (1767–1848) and examines how he balances his creative aspirations and his quotidian life. Though he uses Bakin's journal as a reference, the story is not a historical biography of the famous author.[16] Instead, as his friend Kikuchi Kan (1888–1948) proposed, the story can be understood as Akutagawa's "confessions about his creative philosophies."[17] Kikuchi muses: "I think it is because [Akutagawa] is more artistic than the typical confessional novelist that he had used Bakin as a stand-in, making his confessions through a proxy." Gesaku was the playful, popular fiction genre that Bakin was renowned for in the late Edo period, and Akutagawa's use of this term instead of the more general term of "literature" throughout the story seems to suggest his belief that while its forms and conventions may change, the overall human endeavor of expression through writing remains constant throughout time. And as Kikuchi suggested, the reference to Edo-period literature allows Akutagawa to voice his own views without recourse to the autobiographical realism favored by his Naturalist peers. Akutagawa articulated his belief in the timelessness of literature in a short essay entitled "Kōsei" (Later generations, 1919):[18]

> Sometimes, I think of twenty or fifty or a hundred years later, when an era that does not even know of my existence will arrive. At that time, volumes of my collected works will probably be buried in thick dust, in the corner of a used bookstore somewhere around Kanda, waiting pathetically for a reader. Or if I'm lucky, a single volume might be preserved in a library somewhere, ravaged as food for silverfish, so torn that the characters cannot even be read. However—.
> And I think of a however.
> However, is it impossible that someone might find a volume of my works by chance, and read a short story, or a few lines from a story? To be even more presumptuous, is it impossible that this one story or those several lines might evoke for my unknown future reader a beautiful dream, even just a bit? (ARZ 4: 295)

This quiet hope that perhaps his work would outlast him and retain some portion of its aesthetic-affective impact, despite the inevitably new societal contexts against which it will be read, is also a key motivator for Bakin in Akutagawa's telling. The titular character's solemn meditations about the evanescence—and pettiness—of the present moment, and the potential infinity of literature constitute the central drama of the story.

The opening scene of the story clearly presents this theme. Bakin, in his sixties, relaxes in the warm water of a crowded public bath. The sight of his wrinkled skin causes him to contemplate his long career as a writer and his own mortality: "The shadow of 'death' crossed the old man's heart at this moment. But this 'death' did not harbor any morbid trace as that which used to frighten him previously. Like the sky reflected in the tub, it was quiet and pleasant, a peaceful feeling of rest. If only one could escape the cares of life and rest in this 'death'—how wonderful it would be to sleep dreamlessly like a carefree child. It is not just that he is tired of life. He is also tired from suffering through decades of ceaseless creative production" (ARZ 3: 4–5). As though foreshadowing Akutagawa's own breakdown in his later period, literary labors have exhausted Bakin mentally and physically to the point that he fantasizes about the respite of death. His thoughts are interrupted when he is recognized by a reader who promptly joins him in the bath. He also overhears someone criticizing his works, and he heads home in a dark mood. He knows better than to let an amateur's words bother him, but his ego is bruised. Bakin's fickle moods show that the self-esteem of an artist is delicate. The shifting emotions described in this early episode are accentuated as the tale progresses, showing that an artist's aesthetic contemplations are easily disturbed by interruptions of a nonartistic nature.

Later that afternoon, the writer peruses the *Water Margin*, a Chinese vernacular fiction about historical warriors from the Song period. Like Akutagawa, a voracious reader who incorporated elements from a variety of literary texts into his own stories, Bakin's imagination is also ignited through books: "His novels were, as he declared, the artistic expression of the 'paths trodden by the great beings of the past.' ... But there is an unexpectedly large gap between the value that the 'paths of the great beings of the past' endows to his work, and the value that his own emotions bestow. The ethicist in him affirms the first, while the artist in him inevitably affirms the latter" (*ARZ* 3: 27). Bakin debates whether his literature should emphasize the moral lessons passed on through shared lore from the past or display his own creative genius via his distinctive reworkings of familiar source materials. The issue was familiar to Akutagawa, who faced charges of derivativeness for his liberal references to other literary texts.

In an essay titled "Mukashi" (Long ago, 1918), Akutagawa explains that he uses historical settings and figures in his fictions for the creative latitude this affords him.[19] He claims that "fantastic happenings, in so far as they are fantastic, are difficult to write about as events taking place in contemporary Japan. ... My stories that draw from historical materials are generally driven by this necessity, and I stage them in the past to avoid the obstacle of seeming unnatural" (*ARZ* 3: 88). The assumption is that while stories situated in the present day are expected to adhere to realist standards, such pressures can be skirted with the use of historical settings. But if Akutagawa's only goal were to create a context sufficiently removed from his own where his imagination could unfurl unimpeded, he could have invented entirely new places and people instead of relying on preexistent references. That he does not do this signals the wish to have his stories maintain legible connections to a communally established realm, even as he seeks to safeguard his individual artistic freedoms. While Akutagawa does not delve deeper into this issue in the story, through Bakin's thoughts he evinces his awareness of intertextual referentiality—which in premodern Japanese literature operated according to its own specific conventions—as a persistently fraught issue for writers in each era.

When Bakin's friend, the painter Watanabe Kazan (1793–1841) comes to visit, their conversation turns to the problem of the government's zealous regulation of literary publications. At first, Bakin vociferously complains about the seeming hypocrisy of these censors: "It's because they themselves take bribes that if I write about bribery, they make me rewrite those scenes. And it's because they so easily fall into lurid imaginations that they label as obscene any text if it mentions male-female romance. It is painful to look on while they go on pretending to have higher morals than the writers!" (ARZ 3: 32). The two friends joke about "dying in battle" (uchi jini) for the sake of artistic expression, but as though to temper his outspoken comments, Bakin adds that what is more important is to "survive" (ikinokoru). Bakin is apparently passionate about his artistic rights but unwilling to incur the wrath of the shogunate by actively defying its rules. This mirrors Akutagawa's own uneasy political passivity, which would become more pronounced with the rise of his literary stature. Throughout his career he kept apprised of developments in socialist discourses, but avoided presenting overt political bias in his writings.[20] He once summarized his views as follows: "With a false step, art for art's sake (geijutsu no tame no geijutsu) can fall into a view of art as a mere game. With a false step, art for life's sake (jinsei no tame no geijutsu) can fall into a view of art as a means to an end" (ARZ 5: 164).[21] On the one hand, Akutagawa hoped to preserve the independence of his creative endeavors, but on the other, he recognizes that an art entirely disconnected from broader social contexts could fall into meaningless, self-referential abstraction.

That Bakin's artistic ally Kazan is a painter, and not a fellow writer, is meaningful in the context of "Gesaku zanmai" as an early blueprint for Akutagawa's creative philosophies. In many of his stories, Akutagawa features painters as protagonists and paintings as major plot devices. He also discloses how in his own life, the visual arts had catalyzed his development as a thinker and a writer. For instance, Akutagawa counted the yōga painter Oana Ryūichi (1894–1966) among his closest friends. In a short 1927 essay he departs from his earlier hopefulness that his literary works might survive the test of time and predicts that while Oana's paintings will be admired by future progeny, his own literature might be forgotten: "I say this because I take into account the differences between the plastic arts (*zōkei bijutsu*) and literature (*bungaku*). (Literature—and especially this thing called the novel, will hardly be in circulation in three hundred years or so)" (ARZ 14: 264).²² The late-stage Akutagawa suspected that the novel might not age as well as a painting because it was so distinctively a product of the present zeitgeist. His view that the novel is the medium most capable of expressing the multiple dimensions of modern consciousness is summed in the statement from *Bungei-teki na, Amari ni bungei-teki na* quoted at the start of this book: "I write novels because out of all the arts, novels are the most encompassing, and it is possible to throw everything and anything into them" (ARZ 15: 154). The inverse implication is that the visual arts stand at a dignified, perhaps more purely artistic remove from the messier and more banal aspects of the lived experiences that cumulatively comprise the stuff of literature.

In "Gesaku zanmai," the sole interaction between Bakin and another human being unrelated to his status as a writer occurs when his grandson bounds into his study. "'Grandfather, I'm home!' 'Oh, you were early!' And with these words, the wrinkled face of the *Hakkenden* author lit up with a delight that seemed to belong to someone else" (ARZ 3: 36). This unremarkable scene suggests that quotidian obligations need not always hinder art, and that the bonds of life could give much needed succor to an artist wearied from his solitary battles. That night, Bakin continues his writing with renewed vigor: "There is a strange joy. Or the deep emotion of an entrancing pathos. How can anyone who does not know this emotion understand the mental state of infatuation with gesaku?" (ARZ 3: 41). Bakin's spiritual joy in his literary work seems to represent the triumph of the artist transcending the often-wearisome contexts of his personal life. But outside the sanctuary of his study, life unfolds relentlessly. Bakin's wife and daughter-in-law talk to each other as they sew. When his daughter-in-law casually comments that Bakin must be staying up late engrossed in his writing, his wife harshly replies: "What a nuisance. It doesn't even pay that well" (ARZ 3: 41). This unsympathetic judgment of the author's work based on its monetary potential again revives the theme of the opposition between art and life. Unless we count the extradiegetic fact of Bakin's enduring fame, the story's ending does not signify either a victory or defeat for the writer, who continues to work deep into the night, undeterred.

"Jigoku-hen" (Hell screen, 1918), another work from Akutagawa's early period, furthers the exploration of the artist's relationship to his surrounding realities.[23] From the time of its publication, the work has been hailed as evincing Akutagawa's artistic absolutism, the prioritization of aesthetic achievements over more immediate human concerns such as love and ethics. Upon the story's appearance, the critic Kojima Masajirō wrote: "What moved me most was certainly the main character Yoshihide's genius (*tensai buri*).... It is the artistic ecstasy of his genius that appeals to us with a superhuman (*chō ningen-teki*) power. No, it is the gradual heightening of the author's expression of his poetic qualities."[24] Kojima's remarks point out the double layers of the story, namely that of the painter Yoshihide's passions and of Akutagawa's literary virtuosity, both of which reach impressive heights by the story's end. Later critics have tended to read the story in terms of a struggle between Yoshihide as an artistic genius and Yoshihide as a vulnerable human individual, interpreting Yoshihide's suicide at the tale's conclusion as the ultimate sacrifice by an artist in the name of his calling.[25] In light of Akutagawa's own suicide, these readings take on a darker aspect. Yet the story can be read not just as Akutagawa's unhesitant endorsement of artistic supremacy but also as his cautious critique of such an attitude, or at least, as an open meditation on whether art and quotidian existence must be so antithetical to each other.

Akutagawa took his inspiration for the story from an entry in the twelfth-century Japanese vernacular tale collection, the *Konjaku monogatari*. This setting in the distant literary past enhances Yoshihide's otherworldly quality. Yoshihide, a renowned artist in the court of Lord Horikawa, is not the narrator of this tale. For that role, Akutagawa casts an old servant who functions as an onlooker to the events that unfold around Yoshihide. This added layer of distancing allows Akutagawa to portray the artist at close proximity but without a third-person omniscience to fully reveal his thoughts. Speaking in retrospect, the narrator describes Yoshihide as having been insufferably arrogant about his superior painting skills and kind to no one except his beloved daughter. He thinks nothing of having his assistants pose in uncomfortable and dangerous positions so that he might sketch them, or of using rotting corpses to study the human form. One day Lord Horikawa commissions him to paint a screen depicting the Buddhist image of hell. The narrator, who speaks in retrospect, discloses that although the image of hell (*jigoku-e*) is a conventional trope in Buddhist religious art, the screen that Yoshihide ends up producing was extraordinary in its graphic depictions of sinners burning in the flames of punishment. In a bit of foreshadowing, the narrator states that the most arresting image in Yoshihide's shocking, powerful painting was of an ox-carriage falling from the burning sky: "Behind the carriage's screen which was blown upward by the winds of hell was a woman dressed so richly that she could have been a lady in the imperial household, with her floor-length black hair waving in the flames, writhing in agony with her white neck arched. Every element, from her appearance to the burning carriage, evoked the intense suffering in the inferno. It was as though all the horror in the wide screen was concentrated in this one figure. It was so divinely inspired that anyone seeing the painting thought they could hear her screaming" (ARZ 3: 169–170).

The narrative then goes back in time to describe the methods that fueled Yoshihide as he created his masterpiece. He threw himself into his work, savagely torturing his models in order to paint their pain. He even asked his patron Horikawa to burn a woman in an ox-carriage so that he could portray the scene more accurately. Yoshihide claims: "I absolutely cannot paint anything I have not seen. Even if I manage, I am not satisfied. This is the same as not being able to paint at all" (ARZ 3: 187). Horikawa concedes, but on the day of the torching Yoshihide discovers that the woman on fire in the carriage is his daughter. The narrator recalls: "Most strangely, the man gazed delightedly at his only daughter's death but it wasn't only that. Yoshihide at that moment displayed an awe-inspiring gravitas that for some reason seemed superhuman, like the rage of a lion king in a dream" (ARZ 3: 198). A month later, after presenting the finished screen to Horikawa, Yoshihide hangs himself. A man of few words, he leaves no explanation.

Yoshihide's suicide after completing his magnum opus would seem to indicate that even great artists are not exempt from human frailties, and they are subject to the social and political authority of their rulers. And the narrator's denunciation of the rumors that Lord Horikawa had ordered the torching of Yoshihide's daughter because she had spurned his amorous advances, has the opposite effect of stoking the reader's suspicions that the contest of wills between the artist and his patron had been motivated not by their respective pride, but by less exalted factors. According to this reading, Horikawa is a tyrannical autocrat who executed a woman who would not give into his will, and he punished her father by making him watch her violent death. Yet, whatever the confluence of events leading up to the immolation of his daughter, Yoshihide sacrifices his humanity for the sake of his artistic calling when he turns the horrible spectacle into the subject of his painting. As a product of Yoshihide's artistic brilliance, the painting proves Lord Horikawa's cruelty ineffective. We can thus read "Jigoku-hen" as affirming art's ability to exist on a privileged plane above quotidian hierarchies, or as a warning about the pernicious effects of prioritizing art above the people and values that order our everyday lives.

Akutagawa's decision to cast a painter as the subject of this exploration of artistic absolutism is significant on many levels. For one, the narrator explains that the work was from its inception designated as a hell screen, an artistic trope illustrating notions of hell preestablished in Buddhist lore. Viewers familiar with religious concepts would thus be able to understand and appreciate the scene that Yoshihide depicted without the aid of narrative explanation. Moreover, Akutagawa describes the hell painting as so lifelike that viewers could almost hear its subjects screaming. We might conclude that Yoshihide's antisocial reticence is only natural given how much feeling he could express through visual imagery alone. Such visceral reactions, the story seems to suggest, cannot be evoked through literary language. But the story itself hinges on Akutagawa's ability to provide an ekphrastic description of Yoshihide's painting rich enough to convince readers of its magnificence. For readers, the impact of the work comes from the sum effect of visualizing the infamous painting conjured through the prose, and savoring its linguistic description itself as a work of art.

Yet we also see Akutagawa tipping the scales towards his own medium in the contest he implicitly mounts between image and literary narrative. His liberal deployment of hindsight and foreshadowing—techniques unavailable to the visual arts—draw attention to the inimitable ability of language to express temporality and a multiplicity of dramatic perspectives. The narrator's extradiegetic interjections shroud the story's events in an air of hoary legend rather than crisp reality. Comments like, "There may still be some who would recognize the name 'Yoshihide'" (ARZ 3: 158), or "In my rush to describe that rare hell screen, I may have deviated from the order of events" (ARZ 3: 170), create an uncanny impression since no one "recognizes" Yoshihide until he is spoken of, and there is no "correct" chronology to the story until it is told. They underscore the fact that Yoshihide, Lord Horikawa, and the hell screen only come to exist at all through the narrator's telling of the tale. In sum, we can read the story as a celebration, as well as a lament, of literary writing's self-referential properties that stand in contrast to the more blatant visual impact of a powerful painting.

Disintegrating Perspectives

Akutagawa further pursues the interartistic dynamic of ekphrasis in "Shūzanzu" (Painting of an autumn mountain, 1921), a story inspired by an anecdote that he found in a book about Chinese ink paintings.[26] The story was published in the *Kaizō* magazine in January 1921, two months before Akutagawa set off on a four-month tour of China as a special correspondent for the *Osaka Mainichi* paper. "Shūzanzu" takes place in the Chinese past and reflects the author's enthusiasm for classical Chinese paintings and his romanticized views about China that would be greatly dismantled after his trip.[27] The narrative begins with a conversation between two painters who had been active in late seventeenth- and early eighteenth-century Qing-period China, Yun Nantian and Wang Shigu. Yun Nantian tells his friend that many years ago, his teacher, Wang Yanke, had heard about the splendors of a painting called *The Painting of an Autumn Mountain* by the fourteenth-century Yuan-period artist Huang Yifeng.[28] Intrigued, Wang Yanke sets off on a long journey to see the artwork for himself. Upon viewing its perfect beauty he rhapsodizes in awe: "The painting is composed in shades of blue. Small villages and bridges dot the landscape where the water snakes between the valleys. Above the main mountain peak, elegant clouds are layered in shades of white. High mountains overlap horizontally in shades of green as though after a fresh rainfall, and in the places where the foliage of the woods are brilliantly portrayed with spots of crimson, the beauty is such that there are almost no words fit to describe it" (ARZ 7: 135).

The owner of the painting though, seems surprised by the strong impression it makes on his visitor. Fifty years pass, and Wang Yanke remains unable to forget the beauty of that long-ago image. His student Yun Nantian then locates the painting, which now belongs to a new owner. A viewing party is promptly arranged. Although the other attendees praise the painting when it is unveiled, Wang Yanke is disappointed. He confides in

Yun Nantian that the image before him is certainly a Huang Yifeng painting, but somehow not the one that had so inspired him in his youth. "Everything seems to have been a dream," he says, blinking his eyes (ARZ 7: 145).

The story certainly makes a general aesthetic statement about how an ideal artistic image is the product of the beholder's gaze.[29] But new layers of nuance come to light when considering how the story describes the affective jolt delivered by visual imagery, and how it depicts narrative language's power to diffuse, then multiply refract, initial impressions. To start, when Akutagawa evokes the painting through his narrator's lively recollections, he includes the qualifier that "there are almost no words fit to describe it" (ARZ 7: 135), intimating that there is an unmediated quality about a visual image that does not fully translate into linguistic descriptions. The subsequent turn of events in which Yun Nantian painstakingly tracks down the image through a network of various individuals further implies that not only the remove of time and Wang Yanke's fading memory, but also the repeated recountings and hearsay about the painting, play a role in diffusing Wang Yanke's reactions to the image. Perhaps the newly resurfaced painting was in fact the same one that the artist had encountered as a young man, and over the intervening decades he had come to mentally idealize the image to improbable levels. Or his artistic sensibilities may have become more discerning during that time. It is also possible that, within the fictional world of the story—although it is populated with real art historical personages—the image itself had inexplicably transformed. The "truth" of the story remains undisclosed and beside the point. The rich sense of open possibilities and wonder that remain in the wake of the recovered painting is of a distinctively literary quality.

The story "Yume" (Dreams, 1927) also pits the energies of visual art against the evocative powers of narrative. The manuscript of the story was discovered after Akutagawa's death and first published in 1929.[30] A markedly more muted view of the expressive capacities of the arts—both visual and literary—emerges here than in Akutagawa's previous works on the theme. "Yume" is told from the perspective of an unnamed *yōga* painter as he paints a female model. He is impressed by her mighty physical presence but unable to gain any insight into her interiority, and he deems her "more like an animal than a human being" (ARZ 22: 533) in her inscrutability. For inspiration, he turns to a book of the French Post-Impressionist artist Paul Gauguin's paintings in Tahiti.

One night, the painter dreams that he killed his model in his studio. The following day, she does not show up to pose for him. As he walks the city searching for her, he is overcome with the strange conviction that he had also dreamt taking this very walk. The story concludes: "That I had gone in search of her was no different from what I saw in a dream a few months—or was it a few years?—ago. In that dream too, I seem to have been walking these lonely streets by myself after I left the laundry shop. Beyond that, I couldn't remember what had come next in my dream. I sensed however, that should anything else happen, it too might become a part of my dream" (ARZ 22: 539–540).

It is possible that the narrator murdered his model, or that he had dreamt the whole sequence of his interactions with her. In either case, the painter is depicted as so out of touch with matters beyond his creative work that he cannot be certain about what, if anything, is objectively real. Like Yoshihide in "Jigoku-hen" he needs a model to pose for him, which seems to posit a continuum between the artist's empirical observations of external subjects and his subsequent creative expressions. But even though the story is told from his point of view, Akutagawa's deliberately crafted wording clouds what actually transpired between the painter and his model, and it entirely overlooks the viewpoints and agency of the model. Their conversations are desultory, and the painter is portrayed as an unreliable and rather unsavory narrator, existing in a perpetually self-centered haze. The only point of reference he has beyond his own thoughts is the book of paintings by Paul Gauguin, a male artist whose colorful and bold depictions of often nude Tahitian women nonetheless evince an objectifying, patriarchal gaze that may not be dissimilar to how he too regards his model. The painter's lack of communication with other people show him outside the normal web of human bonds. But his isolation does not give him the focus by which to achieve glorious artistic achievements. At the story's end his painting remains unfinished, and he is left fearful about his own sanity.

The story suggests the limitations of art to reach beyond the closed world of the self when the artist is in dire personal straits. The story opens with the narrator stating how exhausted he feels, describing his bodily aches and his insomnia. But unlike Bakin from "Gesaku zanmai," the artist's physical debilitation is not offset by the spiritual energies he derives from his work. The narrator of "Yume" is in poor health both physically and mentally, and he relies on sleeping pills. This beleaguered character, has a first-person narrative voice steeped in a dreamy uncertainty. Akutagawa abstains from exercising authorial omniscience to give a fuller account of the painter's experiences with his muse. He stays within the painter's limited perspective and uses vague language to describe his impressions of his model:

> [The model's face] was not very pretty. Yet her body—in particular, her breasts—were undeniably impressive. Her combed-back hair was also undeniably luxurious. I was satisfied with this model, and after seating her on a wicker chair decided to get to work right away.... But when I faced the easel I realized, as though I were just discovering this, how exhausted I was. There was only one charcoal brazier in my north-facing room. I of course built a fire in it that almost scorched its rims. But the room would not become warm enough. Perched on the wicker chair, a reflexive shiver would occasionally course through [the model's] thigh muscles. Each time, I felt annoyance as I moved my brush. This was an annoyance aimed more at myself and my inability to buy even a single stove, rather than at her. (ARZ 22: 531–532)

The subject of the story is the artist's inability to paint his model, and so Akutagawa refrains from any ekphrastic descriptions about the painting that his protagonist so desperately wishes to paint. The painter is unable to view, let alone artistically represent, his model apart from the psychological darkness that colors everything for him. The unfinished portrait of the missing woman and the narrative impasse with which "Yume" ends suggest a failure of both the visual and linguistic arts. In retrospect, it is tempting to draw parallels between Akutagawa's state of psychological exhaustion in the final year of his life, and his fictional painter's overwhelming despair in "Yume." By this point, the stresses brought on by family obligations, his standing in the literary community, his creative anxieties, and worsening health had plunged Akutagawa into a state of neuroses and depression.

Writing and Painting the Self

Akutagawa also explored the junction between creative work and the artist's personal welfare in stories that were more explicitly about himself,

AKUTAGAWA RYŪNOSUKE'S LITERARY ANXIETIES

especially in works that were consciously styled after modes of painting. Oana Ryūichi painted an oil portrait of Akutagawa that he entered in the Nika-ten art contest in the fall of 1922 (figure 5.1). In response, Akutagawa wrote "Yasukichi no techō kara" (From the notebooks of Yasukichi, 1923), and in a letter to Oana he explained: "I wanted to extend further what you

FIGURE 5.1 Ryūichi Oana, *Hakui* (Portrait in White Clothes [of Akutagawa Ryūnosuke], 1922). Oil on canvas.
The Museum of Modern Japanese Literature

did, by writing a self-portrait (*jigazō*)" (*ARZ* 20: 287).[31] Then in "Daidōji Shinsuke no hansei: aru seishin-teki fūkeiga" (The early life of Daidōji Shinsuke: A psychological landscape painting, 1925), he experimented with broad landscape perspectives.[32] And shortly before his suicide, Akutagawa wrote "Aru aho no isshō" (The life of a fool, 1927), which in earlier drafts had been subtitled "Jiden-teki esukisu [esquisse]" (An autobiographical sketch).[33] This series of "self-portraiture," "landscape painting," and "sketch" reveals the evolution of Akutagawa's literary attempts to depict himself: he first attempted to observe himself coolly and objectively in Yasukichi's story of 1923, then tried to define himself in relation to his surroundings in Shinsuke's story of 1925, and finally in 1927, he fragmented his perspective into multiple dashes of expressive, personal detail in "Aru aho no isshō."

Akutagawa's turn to the conventions of painting in his self-narrations must be understood within the context of the literary as well as visual artistic discourses of the period. In both domains, the creator's "self" was established as a major subject for representation by the early 1920s. Over the first decade of the century, the literary world had seen the rise of Japanese Naturalism that called for frank revelations of the authors' personal affairs including their baser instincts and actions; Tayama Katai's *Futon* (1907) is frequently cited as a representative work of this movement. Meanwhile, writers like Masaoka Shiki and Natsume Sōseki explored the notion of *shasei*—literally, sketching from life—which sought to dispassionately depict aspects of the world selected through the filters of individual psychologies. This was followed by a more affirmative celebration of individuality by Mushanokōji Saneatsu and his fellow members of the *Shirakaba* magazine. In the visual arts, Kishida Ryūsei, Takamura Kotarō, and many others ushered in bold and intensively subjective styles of painting during the 1910s with imagery inspired by European Post-Impressionism and Fauvism. They painted numerous self-portraits in this period.

But by the early 1920s various avant-garde strains of Western painting such as Cubism, Russian Suprematism, and Dadaism had also started to influence Japanese artists. Painters like Fumon Gyō and Kinoshita Shūichirō established the Mirai-ha kyōkai (Futurist Association) in 1920. Shortly after, the new group was visited by leading Russian Futurist artists David Burliuk and Victor Palmov. The Japanese artists under the sway of new trends began to use formal abstraction and politically motivated content, moving away from the expression of purely individual perspectives. The literary realm too was undergoing major shifts. The explosive growth of the publishing industry produced a growing body of writing that emphasized mass appeal and entertainment over artistic gravitas and philosophical inquiry. Furthermore, in the wake of the Russian Revolution (1917) socialist thought gained ground in the more liberal political climate of the "Taishō Democracy" era. Proletariat writers and the literary establishment alike attempted to question the social purposes and potentials of literature. Modernist writers who experimented with freer modes of perspective and form emerged in the latter Taishō period; as Seiji Lippit has shown, Akutagawa's own late-period works, including "Aru aho no isshō," indeed show these modernist characteristics.[34] Artists and writers queried anew the significance of their work in this period: What did it mean to create art and literature within the rapidly changing world? How should the subjective perspective evolve in response to these changes?

It was amid such an atmosphere of self-reflection that a heated literary debate broke out between the proponents of *honkaku shōsetsu* (authentic novels), who strove to create objective, third person narratives, and the supporters of the so-called *watakushi shōsetsu* (I-novels),[35] who defended the centrality of the author's subjective views. In an article published in the *Shin shōsetsu* magazine in January 1924, Nakamura Murao called for novels that "do not directly express the author's state of mind or feelings, but in which the author's views on life become visible through the depiction of [invented] characters and their lives."[36] The opposite view was taken by Kume Masao, who declared a year later that "novels in which the author reveals himself most directly"[37] were superior because "the basis of all art lies in 'the self.'"[38] Such a dichotomy stymied Akutagawa, who felt chagrin at the prospect of confessing the details of his own life in his stories, but also did not believe in hiding his authorial presence in his works.

In a short piece entitled "Kokuhaku" (Confession, November 1923),[39] he wrote:

> Many of you have periodically urged me: "Write more about your own life, and confess yourself more explicitly!" But it is not that I do not confess anything. My novels are more or less confessions of my own experiences. And yet, you do not accept this. What you recommend is that I make myself the main character [of a story], and write unabashedly about what happened to me. Furthermore, you tell me to include a full index of featured characters at the end of such a work,

listing their fictional names and their actual names, of course with me as the main character. I cannot help but refuse to comply with this.

First of all, it is unpleasant for me to reveal the details of my quotidian life to my esteemed readers. Secondly, it is also unpleasant for me to gain fame and money based on such confessions....

For now, poor as I am, I manage to keep myself afloat. And even if I suffer from physical illnesses, my psychological condition is still rather *norumaru* [normal]. I don't detect signs of masochism. Who would want to take the trouble to do something so embarrassing as to write a confessional novel? (ARZ 10: 282)

Although he acknowledges the public's desire for him to expose more about his own life, Akutagawa states that writing about himself so openly struck him as distasteful and threatened his sense of psychological self-preservation. A line had to be maintained between his art and his personal realities. Also, Akutagawa had been an admirer and acolyte of Sōseki. Traces of Sōseki's views about the role of subjective affect in artistic perspectives—memorably captured in the literary equation "F (intellectual content) + f (emotional factor)" proposed in his *Bungakuron* (1907)—seem to underlie Akutagawa's contention that "my novels are more or less confessions of my own experiences." Akutagawa indicates that he would not write about something he has little or no personal investment in. In other words, everything he writes is already imbued with his affect. But the series of semiautobiographical stories featuring his fictional alter ego Yasukichi, written between 1923 and 1925, could be seen as Akutagawa's efforts to express his lived perspectives more directly while still retaining his artistic freedoms.

Akutagawa's claim that he wrote "Yasukichi no techō kara," the earliest of the Yasukichi stories, as "a self-portrait (*jiga-zō*)" is pertinent here (ARZ 20: 287). That he did not use the term "autobiography" (*jiden*) or "I-novel" (*watakushi shōsetsu*) to describe the work signals his hesitation to align himself with extant literary positions that posited an a priori authorial authenticity. "Self-portraiture" offered an alternative way to represent himself as an artistic subject. In a letter to another friend, Akutagawa briefly mentioned that Oana's painting had made him appear more handsome than he actually was (ARZ 19: 288).[40] Although he might have made this comment as a passing pleasantry, it indicates the disorientation he must have felt upon seeing how his friend had portrayed him. In the "self-portrait" of a story that ensued, Akutagawa channels the uncanny experience of confronting an image of himself as seen through another's gaze. The contradictions between his surface appearance and interior thoughts bring its titular character Yasukichi to life.

"Yasukichi no techō kara" follows the protagonist's day-to-day affairs as an English language lecturer at the Naval Officer's Academy in Yokosuka. Akutagawa had taught at the school from 1916 to 1919 after graduating from his university studies; as befits a literary "self-portrait," the story appears to be based on his own experiences from that time. But there is a palpable division between the perspectives of Akutagawa the writer and Yasukichi his subject. The narrative is presented from Yasukichi's point of view but it gives only partial access to his thoughts and emotions in each scene. Readers gain the impression of looking in on this character within the frame of his environment, rather than of looking out at the world through his eyes.

For example, in one episode, Yasukichi is eating by himself at a restaurant when he notices two naval officers taunting a young beggar. They tell the beggar that if he barks like a dog, they will give him food. Yasukichi briefly identifies with the beggar and their common struggle to sustain themselves in an unforgiving world. It seems that at this point he is gathering the courage to speak up in defense of the beggar, but his next thoughts are unexpectedly dispassionate: "To each his own. If it pleased the officers, they should continue with their experiment" (ARZ 10: 50). Much like the narrator of Sōseki's *Kusamakura*, Yasukichi appears intent on holding himself emotionally apart from the people around him by viewing them as pictures. Watching the cruel scene unfold before him, he recalls that he had "occasionally romanticized the notion of beggars," but that he had "never felt pity or empathy" for them, and he goes on admiring the "Rembrandt-esque effect" of the young beggar's pathetic appearance (ARZ 10: 50).

This initial impression of "unhuman sentiment," to use Sōseki's term, is offset with a coda set several days later when Yasukichi is waiting to pick up his salary at the bursar's office of the school. The administrator behind the desk is one of the two men who had been bullying the beggar. Exasperated by the long wait, Yasukichi asks him, maintaining his polite tone, "Should I too, bark like a dog?" (ARZ 10: 51). The officer's response is not recorded, but his flustered surprise and embarrassment at the implicit rebuke of his dastardly behavior can be imagined. Yasukichi's subsequent thoughts remain hidden to readers but this unexpected verbal jab reveals that he is a more complex character than the narrative had previously implied. This episode illustrates that even when writing a character based on his firsthand experiences, Akutagawa could exercise his authorial prerogative to show or withhold information about his subject as it suits him. The rest of the story consists of vignettes that illustrate the gaps between Yasukichi's outer appearances and his inner thoughts—for example, an oddly animated teaching session inspired by the shame he had felt at having to teach a lackluster text—as well as Yasukichi's encounters with similarly unexpected aspects of his peers' personas.

Rather than the all-confessional ethos that he had hesitated to don, Akutagawa emulates the manner of a portrait painter who selects specific angles from which to view his subjects and then determines the light in which to showcase certain contours and features while downplaying others. This technique grants the writer more creative control over which details of himself he will disclose in his narrative. But it also emphasizes the inevitable slippages between subjects and their external viewers that undermines Akutagawa's implied intent to reveal more of himself through his writing. The gap between Akutagawa's writerly gaze and the inner life of Yasukichi is conspicuous. It is possible, however, to interpret the carefully constructed episodes of the story as effective in expressing Akutagawa's guarded nature.

Following his Yasukichi period, Akutagawa wrote the semiautobiographical story "Daidōji Shinsuke no han-sei: aru seishin-teki fūkeiga" (1925). At the most basic level, the subject of a landscape painting (*fūkei-ga*) is not a central figure but the field itself within which, or against which, the observer stands. As such, a landscape painting reveals not only *what* the painter sees but *how* he sees his surroundings; I discussed in chapter 1 how Karatani Kōjin's famous argument—that the importation of Western landscape imagery had introduced Japanese audiences to the conceptual premise of a fixed, internal "self" gazing out at the world—traces this logic. But although "Daidōji Shinsuke no han-sei" gives a detailed view of the environment surrounding and shaping its titular character, the cold and analytical tone of the narrative negates a sense of intimacy between Akutagawa the writer and the environments that he depicts.

The story opens with a description of the cityscape of the lower-middle-class Shitamachi area of Tokyo where Akutagawa had spent his childhood. It was an area where "the houses, trees, and streets were all oddly dingy" (ARZ 12: 40). Contrary to their attempts to maintain appearances of respectability in keeping with their former samurai background—such as by sending relatives a cheap cake from a neighborhood shop in wrapping paper from a fancier store—Shinsuke's family struggled to support themselves. As a young boy, Shinsuke resents this and dreams of a fuller life. He soon realizes that the only way to better his lot is by attaining an education, and he becomes a top student, as Akutgawa too had done. According to this retrospective account, it was not just ambition but also something less wholesome that took root in the young boy's heart. Akutagawa writes of his protagonist: "Shinsuke learned everything and anything from books. There was, at least, nothing he knew that didn't owe at least something to books. He did not gaze upon passersby on the city streets in order to learn about life.... For Shinsuke, the passersby on the streets were merely transients. In order to understand them—their love, their hate, and their pride—he had no other method than to read books" (ARZ 12: 53).

It was through his reading of books, not his own interactions with the world, that Shinsuke builds his understanding of human nature. Self-awareness allows him to observe, for instance, that "he loved several women in the course of his life, but it was not they who taught him the beauties of woman—or at least nothing beyond what he had already learned from books." In other words, foreknowledge gleaned from reading structured his cognition of the world. He appears unable to trust his own unmediated instincts or impressions. Overall, Akutagawa displays Shinsuke as having a defensive and insecure personality that stems from his desire to escape the meager contexts of his upbringing via the worlds he encounters in books. Akutagawa ends the story with a postscript informing readers about his plans to continue the narrative into Shinsuke's adulthood over several more installments, but this promise remained unfulfilled. Drafts for potential subsequent chapters were discovered after his death.[41] But Akutagawa ultimately abandoned the young Shinsuke to stew in his book-centered hermeticism.

The unflinching examination of Shinsuke's family's straitened economic conditions and his desire to rise above these circumstances through academic achievements show Akutagawa's acknowledgment of rising class and material consciousness in the collective sensibilities of his era. It may be because Akutagawa himself was growing frustrated with the gap between his high literary ideals and his inability to resolve the often-petty stresses of his own life that he portrays his bookish alter ego's diffident attitude toward his surroundings with a coldness bordering on disdain. Whereas young Shinsuke is depicted as trying to live entirely through the sequestered world of bookish imagination, Akutagawa as an adult seems to judge this stance as insufficient for a full life. The narrative does not depict its character's psychological and emotional maturation. Shinsuke is presented in a severely limited light, and at least one critic has suggested: "It is better to see [Shinsuke] not as the bared essence of the author himself."[42] Akutagawa's eventual departure from the Shinsuke character hints at his realization that an individual's psychological state can only be partially conveyed through an account, however candid, of how he perceives his world at a given moment. This is because as an individual moves through his environment and actively engages with the people and things in it, influencing them and being influenced in turn, his outlooks evolve too. A psychological landscape cannot remain static.

Akutagawa wrote "Aru aho no isshō" just prior to taking his own life in July 1927. The story, published posthumously in October of that year, presents a more fluid record of his development as an individual and as a literary artist. It features an unnamed protagonist and is told through a collection of fifty-one scenes identifiably based on events from Akutagawa's own life. These passages are recounted in a third-person narrative voice. When the piece appeared in *Kaizō* magazine, his friend and fellow writer Kume Masao included a notation that Akutagawa had originally labeled the manuscript an "autobiographical sketch," but had later crossed this out.[43] Kume's decision to share this detail with readers was apt since the narrative vignettes are reminiscent of impressionistic sketches. Each scene focuses on key elements and details, with few transitions or explanatory context between them. This approach is reminiscent of Sōseki's attempts at the "haiku-novel," which as we saw in chapter 2 tried to dismantle the linear structure of standard novels in favor of a more decentered, panoramic sprawl associated with the visual arts.

The protagonists' evident love for paintings is disclosed in an early passage and presages the centrality of visuality as a theme in Akutagawa's final autobiographical story. In the scene, the main character experiences a sudden artistic awakening through admiring the paintings of Vincent van Gogh that he encounters in a book. This echoes the events that Akutagawa described in a letter that he sent to his friend Ikawa Kyō as a university student in 1914, during the height of the popularity of the *Shirakaba* magazine which had introduced Post-Impressionist art to the broader Japanese public. In his letter, the young Akutagawa wrote: "I feel as though I have begun to really understand the paintings of Van Gogh. I feel that this might be an understanding that applies to all paintings. And I dare say, it might be a true understanding of all art" (*ARZ* 17: 241). Despite the grandly dramatic tone of this pronouncement, Akutagawa did not describe to his friend how Van Gogh's images had triggered his conceptual revolution. He did not articulate what it was about the colors, forms, and composition that had excited him. In the 1927 story as well, Akutagawa maintains this reticence, and it stands out when compared to the more voluble manner in which he later describes the protagonist's literary influences. For example, Anatole France's "skepticism that smelled of roses" and Voltaire's "cold intellect" are named as inspiring the young author (*ARZ* 16: 47–48). For the protagonist—presumably an older version of the bookish Daidōji Shinsuke—paintings offered a mode of signification that felt more instinctive and immediate than the texts with which he girded his intellect.

But literature too continues to figure prominently in "Aru aho no isshō" as the protagonist embarks on the path to becoming a writer. He finds spiritual solace and guidance from the works of Baudelaire, Ibsen, and numerous other luminaries. Gradually though, he grows disillusioned with the dissonance between the lofty inspirations he gains through his reading and his inability to act upon these insights in the context of his own life; citing the myth of Icarus, he calls literature his "Artificial Wings" (*ARZ* 16: 47). In another scene, he reads the German poet Goethe's poetry collection titled *West-Eastern Diwan*, which explores the exchanges between the Occidental and Oriental lyrical traditions, and he could feel the work "trying to give him a new power to his soul" (*ARZ* 16: 62). Given Akutagawa's position as a Japanese writer celebrated for his knowledge of foreign philosophies and literatures, his fictional counterpart should have reveled in a sense of kinship with Goethe's cosmopolitanist sentiments. Instead, his reactions are far more bitter: "Finishing the *Diwan*, after his raging emotions died down, he could not help but despise himself for having been born so impotent toward life" (ARZ 16: 62–63). He is by this point all too aware that literary exuberance alone could not sustain his will to live.

Throughout his deepening skepticism about literature's ability to intervene in his lived realities, the visual arts continue to offer the protagonist a reprieve. One episode recalls the writer's encounter with a painter—seemingly modeled on Akutagawa's own meeting with Oana Ryūichi—and deems it "one of the most important events of [his] life" (ARZ 16: 49). The protagonist feels that he "discovered in the painter a poetry that no one else knew," reflecting the deep emotional connection that Akutagawa had felt with Oana. In another scene, the protagonist delights in the desolate beauty of an abandoned lot scattered with broken tiles. The scenery reminds him of a Paul Cezanne (1839–1906) painting. He remains instinctively drawn to beauty even as he sinks deeper into depression.

Toward the end of the story, the writer attempts to write an autobiography (*jijo-den*) but finds it unexpectedly difficult "because he still held onto his self-pride, skepticism, and calculations of self-interest. He could not help but look down on himself for this" (ARZ 16: 65). He realizes that he is unable to transcend his everyday ego for the sake of his art. On the other hand, he could not help but think that "Everyone is the same beneath the surface," implying his doubt that there is anything essential and special about his—or anyone's—subjectivity that is worth writing about. The narrative's disembodied literary voice splits more definitively from that of its protagonist when it describes him finishing the writing of "Aru aho no isshō." As Seiji Lippit observes, "With this gesture of self-reference, the text seems to fold back onto itself, even though it is unable to close the circle. It reveals Akutagawa's inability to provide closure to the work, to close the gap between writing and experience, and it remains essentially open, unfinished."[44]

The story concludes with a scene titled "Haiboku" (Defeat) that portrays the protagonist living "day to day in the semidarkness" of creative despair and prescription-drug-induced stupor (ARZ 16: 67). In a macabre twist, Akutagawa was dead by the time the story appeared in print; critics soon after began to interpret his suicide in terms of the defeat of his literary and artistic idealism in the face of pressing political and social conditions, which he could no longer ignore in good conscience, as well as the deteriorating circumstances of his personal life. Still, the story Itself might be counted as a literary success for its blend of emotional intensity and lyricism. Its dreamlike vignettes provide readers with startlingly intimate access to Akutagawa's dilemmas and self-doubts. Especially in light of his earlier "self-portrait" and "landscape" stories, this final literary "sketch" could be seen as the culmination of the author's multimedia investigations into the methods and premises of artistic self-expression.

Searching for Modern Japanese Cultural Identity

In a scene in "Haguruma" (Cogwheels, 1927), another semiautobiographical late-period work, Akutagawa describes the identity crisis that plagued him toward the end of his life: "I suddenly remembered the pen name Juryō Yoshi that I had used in the past. [The third-century BCE Chinese philosopher] Han Feizi had written about a young man from the city of Juryō, who forgot how to walk in [his native] Juryō style before he mastered walking in the [new] Kantan style, and he had to slither home [from Kantan to Juryō] like a snake. To anyone's eyes, I must now appear to be a 'Juryō Yoshi'" (ARZ 15: 58).[45] Akutagawa knew that in addition to the praise he received for the range of philosophical and literary allusions he employed in his elegant writings, he was also criticized as a noncommittal dilettante for these very qualities by the growing ranks of politically minded proletariat writers, as well as the self-confessional "I-novelists." By calling himself Juryō Yoshi after the cautionary legend of a tragicomic man who had put on airs and lost sight of his own core values, Akutagawa notes the breakdown of his self-understanding. The vast literary knowledge and stylistic virtuosity he had delighted in displaying as a younger writer now seemed to be his undoing: What did his core subjectivity consist of, shorn of his countless artistic references?

In addition to examining questions about subjectivity and agency through his own position as a modern writer, or through thinking about fictional individuals in dramatic situations that he encountered in books, Akutagawa also often considered these issues through the collective context of modern Japanese history. In the Taishō period, especially after World War I, there was a widespread sentiment that Japan had now reached a world-class state of modernity. And yet, it was also recognized that barely half a century had passed since Japan entered the imperial world order, and that Japanese modernity had been, as Natsume Sōseki had memorably put it, "externally motivated" by the threat of foreign force as opposed to internally instigated through domestic developments. Akutagawa examined Taishō Japan's sense of cultural discomfort through stories set in the Meiji Enlightenment era of the 1870s and 1880s, when the nation first embarked upon a full-scale mission to learn about Western culture and ideas after centuries of restrictions on contact with other nations. The period is known synecdochally as the Rokumeikan era after the Rokumeikan, a Western-style building in Tokyo that was built in 1883 to serve as a venue for entertaining foreign dignitaries. The project had been conceived of by the foreign minister Inoue Kaoru who had hoped that the ornate building designed by the British architect Josiah Conder, and the fancy parties held there by Japanese diplomats in full Western regalia, would convince visitors that Japan was civilized enough to join the ranks of the world's leading nations despite its late arrival to the imperial world order. But Inoue's eagerness to gain foreign acceptance by blindly imitating European customs eventually earned him the scorn of the Japanese public, and following his resignation in 1887, the Rokumeikan fell into decline. For Akutagawa, the illusion of the ready-made cosmopolitanism that the Rokumeikan had briefly represented seemed to speak to his own deepening sense of spiritual deracination beneath his well-known familiarity with and appreciation of the world's greatest works of literature and art.

The 1920 story "Butōkai" (The ball), based on the short story "Un Bal à Yedo" (A ball in Edo, 1886) by the French writer Pierre Loti, embodies Akutagawa's bittersweet views on the Rokumeikan era.[46] "Un Bal à Yedo" was included in Loti's 1889 collection of writings titled *Japoneries d'Automne* (Japanese autumn). Loti was the pen-name of Julien Viaud (1850–1923), who had traveled to Japan as well as to many other countries in his capacity as a naval lieutenant, and "Un Bal à Yedo," a Frenchman's impressions of an opulent ball held at the Rokumeikan, is semiautobiographical. In Loti's story the Japanese guests in their attempts to appear at ease in formal European clothing and surroundings strike the narrator as awkward, and he deems the ball an "immense farce officielle," but he is intrigued by a young Japanese girl who speaks French and dances with him passably well.[47] Yet she too remains an object of his Orientalist gaze as he idly imagines her going home to a house of paper and bamboo. Loti ends the story with a few remarks about his lack of cruel intentions behind the disparaging comments he makes about the Japanese. He writes that the Japanese are marvelous imitators who are very rapidly learning European customs, and that one of their principle strengths as a people lay in their power of adaptation. In closing, he muses that perhaps future generations of Japanese readers will be able to look back upon this record and be amused.

"Un Bal à Yedo" was translated into Japanese in 1893 by Iida Hatanoki and in 1914 by Takase Toshio. Akutagawa's story is believed to be based on the latter version.[48] "Butōkai" adds a range of creative details to Loti's fictional account of an encounter between a French officer and the young Japanese girl he dances with at the ball. Akutagawa names this character Akiko and she supplants the Frenchman as the main character. This textual reworking might be seen as a confident answer to Loti's call for future Japanese readers to reflect upon his account of the inchoate state of Japanese modernity in 1886 in light of the cultural progress made since then. Akutagawa's decision to actively respond to the passages from Loti's text that portray the Japanese in an unflattering light, rather than to suppress them, support this reading. For example, although in Loti's story the Frenchman stares at the Japanese girl's feet because they "turn inward in the old style that was considered elegant in Japan, and so they had a certain heaviness," Akutagawa has Akiko interpret her partner's downward gaze as one of admiration directed at her new shoes.[49] Because of this misperception, Akiko's charming confidence does not flag. And though Loti in his story consistently makes condescending comments about his partner's dress being "a bit provincial" and about the other Japanese guests looking "un peu Louis XV," Akiko interprets her dance partner's comparison of her to a painting by Jean-Antoine Watteau, an eighteenth-century painter, as praise.[50] Akutagawa accentuates Akiko's appealing innocence by leaving her immune to Loti's veiled insults.

Akutagawa's story begins with a description of Akiko's excitement at attending her first formal ball. She is nervous but proud of how beautiful she looks in her Western outfit; she notices that a Chinese official wearing his hair in the traditional long queue and a young Japanese man in a tailcoat stare at her in astonishment as they pass her on the staircase: "Her innocently sweet rose-colored ball gown, the light blue ribbon arranged tastefully on her neck, and the single rose fragrantly gracing her thick hair—in truth, Akiko's appearance that night represented the full and unreserved beauty of a Japanese girl of the Enlightenment" (ARZ 5: 249).

But she is not unflappably confident, for the French officer's invitation to dance—Akutagawa does not mention him by name at this point—causes her to blush involuntarily. Waltzing together, she sees him stealing glimpses of her feet clad in new, rose-colored dancing shoes, and interpreting this to be a sign of admiration she enlivens her steps. Akiko's fleeting concerns about how her dance partner sees her seem more rooted in a young girl's self-consciousness than in a sense of cultural inferiority. When she exclaims upon the beauty of European women, the suave French officer tells her that Japanese women are as pretty as Western ones. Akiko expresses her desire to go to Paris one day, but the officer assures her that balls are the same everywhere. His world-weariness is lost on her, and she goes on enjoying her beautiful evening as he falls into a pensive melancholy. Later on, the two characters watch a display of fireworks in the night sky, and the Frenchman poetically compares their fleeting brilliance to life itself.

The story ends with a coda that takes place in 1918, more than three decades after the ball. The now matronly Akiko recounts her memory of her evening at the Rokumeikan to a young writer that she meets in the quintessentially modern space of a traveling train. In the original story that Akutagawa published in the *Shinchō* magazine in January 1920, when the writer asks Akiko the name of the French officer she had danced with, she informs him: "He was named Julien Viaud. You surely know of him too, for this is the real name of Pierre Loti who wrote *Madame Chrysanthème*" (ARZ 5: 379–380). But in the revised version of the story that was included in Akutagawa's anthology collection *Yarai no hana* published in March 1921, the conversation between the young writer and Akiko unfolds differently:

"He was named Julien Viaud."
"So it was Loti? The Pierre Loti who wrote *Madame Chrysanthème*?"
The young man felt an amused excitement. But the older woman gazed curiously at him, muttering repeatedly, "No, I do not know anyone named Loti. He was named Julien Viaud." (ARZ 5: 257)

The implications of this revision are far-reaching. In the first version, Akutagawa's punchline that Akiko had in fact been the girl that Loti had written about in his notoriously Orientalist "Un Bal à Yedo" would only have been legible to members of the Taishō period intellectual class familiar with the French author's writings. It therefore presumes an elitist form of literary cosmopolitanism that answers in its own way Loti's call for future generations of Japanese to become more worldly. If we are to read Akiko as representative of Japanese cultural and intellectual sensibilities, her evolution from the naive but curious young girl of the Enlightenment era to the savvy and well-read matron of the Taishō period in the first version of the story would represent a positive view of Japan's modern advances. Her arch amusement at having once been depicted as a silly young girl would emphasize her present worldly wisdom.

But in the new ending, Akiko's professed ignorance about the writer Loti suggests a less robust view of Japanese modernity. It shows her stuck inside the Rokumeikan era, not having kept up with the momentous changes that have taken place in the world since then. In this reading, Akiko's—that is to say, Japan's—lack of progress symbolizes her failure to meet the promise she had shown in her youth. Her naivete, appealing for a young girl finding her footing in the world, now takes on an air of pathos and begs the question of where she had lost her way. As cultural critique, this ending alleges that despite its appearances of prosperous maturity, Taishō Japanese society is still unable to rebut Loti's earlier charges of the contradictions between its superficially modernized appearances and its entrenched premodern values. Alternatively, Akiko's denial about knowing Loti might be read as a willful performative stance. It could be that the full-grown Akiko was apprised of "Un Bal à Yedo" and how unflatteringly it had depicted her and her country, and she made a conscious decision to excise references to this text from her account of her meeting with Viaud. This way, she could preserve the memory of her poetic evening with him when she had been young and full of possibilities.

The early Meiji period, when the direction of Japan's future directions was still undecided, thus represented to Akutagawa a time of opportunity when the Western values being introduced to the nation could have been dialectically synthesized with traditional Japanese worldviews. Another story set in this era, "Kaika no otto" (A husband of the Enlightenment, 1919), begins with nostalgia for the distinctive artworks produced in this period.[51] The story opens at a museum exhibit about Meiji Enlightenment culture where the nameless narrator and his friend Count Honda observe a mix of traditional woodblock prints and Western-style etchings from the period. They admire a copperplate print of a map of the old Tsukiji foreign settlement area and find: "There was a certain type of East-West eclecticism (*wa-yō setchū*) in both content and form that was beautifully harmonious in a way specific to that period. The arts have since lost this harmony. The city of Tokyo in which we live too has lost this harmony" (ARZ 4: 178). Made sentimental by the images around him, Count Honda remarks to the narrator: "It's as if that era—which cannot be defined as either Edo or Tokyo, and like the conjoining of night and day—rises before my eyes" (ARZ 4: 179). Honda then launches into a story from his youth. His account fittingly begins in the aesthetic space of a museum exhibition hall. Honda's reveries transport him and the narrator back to a past when there had been hope of achieving "East-West eclecticism" as an actual way of life, an ideal that has since been discarded and—Akutagawa seems to say—now operates only as an artistic vision. That they are at a special exhibit dedicated to the Enlightenment era shows how distant it already seemed to Taishō sensibilities, although older individuals like Honda are still alive to remember it vividly.

Honda's story is about his friend Miura, a fellow aristocrat and firm adherent of the concepts of individualism and romantic love newly imported from the West. The two had met and become fast friends aboard a ship headed back to Japan from France where they had each been studying. Miura refuses to be introduced to prospective marriage partners as was customary in Japan for someone of his social class, and he holds out for "a marriage of *amour*" (ARZ 4: 184). Honda, out of consideration for his friend's happiness, advises: "If you must examine your feelings so thoroughly before you do anything, you will be barely able to move or stand. So why not accept that the world is not ideal, and settle for someone passable?" (ARZ 4: 184). Akutagawa might have been addressing the sentiment to modern Japanese individuals like himself, who appreciate progressive ideals on an intellectual level and enjoy seeing them depicted in art, but who find it difficult to uphold them as their own lives continue to be ruled by ingrained conventions. As Honda suggests, to pragmatically accept this gap would prevent much heartache. But Miura refuses to compromise and continues to seclude himself with his foreign books. Honda, a diplomat, is subsequently sent to a new post in Korea and falls out of regular contact with Miura. It is noteworthy that Akutagawa had included this detail—apparently an allusion to the Japan-Korea Treaty of 1876, which had used gunboat diplomacy to force Korea to establish trade relations with Meiji Japan—because it acknowledges that the early Meiji enthusiasm to learn

Western ideals had not been limited to the realm of art and ideas, and that it had extended to the sphere of imperial geopolitics.

Shortly after arriving in Korea, Honda is surprised to receive a marriage announcement from Miura. Honda is a bit disturbed to learn that Miura had first met his wife Katsumi while strolling the grounds of a picturesque temple, a scenario that sounded oddly old-fashioned for his progressive friend. But he dismisses his doubts because Miura seems thrilled by his *amour*. Miura's letters to his friend convey his joy, and Honda is struck by how Miura proudly recounts that he had the *yōga* painter Goseda Hōbai execute a portrait of his new wife. Miura hung the portrait in his study so that he might always gaze upon Katsumi's visage. While Hōbai seems to be a fictional figure, the Goseda clan was known for their pioneering techniques in Western oil painting in the early Meiji period. Inserting the Goseda name into the narrative enhances the story's historical setting, and it also reprises the start of Honda's retrospective recitation of Miura's tale in the Taishō period within the aesthetically demarcated space of an art gallery.

Honda returns to Japan and is not entirely impressed when Miura introduces him to his new wife. Her busily energetic mannerisms upon their meeting cause him to exclaim: "You should have been born in some place like France rather than here in Japan!" (*ARZ* 4: 188). The wrathful and shockingly lewd look that Katsumi shoots toward her husband give Honda a sense of foreboding. In the subsequent months, a series of clues lead Honda to begin suspecting that Katsumi is engaged in an extramarital affair, and he finally confronts Miura. Miura admits that his friend's suspicions were indeed correct, and that he had just separated from Katsumi. Miura says that when he first discovered her infidelity, he had believed that his wife was acting on her own feelings of pure *amour*. Ever the idealist, he was thus ready to support her despite her betrayal of their matrimonial bond. But upon learning that she was involved in relationships with multiple men, he became jaded. Miura starts to mention the foolishness of the ideals he had held about his marriage and the possibility of attaining a real romantic love in Japan, but Honda finishes the sentiment for him: "Indeed, it may have been a naive dream. But this project of Enlightenment that we are pursuing as our goal too might be revealed as a naive dream in a hundred years" (*ARZ* 4: 201). The comment shows the Meiji men's comprehension of the profound societal and cultural changes that would have to be implemented for their nation to reach Western "Enlightenment" in a full sense, and hence the likeliness that their project may fail. Honda and the original narrator leave the exhibition space in contemplative silence, "as though they were ghosts who had stepped out from the past." The story suggests that while the early Meiji Japanese had envisioned a world in which the key themes of Western civilization could be smoothly integrated with their Eastern traditions, the Japanese of the Taishō period were already looking back at the notion of such syncretism as having been an impossible folly. It is only in the "ghostly" forms of memory and fiction that this former idealism can be recalled.

Akutagawa portrays Miura, who was born a generation before him, as unable to foster the flowery notion of *amour* learned from Western literature and art within his Japanese life. In doing so he casts doubt upon the viability of other Western-inspired universalist values still being touted in the Taishō period. He presents Miura's wife as a femme fatale—a trope familiar across multiple artistic and literary traditions in Japan and elsewhere—whose overpowering sexuality threatens to upend the rational order of her admirers. Through his infatuation with the progressive-sounding notion of *amour*, Miura becomes unable to perceive Katsumi as an individual, and in the breakdown of communication between them she develops into a force that he cannot subjugate. In the story, she seems to stand for the dangers that foreign liberal values might pose to vulnerable Japanese men unless they proceed with a firm grasp of their core principles. But we can also argue that Miura's chief vulnerability derives from his inability to perceive that his own expectations—that his wife should have been controllable at all, and that she should have conformed to his images of her—were antithetical to the modern ideals of equality and pure love he had aspired to. It is not surprising that he had been unable to detect the faults in their relationship for so long. In this light, the pride that Miura had felt in owning a Goseda Hōbai portrait of Katsumi takes on ominous undertones. Miura ultimately remained unable to see her as more than a romanticized beauty, a perennial Other whose perspectives he could not access.

The Power to Remake

Akutagawa does not offer facile, prescriptive answers about whether a complete acceptance of all modes of cultural Otherness is possible, and if so, what form such a cosmopolitanism would take. He is more focused on the affective and cognitive tensions that arise when new concepts first enter into an established discursive sphere. In addition to the Meiji Enlightenment period, another historical juncture that thus interested him was the period of Japan's first encounters with Christianity, as introduced by Jesuit missionaries in the sixteenth-century Muromachi era before the Tokugawa shogunate government forbade foreign religions in 1612. In the so-called *kirishitan* stories—the early Japanese Christians referred to themselves by this term—Akutagawa attempts to examine his Japanese characters' reactions to the belief systems of their European visitors at a remove from the discourses of politics, progress, and profit that more overtly colored cross-cultural contact in the Meiji period and beyond. Although power differentials obviously exist in all encounters, the dynamics that are emphasized in Akutagawa's premodern stories are different from those in his Enlightenment era ones in which Japan is depicted as a latecomer to the inevitable path of an imperial, Western-inspired modernity. His stories set in the further past weigh in a more hypothetical sense the possibilities, as well as the limits, of achieving mutual understandings between competing worldviews.

An example of such a work is "Kamigami no bishō" (The faint smiles of the gods, 1922).[52] The story unfolds in the sixteenth century at the Namban-ji Catholic Church in Kyoto, and its main character is Padre Organtino, a Jesuit missionary. The term "Namban," literally "Southern Barbarian," was widely used to designate the Christian missionaries who arrived in Japan during this period. The character of Organtino is loosely based on the Gnecchi-Soldi Organtino, an Italian priest who came to Japan in 1570 and stayed until his death in 1609 in Nagasaki.[53] But Rebecca Suter observes that the narrative's description of Organtino as "red-haired" (*kōmō*) and "green-eyed" (*hekigan*) is "a willful anachronism that replicates and subverts Western essentialist representations of Japanese people" because before the Tokugawa era these epithets had specifically been used to designate the Dutch people who came to Japan for commercial purposes, and the term "Namban jin" was reserved for the Portuguese, Spanish, and Italian missionaries.[54] Indeed, this preliminary mislabeling of Organtino presages the inability on the part of both he and his host country to accurately comprehend each other.

Despite the growing numbers of converts to his church, Organtino has been harboring an uneasy suspicion that his new followers, whom he derisively thinks of as the "little yellow-faced people," do not truly accept the Christian God that they refer to as "Deusu," a name that Akutagawa uses kanji characters to write (ARZ 8: 188–189). Organtino's anxieties are substantiated when an old man who identifies himself as one of the many native deities of Japan appears to him and predicts that the Christian mission in Japan will fail. The spirit says that many teachings have come to Japan from overseas—those of Confucius, Mencius, Chuang-tzu, and others from China, as well as of Siddhartha's Buddhism from India—only to be absorbed into the scope of traditional Japanese worldviews. He also states that from the time of Kakinomoto Hitomaro's poetry in the eighth century, even the writing system imported from China underwent an alteration to become a phonetic alphabet for transcribing the Japanese syllabary, and that in the process of assimilation into the Japanese linguistic sphere, the Chinese characters lost their original significations. The old god declares: "Instead of conquering us, Chinese writing was conquered by us" (ARZ 8: 199). He tells Organtino that the strength of the Japanese spirit lies in "the power not to destroy [other teachings] but to remake (*tsukuri-kaeru*) them" (ARZ 8: 201). He warns Organtino that the Japanese will inevitably adapt the Western concept of an omnipotent Deus rather than allow it to conquer the cultural status quo of polytheism.

When the story was first published in the *Shin shōsetsu* magazine, its ending seemed to emphasize that Japan's penchant for syncretism would reign victorious over any imported notions of singularity. That night, after meeting with the nameless Japanese deity, Organtino is praying in the chapel when he sees a mural of Christ at the Last Supper come to life. The face of Saint Peter now resembles the old Japanese god he had seen that afternoon. Much to his horror, the Christ figure also turns into a beautiful woman. The twelve disciples chant "Hosannah to Ohirumemuchi," praising the Japanese sun goddess (ARZ 8: 207). The dissolution of the Christian imagery confirms Organtino's fears that despite his efforts, the Japanese literally "see" God not as an absolute and all-powerful being but in terms of their native pantheism. Such a notion would not have been unfamiliar to Akutagawa's readers, for Japanese culture's allegedly exceptional ability to ingest and domesticate various external influences, if in a skewed form,

FIGURE 5.2 Naizen Kanō, Namban screen painting, left section. Pigment and gold leaf on paper. Late sixteenth to early seventeenth century. The painting appears to depict a Portuguese ship from a port that could be Goa, India, from where ships sailed to Japan.
Kobe City Museum

FIGURE 5.3 Naizen Kanō, Namban screen painting, right section. Pigment and gold leaf on paper. Late sixteenth to early seventeenth century. The painting appears to depict a Portuguese ship docked in the port of Nagasaki. Foreign missionaries and local Japanese people greet the European visitors.
Kobe City Museum

has been noted by previous cultural commentators. For example, the art impresario Okakura Kakuzō famously described Japan as a "repository of the trust of Asiatic thought and culture" in his book *Ideals of the East with Special Reference to the Art of Japan* (1903), which he wrote in English for an overseas audience.[55]

But the new ending that Akutagawa gave to the story when he included it in an anthology in 1923 destabilizes the affirmation of Japanese culture's purported propensity for a selective cosmopolitanism. In this version, the extradiegetic narrative voice reveals that Organtino is actually a figure in a painting, and that the preceding account of his visions and monologues had been imagined by a viewer of the artwork. The narrative describes that "the foreigners with tall noses, elegantly trailing the skirts of their habits, returned into the folding screen painting amid the imaginary laurels and roses floating in the golden light of dusk. They went back into the screen painting of three centuries ago depicting the arrival of the Namban ships" (*ARZ* 8: 203). Ornate folding screen paintings picturing Spanish and Portuguese visitors to Japan had been popular until around the mid-seventeenth century when the persecution of Christians caused the exoticism of Namban-themed artworks to fall out of style (figures 5.2 and 5.3). By defining Organtino as a figure in such a screen painting, Akutagawa appears to wrest back narrative authority from him and confer it to his disembodied narrator. Read as a story of ekphrasis, the painted priest is framed as an object at the mercy of the narrator's gaze, while literary language exercises its active agency to comment on his plight. And this narrative voice is linguistically a Japanese one. By the end of the text, Organtino—whose name had first been written in Roman script, then in katakana throughout the story—is finally addressed as "Bateren Urugan of Nambanji" in kanji, marking his linguistic subjugation to Japanese.

Yet the identification of this narrative perspective as fully representative of a collective sense of Japaneseness is left ambiguous. The story ends with the following remarks:

Goodbye, Padre Organtino! As you and your companions pace the shore, you gaze at the great Namban vessel with its flags raised in the gilded mist. Whether Deusu or Ohirumemuchi will win—perhaps we cannot easily answer that, even today. But this is an issue that our endeavors (*ware-ware no jigyō*) must soon decide. Watch us quietly from the shores of the past. Even as you are sunk in a deep slumber of oblivion along with the other figures in this painting—like the ship's captain leading a dog, and a dark-skinned slave child carrying a parasol—the sound of the cannons of our Black Ships that recently appeared on the horizon will surely tear apart your old-fashioned dreams. Until then—goodbye, Padre Organtino! Goodbye, Bateren Urugan of Nambanji! (ARZ 8: 203)[56]

The evocation of "our Black Ships" suggests that the narrator does not fully identify with Japan; the term broadly refers to the display of Western military might that had forced Japan to open up to international commerce and diplomacy in the nineteenth century. Perhaps then, the narrative voice could be interpreted as the spirit of Japan's Meiji- and Taishō-period modernity claiming the Black Ships as an aspect of its constitutive experiences. More so than a straightforward East-West binary, this reading seems to accentuate the gaps between the sensibilities of the present and that of the past. The contrast between the narrative's capacity to nimbly reflect on ideas across time periods and viewpoints, and Organtino's anxiety as a subject suspended in the still medium of a painting, seems to underscore the literary medium's unique suitability for commenting on the sense of discontinuities and contradictions that characterize much of modern experience. But diegetically placing Organtino into a painting, an artwork within the story, does not make the extradiegetic narrator of the fictional story any more real. Organtino's basis in history adds a further twist to the issue but, overall, Akutagawa's use of multiple narrative layers calls attention to itself. More so than Akutagawa's optimistic or pessimistic views on the future trajectories and tendencies of Japanese culture, what remains particularly salient at the conclusion of the story is its status as a work of literature. Any sociohistorical insights it offers are ultimately bracketed within the self-reflexive context of the literary.

Moreover, as he often did, Akutagawa wrote "Kamigami no bishō" in response to another literary text. Scholars have noted the influence on the story of the Japanologist Lafcadio Hearn's *Glimpses of Unfamiliar Japan* (1894)—especially the observation that "eclectic like the genius of the race, [the Shinto religion] had appropriated and assimilated all forms of foreign thought which could aid its material manifestations or fortify its ethics."[57] "Kamigami no bishō" also explicitly celebrates literary imagination as a grounds where intercultural exchange could prove fruitful. At one point in their conversation, the unnamed Japanese deity tells Organtino: "Four or five days ago, I met a Greek sailor who had landed on Western shores. That man was not a god. He was just a human. I sat with this sailor on a rock under the moonlight and heard various stories from him. Tales about being captured by one-eyed gods, a goddess who turns humans into pigs, mermaids with beautiful voices—do you know the name of this man? From the moment he met me, this man turned into a native of this land. He now calls himself Yuriwaka" (*ARZ* 8: 202).

Readers familiar with Western literary canons might recognize the allusion here to the epic journey of the ancient Greek hero Odysseus. Scholars have suggested that the origins of the legend of the itinerant warrior Yuriwaka, which has existed in the Japanese dramatic repertory since at least the sixteenth century, lay in the Latinized version of the story imported by European missionaries, in which the hero was named Ulysses.[58] The theory of Yuriwaka's Western roots has since come under question, but in Akutagawa's time, no less a figure than Tsubouchi Shōyō, the author of *Shōsetsu shinzui*, had supported it.[59] Whatever its origins, foreign or domestic, the Yuriwaka story proved popular and it was adapted into multiple kabuki and *jōruri* plays. By including Yuriwaka in the Japanese deity's spiel about his culture's special ability to "remake" ideas so that they gain legibility within its new parameters, Akutagawa appears to propose that at least in the sphere of literature, unintentional misapprehensions or intentional subversions of source material can have positive outcomes. Aesthetic cosmopolitanism is celebrated, even as the story remains less strident about what it would entail to attain and live by a more critical understanding of cultural, religious, or linguistic differences.

The productive transformations that can result from an exclusively artistic mode of cross-cultural exchanges is the subject of the story "Nagasaki shōhin" (A short Nagasaki piece, 1922).[60] It is not a *kirishitan* work per se since it is not directly about Christianity, but it takes up the theme of Namban-era cultural, if not spiritual, hybridity. The story takes place as a Taishō-period dialogue among a collection of art objects from the port city of Nagasaki that date back to the Edo period, when Japan's foreign contact had been restricted to Chinese, Korean, and Dutch traders. The figurines, plates, ceramics, and paintings on display are a mix of foreign-made works, and Japanese works made under foreign influence. The main character of the story is a Dutchman painted by Shiba Kōkan (1747–1818), a very early proto-Western-style artist. He is in love with a woman painted on a plate imported from Holland. Among the other characters is a "Maria-Kannon" statuette—after the ban on Christianity in 1612, some hidden converts continued their worship by using statues of the Buddhist goddess Kannon in place of the Virgin Mary. There is also a Catholic priest depicted in gold inlay on a Japanese sword handle, and a Western woman painted on Japanese Kameyama porcelain. The Maria-Kannon tries to relay the Shiba Kōkan Dutchman's love to the woman on the plate from Holland who sniffs: "He might pass as a Dutchman here in this country. But in truth, he's not Dutch, and is a weird person who is neither Western nor Eastern" (ARZ 9: 147). The other objects are insulted by her haughtiness.

The owner of the art collection enters the room at this point with guests who exclaim over the variety of objects. One immediately compliments the Shiba Kōkan Dutchman, who had been reduced to tears before the humans' arrival. Another guest admires the Japanese porcelain of the Western woman and says she is much more beautiful than the one on the imported plate from Holland. The guests converse among themselves: "There is a distinct taste to Western-style works made by the Japanese, which are lacking in Western works. . . . Indeed, for this is where today's civilization was born. In the future, there will be greater works to come" (ARZ 9: 149). The "distinct taste" of these hybrid art objects seem to point to Akutagawa's ideal manifestation of multiculturalism, wherein Japanese sensibilities are maintained while Western styles and techniques are recast in new ways.

In an essay written in the aftermath of the Kantō earthquake of 1923, in which downtown Tokyo was destroyed and had to be completely rebuilt, Akutagawa describes what he will miss most about the old city: it is not the olden romance of the Edo-flavored Tokyo, which was unfamiliar to his sensibilities, but "the Ginza landscaped with willow trees, where cafés did not replace *shiruko* shops, a more generally balanced Tokyo—you probably know this Tokyo, which wore a light *haori* even while donning a straw hat" (ARZ 10: 161). Akutagawa mourns the last vestiges of this organic coexistence of Eastern and Western—or traditional and modern—elements within the urban sprawl of Tokyo. He seems resigned that when the city is reconstructed, it would be along a more unified modern, Western style. Despite his fondness for European art and literature he does not want Japan to lose sight of its heritage. Thus it is neither a pre-Western, premodern Japan of the past, nor an entirely Westernized Japan of some yet unforeseen future that appeals to Akutagawa. He envisions a polyphonic coexistence of multiple cultural registers that had been possible, he believed, for brief periods in the Japanese past, and can still be accessed in the artistic and literary realms.

The Poetic Spirit

The essay collection *Bungei-teki na, Amari ni bungei-teki na* (1927), which I have already mentioned a few times in this book, reveals Akutagawa's final philosophies on the craft and ethos of writing. It was catalyzed by a debate with fellow writer Tanizaki Jun'ichirō (1886–1965) over the question of plot, a theme of ongoing concern for literary writers. Tanizaki had claimed: "What is most lacking in Japanese novels is the power to construct and the talent to geometrically assemble complex plot lines."[61] Akutagawa countered by stating that more than the ability to structure a solid plot, novels should depend on a "poetic spirit that enlivens [the materials of a story]" (ARZ 15: 153). He declared that the "poetic spirit" is the most important element of a literary work, and the quality that separates literature from other nonartistic modes of writing. This logic echoes his mentor Natsume Sōseki's literary formula "F (intellectual content) + f (emotional factor)," wherein the presence of the emotional factor "f" determines a text as literature. It also resonates with Mori Ogai's contention that the "inner flame" emanating through an object's form is the source of its beauty (OZ 7: 197). But as with Sōseki's emotional "f" or Ogai's "inner flame," "poetic spirit" proved difficult to explain precisely. The various topics covered throughout Akutagawa's essay collection circle the fundamental attempt to define this literary essence.

Given his repeated allusions to the visual arts, not just in this essay but in his oeuvre at large, Akutagawa seems to posit poetic spirit as a value that governs all aesthetic works, not just literary writing. Yet he states that it is especially crucial in literature because novels are a capacious medium that can accommodate "everything" (*nandemo*) (ARZ 15: 154), including "vulgar concerns" (*tsūzoku-teki kyōmi*) (ARZ 15: 150). He contends that for a novel to avoid vulgarity—to recall, this had been a central concern for him when he began to experiment with autofiction—it requires the infusion of poetic spirit. He names Jules Renard's *Les Philippe* (1907) as representing this dynamic, noting that "Philippe—who arrives to us distilled through the eyes and heart of a poet—interests us partly because he is an average person like us." Akutagawa estimates that the unremarkable Philippe comes alive for readers not because of any notable qualities on his part but for how he is depicted through Renard's gaze. The novel depends more on the writer's innate sensibilities and spirit rather than on what topic he writes about, or the plot that he imposes over his subjects. This view is somewhat reminiscent of the notion of *shasei* writing endorsed by Sōseki and others, in which the author is to be a detached observer who refrains from forcing his characters into a linear storyline.

But according to Akutagawa, poetic spirit need not necessarily negate authorial design. He elaborates: "There can be no painting without a *dessin* (outline, drawing). Several of Kandinsky's paintings titled 'Improvisations' are an exception. However, there are paintings that entrust their spirits more to color than to outlines. Fortunately, several Cezanne paintings that have come to Japan clearly prove this. I am interested in novels that, in this way, are closer to painting" (*ARZ* 15: 148). This admission that some underlying outline is necessary in the composition of any image can be extended to mean that artistic creation—whether of a novel or a painting—requires the artist's active intentions. In fact, Akutagawa had stated in an earlier essay that: "Artistic activity, no matter how great a genius one may be, is conscious (*ishiki-teki*)" (*ARZ* 5: 169).[62] It seems that he would concur with abstract painters like Wassily Kandinsky that while the clear and realistic delineation of a central subject is not always required in a painting, the final image must be realized in a nonrandom form. It would follow that novels require a similar sort of constructive will. As we saw at the start of this chapter, Akutagawa names Shiga Naoya as a writer who manages to balance the twin conditions of inherent artistic spirit and rational intent. He admires the older author's seemingly effortless ability to infuse his writings with detailed realism and "a poetic spirit that stands on the basis of Eastern tradition" (*ARZ* 15: 155). In view of the cross-cultural analyses Akutagawa undertook in his writings, the appeal to "Eastern" spirit in this instance might be understood as a shorthand for an alternative to the authorial certitude, and the wider metaphysics of presence this implies, that he perceived in conventional Western literary works.

A central theme that Akutagawa explores in *Bungei-teki na, Amari ni bungei-teki na* is how literature grants readers access to new ways of seeing and feeling beyond their limited perspectives. Akutagawa is under no illusion that Western and Japanese cultures could achieve a full mutual comprehension of each other solely through dint of empirical observation and scholarly study. He remarks: "Surely, they [Westerners] cannot help laughing at our customs and traditions. At the same time, their customs and traditions seem hilarious to us" (ARZ 15: 186–187). He concedes that books offer some entree into Western sensibilities, observing: "Thanks to [the bookstore] Maruzen, it is certain that we do know a bit about their souls (*tamashii*)" (ARZ 15: 186–187). This is a more muted view of literature's ability to provide knowledge of the world than might be suggested by the reputation that Akutagawa had gained as a representative of the Taishō-era ethos of cosmopolitan erudition. His caution evinces his hard-won awareness that undergoing serious dialogic confrontations with new ideas is necessary for truly expanding one's conceptual horizons. As implied in his cool treatment of his fictional alter ego Daidōji Shinsuke, Akutagawa had soured on the illusion that reading books could wholly substitute for lived experiences.

He also offers: "The extreme pole (*kyokuhoku*) of literature, or the most literary of all literatures, can only quiet us. We can only become entranced when we come into contact with such works. Literature—or perhaps art—has a terrifying appeal. If we prioritize the various practical aspects of life, we can say that all art fundamentally has some power to castrate (*kyosei*) us" (ARZ 15: 227). Akutagawa recognizes aesthetic sentiment as that which defines literature and other works of art as such, and that it can "castrate" the critical faculties governing everyday living. This core element becomes impossible to comprehend when reduced to its bare essence, much like Theodor Adorno's aforementioned notion of a powerful "truth content" that is apprehended through the philosophical reflection of an artwork.[63] Such an element is not isolable from the artwork's forms and content, which are legible as objects of interpretation for the viewer. Truth content cannot be distilled in a pure form. It is this sort rationally inaccessible core that Akutagawa attributes as the "poetic spirit" of literary texts.

Akutagawa sees the visual arts, rather than literature, as offering a more direct path to this enigmatic aesthetic essence. In a section of the essay collection titled "Seiyō no yobi-goe" (Call of the West), he compares a seemingly instinctive appreciation of visual artworks to the more intellectually-based comprehension of literary works. He muses:

It is always through the plastic arts that "The West" calls out to me. Unexpectedly, the literary arts—especially prose writing—are less plaintive in this regard. For one, this is because there is little difference between East and West about the fact that human beings have an animal nature [so stories about human nature tend to be universal.] ... Also, our linguistic skills are clearly not enough to grasp the beauty of an imported literary work. It is not that we, or in any case I, cannot at least semantically understand the poems written by the Westerners. But we cannot savor each letter and syllable of their works in the way we face the poetic writings of our own ancestors. (ARZ 15: 205)

Stories like "Shūzanzu" (1921) and "Yume" (1927) have shown Akutagawa's recognition that the vagaries of shifting human perspectives in fact affect viewership of visual artworks too, despite their seeming to have a more fixed presence than literary texts. But this passage revisits the assumption from stories like "Jigoku-hen" (1918) that the visual arts do nonetheless have a raw communicative potential that trumps the mediated nature of linguistic signification. Rather than empowering him with a cosmopolitan worldview, Akutagawa's connoisseurship and enjoyment of foreign literatures and philosophies had the effect of making him realize the multitudes of references contained in each text, the vastness of the linguistic and cultural fields that contextualize each work. He was thus humbled by the impossibility of fully grasping the nuances of "the West" through reading, and like the Shirakaba writers before him, he believed that pictorial representations seemed to bypass these challenges. Akutagawa distinguishes between his carefully honed attention to the linguistic cadences and the intertextual allusions in foreign literary works, and his unhesitant, "animal nature" attraction to imported visual imagery.

Akutagawa also recognizes "the West" as a slippery notion that signifies something distinct for each beholder. He acknowledges that while some see it epitomized in the "German Expressionism that died around 1914 or 1915," or "within Rembrandt and Balzac," or in the "arts of the Rococo period," it is in the arts from ancient, "mysterious Greece (fukashigi na Girisha)" that he most keenly perceives the essence of Western cultures (ARZ 15: 207). He struggles to explain in words this perception of exotic otherness: "If I were to explain this [spirit of] Greece most succinctly, I would recommend that you take a look at some of the Greek ceramics that exist in Japan. Or I would recommend you look at photographs of Greek sculptures. The beauty of these works is the beauty of the Greek gods. A thoroughly sensuous beauty—a beauty that includes within its physicality some appeal to what we could only call the sublime (*chō-shizen*)" (ARZ 15: 205). It is therefore not the monotheism of Judeo-Christianity and logocentrism that most clearly represents the "Western" spirit for Akutagawa, but the pantheistic world of ancient Greek mythology that came before these developments. In this view, Hebraic culture acts as something of a domesticating force over the ancient Greek world he judges to be still residing at the foundation of Western culture: "Even after the West has received the baptism of Hebraism, it still has a different bloodline (*kettō*) than our Eastern world. The most trenchant example of this may be in pornography. Even the Westerners' physicality itself has a different sensibility (*omomuki*) than ours" (ARZ 15: 206–207). More so than the logical opposition he had located between Western monotheism and Japanese syncretism in "Kamigami no bishō," Akutagawa sees the realm of Greek mythology as irreducibly foreign to Japanese sensibilities. It is a difference that cannot be precisely articulated through his Japanese vocabulary and frames of reference.

Akutagawa seems to sense the limitations of his attempts to verbally describe the visceral sense of disorientation he feels vis à vis the mysterious spirit of "the West." Instead, he names the French symbolist painter Odilon Redon's oil painting *The Young Buddha* (1905) as a concrete example of an artwork that captures it.[64] Redon (1840–1916), known today as a precursor to Surrealism and Dadaism, was interested in dreams and psychology as well as in the Eastern philosophies of Buddhism and Hinduism.[65] He experimented with color and form, and was—somewhat ironically, from our standpoint—inspired by Japanese graphic art. The painter Tsuchida Bakusen purchased *The Young Buddha* along with one other image during his time studying in Paris in 1921, and these became the first works by Redon to enter Japan. The painting shows its titular subject in profile with his eyes peacefully closed, clad in a brilliant red and gold garment. Around him, clouds of gold and white billow against a background that is a swirl of deep blues, lighter blues, purples, and greens. The interplay of flat surfaces and the illusion of depth created by the diaphanous gradations of color give a dreamy opacity to the image. As the Italian Jesuit Organtino was coopted into the confines of a Japanese screen painting and his name retranscribed to fit the Japanese language by the present-day narrator of "Kamigami no bishō" (1922), the Buddha in Redon's painting has been removed from his

Asian origins and recast in a new, visually striking artistic fashion that strikes Akutagawa as irresistibly exotic.

Despite his claims about an intuitive approach to visual imagery, we see that some intellectual consciousness about his position as a viewer often colored Akutagawa's interest in foreign artworks as it did in his readings of foreign works of literature. He was knowledgeable about the art-historical significance of the European painters who became his aesthetic touchstones, and his artistic preferences were aligned with his own evolving stances as a writer. For example, in a letter that he sent to a friend in 1914 while still a university student, Akutagawa explained that while "there are many paintings, such as by Picasso, that I don't understand at all," he liked the work of Matisse whose "art is flooded with life energy, like sunlit grass actively growing toward the sky" (ARZ 17: 238).[66] Akutagawa then added, "In this sense, I do not agree with art for the sake of art." He stressed his desire to create work that naturally coheres with and affirms lived conditions, instead of raising questions about form and medium that destabilize the conceptual grounds of what artworks are. Here, Akutagawa appears to criticize the conceptual boldness of Pablo Picasso's experimentations with abstraction, against the organic expressivity of Henri Matisse's brilliantly colored figures and scenes from the same period. At this preliminary stage of his literary trajectory, the author had aligned himself with the principles "of balance, of purity and serenity" that Matisse had taken as the guiding principles in his art, rather than Picasso's challenges to the conventions of artistic representation.[67]

As Akutagawa's views about the symbiosis of art and life grew darker over time, his views of the European painters too underwent a shift. Shortly before his death, he wrote in an essay titled "Futari no kōmō gaka" (Two Western painters, 1927)[68]:

> Picasso is always attacking the citadel.... I am not the only one that feels a kind of ease when I turn to Matisse after looking at Picasso. Matisse sails a yacht across the ocean. No sounds of war or odors of nitric acid arise from there. His pink and white striped sails just swell with the wind. When I happened to see paintings by these two together, I felt sympathy for Picasso and a sense of familiarity and envy toward Matisse.... If I had to choose between them, Picasso would be my choice. Picasso, with the fur trim of his armor scorched by flames, with the handle of his spear broken. (ARZ 15: 91)

After his own battles to achieve high artistic ideals as well as authentic self-expression through Japanese literary language, Akutagawa had apparently reached the conclusion that whatever the medium or cultural context, all endeavors of representation required navigation between these competing impetuses. His feelings of fondness and jealousy toward the seemingly untroubled, positive energies of Matisse's imagery echo his regard for Shiga Naoya's graceful novels. But in his final stage, Akutagawa cast his lot with Picasso's fearless questioning of the potentials of visual art, apparently coming to terms with his desire to become Picasso's Japanese literary counterpart in "attacking the citadel" of representational practices. Indeed, the range of his works ending with the formal and perspectival dissolution of late stories like "Aru aho no isshō" (1927) and "Haguruma" (1927)—and his experimental dramas "Yūwaku" (Temptation, 1927) and "Asakusa Kōen" (Asakusa Park, 1927)—presents a sustained inquiry into the conceptual and formal licenses afforded to the writing of fiction. Akutagawa's attempts to cross literature's multiple divisions—its potential to depict lived, subjective particularities and artistic ideals aspiring to a timeless universalism; the exhilaration and dread attendant to the ultimately referential nature of language and textuality; the particular powers of the linguistic arts as compared to the visual arts and the overarching, cross-media notion of "art" at large—by embracing them fully, have not lost their relevance to literary discourse today.

Epilogue

Why Aesthetics?

AS THIS BOOK goes into production, 2023 draws to a close. Across institutions in all spheres—including the corporate world, media, the arts, and education—there has been an air of anxious self-examination as the world moves on from the emergency phase of the Covid-19 pandemic that upended operations as usual. Former practices and ideals are being questioned as workers and consumers alike are no longer content with a return to "normalcy" and demand a longer-term shift to more sustainable and livable conditions. In the wake of semesters taught online and enrollment figures still below prepandemic levels,[1] universities have been under pressure to reaffirm their missions and purposes in light of ever-rising tuition costs and the new skillsets needed to succeed in today's rapidly shifting workplace. The crisis of the humanities, brewing for decades now, has become especially pressing under these circumstances.

According to an article in the March 6, 2023, issue of the *New Yorker* titled "The End of the English Major":

> During the past decade, the study of English and history at the collegiate level has fallen by a full third. Humanities enrollment in the United States has declined over all by seventeen percent.... What's going on? The trend mirrors a global one; four-fifths of countries in the Organization for Economic Cooperation reported falling humanities enrollments in the past decade. But that brings little comfort to American scholars, who have begun to wonder what it might

EPILOGUE: WHY AESTHETICS?

mean to graduate a college generation with less education in the human past than any that has come before.²

That the declining number of students in humanities departments merited discussion in the *New Yorker* shows that the matter has developed into a cause for concern beyond the precincts of higher education. The article delivers the finding that this trend does not appear to be solely linked to students' sense of economic precarity and their hopes of gaining greater postgraduation employment opportunities from more career-oriented studies, since humanities enrollment figures have been falling even during periods of robust economic growth. The bigger issue seems to be a cultural shift in how we perceive humanities skills and knowledge as abstract or impractical in an era ruled by quantifiable rigor, and in how rather than the cultivation of our collective aesthetic sensibilities through studying and appreciating a canonical body of literary and artistic works, humanities research can seem more intent on joylessly assessing cultural products for evidence of social ills. Meanwhile, universities continue to invest more money and resources into the STEM fields, reenforcing the general narrative that the uplift of humanity will not come from the world's literatures, languages, or arts but from data-driven technologies. The *New Yorker* article, however, quotes an engineering professor who opines: "I think the future belongs to the humanities," because AI technologies will be unable to achieve the higher-order critical and emotional skills needed, for example, to "conceive 'Mrs. Dalloway'" or "guide and people-manage an organization."³ The article also features the voices of college students who still sincerely believe in studying literary texts, and it concludes on a cautiously hopeful note.

Ironically, the present-day efforts in academic and mass media settings to articulate the value of literary studies and the humanities—and to staunch their decline in higher education and in public discourse—find echoes in the thought of the writers I examined in this book: the Meiji-period authors Natsume Sōseki and Mori Ōgai, who contributed to the rise of literature as a new cornerstone of cultural and intellectual life in modern Japan, and the Taishō-period authors Mushanokōji Saneatsu and Akutagawa Ryūnosuke, who further expanded the conceptual parameters and potentials of literary thought. The apprehension about the "ephemeral" nature of literature as compared to envy for the "solid" nature of the

EPILOGUE: WHY AESTHETICS?

sciences (*SZ* 25: 282)[4] that had spurred Sōseki to undertake the "Bungakuron" project to delineate literature in a mathematical manner rings close to the solicitude of those today who seek to champion the humanities using quantitative terms. Mizumura Minae, for one, conjectures that if Sōseki were alive today, as a man of talent he would likely have focused his energies on the sciences and not have become a literary writer.[5] Mizumura's argument unfolds mainly in the context of the Japanese language's declining import in today's English-centric global culture, but also in view of the major strides made in scientific knowledge. She observes: "Today, people who wish to explore the eternal question that haunts the human race—what is a human being?—are turning increasingly to the latest scientific advances, particularly in fields such as genetics and brain science" rather than literature.[6] The ideas of Ogai, who in contrast to Sōseki had trained in medicine and the natural sciences before turning to literature, are also strikingly timely. His intuition of a meaningful realm beyond science and empirical logic led him to emphasize literature's unquantifiable aesthetic elements, in line with today's defenders of the humanities who celebrate qualities that elide systematization and automation. And the Shirakaba group and Akutagawa sought from literature a markedly personal sense of validation, as do many contemporary writers and readers. With the diversification of the perspectives and stories expressed and promoted in today's literary sphere, there are now more openings than ever for more people to develop individualized and intimate affective roots therein.

The uncertainty about the position of literature in the intellectual landscape that inspired the Meiji- and Taishō-period Japanese writers and roils present-day academe can also be examined against the emergence of literary studies as a scholastic discipline in the modern period. In *Professing Criticism* (2023), John Guillory chronicles how literary criticism evolved into a specialized profession within the American university with influences from European educational systems. He describes how in the nineteenth century, "criticism" had referred to writings propagated in the public sphere by those who did not necessary hold academic degrees in the subjects they discussed. "The *self-authorization* of the critic-journalists licensed the diverse subjects of their criticism, which were not restricted to the literary. The critics of the great nineteenth-century periodicals, the so-called Victorian sages, saw all of society as their legitimate concern."[7] Guillory states that the critics who dominated the journalistic realm took as their mission the analysis of society as a whole via their analysis of its literary artifacts. He then examines how even as the practice of literary criticism gained autonomy from the forces of the marketplace by becoming organized as an academic field requiring formal training and expertise, it still purported to maintain its original goal of speaking to the conditions of society at large. Guillory summarizes this incongruity: "The very insistence of the discipline on its professional status raises the question of whether the academic study of literature can in fact be comprehended under the name of criticism and whether this name really legitimizes a special claim on the criticism of society."[8] Many literary scholars today use the method of close reading to analyze the relationship between the form and content of literary texts as a basis for considering the sociohistorical contexts they were written in, and for diagnosing the political and ideological perspectives clearly or latently manifest in them. The asymmetry between the means of close reading, and the professed ends of social insight, informs the current identity crisis of the professional literary studies sphere. And as I discussed in chapter 1, the emphasis on socially oriented literary criticisms has also diverted academic attentions away from the aesthetic aspects of texts that render them literary, and hence uniquely compelling to readers, in the first place.

In *Metaphorical Circuit: Negotiations Between Literature and Science in Twentieth-Century Japan* (2004), Joseph A. Murphy examines the organization of the fields of learning in the modern Japanese university system established in the 1880s. Comparing it to the European and American systems, he finds that "the pairing of '*bungaku vs. kagaku*' does not call up the same clear opposition as 'literature vs. science.'"[9] Murphy contends that "the odd prominence of literature in major histories of Japanese thought, indicat[es] a different status for literature in the intellectual field," and, naming literary writers trained in the sciences including Mori Ogai, he also points to the "manifest investment by scientists in the practice of literature."[10] He seems to imply that in Japan, unlike in the West, literature has continued to be held in high public regard because of an intellectual legacy of interdisciplinarity. This is a questionable argument, and Japanese commentators too have been decrying the decline of literature's public prominence and relevance for several decades. Karatani Kōjin, for example, stated in the provocatively titled essay "Kindai bungaku no owari" (The end of modern literature, 2004): "Literature used to be accorded a special meaning

EPILOGUE: WHY AESTHETICS?

in modernity and have a particular significance, and this is no longer so."[11] Karatani locates literary decline in Japan as starting in the 1980s, while he sees it a few decades earlier in America and more recently in South Korea.[12] And the cultural critic Azuma Hiroki assessed in 2013: "We seem to live in an era in which the imagination and reality, fiction and reality, literature and society are set apart from each other. Literature's impact on society is smaller than ever, and on the other hand, society's impact on literature too is unprecedentedly small."[13]

These observations, however, do not directly negate Murphy's earlier point that until its more recent demise, there had seemed to exist in at least some sectors of Japanese culture a view that literature has the capacity to comprehend the modern world in a vital way that could hold its own against the social and natural sciences. There had prevailed, it seems, an expectation that literature could offer valuable ways of knowing and feeling to complement technological advancements. My foregoing chapters examined key writers from the period when literature was apparently coming to hold such an esteemed position in Japanese public life. These writers sought to explain the special potentials of their literary medium by confronting its rootedness in aesthetic sentiments and imaginations that they found to be urgently felt but largely ineffable, subjectively derived though presumed to be universally evident, disinterested and yet somehow edifying. As a result, these authors came to see literature as an inherently volatile and exceptionally capacious mode of interfacing with the world.

To reiterate, the writers in my study envisioned literary thought to include felt aesthetic judgments *and* critically reasoned responses to the people and objects of the world that it takes up. Sōseki attempted to explain literature's conceptual hybridity through his "F (content) +f (personal affect)" formula. And in the novels of his that I have analyzed, the characters gradually come to accept the compatibility of private aesthetic sentiments and participation in the fuller dynamism of a shared humanity. Ogai followed a similar trajectory in moving from a binary notion of beauty as an interior province set at odds with publicly legible pragmatic reason, to interrogating how art and quotidian realities can coexist. For all the Shirakaba writers' blithe expectations that their personal pursuits of beauty could transcend social contexts, they also were not entirely oblivious to the worldly situations they turned their backs to, and they nursed a belief that their artistic endeavors would ultimately benefit humankind. Akutagawa's oeuvre could be read as an extended meditation on the literary episteme as both aesthetically disconnected from, and critically entrenched in, lived conditions. These writers would not—I believe—have disputed contemporary scholars who claim that literary texts reflect ideological horizons and cultural premises, and can hence serve as the grounds for social critique and new modes of political agency. But their key insight was that literature is also shot through with aesthetic affects that enliven texts and enable them to call to us in potent and irreducible ways, and which also deserve serious examination and analysis. In recognizing its fundamentally mixed valences, these modern Japanese authors illuminate literature's unique contributions to our continued, species-wide quest to understand what it means to be human. And in today's ever-mechanized and commercialized world, such affirmations might matter more than ever.

Notes

1. Modern Japanese Literature and Aesthetics

1. *Bungei-teki na, Amari ni bungei-teki na* was originally published in *Kaizō* from April to August 1927, skipping the July issue because Akutagawa died that month.
2. John Whittier Treat, *The Rise and Fall of Modern Japanese Literature* (Chicago: The University of Chicago Press, 2018), 20. Treat goes on to refute the notion that modern Japanese literature is devoid of the effects of extraliterary, sociohistorical contexts. He writes: "The history of modern Japanese literature is coordinate with how the exercise of power—on behalf of the state and against it—was woven in ways both Japanese and generically modern" (21).
3. Quote about Naturalism from Donald Keene, *Dawn to the West: Japanese Literature of the Modern Era* (New York: Holt, Rinehart, and Winston, 1984), 7.
4. See for example Seiji Lippit, *Topographies of Japanese Modernism* (New York: Columbia University Press, 2004), 19. Lippit refers to H. D. Harootunian, "Between Politics and Culture: Authority and the Ambiguities of Intellectual Choice in Imperial Japan," in *Japan in Crisis: Essays on Taishō Democracy*, ed. Bernard S. Silberman and H. D. Harootunian (Princeton, NJ: Princeton University Press, 1974), 110–155. Lippit also refers to Leslie Pincus, *Authenticating Culture in Imperial Japan* (Berkeley: University of California Press, 1996).
5. See Odagiri Hideo, *Kitamura Tōkoku ron* (Tokyo: Yagi shoten, 1970).
6. Tsubouchi Shōyō, *Shōsetsu shinzui* (1885–1886), in *Meiji bungaku zenshū*, vol. 16, *Tsubouchi Shōyō shū*, ed. Inagaki Tatsurō (Tokyo: Chikuma shobō, 1969), 17. I reference and quote from Nanette Twine's translation of the text, titled *The Essence of the Novel*, available online in its entirety at https://archive.nyu.edu/html/2451/14945/shoyo.htm#electronic. I note when I diverge from Twine's translation.
7. Tsubouchi Shōyō, *Shōsetsu shinzui*, 19. Here I diverge from Twine's translation by changing the tense.

1. MODERN JAPANESE LITERATURE AND AESTHETICS

8. Regarding literature's appeal to a new generation, Tomi Suzuki and Donald Keene both quote the writer Uchida Roan's (1868–1929) retrospective remarks from his essay "Futabatei Shimei no isshō" (1925): "Aspiring young men of the time, who had hitherto considered politics the only way to realize their ambitions, discovered a new world and rushed into literature as if they had suddenly been awakened." Futabatei's *Ukigumo* (1887) is regarded as Japan's first modern novel. I use Suzuki's translation here. Tomi Suzuki, *Narrating the Self* (Stanford, CA: Stanford University Press, 1996), 28; Keene, *Dawn to the West*, 105.
9. Atsuko Ueda, *Concealment of Politics, Politics of Concealment: The Production of 'Literature' in Meiji Japan* (Princeton, NJ: Princeton University Press, 2005). See also H. D. Harootunian, "Between Politics and Culture." Harootunian offers the following assessment of Japanese writers in the late nineteenth century: "Whatever they do or think is without importance to others, and what is important to others is of no interest to them. From this idea arose the consistent trivialization of experience and of consciousness itself in the confessional novel (*shishōsetsu*). For the only alternative Japanese society offered was a totally public life, lived under conditions of complete visibility and exposure in the fulfillment of publicly sanctioned goals. The narrow corridor between these alternatives—complete concealment and complete visibility—offered a precarious sanctuary at best. But it was here that the impulse to *act* was satisfied by art, the creation of culture, active negation of politics, and violence" (114).
10. Kōjin Karatani, "The Discovery of Landscape," in *Origins of Modern Japanese Literature*, trans. and ed. Brett de Bary (Durham, NC: Duke University Press, 1993), 11–44.
11. Suzuki, *Narrating the Self*.
12. Suzuki, *Narrating the Self*, 2.
13. Suzuki, *Narrating the Self*, 1.
14. Akutagawa Ryūnosuke, "Taishō hachi nen-do no bungei kai." Originally published in December 1919 in *Mainichi nenkan* (*Taishō kyū nen, 1920 ban*). Tayama Katai (1872–1930) is considered a leading Japanese Naturalist writer and will be mentioned again in chapter 3.
15. For how critics contemporary to Sōseki assessed him through the rubrics of Naturalism and anti-Naturalism, see Kumasaka Atsuko, "Sōseki to 'Asahi bungei ran,'" in *Meiji han shizen-ha bungaku shū*, vol. 2, ed. Naruse Masakatasu (Tokyo: Chikuma shobō, 1968), 362–387. The article discusses how Sōseki and his acolytes were variably viewed as Naturalist and anti-Naturalist by critics during the span that Sōseki's *bungei ran* (literary critique) column ran in the Asahi newspaper from 1909 to 1911. For how critics speculated on Ogai's views about Naturalist and anti-Naturalist literature in light of his 1908 idea to establish a government-backed *bungei'in* (literary council) to support the literary arts, see Itō Sei, *Nihon bundan shi 14: Han shizen shugi no hito tachi* (Tokyo: Kōdansha, 1997), 106–124. For examples of scholarship that retrospectively view Sōseki and Ogai as anti-Naturalists, see, Takada Mizuho, *Han shizen shugi bungaku* (Tokyo: Meiji shoin, 1963) and Miyagi Tatsurō and Hiroshi Sakagami, *Kindai bungaku no chōryū: Shizen shugi to han shizen shugi* (Tokyo: Sōbunsha shuppan, 1977).
16. Takada Mizuho, *Han shizen shugi bungaku*, 25.

1. MODERN JAPANESE LITERATURE AND AESTHETICS

17. Maruyama Masao, "Nikutai bungaku kara nikutai seiji made," in *Zōho ban: Gendai seiji no shisō to kōdō* (Tokyo: Miraisha, 1964), 380. Originally published in October 1949 in *Tenbō* magazine. Emphasis on the word *sōsaku* and the phrase *baikai sareta genjitsu* are in the original.
18. Nakamura Mitsuo, "Fūzoku shōsetsuron" (1950), in *Nakamura Mitsuo zenshū* (Tokyo: Chikuma shobō, 1972), 7: 525-618. Originally published in 1950 by Kawade shobō.
19. William J. Tyler, "Anti-Naturalism: Illuminating the Spectacle," in *Modanizumu: Modernist Fiction from Japan, 1913-1918* (Honolulu: University of Hawai'i Press, 2008), 57.
20. In addition to Seiji Lippit's *Topographies of Japanese Modernism* and William J. Tyler's *Modanizumu: Modernist Fiction from Japan, 1913-1918* already cited, see for example William O. Gardner, *Advertising Tower: Japanese Modernism and Modernity in the 1920s* (Cambridge, MA: Harvard University Press, 2006); Gregory Golley, *When Our Eyes No Longer See: Realism, Science, and Ecology in Japanese Literary Modernism* (Cambridge, MA: Harvard University Press, 2008); Arthur M. Mitchell, *Disruptions of Daily Life: Japanese Literary Modernism in the World* (Ithaca, NY: Cornell University Press, 2020).
21. Lippit, *Topographies of Japanese Modernism*, 31.
22. Brian Hurley, *Confluence and Conflict: Reading Transwar Japanese Literature and Thought* (Cambridge, MA: Harvard University Press, 2022), 7. Unlike the other books I have mentioned, Hurley's book is not explicitly about literary modernism, but about the convergence of critical theories and literature in the 1930s to the 1950s.
23. Immanuel Kant, *Critique of Judgement* (1790), trans. James Creed Meredith, ed. Nicholas Walker (Oxford: Oxford University Press, 2007), 43.
24. Steve Odin, *Artistic Detachment in Japan and the West: Psychic Distance in Comparative Aesthetics* (Honolulu: University of Hawai'i Press, 2001), 6-7.
25. Odin, *Artistic Detachment in Japan and the West*, 19.
26. Nicholas Walker, "Introduction," in Kant, *Critique of Judgement*, xiv-xv.
27. Elaine Scarry, *On Beauty and Being Just* (Princeton, NJ: Princeton University Press, 1999), 7.
28. Taking Natsume Sōseki's writings as an example, in *When Our Eyes No Longer See*, Gregory Golley describes modern Japanese literature before the 1920s and 1930s as characterized by "a positivistic obsession with *unmediated sensory experience*" (11-12).
29. Tsubouchi Shōyō, *Shōsetsu shinzui*, 5. To get closer to the meaning of the original wording, I diverge slightly from Twine's translation in *The Essence of the Novel*.
30. Tsubouchi Shōyō, *Shōsetsu shinzui*, 19. To get closer to the meaning of the original wording I diverge slightly from Twine's translation in *The Essence of the Novel*.
31. Tsubouchi Shōyō, *Shōsetsu shinzui*, 5. To get closer to the meaning of the original wording I use here Twine's translation in *The Essence of the Novel*.
32. Elizabeth S. Anker and Rita Felski, "Introduction," in Elizabeth S. Anker and Rita Felski, ed., *Critique and Postcritique* (Durham, NC: Duke University Press, 2017), 4.
33. Anker and Felski, "Introduction," 7.

1. MODERN JAPANESE LITERATURE AND AESTHETICS

34. Bruno Latour, "Why Has Critique Run Out of Steam? From Matters of Fact to Matters of Concern," *Critical Inquiry* 30 (December 2004). Cited in Anker and Felski, "Introduction," 15.
35. The growing corpus of recent academic studies on aesthetics includes, for example, Scarry, *On Beauty and Being Just*, cited above; Peter De Bolla, *Art Matters* (Cambridge, MA: Harvard University Press, 2003); Michael Bérubé, ed., *The Aesthetics of Cultural Studies* (Malden, MA: Blackwell, 2004); Peter Uwe Hohendahl, *The Fleeting Promise of Art: Adorno's Aesthetic Theory Revisited* (Ithaca, NY: Cornell University Press, 2013); W. Michelle Wang, *Eternalized Fragments: Reclaiming Aesthetics in Contemporary World Fiction* (Columbus: Ohio State University Press, 2020); Alva Noë, *The Entanglement: How Art and Philosophy Make Us What We Are* (Princeton, NJ: Princeton University Press, 2023). See Wang, *Eternalized Fragments*, 3, for a fuller list of academic works on the topic of aesthetics from the last decade of the twentieth century and later.
36. Anker and Felski, "Introduction," 15.
37. Rita Felski, *The Limits of Critique* (Chicago: University of Chicago Press, 2015), 11.
38. See Sadoya Shigenobu, *Sōseki to seikimatsu geijutsu* (Tokyo: Kōdansha, 1994), 65–67.
39. Stephen Cheeke, *Writing for Art: The Aesthetics of Ekphrasis* (Manchester, UK: Manchester University Press, 2008), 21.
40. Alfreda Murck and Wen C. Fong, *Words and Images: Chinese Poetry, Calligraphy, and Painting* (New York: Metropolitan Museum of Art, 1991), xv.
41. Cheeke, *Writing for Art*, 24–25.
42. Kinoshita Naoyuki, *Bijutsu to iu misemono: Abura-e jaya no jidai* (1993) (Tokyo: Kōdansha, 2010), 228–230.
43. Kinoshita Naoyuki, *Bijutsu to iu misemono*, 232–237.
44. For an overview on the topic of the Meiji emperor's portraiture, see Taki Kōji, *Tennō no shōzō* (Tokyo: Iwanami shoten, 1988), 113–138; and Inose Naoki, *Mikado no shōzō* (Tokyo: Shōgakkan, 1986), 424–437.
45. See Kaneko Ryūichi, "The Origins and Development of Japanese Art Photography," in *The History of Japanese Photography* (New Haven, CT: Yale University Press, 2003), 100–141.
46. Kinoshita Naoyuki, *Bijutsu to iu misemono*.
47. Kanbayashi Tsunemichi, *Kindai nihon "bigaku" no tanjō* (Tokyo: Kōdansha, 2006), 22. See also Amagai Yoshinori, "Kōbu bijutsu gakkō no setsuritsu mokuteki ni tsuite," in *Bigaku* 55, no. 3 (2004): 50. Amagai suggests that the school was intended as a commercial design school.
48. On the creation of the discourse of "art" in modern Japan, see also Satō Dōshin, *'Nihon bijutsu' tanjō: kindai Nihon 'kotoba' to senryaku* (Tokyo: Kōdansha, 1996); and Kitazawa Noriaki, *Me no shinden: 'bijutsu' juyō shi nōto* (1989) (Tokyo: Buryukke, 2010).
49. Omuka Toshiharu, *Kanshū no seiritsu: Bijutsu-ten, bijutsu zasshi, bijutsushi* (Tokyo: Tokyo daigaku shuppankai, 2008), 23.
50. For information on Fenollosa and his lecture, see J. Thomas Rimer, "Hegel in Tokyo: Ernest Fenollosa and His 1882 Lecture on the Truth of Art," in *Japanese Hermeneutics: Current Debates on Aesthetics and Interpretation*, ed. Michael F. Marra

1. MODERN JAPANESE LITERATURE AND AESTHETICS

(Honolulu: University of Hawai'i Press, 2002), 97–108. The lecture was originally delivered in English but only remains in the form of notes taken in Japanese by Omori Ichū.
51. Tsubouchi Shōyō, *Shōsetsu shinzui*, 5. I use Twine's translation here.
52. Tsubouchi Shōyō, *Shōsetsu shinzui*, 6. I use Twine's translation here.
53. Theodor W. Adorno, *Aesthetic Theory* (1970), trans. and ed. Robert Hullot-Kentor (Minneapolis: University of Minnesota, 1997), 225–226.
54. Adorno, *Aesthetic Theory*, 260.
55. Adorno, *Aesthetic Theory*, 127–128.
56. Henceforth I quote from this work in Natsume Sōseki, *Theory of Literature*, in *Theory of Literature and Other Critical Writings*, trans. and ed. Michael K. Bourdaghs, Atsuko Ueda, and Joseph A. Murphy (New York: Columbia University Press, 2009), in addition to citing Sōseki's original Japanese text.
57. Adorno, *Aesthetic Theory*, 129.
58. Robert Hullot-Kentor, "Translator's Introduction," in Adorno, *Aesthetic Theory*, xii.
59. Frank Kermode, "Life and Death of the Novel," *The New York Review of Books*, October 28, 1965. Retrieved from: https://www.nybooks.com/articles/1965/10/28/life-and-death-of-the-novel/.
60. Akira Iriye, "Japan's Drive to Great Power Status," in *Cambridge History of Japan*, vol. 5, ed. Marius Jansen (Cambridge: Cambridge University Press, 1989), 740.
61. Iriye, "Japan's Drive to Great Power Status," 741.
62. Natsume Sōseki, "Gendai Nihon no kaika." Originally delivered as a lecture in August 1911 and then published in the anthology *Asahi kōen shū* (Tokyo: Asahi Shinbun, 1911).
63. Grace Lavery, *Quaint, Exquisite: Victorian Aesthetics and the Idea of Japan* (Princeton, NJ: Princeton University Press, 2019).
64. Lavery, *Quaint, Exquisite*, 4.
65. Christopher Reed, *Bachelor Japanists: Japanese Aesthetics and Western Masculinity* (New York: Columbia University Press, 2017), 10.
66. Kant, *Critique of Judgment*, section 22, as quoted in Lavery, *Quaint, Exquisite*, 10.
67. Lavery, *Quaint, Exquisite*, 11.
68. Lavery, *Quaint, Exquisite*, 31.
69. Abe Jirō, *Santarō no nikki* (1914) (Tokyo: Iwanami shoten, 1918), 74–75.
70. For general information about this movement, see Uozumi Takashi, "Kyōyō shugi," in Koyasu Nobukuni et al., *Nihon shisōshi jiten* (Tokyo: Perikansha, 2001), 126–127; Hashikawa Bunzō, *Kindai Nihon shisōshi no kiso chishiki: Ishin zen'ya kara haisen made* (Tokyo:Yūhikaku, 1971), 238–239. Seiji Lippit also discusses how the Taishō period discourse of "self-cultivation" was based on a conception of universality enabled by a familiarity with European and Asian literatures in *Topographies of Japanese Modernism*, 41–42. There has also been debate about how the Taishō "self-cultivation" movement seemed to promote idealistic, esoteric learning over engagement with local social and political realities. Karaki Junzō's *Gendai shi e no kokoromi* (1949) is often identified as the origin of such critical readings.

1. MODERN JAPANESE LITERATURE AND AESTHETICS

71. Abe Jirō, "Bunka no chūshin mondai to shite no kyōyō" (1933), cited in Tanaka Yūsuke, "Shikō yōshiki to shite no Taishō kyōyō shugi: Karaki Junzō ni yoru Abe Jirō no hihan no saikentō wo tsūjite," in *Ajia bunka kenkyū* 30 (2004), 64.
72. Miyamoto Kenji, "'Haiboku' no bungaku: Akutagawa Ryūnosuke no bungaku ni tsuite," in *Kindai bungaku hyōron taikei*, vol. 6, ed. Miyoshi Yukio and Sofue Shōji (Tokyo: Kadokawa shoten, 1972). Originally published in August 1929 in *Kaizō* magazine.

2. Natsume Sōseki's Quest for "A Feeling of Beauty"

1. *Kusamakura* was originally published in *Shin shōsetsu* magazine in September 1906.
2. *Bungakuron* was originally published by Okura shoten in May 1907. It has been translated as *Theory of Literature*, in Natsume Sōseki, *Theory of Literature and Other Critical Writings*, trans. and ed. Michael K. Bourdaghs, Atsuko Ueda, and Joseph A. Murphy (New York: Columbia University Press, 2009). I use the translation of Bourdaghs et al. for this text.
3. Natsume Sōseki, "Tower of London," trans. Damian Flanagan, in *Tower of London* (London: Peter Owen Publishers, 2004), 91–92. I use Flanagan's translation for this text. "Rondon tō" was published in January 1905 in *Teikoku bungaku*.
4. Natsume Sōseki, "Letter from London," trans. Damian Flanagan, in *Tower of London*. 62. I use Flanagan's translation for this text. "Rondon shōsoku" was published in May and June 1901 in *Hototogisu*.
5. Natsume Sōseki, letter to Nakane Shigekazu, March 15, 1902.
6. Natsume Sōseki, *Theory of Literature*, trans. Bourdaghs et al., 52.
7. Natsume Sōseki, *Theory of Literature*, trans. Bourdaghs et al., 47.
8. For a discussion on the scholarly attention accorded to the preface, see Atsuko Ueda, "Bungakuron and 'Literature' in the Making," *Japan Forum* 20, no. 1 (2008): 25–27.
9. Natsume Sōseki, *Theory of Literature*, trans. Bourdaghs et al., 44.
10. This is the fifteenth of the sixteen topics that Sōseki lists in his plans for literary research. Muraoka Isamu, *Sōseki shiryō: Bungakuron nōto* (Tokyo: Iwanami shoten, 1976), 9.
11. Michael K. Bourdaghs, *A Fictional Commons* (Durham, NC: Duke University Press, 2021), 8.
12. Natsume Sōseki, "Letter From London," trans. Flanagan, 53.
13. Natsume Sōseki, *Theory of Literature*, trans. Bourdaghs et al., 48.
14. Natsume Sōseki, letter to Masaoka Shiki, August 9, 1890.
15. Natsume Sōseki, letter to Masaoka Shiki, November 11, 1891.
16. Natsume Sōseki, letter to Masaoka Shiki, August 3, 1891.
17. Masaoka Shiki, "Hitobito ni kotau," part 6, April 2, 1898, in *Shiki zenshū* (25 vols.) (Tokyo: Kōdansha, 1975–1978), 7: 68. The essay was published in thirteen installments in the *Nippon* newspaper from March to May 1898.
18. Nakamura Fusetsu, "Shinobazu jukkei," in *Shiki zenshū*, 12: 601.

2. NATSUME SŌSEKI'S QUEST FOR "A FEELING OF BEAUTY"

19. Masaoka Shiki, "Meiji nijū-kyū nen no haiku-kai," part 3, January 4, 1897, in *Shiki zenshū*, 4: 503. The essay was published in twenty-three installments in the *Nippon* newspaper from January to March 1897.
20. Masaoka Shiki, "Meiji nijū-kyū nen no haiku-kai," part 3, 504.
21. Masaoka Shiki, "Meiji nijū-kyū nen no haiku-kai," part 6, January 11, 1897, 512.
22. Natsume Sōseki, *Theory of Literature and Other Critical Writings*, trans. Bourdaghs et al., 89.
23. In chapter 1 of this book I mention Fenollosa's influential 1882 lecture "Bijutsu shinsetsu" (An explanation of the truth of art).
24. Masaoka Shiki, "Joji bun" (1900), published in *Nippon furoku shūhō*, in *Shiki zenshū*, 14: 241.
25. Masaoka Shiki, "Joji bun," 247.
26. Natsume Sōseki, "Kyoshi cho 'Keitō' jo," was published in the *Tokyo Asahi* newspaper on December 23, 1907, before appearing as the preface to Kyoshi's *Keitō*, published by Shun'yōdō in January 1908.
27. Natsume Sōseki, "Tower of London," trans. Flanagan, 92.
28. Joseph A. Murphy, "The Fourth Possibility in Sōseki's *Theory of Literature*," in *Metaphorical Circuit: Negotiations Between Literature and Science in 20th-Century Japan* (Ithaca, NY: Cornell University East Asia Program, 2004), 24–54.
29. "Maboroshi no tate" was published in *Hototogisu* in April 1905. "Kairo kō" was published in *Chūō kōron* in November 1905.
30. Published September 1905 in *Chūō kōron*. Translated by Alan Turney as "One Night." See Natsume Sōseki, "One Night," trans. Alan Turney, *Monumenta Nipponica* 33, no. 3 (Autumn 1978), 289–297. I use Turney's translation for this text.
31. Alan Turney, "A Feeling of Beauty: Natsume Sōseki's Ichiya," *Monumenta Nipponica* 33, no. 3 (Autumn 1978): 285–288; 286.
32. Turney, "A Feeling of Beauty," 287.
33. Natsume Sōseki, "One Night," trans. Turney, 291.
34. Natsume Sōseki, "One Night," trans. Turney, 296.
35. Natsume Sōseki, "One Night," trans. Turney, 296.
36. Natsume Sōseki, "One Night," trans. Turney, 297.
37. Natsume Sōseki, "One Night," trans. Turney, 290.
38. "Yo ga *Kusamakura*" was published in *Bunshō sekai* in November 1906.
39. Immanuel Kant, *Critique of Judgement* (1790), trans. James Creed Meredith and ed. Nicholas Walker (Oxford: Oxford University Press, 2007), 37.
40. Kant, *Critique of Judgement*, 43.
41. Kant, *Critique of Judgement*, 36.
42. Komori Yōichi, *Seikimatsu no yogensha: Natsume Sōseki* (Tokyo: Kōdansha, 1999), 118–120.
43. In classical Chinese lore, the Taoist sages live in a lofty realm of peach blossoms (*tōgen*) blissfully aloof to the world.
44. Jonathan Crary, *24/7* (London: Verso, 2013), 126.
45. Kin'ya Tsuruta, "Sōseki's *Kusamakura*: A Journey to 'The Other Side,'" *The Journal of the Association of Teachers of Japanese* 22, no. 2 (November 1988): 170.
46. See Steve Odin, *Artistic Detachment in Japan and the West: Psychic Distance in Comparative Aesthetics* (Honolulu: University of Hawai'i Press, 2001). The cover

2. NATSUME SŌSEKI'S QUEST FOR "A FEELING OF BEAUTY"

features an image that was included in Matsuoka Eikyū's *emaki* of *Kusamakura*, the painting *Mizu no ue no Oferia* (Ophelia in the water) by Yamamoto Masayuki.
47. Sadoya Shigenobu, *Sōseki to seiki-matsu bijutsu* (Tokyo: Kōdansha, 1994), 224. Odin refers to *Kusamakura* as *Grass Pillow*, although the novel has not been translated in English with that title; it has been translated as *The Three-Cornered World* by Alan Turney (London: Peter Owen, 1965) and as *Kusamakura* by Meredith McKinney (New York: Penguin Books, 2008).
48. Odin, *Artistic Detachment in Japan and the West*, 256.
49. Itō Junko, "Meiga to meiku de tadoru 'Nihonjin to ame:' Edo jidai no ukiyo-e, haiku kara," *Science Window* 4, no. 20 (Spring 2010): 31.
50. Yoon Sang, in *Seikimatsu to Sōseki* (Tokyo: Iwanami shoten,1994), 126; and Sadoya Shigenobu, *Sōseki to seiki-matsu bijutsu*, 225–227.
51. Kin'ya Tsuruta, "Sōseki's *Kusamakura*," 186.
52. Steve Odin cites Makoto Ueda in describing *yūgen* as a medieval Japanese concept of "mystery and depth" or "shadows and darkness." See Odin, *Artistic Detachment in Japan and the West*, 246. Odin cites Makoto Ueda, *Modern Japanese Writers* (Stanford, CA: Stanford University Press, 1976), 11.
53. Natsume Sōseki, *Theory of Literature*, trans. Bourdaghs et al., 95.
54. *Sanshirō* was originally serialized in the *Tokyo Asahi* and *Osaka Asahi* newspapers from September to December 1908. Natsume Sōseki, *Sanshirō*, trans. Jay Rubin (New York: Penguin Classics, 2009).
55. Natsume Sōseki, "*Sanshirō* yokoku," was published in the *Tokyo Asahi* and *Osaka Asahi* newspapers on August 19, 1908.
56. Karatani Kōjin, "*Sanshirō*," in *Sōseki ron shūsei* (Tokyo: Daisan bunmei-sha, 1992), 287.
57. See for example Mizumura Minae, *The Fall of Language in the Age of English*, trans. Juliet Winters (New York: Columbia University Press, 2017), 138. Ochi Haruo discusses how Hasegawa Izumi deemed the novel a story of Sanshirō's awakening and growth in *Kindai meisaku kanshō* (1958) but then refutes this conclusion. See Ochi Haruo, "*Sanshirō* no seishun," in *Sōseki sakuhinron shūsei*, vol. 5, *Sanshirō*, ed. Tamai Takayuki and Murata Yoshiya (Tokyo: Ofusha, 1991), 24. Ebii Eiji also argues that Sanshirō experiences no growth and that he remains a "tabula rasa" from start to finish. Ebii Eiji, *Kaika, ren'ai, Tokyo: Sōseki, Ryūnosuke* (Tokyo: Ofūsha, 2001), 14–15.
58. Ishihara Chiaki, "Kagami no naka no *Sanshirō*," in *Natsume Sōseki 'Sanshirō' o dō yomu ka*, ed. Ishihara Chiaki (Tokyo: Kawade shobō, 2014), 141–142.
59. Haga Tōru, "Natsume Sōseki: kaiga no ryōbun," in *Kaiga no ryōbun: Kindai Nihon hikaku bunka-shi kenkyū* (Tokyo: Asahi, 1990), 353–518, remains influential. See also Nīzeki Kimiko, *Sōseki no bijutsu ai suiri nōto* (Tokyo: Heibon-sha, 1998), 29–31 and 132–139; and Furuta Ryō, *Toku kō: Sōseki no bijutsu sekai* (Tokyo: Iwanami, 2014), 82–105.
60. See for example Miya Elise Mizuta Lippit, *Aesthetic Life: Beauty and Art in Modern Japan* (Cambridge, MA: Harvard University Press, 2019), 171–189; Kanda Shōko, *Sōseki 'bungaku' no reimei* (Tokyo: Seikan sha, 2015), 216–227; and Murase Shirō, "'San' to 'Yon' no zushō-gaku: *Sanshirō*, setsudan sareru shōjo tachi," *Sōseki kenkyū* 2 (May 1994): 82–100.

3. MORI OGAI AND THE "INNER FLAME" OF BEAUTY

61. See for example Hashikawa Toshiki, "Satomi Mineko: Jogakusei agari no 'mayoeru hitsuji,'" *Kyōritsu kokusai kenkyū: Kyōritsu joshi daigaku kokusai gakubu kiyō* 29 (March 2012): 101–122; He Wei, "Natsume Sōseki 'Sanshirō'ron: Atarashī onna no Mineko to Yoshiko," *Hiroshima jogakuin daigaku daigakuin gengo bunka rongyō* 18 (March 2015): 23–41; and Ishihara Chiaki, "Jidai no naka no 'Sanshirō,'" *Kokubungaku: kaishaku to kyōzai no kenkyū* 53 (9), no. 769 (June 2008): 140–151.
62. Shiozaki Fumio, "Onna ga otoko wo sasou toki," *Sōseki kenkyū* 16 (October 2003): 24–36, quoted in Ishihara Chiaki, "Jidai no naka no 'Sanshirō,'" 142.
63. The speech was delivered in August 1911 as part of a lecture series organized by the *Osaka Asahi* newspaper and first published in the *Asahi kōen shū* (Asahi, November 1911) anthology. This was the second in a series of four lectures.
64. Sōseki provides the English term "anachronism" rendered in katakana as a gloss for the term *jidai sakugo*.
65. Koyama Keita, *Sōseki ga mita butsurigaku: Kubitsuri no rikigaku kara sōtaise riron made* (Tokyo: Chūkō shinsho, 1991), 6–7.
66. Senuma Shigeki, *Natsume Sōseki* (Tokyo: Tōdai shuppankai, 1970), 38; and Takemura Tamio, "Kagaku to geijutsu no aida: Ikeda Kikunae to Natsume Sōseki no ba'ai," in *Kōza Natsume Sōseki*, vol. 1, *Sōseki no hito to shūhen*, ed. Miyoshi Yukio (Tokyo: Yūhikaku, 1981), 271.
67. See Joseph A. Murphy, *Metaphorical. Circuit: Negotiations Between Literature and Science in 20th-Century Japan* (Ithaca, NY: Cornell University East Asia Program, 2004), and Sawa Hidehiko, *Sōseki to Torahiko* (Tokyo: Chūseki-sha, 2002).
68. Koyama Keita, *Sōseki ga mita butsurigaku*, 104–112.
69. The English term "cosmopolitan" is used in the original.
70. Natsume Sōseki, letter to Terada Torahiko, September 12, 1901.
71. Minae Mizumura. *The Fall of Language in the Age of English*, 144.
72. Originally delivered as a lecture in August 1911 and then published in the anthology *Asahi kōen shū* (Tokyo: Asahi Shinbun, 1911). This was the first in a series of four lectures.
73. Komori Yōichi, "3/11 to Natsume Sōseki: 'Gendai Nihon no kaika' kara 100 nen," *Subaru* 33, no. 11 (November 2011), 224.
74. See for example Kanda Shōko, *Sōseki 'bungaku'no ryūmei*, 117; Karatani Kōjin, "Sanshirō," 284–285; and Ebii Eiji, *Kaika, ren'ai, Tokyo*, 13–14.
75. Ebii Eiji, *Kaika, ren'ai, Tokyo*, 13.

3. Mori Ogai and the "Inner Flame" of Beauty

1. Mori Ogai, "Nakajikiri," published in *Shiron* in September 1917.
2. J. Thomas Rimer, "Introduction," in Mori Ogai, *Youth and Other Stories*, ed. J. Thomas Rimer (Honolulu: University of Hawai'i Press, 1994), ix.
3. "Maihime" was originally published in January 1890 in *Kokumin no tomo*. "Utakata no ki" was published in August 1890 in *Shigarami zōshi*. "Fumizukai" was published in January 1891 in the *Shincho hyakushu* anthology.

3. MORI OGAI AND THE "INNER FLAME" OF BEAUTY

4. He later retitled the essay "I ni shite shōsetsu o ronzu" (Theorizing on the novel as a medical doctor, 1892) for its publication in the *Shigarami zōshi* magazine, and again retitled it as "Igaku no setsu yori idetaru shōsetsu ron" (Theory on the novel based on medical theories) when he included it in his critical essay anthology *Tsukikusa* (Moonflowers, 1896).
5. Kobori Kei'ichirō, *Wakaki hi no Mori Ogai* (Tokyo: Tokyo daigaku shuppankai, 1969), 384.
6. Kobori Kei'ichirō, *Wakaki hi no Mori Ogai*, 385.
7. Full images of Gottschall's *Literatische Todtenklänge und Lebensfragen* are available at the Ogai Bunko Collection online: http://rarebook.dl.itc.u-tokyo.ac.jp/ogai/data/A100_1666.html. For more information on Ogai's essay see: Kobori Kei'ichirō, *Wakaki hi no Mori Ogai*, 377–389; Kanda Takao, "Ogai shoki no bungei hyōron," *Hikaku bungaku kenkyū* 1-2, no. 6 (December 1957), 29; Kabe Yoshitaka, "Mori Ogai bungei hyōron on kenkyū (ichi): 'Shōsetsuron'no kaikō no ito to hōhō," *Shoin kokubungaku* 14 (September–October 1976): 69–70.
8. Mori Ogai, "Shōsetsuron: cfr. Rudolph von Gottschall." Claude Bernard (1813–1878) was a French scientist who promoted empirical experimentation.
9. It has been suggested that despite his strident tone, Ogai had not read the French writers that Gottschall cites, even in German translation, at the time he wrote "Shōsetsuron." See Kobori Kei'ichirō, *Wakaki hi no Mori Ogai*, 380; Kabe Yoshitaka, "Mori Ogai bungei hyōron on kenkyū (ichi)," 70.
10. Ozaki Kōyō, "Kokumin no tomo dai 37 gō furoku ni te Kochō dono" (January 1889), cited in Nakayama Akihiko, "Ratai-ga/Ratai/Nihonjin: Meiji-ki 'Ratai-ga ronsō'dai ichi maku," in *Disukūru no teikoku: Meiji 30 nendai no bunka kenkyū*, ed. Kaneko Akio et al. (Tokyo: Shin'yōsha, 2000), 23.
11. Futabatei Shimei, "Ochiba no haki-yose, ni kagome," quoted in Nakayama Akihiko, "Ratai-ga/Ratai/Nihonjin," 24.
12. Nanette Gottlieb, *Language and the Modern State: The Reform of Written Japanese* [1991] (London: Routledge, 2018), 151–152.
13. Nakayama Akihiko, "Ratai-ga/Ratai/Nihonjin," esp. 26–27.
14. See for example: Niizeki Kimiko, *Mori Ogai to Harada Naojirō: Myunhen ni mebaeta yūjōno yukue* (Tokyo: Tokyo geijutsu daigaku shuppankai, 2008); Haga Tōru, "Mori Ogai to Harada Naojirō," in *Kaiga no ryōbun: Kindai Nihon hikaku bunka-shi kenkyū* (Tokyo: Asahi shinbunsha, 1990); Suzuki Susumu, "Sono kaikō: Ogai to Harada Naojirō," *Mori Ogai no dansō satsuei zō*, in *Kokubungaku: kaishaku to kanshō* 49, no. 2 (January 1984) 201–208; Oishi Naoki, "Ogai no kaiga-ron: Harada Naojirō to no kanren ni furete," in *Kokubungaku: kaishaku to kyōzai no kenkyū* 45 (8), no. 657 (July 2000).
15. See Kevin Doak, *A History of Nationalism in Modern Japan: Placing the People* (Leiden: Brill, 2007) for a study on the rise of Japanese national identity in political, cultural, social, and ethnic discourses from the Bakumatsu to the postwar period; for the nationalist implications of Fenollosa's aesthetic theories, see 180–181.
16. The essay was retitled as "Kanba-dai no tenrankai" when it was compiled in the *Tsukikusa* anthology in 1896.

3. MORI OGAI AND THE "INNER FLAME" OF BEAUTY

17. Justus Brinkman (1843–1915), the first director of the Museum of Art and Design in Hamburg, was an enthusiast of traditional Japanese craftwork.
18. For more information on Ogai's debate with Naumann see Kobori Kei'ichirō, *Wakaki hi no Mori Ogai*, 185–294; and Sarah Cox Smith, "The Truth about Japan: Two Articles," in Mori Ogai, *Not a Song Like Any Other*, 50–73.
19. Hirayama Mikiko, "Japanese Art Criticism: The First Fifty Years," in *Since Meiji: Perspectives on the Japanese Visual Arts, 1868-2000*, ed. J. Thomas Rimer (Honolulu: University of Hawai'i Press, 2012), 261.
20. The essay was published in April 1890 in *Shigarami zōshi*.
21. For recent examples in English, see Goto Miyabi, "'Maihime' and the Space of Criticism in Meiji Japan," *The Journal of Japanese Studies* 46, no. 2 (Summer 2020); Christopher Hill, "Mori Ogai's Resentful Narrator: Trauma and the National Subject in 'The Dancing Girl,'" *Positions: East Asia Cultures Critique* 10, no. 2 (Fall 2020); and Tomiko Yoda, "First-Person Narration and Citizen-Subject: The Modernity of Mori Ogai's 'Dancing Girl,'" *The Journal of Asian Studies* 65, no. 2 (May 2006).
22. See, for example, Rokusō Ichika, *Sorekara no Erisu: ima akiraka ni naru Ogai 'Maihime' no omokage* (Tokyo: Kōdansha, 2013) and *Ogai no koibito Erisu no shinjitsu* (Tokyo: Kōdansha, 2011); Konno Tsutomu, *Ogai no koibito: hyaku-nijū nen go no shinjitsu* (Tokyo: NHK shuppan, 2010); Ueki Satoshi, *Shin-setsu Ogai no koibito erisu* (Tokyo: Shinchōsha, 2000); Chiba Shunji, *Erisu no ekubo* (Tokyo: Ozawa shoten, 1997).
23. Mori Ogai, "Harada Naojirō," in *OZ* 25. Originally published in four installments from January 11 to 14, 1900, in the *Tokyo nichi-nichi shinbun*. Later included in the catalog *Harada Sensei kinen-chō* (1910), and then in Ogai's *Mōjin mōgo* (1915) essay collection.
24. Ogai writes in "Harada Naojirō": "If one were intentionally hiding [his married state] to play with the emotions [of a suitor], that is an ignoble person. There are many such Japanese. In the West too, there are many who hide their so-called wedding bands. Harada was certainly not one of these. He was so modest that he was embarrassed even mentioning his wife, and even to me, a close friend" (*OZ* 25:132).
25. Mori Ogai, "Doitsu nikki," entry for November 21, 1886.
26. Niizeki Kimiko, *Mori Ogai to Harada Naojirō*, 36.
27. Richard Bowring proposes that the story may also have been inspired by Ogai's fellow army colleague Takeshima Tsutomu. See Richard Bowring, *Mori Ogai and the Modernization of Japanese Culture* (Cambridge: Cambridge University Press, 1979), 52.
28. Sigmund Freud, *The Interpretation of Dreams* (1900), trans. James Strachey (New York: Avon Books, 1965), 564.
29. Jacques Derrida, *Resistances of Psychoanalysis*, trans. Peggy Kamuf et al. (Stanford, CA: Stanford University Press, 1998), 11.
30. For example, in Iwamoto Zenji's review in *Jogaku zasshi* (January 1890), and Takuten Jōsen and Yamaguchi Toratarō's reviews in *Shigarami zōshi* (January 1890).
31. Ishibashi Ningetsu's critiques in *Kokumin no tomo* (February 1890) prompted a series of exchanges with Ogai that came to be known as the "Maihime debates."

3. MORI OGAI AND THE "INNER FLAME" OF BEAUTY

Ogai published his defensive responses in *Shigarami zōshi* (April–May 1890) as "Aizawa Kenkichi," a pen name after the character in the story.
32. Otsuka Miho, "'Maihime' ga 'kindai-teki jiga' no bungaku ni naru made," in *Mori Ogai ronshū: Kare yori hajimaru*, ed. Sakai Satoshi and Hara Kunito (Tokyo: Shintensha, 2004), 66.
33. "Utakata no ki" is clearly modeled on Harada Naojirō. The story narrates the painter's encounters with a beautiful and tragically fated model. For analysis on the story as a '*kaiga shōsetsu*' (painting story), see Sadoya Shigenobu, *Ogai to seiyō bijutsu* (Bijutsu kōron sha, 1984), 161–166. I have written about "Utakata no ki" in a chapter titled "Multivalent Muses in Mori Ogai's Fictions," in *The Routledge Companion to Literature and Art*, ed. Neil Murphy, W. Michelle Wang, and Cheryl Julia Lee (Routledge, forthcoming 2024).
34. Kobori, *Wakaki hi no Mori Ogai*, 563. Kobori cites the poet and critic Yosano Hiroshi who worked closely with Ogai, especially in producing the *Subaru* literary magazine (1909–1913), the novelist Satō Haruo (1892–1964) who was close with Yosano and Ogai, and Ogai's brother Mori Junzaburō (1870–1944), all of whom claim to have heard that "Utakata" had been Ogai's first story.
35. Naikoku kangyō hakurankai, a government sponsored exposition to display products for trade promotion, was held five times from 1877 to 1903.
36. Nakamura Giichi, *Nihon bijutsu ronsō-shi* (Tokyo: Kyūryūdō, 1981), 33.
37. Reprinted in Toyama Masakazu, *Meiji bungaku zenshū*, vol. 79, *Meiji geijutsu bungaku ronshū*, ed. Hijikata Teiichi (Tokyo: Chikuma shobō, 1975).
38. Toyama Masakazu, "Nihon kaiga no mirai," in *Meiji bungaku shū*, vol. 79, 153. Toyama uses the English word in katakana.
39. Toyama Masakazu, "Nihon kaiga no mirai," 158.
40. Toyama uses the phrase "*charine no onna*." Nakamura Giichi writes that *charine* was a vernacular term referring to circus troupes, likely inspired by the popularity of an Italian troupe that toured Japan in 1886: Nakamura Giichi, *Nihon bijutsu ronsō-shi*, 35.
41. Toyama Masakazu, "Nihon kaiga no mirai," 160.
42. Toyama Masakazu, "Nihon kaiga no mirai," 162.
43. Isogai Hideo, *Mori Ogai—Meiji 21 nen o chūshin ni* (Tokyo: Meiji sho'in, 1979), 144. Isogai also notes that Ogai's first mention of Hartmann by name occurs in April 1890 in "Hōchi ibun ni daisu," a short essay that expresses his support of Yano Ryūkei's adventure novel *Hōchi ibun*.
44. The notes on the text in *OZ* 22 give the German gloss from the essay's original publication (*OZ* 22:573).
45. It is not clear which painting by Max that Ogai had in mind.
46. Mori Ogai, "Shōyō shi no sho hyōgo," in "Shigarami zōshi no sanbō ronbun" (September 1891).
47. Hartmann's "ruisō," "kosō," and "shōtenchi" hierarchy is presented in *Shinbi kōryō*, *OZ* 21: 247–252. Reflecting on this work in July 1900, Ogai wrote: "The *Shinbi kōryō* is a boring book but there are no parts in it that blatantly take from the hard work of others, so even if it were translated into German, I shall not have to blush in shame." This emphasizes how the work was not merely a verbatim translation of

3. MORI OGAI AND THE "INNER FLAME" OF BEAUTY

Hartmann's work but was the result of his active internalization of its cumulative contents. Quoted in Kinoshita Mokutarō et al., "Kōki," *Shinbi kōryō, OZ* 21: 507.
48. Haga Tōru, "Mori Ogai to Harada Naojirō," 249.
49. See for example Kagioka Masanori, "Harada Naojirō Kiryū kannon no moderu," in *Okayama kenritsu bijutsukan kiyō* 7 (2016), 1. In the article, however, Kagioka argues against the theory that Yamamoto Take had been Harada's model and argues instead that there are other women Harada based his painting on.
50. Jo-Anne Birnie Danzker, ed., *Gabriel von Max: Be-tailed Cousins and Phantasms of the Soul* (Seattle: Frye Museum, 2011), 14.
51. Joseph Beavington Atkinson, *The Schools of Modern Art in Germany* (1881), quoted in Danzker, *Gabriel von Max*, 15.
52. Danzker, *Gabriel von Max*, 6.
53. Kuroda Seiki in *Harada Sensei kinen chō* (Harada Naojirō-shi kinen-kai, 1910), quoted in Takemori Ten'yū, "Ogai sono shuppatsu (122) Horon: Harada Naojirō kara no shōsha: 'Utakata no ki' o megutte (26)," *Kokubungaku: kaishaku to kanshō* 71, no. 5 (May 2006): 200.
54. Theodor W. Adorno, *Aesthetic Theory* [1970], trans. and ed. Robert Hullot-Kentor (Minneapolis: University of Minnesota Press, 1997), 121.
55. See for example Niizeki Kimiko, *Mori Ogai to Harada Naojirō*, 51–53; Kobori Kei'ichirō, *Wakaki hi no Mori Ogai*, 664–683; Shimizu Shigeru, "Iida hime—'Fumizukai:' 'Hijō' no sentaku to 'ri'in' e no yume," *Mori Ogai no dansō satsuei zō*, in *Kokubungaku: kaishaku to kanshō* 49, no. 2 (January 1984), 33–35.
56. Niizeki Kimiko, *Mori Ogai to Harada Naojirō*, 52–53.
57. Yamamoto Masahide, *Genbun itchi no rekishi ronkō: zoku-hen* (Tokyo: Ofūsha, 1981), 236.
58. Published in the *Tōa no hikari* magazine.
59. There are stress marks alongside the entire sentence in the original. "Yume" was originally published in September 1889 in *Eisei shinshi* magazine.
60. The first mention of Freud in Japanese psychiatry was an article about the notion of repression, published in 1912 in the magazine *Shinri kenkyū* (Psychology research), which was founded in 1910. Freud's theories were introduced to Japanese readers, primarily through this magazine, throughout the decade. See Yamashita Tsuneo, *Nihonjin no 'kokoro' to shinrigaku no mondai* (Tokyo: Gendai shokan, 2004), especially chap. 7.
61. Yoshiyuki Nakai, "Ogai's Craft: Literary Techniques and Themes in *Vita Sexualis*," *Monumenta Nipponica* 35, no. 2 (Summer 1980), 229.
62. Iwasa Sōshirō, "Mori Ogai, Shunittsurā, Yamamoto Yuzō: Furoito no kage," in *Nihon kindai bungaku no danmen: 1890–1920* (Tokyo: Sairyūsha, 2009).
63. Ogai uses the Western term here.
64. The story was published in July 1910 in the *Mita bungaku* magazine.
65. Nakajima Kunihiko, "Jikkan, bikan, kankyō—Kindai bungaku ni kakareta kanjusei, 18: 'Shōma kyō'to shite no Rodan—Kōtarō to Ogai to no aida," *Waseda bungaku* 171 (August 1990), 101; 100–113.
66. Takamura Kōtarō, "Rodan no shuki danwaroku" (1942), in *Bōgetsu bōjitsu: zuihitsu* (Tokyo: Ryūseikaku, 1943), 74–75.

3. MORI OGAI AND THE "INNER FLAME" OF BEAUTY

67. Satō Yōko, "Chōkoku-ka Rodan to Nihon ni okeru kindai no keisei," in *Waseda daigaku kyōiku kenkyū sentā kiyō* 18 (2004): 35.
68. *Shirakaba*, November 1910.
69. Akira Mizuta Lippit, *Atomic Light (Shadow Optics)* (Minneapolis: University of Minnesota Press, 2005), 53. This new mode of avisual vision that Lippit observes is described by Gregory Golley as the basis of a high-modern, realist epistemology. See Gregory Golley, *When Our Eyes No Longer See* (Cambridge, MA: Harvard University Press, 2008).
70. For more details on Hanako's life, see Isao Sukenobu, *Maruseiyu no Rodan to Hanako* (Tokyo: Bungeisha, 2001); and Sawada Suketarō, *Puchito Anako* (Nagoya: Chūnichi shuppansha, 1983).
71. Francesco Adinolfi, *Mondo Exotica: Sounds, Visions, Obsessions of the Cocktail Generation* (Durham, NC: Duke University Press, 2008), 73.
72. Recall that Hanako was born in 1868.
73. Yoshikawa Yūsuke, "Hanako wo mono ni suruno wa dare?" in *Mori Ogai ronshū: kare yori hajimaru*, ed. Sakai Satoshi and Hara Kunito (Tokyo: Shintensha, 2004), 114–116.
74. This sentence of the essay is not included in Ogai's story. I quote from Charles Baudelaire, "The Philosophy of Toys" (1853), in *Painter of Modern Life and Other Essays* [1863], trans. and ed. Jonathan Mayne (London: Phaidon Press, 1995), 202.
75. See Miya Yoshihei, *Miya Yoshihei jiden: Mori Ogai ni aisareta gagakusei M-kun no shōgai*, ed. Horikiri Masato (Tokyo: Kyūryūdō, 2010).
76. Miya Yoshihei, *Miya Yoshihei Jiden*, 549–550.
77. Hasegawa Tenkei, "Bungei'in no setsuritsu o nozomu," in *Taiyō*, June 1906, 155.
78. Satō Haruo, *Shibun han-seiki* (Tokyo: Yomiuri shinbun-sha, 1963), 55.
79. Mizusawa Fujio quotes an editorial in the August 1909 *Teikoku bungaku* magazine: "The censors, intimidated by the author's prestige (*ikō*), seem unlikely to prevent the *Subaru* magazine's sales:" Mizusawa Fujio, "Mori Ogai to ken'etsu," in *Tokushū: Mori Ogai no Mondai-kei*, in *Kokubungaku: kaishaku to kyōzai no kenkyū* 50 (2), no. 720 (February 2005), 59–60. For more on the circumstances surrounding the censoring of *Vita Sexualis*, see also Jay Rubin, *Injurious to Public Morals: Writers and the Meiji State* (Seattle: University of Washington Press, 1984), 130–135.
80. It is somewhat ironic that Tayama Katai had in fact been heavily influenced by Ogai's introductions of German aesthetic thought, especially his translations of Johannes Volkelt's philosophies. Volkelt's explanation of Naturalism appears to have directly informed Katai's calls for writings based on *heimen byōsha* (flat descriptions). See Suda Kiyoji, "Ogai to Katai: 'Shinbi shin-setsu' o jiku to shite," in *Kōza Mori Ogai*, vol. 1, *Ogai no hito to shūhen*, ed. Hirakawa Sukehiro et al. (Tokyo: Shin'yōsha, 1997).
81. Tayama Katai, "Rokotsu naru byōsha" (1904), in *Kindai bungaku hyōron taikei*, vol. 2, ed. Inagaki Tatsurō and Satō Masaru (Tokyo: Kadokawa shoten, 1972), 360. Originally published in *Taiyō*, February 1904.
82. Mori Ogai, "Yo ga tachiba," published in *Shinchō* 11, no. 6 (December 1909).
83. Ogai uses the English word in this essay.
84. Journal entry, July 9, 1922, in Arishima Takeo, *Arishima Takeo zenshū*, 16 vols. (Tokyo: Chikuma shobō, 1979–1986), 12: 327.

85. Shinohara Yoshihiko, "Mori Ogai to Taigyaku jiken: 'Dekigoto chūshin no seken jūō ki'no mondai," in *Kōchi daigaku gakujutsu kenkyū hōkoku: jinbungaku-hen* 40 (1991), 66–67; and Nakamura Fumio, *Mori Ogai to Meiji kokka*, 184–185. Shinohara and Nakamura refer to the former *Mainichi denpō* journalist Inomata Denka's August 1923 essay, "Dekigoto chūshin no seken jūōki," published in *Shin shōsetsu* magazine.
86. See for example Nakamura Fumio, *Mori Ogai to Meiji kokka*, 179–180.
87. Hiraide Shū, "Gyakuto" (September 1913), in *Gyakuto: 'Taigyaku jiken'no bungaku*, ed. Ikeda Hiroshi (Tokyo: Inpakuto shuppan-kai, 2010), 232. The story, originally published in *Taiyō* magazine in September 1913, was immediately censored when it appeared, and Hiraide wrote a rebuttal protesting this in the October 1913 issue of the same magazine.
88. Nakamura Fumio, *Mori Ogai to Meiji kokka*, 186–187.
89. All of these stories were originally published in *Mita bungaku*.
90. The proceedings were compiled in the April 1910 issue of the *Chūō kōron* magazine.
91. Imamura Yasutarō, "Kanken to bungei," *Taiyō*, August 1910, 102.
92. Shigeta Kanjirō, *Sekai fūzoku-shi* (Hakubunkan, 1904), quoted in Shinbo Kunihiro, "Ogai 'Chinmoku no tō:' ichimei gaisei hika 'Pāshī'sōdō shimatsu ki," *Kōhon kindai bungaku* 12 (December 2000), 2.
93. Shinbo Kunihiro, "Ogai 'Chinmoku no tō,'" 2–3.
94. Imamura Yasutarō, "Kanken to bungei," 100.
95. Uozumi Setsuro, "Onken-naru jiyū shisōka" (September 16, 1910), in *Gendai Nihon bungaku taikei*, vol. 40 (Tokyo: Chikuma shobō, 1973), 9–11.

4. Mushanokōji Saneatsu and the Early Shirakaba's Artistic Cosmopolitanism

1. The first iteration of the *Mita bungaku* magazine ceased publication in 1925 but it was restarted in 1926. The magazine has started and ceased publication seven times, and it continues into the present.
2. The *Shin-shichō* magazine started and ceased publication twenty-one times. The latest iteration started up in 2022.
3. Mushanokōji Saneatsu, *Aru otoko* (1921–1923). *Aru otoko* was published in installments in *Kaizō* magazine from July 1921 to November 1923.
4. Shiga Naoya, "Inamura zatsudan" (1948), in *Shiga Naoya zenshū*, 15 vols. (Tokyo: Iwanami shoten, 1973–1974), 8: 62. "Inamura zatsudan" was published in installments in *Sakuhin* magazine from August 1948 to March 1949.
5. Shiga Naoya, "Inamura zatsudan," 66.
6. Yamamoto Masahide, *Genbun itchi no rekishi ronkō* (Tokyo: Ofūsha, 1971), 23–24.
7. Uno Kōji, "'Watakushi shōsetsu' shiken" (1925), in *Kindai bungaku hyōron taikei*, vol. 6, ed. Miyoshi Yukio and Sofue Shōji (Tokyo: Kadokawa shoten, 1972), 62. Originally published in *Shinchō*, October 1925.
8. The novel was published in February 1911 by Rakuyōdō.

4. MUSHANOKŌJI SANEATSU AND THE EARLY SHIRAKABA

9. Honda Shūgo, *'Shirakaba'-ha no bungaku* (Tokyo: Shinchōsha, 1960), 76.
10. Senuma Shigeki, *Nihon bundanshi*, vol. 19, in *Shirakaba-ha no wakōdo tachi* (Tokyo: Kōdansha, 1997), 82–85.
11. Miyoshi Yukio, "Shirakabaha no seishun," in *Kokubungaku: kaishaku to kanshō* 22, no. 8 (August 1957): 12.
12. Miyoshi, "Shirakabaha no seishun," 12.
13. Ishikawa Takuboku, "Jidai heisoku no genjō" (1910), in *Nihon kindai bungaku hyōron-sen: Meiji-Taishō hen* (Tokyo: Iwanami bunko, 2003), 160. The essay was published after Takuboku's death in a volume of his collected works in 1913.
14. Shiga Naoya recalls this insult in "Hosokawa shoten ban 'Abashiri made' atogaki" (1947), *Shiga Naoya zenshū*, 8: 150. This piece was written as an afterword to the anthology *Abashiri made* published by Hosokawa shoten in July 1947.
15. Mushanokōji Saneatsu, *Jibun no aruita michi* (1955). *Jibun no aruita michi* was serialized in *Kaizō* magazine from February to December 1955.
16. Ikuta Chōkō, "Shizen shugi zenha no chōryō" (1916), in *Nihon kindai bungaku hyōron-sen: Meiji-Taishō hen* (Tokyo: Iwanami bunko, 2003), 254.
17. See Usui Yoshimi, "Shirakaba ronsō," in *Kindai bungaku ronsō: jō*, ed. Usui Yoshimi (Tokyo: Chikuma shobō, 1975), 115–139.
18. Arishima Takeo, "*Omedetaki hito* wo yomite" (1911), in *Arishima Takeo zenshū*, 7: 39. Originally in *Shirakaba*, April 1911.
19. Arishima Takeo, "*Omedetaki hito* wo yomite," 40.
20. Arishima Takeo, "*Omedetaki hito* wo yomite," 42–43.
21. Mushanokōji Saneatsu, "Takeo-san ni" (1911). Originally in *Shirakaba*, April 1911.
22. Abe Gunji discusses Mushanokōji's gradual resistance to the Tolstoyan morals he had adopted as a younger man in Abe Gunji, *Shirakaba-ha to Torusutoi: Mushanokōji Saneatsu, Arishima Takeo, Shiga Naoya o chūshin ni* (Tokyo: Sairyūsha, 2008), 78–84.
23. Shiga Naoya, "Abashiri made" (1910), in *Shiga Naoya zenshū*, 1: 24. Originally published in *Shirakaba*, April 1910. The story was edited when it was included in the Shirakaba group's anthology collection *Shirakaba no mori* in 1918, and this edited version was included in Shiga's 1921 collection *Ara ginu*. The *Shiga Naoya zenshū* includes the updated version of the story. I quote from passages that have remained unchanged from the story as it first appeared in *Shirakaba*.
24. Shiga Naoya, "Abashiri made," 24.
25. Shiga Naoya, "Abashiri made," 27.
26. Ogimachi Kinkazu, "Yorozuya," *Shirakaba* (April 1910), appendix, 33.
27. Ogimachi Kinkazu, "Yorozuya," *Shirakaba* (April 1910), appendix, 38.
28. Ogimachi Kinkazu, "Yorozuya," *Shirakaba* (April 1910), appendix, 42.
29. Akutagawa Ryunosuke, "Ano koro no jibun no koto" (1919). In chapter 5, I revisit this essay (see ch. 5, n. 1).
30. Sianne Ngai, *The Theory of the Gimmick: Aesthetic Judgment and Capitalist Form* (Cambridge, MA: Harvard University Press, 2020), 1.
31. Ngai, *The Theory of the Gimmick*, 110.
32. See for example Honda Shūgo, *'Shirakaba'-ha no bungaku*, 82.

4. MUSHANOKŌJI SANEATSU AND THE EARLY SHIRAKABA

33. Miyoshi Yukio, "Mushanokōji saneatsu shi ni kiku," in *Kokubungaku: kaishaku to kanshō* 22, no. 8 (August 1957): 67.
34. Mushanokōji Saneatsu, "Jibun no fude de suru shigoto" (1911). Originally in *Shirakaba*, March 1911.
35. Shimazaki Tōson (1872–1943) and Tokuda Shūsei (1872–1943) are representative Japanese Naturalist writers. Shiga Naoya, "Hosokawa shoten ban 'Abashiri made' atogaki" (1947), in *Shiga Naoya zenshū*, vol. 8, 150–151.
36. Kunikida Doppo (1871–1908), regarded as a precursor to Japanese Naturalism. Mushanokōji Saneatsu, "Kosei ni tsuite no zakkan." Originally in *Shirakaba*, October 1912.
37. W. J. T. Mitchell, *Picture Theory* (Chicago: University of Chicago Press, 1994), 14.
38. Honda Shūgo, '*Shirakaba*'-ha no bungaku, 29.
39. Mushanokōji Saneatsu, *Aru otoko*.
40. Mushanokōji Saneatsu, "*Shirakaba* wo dasu made." Originally in *Shirakaba*, December 1917.
41. Mushanokōji Saneatsu, "Jinrui kara kuru jiyōbun." Originally in *Shirakaba*, September 1911.
42. See for example Martha Nussbaum, "Patriotism and Cosmopolitanism," David Miller, "Cosmopolitanism," and Will Kymlicka, "Citizenship in an Era of Globalization," in *The Cosmopolitanism Reader*, ed. Garrett Wallace Brown and David Held (Malden, MA: Polity Press, 2010).
43. Maya Mortimer, *Meeting the Sensei: The Role of the Master in Shirakaba Writers* (Leiden: Brill, 2000), 53–57; Donald Keene, *Emperor of Japan: Meiji and His World, 1852-1912* (New York: Columbia University Press, 2002), 714; and Otsuyama Kunio, *Mushanokōji Saneatsu ron* (Tokyo: Tokyo daigaku shuppan, 1974), 338–339.
44. Mushanokōji Saneatsu, "Mitsui kōshi kun ni." Originally in *Shirakaba*, December 1912.
45. Fusako was Shiga's younger stepsister. Shiga Naoya, diary entry from September 14, 1912, in *Shiga Naoya zenshū*, 10: 636.
46. Mushanokōji Saneatsu, "Tōzoku," in "Zakkan" (1915). Originally in *Shirakaba*, April 1915.
47. Mushanokōji Saneatsu, "Jinrui wa sakebuyo," in "Aru hito wa itta" (1915). Originally in *Shirakaba*, June 1915. Otsuyama Kunio also cites this short piece in Otsuyama, *Mushanokōji Saneatsu ron*, 349.
48. Mushanokōji Saneatsu, "Jinrui dōshi," in "Aru hito wa itta" (1915). Originally in *Shirakaba*, June 1915.
49. For information on the uprising and its aftermath, see Paul Katz, "Governmentality and Its Consequences in Colonial Taiwan: A Case Study of the Ta-pa-ni Incident of 1915," *The Journal of Asian Studies* 64, no. 2 (May 2005): 387–424.
50. Mushanokōji uses the term *dojin*, translated here as "aborigines," which today is a pejorative that implies primitiveness but was widely used in Japan in this time period. Mushanokōji Saneatstu, "Happyaku-nin no shikei." Originally in *Shirakaba*, November 1915.
51. Mushanokōji Saneatstu, "Roku-gō zakki." Originally in *Shirakaba*, December 1915.

4. MUSHANOKŌJI SANEATSU AND THE EARLY SHIRAKABA

52. For example, *Gendai no yōga* (est. 1912), *Takujō* (est. 1914), and *Geibi* (est. 1915). See Kanagawa Kenristu Bijutsukan, ed., *Shijō no yūtopia: kindai Nihon no kaiga to bijutsu zasshi 1889-1915* (Tokyo: Kanagawa Kenristu Bijutsukan renraku kyōgikai, 2008).
53. Mushanokōji Saneatsu, "Ban Gōho," in "Seichō" (1911). Originally in *Shirakaba*, July 1911.
54. Kojima Kikuo, Yamauchi Hideo, and Shiga Naoya, "Kosumosu kaiga gappyō," *Shirakaba*, May 1910, 60.
55. "Henshū-shitsu ni te," *Shirakaba*, January 1912, 158.
56. The gallery was named after the "grotta azzurra," which figures prominently in Hans Christian Andersen's autobiographical novel *Improvisatoren* (1853). Mori Ogai translated the work into Japanese as *Sokkyō shijin* in installments between 1892 and 1901, and then in its entirety in 1902, to great acclaim. Ogai evocatively translated "grotta azzurra" (blue cave) as *rōkan-dō* (jade cave).
57. Kinoshita Mokutarō, "Gakai kinji" (1911), in *Kinoshita Mokutarō zenshū*, vol. 7 (Tokyo: Iwanami shoten, 1981), 368.
58. Yamawaki Shintoku, "Danpen," *Shirakaba*, September 1911, 105.
59. Yamawaki Shintoku, "Danpen," 105.
60. Kinoshita Mokutarō, "Yamawaki Shintoku kun ni kotau" (1911), in *Kinoshita Mokutarō zenshū*, vol. 8 (Tokyo: Iwanami shoten, 1981), 5.
61. Nakamura Giichi, *Zoku: Nihon kindai bijutsu ronsō shi* (Tokyo: Kyūryū-dō, 1982), 98.
62. Mushanokōji Saneatsu, "Tegami yottsu," *Shirakaba*, December 1911, 50.
63. C. Lewis Hind, *The Post Impressionists* (1911) (Freeport, NY: Books for Libraries Press, 1969). Hind explains that his insights were first inspired by his repeated visits to the art exhibit titled, *Manet and the Post-Impressionists*, held at the Grafton Gallery in London the previous year in 1910 (14). The critic Roger Fry, who first coined the term "Post-Impressionism," curated the exhibition.
64. Yanagi Muneyoshi, "Kakumei no gaka" (1912), in *Yanagi Muneyoshi zenshū*, vol. 1 (Tokyo: Chikuma shobō, 1981), 545. Originally in *Shirakaba*, January 1912. Hind similarly wrote: "Art is more than the emotional Utterance of Life. It is the Expression of Personality in all its littleness, in all its sincerity. A man who expresses himself sincerely can extract beauty from anything.... Post Expressionism or Expressionism seeks synthesis in the soul of man, and in the substance of things; it lifts mere craftsmanship into the region of mysticism, and proclaims that art may be a stimulation as well as solace." Hind, *The Post Impressionists*, 2–3.
65. See Kim Brandt, *Kingdom of Beauty: Mingei and the Politics of Folk Art in Imperial Japan*. (Durham, NC: Duke University Press, 2008).
66. Yanagi Muneyoshi, "Kakumei no gaka," 548.
67. Yanagi Muneyoshi, "Kakumei no gaka," 550. C. Lewis Hind describes Cezanne, Van Gogh, and Gauguin as "The Three Pioneers" of the Post-Impressionist movement: Hind, *The Post Impressionists*, 31–35.
68. Yanagi Muneyoshi, "Kakumei no gaka," 553. Hind writes that Cezanne "was a recluse, a seer, not a clubbable man, ... the boldest and profoundest spirit of the artistic revolutionaries who gathered around Manet." Hind, *The Post Impressionists*, 32.

4. MUSHANOKŌJI SANEATSU AND THE EARLY SHIRAKABA

69. Yanagi Muneyoshi, "Kakumei no gaka," 556. Hind writes of Van Gogh: "The intensity of his temperament, his mania for expression, outraged, outwore his body." Hind, *The Post Impressionists*, 33.
70. Yanagi Muneyoshi, "Kakumei no gaka," 557, 560. Hind writes that Gauguin was a "'great barbarian,' who fled from Europe and civilization, painted the walls of mud-huts in Tahiti, and died on one of the islands." Hind, *The Post Impressionists*, 11.
71. Yanagi Muneyoshi, "Kakumei no gaka," 562. Hind writes: "I realized that Matisse paints his sensations, never the mere imitation of objects; his temperament, never contemporary ideals. To state that sensation he will use drawing and color arbitrarily, caring little for accuracy and less for realism, so long as his sensation is expressed." Hind, *The Post Impressionists*, 46. Yanagi Muneyoshi, "Kakumei no gaka," 563. Hind writes: "Death, I fancy, will find me still trying to explain Matisse," and "He has pressed the expression of his primitive sensations to its logical limit." Hind, *The Post Impressionists*, 52, 58.
72. Ikuma studied in first Rome, then Paris, between 1906 and 1910. Umehara studied in Paris from 1908 to 1913.
73. Shiga Naoya, "Nijūdai ichimen" (1923), in *Shiga Naoya zenshū*, 1: 414.
74. Abe Jirō, *Santarō no nikki* (Tokyo: Iwanami shoten, 1918), 607–608.
75. "Henshū-shitsu nite," in *Shirakaba*, January 1912, 158.
76. "Henshū-shitsu nite," in *Shirakaba*, August 1911, 172.
77. "Henshū kiji," in *Shirakaba*, November 1910. But decades later in "Inamura zatsudan" (1948), Shiga Naoya recounts that it had in fact been two or three years prior to the Rodin issue—not five years prior, as the editorial then had claimed—that his friend Tanaka Hei'ichi sent him the magazine that introduced him to Rodin. "Inamura zatsudan," in *Shiga Naoya zenshū*, 8: 69.
78. Mushanokōji Saneatsu, "Rodan to jinsei" (1910). Originally in *Shirakaba*, November 1910.
79. Yanagi Muneyoshi, "Shūkyōka to shite no Rodan" (1910), in *Yanagi Muneyoshi zenshū*, 1: 481. Originally in *Shirakaba*, November 1910.
80. Mushanokōji Saneatsu, "Rodan no chōkoku no kita koto ni tsuite," *Shirakaba*, March 1912, 149. But in *Aru otoko*, Mushanokōji writes that it had been Rodin who suggested exchanging ukiyo-e for some sketches by him.
81. Dominique Viéville, *Rodin, le Rêve Japonais* (Paris: Flammarion, 2007), 202.
82. Mushanokōji Saneatsu, "Rodan no chōkoku no kita koto ni tsuite," *Shirakaba*, February 1912, 150. The quoted passage was repeated in *Aru otoko*, which includes some segments of the 1912 editorial. Kayano Hatakazu was the pen name of Shirakaba member Kōri Torahiko. Hirasawa Chūji was the pen name of Shirakaba member Nagayo Yoshirō.
83. Yanagi's account of picking up the Rodin bronzes at the port in Yokohama hints at the awkward juxtaposition of the increasingly international discourses of art and commerce. He recounts a conversation he had in English with a customs agent: "'Don't you know the name of Auguste Rodin? The greatest living sculptor?' 'O, I don't know.' 'It's pity! You poor—,' but just then the box opened and I forgot all about what I was saying." Yanagi Muneyoshi, "Rodan chōkoku nyūkyo ki" (1912), in *Yanagi Muneyoshi zenshū*, vol. 1, 571–572. Originally in *Shirakaba*, February 1912. Azuma Tamaki mentions but does not cite an anecdote

4. MUSHANOKŌJI SANEATSU AND THE EARLY SHIRAKABA

that because the customs agent did not appreciate the artistic value of the statues, he ended up calculating the import taxes based on the raw weight of the bronze as though they were scrap metal. Azuma Tamaki, *Shirakaba-ha to kindai bijutsu* (Tokyo: Azuma shuppan, 1980), 34.

84. For more about the Atarashiki Mura, see Otsuyama Kunio, *Mushanokōji Saneatsu kenkyū: Saneatsu to Atarashiki Mura* (Tokyo: Meiji shoin, 1997); Sekikawa Natsuo, *Shirakaba tachi no Taishō* (Tokyo: Bungei shunjū, 2005); and Angela Yiu, "Atarashikimura: The Intellectual and Literary Contexts of a Taishō Utopian Village," *Japan Review*, no. 20 (2008).
85. Mushanokōji Saneatsu, "Atarashii seikatsu ni hairu michi" (1918), in "Atarashiki Mura ni tsuite no taiwa."
86. Katō Kazuo, "'Atarashiki Mura' ni taisuru gigi" (1919), in *Kindai bungaku hyōron taikei*, vol. 5 (Tokyo: Kadokawa shoten, 1972), 116. Originally published in installments in *Jiji shinpō*, March 25–30, 1919. The quote comes from part III, published on March 27, 1919.
87. Shiga Naoya, "Jibun wa kare wo shin'yō shiteiru: Atarashiki mura no tame ni" (1918), in *Shiga Naoya zenshū*, vol. 7.
88. Shiga Naoya, "Inamura zatsudan," in *Shiga Naoya zenshū*, 8: 73.
89. Hirotsu Kazuo, "Shiga Naoya ron" (1919). Originally published in *Shinchō*, April 1919. In *Kindai bungaku hyōron taikei*, vol. 5, 353.
90. Arishima Takeo, "Mushanokōji-kei e" (1918). Originally in *Chūō kōron*, July 1918. In *Arishima Takeo zenshū*, 7: 208.
91. Arishima Takeo, "Mushanokōji-kei e," 210.
92. Arishima Takeo, "Sengen hitotsu" (1922), in *Arishima Takeo zenshū*, 9: 5–10. Originally published in *Kaizō*, January 1922.
93. For the Atarashiki mura website, see: http://atarashiki-mura.or.jp/.

5. Akutagawa Ryūnosuke's Literary Anxieties and the "Power to Remake"

1. Akutagawa Ryūnosuke, "Ano koro no jibun no koto." Originally published in *Chūō kōron*, January 1919.
2. Akutagawa Ryūnosuke, *Bungei-teki na, Amari ni bungei-teki na* (1927). Originally serialized in *Kaizō*, April to August 1927, skipping the July issue.
3. Since their meeting in 1915, Akutagawa looked up to Natsume Sōseki as a mentor. Their friendship was short—Sōseki died the following December—but it left a profound impression on Akutagawa. See Sasaki Mitsuru, "Sōseki to Ryūnosuke," in *Kōza Natsume Sōseki*, vol. 1, *Sōseki no hito to shūhen*, ed. Miyoshi Yukio (Tokyo: Yūhikaku, 1981).
4. Tsuchiya Michio, *Kokugo mondai ronsōshi* (Tokyo: Tamagawa daigaku shuppanbu, 2005), 152–155.
5. Akutagawa Ryūnosuke, "Monbu-shō no kana-zukai kaitei an ni tsuite" (1925).
6. Jacques Derrida, *Of Grammatology*, trans. Gayatri Spivak (Baltimore: The Johns Hopkins University Press, 1997), 12.

5. AKUTAGAWA RYŪNOSUKE'S LITERARY ANXIETIES

7. Gayatri Spivak, "Translator's Preface," in Derrida, *Of Grammatology*, lxix.
8. This was the first story he published under his real name. Previously, he published several translations and stories under the pen name Yangikawa Ryūnosuke, or as Akutagawa Ryūnosuke using a different character for "Ryū."
9. Hori Tatsuo, "Akutagawa Ryūnosuke ron: geijutstuka to shite no kare wo ronzu" (1929), in *Hori tatsuo zenshū*, vol. 4 (Tokyo: Chikuma shobō, 1978), 564. Hori originally wrote this essay as his graduation thesis from Tokyo Imperial University.
10. Hirotsu Kazuo, "Waga kokoro wo kataru" (1931), in *Kindai bungaku hyōron taikei*, vol. 6, ed. Miyoshi Yukio and Sofue Shōji (Tokyo: Kadokawa shoten, 1973), 209. Originally published in *Kaizō*, June 1931.
11. Miyamoto Kenji, "'Haiboku' no bungaku: Akutagawa Ryūnosuke no bungaku ni tsuite" (1929), in *Kindai bungaku hyōron taikei*, vol. 6, ed. Miyoshi Yukio and Sofue Shōji (Tokyo: Kadokawa shoten, 1973), 225. Originally published in *Kaizō*, August 1929.
12. Shiga Naoya, "Kutsukake nite" (1927), in *Shiga Naoya zenshū*, vol. 3 (Tokyo: Iwanami shoten, 1973), 426. Originally published in *Chūō kōron*, September 1927.
13. In popular lore, Saigō Takamori's physical stature has been described as gigantic.
14. Shiga Naoya, "Kutsukake nite," 427.
15. The story was serialized in the *Osaka Mainichi* newspaper from October 20 to November 4, 1917.
16. Ishiwari Tōru cites Yoshida Seiichi, who has pointed out that Akutagawa referenced the *Bakin nikki shō* edited by Aeba Kōson. Ishiwari describes a "Bakin boom" in the late Meiji period. Ishiwari Tōru. *'Akutagawa' to yobareta geijutsuka* (Tokyo: Yūseidō shuppan, 1992), 53–54.
17. Ishiwari Tōru, *'Akutagawa' to yobareta geijutsuka*, 55, cites Kikuchi Kan, "Akutagawa Ryūnosuke ni atauru sho," in *Shinchō*, January 1918.
18. Originally published in *Tokyo Nichi-nichi shinbun*, July 27, 1919.
19. Originally published in *Tokyo Nichi-nichi shinbun*, January 1, 1918.
20. See for example Sekiguchu Yasuyoshi, *Akutagawa Ryūnosuke no rekishi ninshiki* (Tokyo: Shin Nihon shuppan-sha, 2004), esp. 27–42 and 159–174.
21. Akutagawa Ryūnosuke, "Geijutsu sono ta." Originally published in *Shinchō*, November 1919.
22. Akutagawa Ryūnosuke, "Boku no tomodachi ni san." Originally published in *Bunshō kurabu*, May 1927.
23. "Jigoku-hen" was originally published in the evening edition of the *Osaka Mainichi* from May 1 to May 22, 1918, and in the *Tokyo Nichi-nichi* newspaper from May 2 to May 22, 1918.
24. Kojima wrote under the pen name Nakatani Chōzō. Nakatani Chōzō, "Jigoku-hen," in *Mita Bungaku*, June 1918, quoted in Kunisue Yasuhira, *Akutagawa Ryūnosuke no bungaku* (Tokyo: Izumi shoin, 1997), 69.
25. See for example Takemori Ten'yū, "Jigoku-hen," in *Hihyō to kenkyū: Akutagawa Ryūnosuke*, ed. Inagaki Tatsuo and Itō Sei (Tokyo: Haga shoten,1972).
26. Yoshida Morio, "Chūkai (Shūzan zu)," in *ARZ* 7: 325. Yoshida explains that in writing the story Akutagawa referred to Imaseki Hisamaro, *Tōyō garon shūsei* (Tokyo: Dokuga shoin, 1915).

27. For a discussion of Akutagawa's visit to China, see for example Sekiguchi Yasuyoshi, *Tokuha'in Akutagawa Ryūnosuke—Chūgoku de nani o mita no ka* (Tokyo: Mainichi shinbunsha, 1997).
28. Yun Nantian is pronounced in Japanese as Un Nanden, also known as Yun Shouping (1633–1690). Wang Shigu is pronounced in Japanese as Ō Sekkoku, also known as Wang Hui (1632–1717). Wang Yanke is pronounced in Japanese as Enkaku Ō, also known as Wang Shimin (1592–1680). Huang Yifeng is pronounced in Japanese as Kō Ippō, also known as Huang Gongwang (1269–1354).
29. Yoshida Seiichi, *Yoshida Seiichi chosakushū*, vol. 2, *Akutagawa Ryūnosuke kenkyū II* (Tokyo: Ōfūsha, 1981), 184. Qiu Yafen has observed that Yoshida's readings have influenced subsequent critical interpretations of the story. Qiu Yafen, *Akutagawa Ryūnosuke no Chūgoku: shinwa to genjitsu* (Fukuoka-shi: Hana shoin, 2010), 94–98.
30. "Yume" was first published in *Akutagawa Ryūnosuke zenshū*, vol. 8: *Bessatsu* (Tokyo: Iwanami shoten, 1929). This *zenshū* is a precursor to the current edition of the *ARZ*.
31. "Yasukichi no techō kara" was published in *Kaizō* magazine in May 1923. Akutagawa Ryūnosuke, letter to Oana Ryūichi, April 13, 1923.
32. "Daidōji Shinsuke no han-sei: aru seishin-teki fūkeiga" was published in *Chūō kōron*, January 1925.
33. "Aru aho no isshō" was published in *Kaizō* in October 1927.
34. Seiji Lippit, *Topographies of Japanese Modernism* (New York: Columbia University Press, 2004), 50–56.
35. As I discussed in chapter 1, the term "I-novel" began appearing in discursive usage between 1920 and 1921. See Tomi Suzuki, *Narrating the Self: Fictions of Japanese Modernity* (Stanford, CA: Stanford University Press, 1996), 48.
36. Nakamura Murao, "Honkaku shōsetsu to shinkyō shōsetsu to" (1924), in *Gendai nihon bungaku ronsōshi: jō*, ed. Hirano Ken et al. (Tokyo: Miraisha, 2006), 139.
37. Kume Masao, "'Watakushi' shōsetsu to 'shinkyō' shōsetsu" (1925), in *Kindai bungaku hyōron taikei*, vol. 6, 51. Originally published in *Bungei kōza*, May 1925.
38. Kume Masao, "'Watakushi' shōsetsu to 'shinkyō' shōsetsu," 53.
39. The essay was originally published in the November 1923 issue of the *Zuihitsu* magazine as part of an essay series.
40. Akutagawa Ryūnosuke, letter to Mano Yūjirō, September 8, 1922.
41. Akutagawa Ryūnosuke, draft for "Daidōji Shinsuke no hansei: Aru seishin-teki fūkeiga" (1925), in *ARZ* 21: 411–417.
42. Ebii Eiji, *Akutagawa Ryūnosuke ronkō—jiko kakusei kara kaitai e* (Tokyo: Ōfūsha, 1988), 374.
43. Quoted in Ebii Eiji, "Kōki (Aru aho no isshō)," in *ARZ* 16: 351.
44. Lippit, *Topographies of Japanese Modernism*, 53.
45. The first section of the story was published in June 1927 in *Dai chōwa*. The complete story was published in October 1927 in *Bungei shunjū* after Akutagawa's death.
46. "Butōkai" was published in *Shinchō* magazine in January 1920.
47. Pierre Loti, "Un Bal à Yedo," *Oeuvres Completes de Pierre Loti*, vol. 6 (Paris: Calman-Lévy, 1893–1911), 488.
48. Nakajima Reiko, "Chūkai (Butōkai)," in *ARZ* 5: 343.

5. AKUTAGAWA RYŪNOSUKE'S LITERARY ANXIETIES

49. Loti, "Un Bal à Yedo," 484.
50. Loti, "Un Bal à Yedo," 478.
51. Originally published in *Chūgai*, February 1919.
52. Originally published in *Shin shōsetsu* in January 1922.
53. Akutagawa seems to have referenced Shinmura Izuru, "Kyoto Namban-ji kōhai kō," published in *Shirin*, July 1918. Kawada Kazuko, "Akutagawa Ryūnosuke 'Kami gami no bishō'to Taishōki no bunka ishiki: Oshū taisen ikō no 'Nihon-teki na mono' no hyōshō," in *Kyūdai Nichi-bun* 30 (October 2017): 35–38.
54. Rebecca Suter, *Holy Ghosts* (Honolulu: University of Hawai'i Press, 2015), 63.
55. Okakura Kakuzō, *The Ideals of the East, With Special Reference to the Art of Japan* (1903) (New York: Dutton, 1920), 5.
56. Akutagawa uses the term *kuronbo*, which today is a pejorative.
57. Kawada Kazuko, "Akutagawa Ryūnosuke 'Kamigami no bishō'to Taishō-ki no bunka ishiki," 40. Kawada cites a Japanese translation, but I cite here from the original English in Lafcadio Hearn, *Glimpses of Unfamiliar Japan* (Boston: Houghton, Mifflin and Company, 1894), 385.
58. See Sakai Hiroki, "Chūō Yūrashia to Nihon no minwa denshō no hikaku kenkyū no tame ni," *Wakō daigaku hyōgen-gakubu kiyō* 16 (2015): 43–45. Sakai explains that the theory of Yuriwaka as a retelling of the Ulysses story by Christian missionaries in the mid-sixteenth century has been debunked, and he suggests that the story may have reached Japan earlier from Central Asia.
59. Tsubouchi Shōyō, "Yuriwaka densetsu no hongen" (1906), in *Shōyō senshū*, vol. 11 (Tokyo: Shun'yōdō, 1927). Originally published in *Waseda bungaku*, January 1906. For more on this topic, see Inoue Shōichi, *Namban gensō: Yurishīzu densetsu to Azuchi-jō* (Tokyo: Bungei shunjū, 1998).
60. Originally published in *Sunday Mainichi*, June 4, 1922.
61. Tanizaki Jun'ichirō, "Jōzetsu-roku" (1927), in *Gendai nihon bungaku ronsōshi*, vol. 1, ed. Hirano Ken et al. (Tokyo: Miraisha, 2006), 219. Originally published in *Kaizō*, March 1927. "Jōzetsu-roku" was a regular column that Tanizaki wrote in *Kaizō*, and he used it as a platform for responding to Akutagawa's critiques.
62. Akutagawa Ryūnosuke, "Geijutsu sono ta" (1919).
63. Theodor W. Adorno, *Aesthetic Theory* (1970), trans. and ed. Robert Hullot-Kentor (Minneapolis: University of Minnesota Press, 1997), 128.
64. This image appears on the cover of this book.
65. For an introduction to Redon's work, see for example Douglas W. Druick, ed., *Odilon Redon: Prince of Dreams, 1840–1916* (Chicago: Art Institute of Chicago, 1994).
66. Akutagawa Ryūnosuke, letter to Hara Zen'ichirō, November 14, 1914.
67. Henri Matisse, "Notes d'un Peintre" (1908), trans. Alfred H. Barr Jr. (1951), in *Theories of Modern Art: A Source Book by Artists and Critics*, ed. Herschel B. Chipp et al. (Berkeley: University of California Press, 1996), 135.
68. Originally published in *Bungei shunjū*, June 1927.

Epilogue

1. According to the National Student Clearinghouse Research Center, "Total post-secondary enrollment remains well below pre-pandemic levels, down about 1.09 million students overall and about 1.16 million undergraduates alone, compared to spring 2020." "Spring 2023 Current Enrollment Estimates," National Student Clearinghouse Research Center, accessed May 25, 2023, https://nscresearchcenter.org/current-term-enrollment-estimates/.
2. Nathan Heller, "The End of the English Major," *New Yorker*, March 6, 2023, 28.
3. Heller, "The End of the English Major," 37.
4. Natsume Sōseki, "Jiki ga kite itanda: shojosaku tsuikai dan" (1908).
5. Mizumura Minae, *The Fall of Language in the Age of English*, trans. Juliet Winters (New York: Columbia University Press, 2017), 173.
6. Mizumura Minae, *The Fall of Language in the Age of English*, 157.
7. John Guillory, *Professing Criticism: Essays on the Organization of Literary Study* (Chicago: University of Chicago Press, 2023), 45.
8. Guillory, *Professing Criticism*, 49.
9. Joseph A. Murphy, *Metaphorical Circuit: Negotiations Between Literature and Science in 20th Century Japan* (Ithaca, NY: Cornell University East Asia Program, 2004), 8.
10. Murphy, *Metaphorical Circuit*, 7.
11. Karatani Kōjin, "Kindai bungaku no owari," in *Kindai bungaku no owari: Karatani Kōjin no genzai* (Tokyo: Insukuriputo, 2005), 36.
12. Karatani Kōjin, "Kindai bungaku no owari," 40–41.
13. Azuma Hiroki, *Sekai kara motto chikaku ni: genjitsu kara kiri-hanasareta bungaku no shomondai* (Tokyo: Tokyo Sōgensha, 2013), 4.

Bibliography

Primary Source Abbreviations

Throughout this book I have used an in-text parenthetical citation (including the abbreviated name, plus the volume sand page numbers) for works included in the following four primary sources.

ARZ *Akutagawa Ryūnosuke zenshū*, 24 vols. Tokyo: Iwanami shoten, 1995–1998.
MSZ *Mushanokōji Saneatsu zenshū*, 18 vols. Tokyo: Shōgakkan, 1987–1991.
OZ   *Ogai zenshū*, 38 vols. Tokyo: Iwanami shoten, 1971–1975.
SZ   *Teihon Sōseki zenshū*, 28 vols. Tokyo: Iwanami shoten, 2016–2020.

All Other Works

Abe Gunji. *Shirakaba-ha to Torusutoi: Mushanokōji Saneatsu, Arishima Takeo, Shiga Naoya wo chūshin ni*. Tokyo: Sairyūsha, 2008.
Abe Jirō. *Santarō no nikki*. [1914] Tokyo: Iwanami Shoten, 1918.
Adinolfi, Francesco. *Mondo Exotica: Sounds, Visions, Obsessions of the Cocktail Generation*. Durham, NC: Duke University Press, 2008.
Adorno, Theodor W. *Aesthetic Theory*. [1970] Trans. and ed. Robert Hullot-Kentor. Minneapolis: University of Minnesota Press, 1997.
Amagai Yoshinori. "Kōbu bijutsu gakkō no setsuritsu mokuteki ni tsuite (Dai 55 kai Bigaku kai zenkoku taikai happyō yōshi)." *Bigaku* 55, no. 3 (2004): 50–55.
Anker, Elizabeth S., and Rita Felski. "Introduction." In *Critique and Postcritique*. Ed. Elizabeth S. Anker and Rita Felski, 1–28. Durham, NC: Duke University Press, 2017.

BIBLIOGRAPHY

Arishima Takeo. *Arishima Takeo zenshū*. 16 vols. Tokyo: Chikuma shobō, 1979–1986.
Atarashiki Mura. "Ippan zaidan hōjin Atarashiki Mura." Accessed May 1, 2023, http://atarashiki-mura.or.jp/.
Azuma Hiroki. *Sekai kara motto chikaku ni: genjitsu kara kiri-hanasareta bungaku no shomondai*. Tokyo: Tokyo Sōgensha, 2013.
Azuma Tamaki. *Shirakaba-ha to kindai bijutsu*. Tokyo: Azuma shuppan, 1980.
Baudelaire, Charles. "The Philosophy of Toys." [1853] In *Painter of Modern Life and Other Essays*. Trans. and ed. Jonathan Mayne, 198–204. London: Phaidon Press, 1995.
Bérubé, Michael, ed. *The Aesthetics of Cultural Studies*. Malden, MA: Blackwell, 2004.
Bourdaghs, Michael K. *A Fictional Commons*. Durham, NC: Duke University Press, 2021.
Bowring, Richard. *Mori Ogai and the Modernization of Japanese Culture*. Cambridge: Cambridge University Press, 1979.
Brandt, Kim. *Kingdom of Beauty: Mingei and the Politics of Folk Art in Imperial Japan*. Durham, NC: Duke University Press, 2008.
Cheeke, Stephen. *Writing for Art: The Aesthetics of Ekphrasis*. Manchester, UK: Manchester University Press, 2008.
Chiba Shunji. *Erisu no ekubo*. Tokyo: Ozawa shoten, 1997.
Crary, Jonathan. *24/7*. London: Verso, 2013.
Danzker, Jo-Anne Birnie, ed. *Gabriel von Max: Be-tailed Cousins and Phantasms of the Soul*. Seattle: Frye Museum, 2011.
De Bolla, Peter. *Art Matters*. Cambridge, MA: Harvard University Press, 2003.
Derrida, Jacques. *Of Grammatology*. Trans. Gayatri Spivak. Baltimore: The Johns Hopkins University Press, 1997.
——. *Resistances of Psychoanalysis*. Trans. Peggy Kamuf et al. Stanford, CA: Stanford University Press, 1998.
Doak, Kevin. *A History of Nationalism in Modern Japan: Placing the People*. Leiden: Brill, 2007.
Druick, Douglas W, ed. *Odilon Redon: Prince of Dreams, 1840–1916*. Chicago: Art Institute of Chicago, 1994.
Ebii Eiji, *Akutagawa Ryūnosuke ronkō—jiko kakusei kara kaitai e* (Tokyo: Ōfūsha, 1988).
——. *Kaika, ren'ai, Tokyo: Sōseki, Ryūnosuke*. Tokyo: Ofūsha, 2001.
——. "Kōki (Aru aho no isshō)." In *Akutagawa Ryūnosuke zenshū*, 16, 351–354. Tokyo: Iwanami shoten, 1997.
Felski, Rita. *The Limits of Critique*. Chicago: University of Chicago Press, 2015.
Freud, Sigmund. *The Interpretation of Dreams*. [1900] Trans. James Strachey. New York: Avon Books, 1965.
Furuta, Ryō. *Toku kō: Sōseki no bijutsu sekai*. Tokyo: Iwanami, 2014.
Gardner, William O. *Advertising Tower: Japanese Modernism and Modernity in the 1920s*. Cambridge, MA: Harvard University Press, 2006.
Golley, Gregory. *When Our Eyes No Longer See: Realism, Science, and Ecology in Japanese Literary Modernism*. Cambridge, MA: Harvard University Press, 2008.
Goto Miyabi. "'Maihime' and the Space of Criticism in Meiji Japan." *The Journal of Japanese Studies* 46, no. 2 (Summer 2020): 345–368.
Gottlieb, Nanette. *Language and the Modern State: The Reform of Written Japanese*. [1991] London: Routledge, 2018.

Guillory, John. *Professing Criticism: Essays on the Organization of Literary Study.* Chicago: University of Chicago Press, 2023.
Haga Tōru. "Mori Ogai to Harada Naojirō." In *Kaiga no ryōbun: Kindai Nihon hikaku bunka-shi kenkyū.* Tokyo: Asahi, 1990.
Harootunian, H. D. "Between Politics and Culture: Authority and the Ambiguities of Intellectual Choice in Imperial Japan." In *Japan in Crisis: Essays on Taishō Democracy.* Ed. Bernard S. Silberman and H. D. Harootunian, 110–155. Princeton, NJ: Princeton University Press, 1974.
Hasegawa Tenkei, "Bungei'in no setsuritsu o nozomu." *Taiyō,* June 1906.
Hashikawa Bunzō. *Kindai Nihon shisōshi no kiso chishiki: Ishin zen'ya kara haisen made.* Tokyo: Yūhikaku, 1971.
Hashikawa Toshiki. "Satomi Mineko: Jogakusei agari no 'mayoeru hitsuji." *Kyōritsu kokusai kenkyū: Kyōritsu joshi daigaku kokusai gakubu kiyō,* 29 (March 2012): 101–122.
He Wei. "Natsume Sōseki 'Sanshirō'ron: Atarashī onna no Mineko to Yoshiko." *Hiroshima jogakuin daigaku daigakuin gengo bunka rongyō* 18 (March 2015): 23–41.
Hearn, Lafcadio. *Glimpses of Unfamiliar Japan.* Boston: Houghton, Mifflin and Company, 1894.
Heller, Nathan. "The End of the English Major." *New Yorker,* March 6, 2023, 28–39.
Hijikata Teiichi, ed. *Meiji bungaku zenshū,* vol. 79. *Meiji geijutsu bungaku ronshū.* Tokyo: Chikuma shobō, 1975.
Hill, Christopher. "Mori Ogai's Resentful Narrator: Trauma and the National Subject in 'The Dancing Girl.'" *Positions: East Asia Cultures Critique* 10, no. 2 (Fall 2020): 365–397.
Hind, C. Lewis. *The Post Impressionists.* [1911] Freeport, NY: Books for Libraries Press, 1969.
Hiraide Shū. "Gyakuto." [1913] In *Gyakuto: 'Taigyaku jiken' no bungaku.* Ed. Ikeda Hiroshi, 231–263. Tokyo: Inpakuto shuppan-kai, 2010.
Hirayama Mikiko. "Japanese Art Criticism: The First Fifty Years." In *Since Meiji: Perspectives on the Japanese Visual Arts, 1868–2000.* Ed. J. Thomas Rimer, 257–280. Honolulu: University of Hawai'i Press, 2012.
Hirotsu, Kazuo. "Shiga Naoya ron." [1919] In *Kindai bungaku hyōron taikei,* vol. 5. Ed. Endō Tasuku and Sofue Shōji, 368–376. Tokyo: Kadokawa shoten, 1972.
———. "Waga kokoro wo kataru." [1931] In *Kindai bungaku hyōron taikei,* vol. 6. Ed. Miyoshi Yukio and Sofue Shōji, 200–210. Tokyo: Kadokawa shoten, 1973.
Hohendahl, Peter Uwe. *The Fleeting Promise of Art: Adorno's Aesthetic Theory Revisited.* Ithaca, NY: Cornell University Press, 2013.
Honda Shūgo. *'Shirakaba'-ha no bungaku.* Tokyo: Shinchōsha, 1960.
Hori Tatsuo. "Akutagawa Ryūnosuke ron: geijustuka to shite no kare wo ronzu." [1929] In *Hori tatsuo zenshū,* vol. 4, 559–610. Tokyo: Kadokawa shoten, 1964.
Hullot-Kentor, Robert. Translator's Introduction." In Theodor W. Adorno, *Aesthetic Theory,* xi–xii. Minneapolis: University of Minnesota Press, 1997.
Hurley, Brian. *Confluence and Conflict: Reading Transwar Japanese Literature and Thought.* Cambridge, MA: Harvard University Press, 2022.
Ikuta Chōkō. "Shizen shugi zenha no chōryō." [1916] In *Nihon kindai bungaku hyōronsen: Meiji-Taishō hen.* Ed. Chiba Shunji and Tsubouchi Yūzō, 249–261. Tokyo: Iwanami bunko, 2003.

Imamura Yasutarō. "Kanken to bungei." *Taiyō*, August 1910.
Imaseki, Hisamaro. *Tōyō garon shūsei*. Tokyo: Dokuga shoin, 1915.
Inose Naoki. *Mikado no shōzō*. Tokyo: Shōgakkan, 1986.
Inoue Shōichi. *Namban gensō: Yurishīzu densetsu to Azuchi-jō*. Tokyo: Bungei shunjū, 1998.
Iriye, Akira. "Japan's Drive to Great Power Status." In *The Cambridge History of Japan*, vol. 5. Ed. Marius Jansen, 721–782. Cambridge: Cambridge University Press, 1989.
Isao Sukenobu. *Maruseiyu no Rodan to Hanako*. Tokyo: Bungeisha, 2001.
Ishihara Chiaki. "Jidai no naka no 'Sanshirō.'" In *Kokubungaku: kaishaku to kyōzai no kenkyū*, 53 (9), no. 769 (June 2008): 140–151.
———. "Kagami no naka no *Sanshirō*." In *Natsume Sōseki: 'Sanshirō'wo dō yomu ka*. Ed. Ishihara Chiaki, 141–156. Tokyo: Kawade shobō, 2014.
Ishikawa Takuboku. "Jidai heisoku no genjō." [1910] In *Nihon kindai bungaku hyōronsen: Meiji-Taishō hen*. Ed. Chiba Shunji and Tsubouchi Yūzō, 157–174. Tokyo: Iwanami bunko, 2003.
Ishiwari Tōru. *'Akutagawa' to yobareta geijutsuka*. Tokyo: Yūseidō shuppan, 1992.
Isogai Hideo. *Mori Ogai—Meiji 21nen wo chūshin ni*. Tokyo: Meiji sho'in, 1979.
Itō Junko. "Meiga to meiku de tadoru 'Nihonjin to ame:' Edo jidai no ukiyo-e, haiku kara." In *Science Window* 4, no. 20 (Spring 2010): 30–31.
Itō Sei. *Nihon bundan shi 14: Han shizen shugi no hito tachi*. Tokyo: Kōdansha, 1997.
Iwasa Sōshirō. "Mori Ogai—Schnitzler—Yamamoto Yuzō—Furoito no kage." In *Nihon kindai bungaku no danmen—1890-1920*. Ed. Iwasa Sōshirō, 222–227. Tokyo: Sairyūsha, 2009.
Kabe Yoshitaka. "Mori Ogai bungei hyōron on kenkyū (ichi): 'Shōsetsuron'no kaikō no ito to hōhō," *Shōin koku-bungaku* 14 (September–October 1976): 67–75.
Kagioka Masanori. "Harada Naojirō *Kiryū kannon* no moderu." In *Okayama kenritsu bijutsukan kiyō* 7 (2016): 1–9.
Kanagawa Kenristu Bijutsukan, ed. *Shijō no yūtopia: kindai Nihon no kaiga to bijutsu zasshi 1889-1915*. Tokyo: Kanagawa Kenristu Bijutsukan renraku kyōgikai, 2008.
Kanbayashi Tsunemichi. *Kindai nihon 'bigaku'no tanjō*. Tokyo: Kōdansha, 2006.
Kanda Shōko. *Sōseki 'bungaku' no reimei*. Tokyo: Seikan sha, 2015.
Kanda Takao. "Ogai shoki no bungei hyōron." *Hikaku bungaku kenkyū* 1–2, no. 6 (December 1957): 27–53.
Kaneko Ryūichi. "The Origins and Development of Japanese Art Photography." In *The History of Japanese Photography*. Ed. Anne Wilkes Tucker et al., 100–141. New Haven, CT: Yale University Press, 2003.
Kant, Immanuel. *Critique of Judgement*. [1790] Trans. James Creed Meredith, ed. Nicholas Walker. Oxford: Oxford University Press, 2007.
Karaki Junzō. *Gendai shi e no kokoromi*. Tokyo: Chikuma shobō, 1949.
Karatani Kōjin. "The Discovery of Landscape." In *Origins of Modern Japanese Literature*. Trans. and ed. Brett de Bary, 11–44. Durham, NC: Duke University Press.
———. "Kindai bungaku no owari." In *Kindai bungaku no owari: Karatani Kōjin no genzai*, 35–80. Tokyo: Insukuriputo, 2005.
———. "*Sanshirō*." In *Sōseki ron shūsei*, 284–290. Tokyo: Daisan bunmei-sha, 1992.
Katō Kazuo. "'Atarashiki Mura'ni taisuru gigi." [1919] In *Kindai bungaku hyōron taikei*, vol. 5. Ed. Endō Tasuku and Sofue Shōji, 114–120. Tokyo: Kadokawa shoten, 1972.

Katz, Paul. "Governmentality and Its Consequences in Colonial Taiwan: A Case Study of the Ta-pa-ni Incident of 1915." *The Journal of Asian Studies* 64, no. 2 (May 2005): 387–424.

Kawada Kazuko. "Akutagawa Ryūnosuke 'Kamigami no bishō'to Taishō-ki no bunka ishiki: Oshū taisen ikō no 'Nihon-teki na mono'no hyōshō." *Kyūdai Nichi-bun* 30 (October 2017): 34–47.

Keene, Donald. *Dawn to the West: Japanese Literature of the Modern Era*. New York: Holt, Rinehart, and Winston, 1984.

———. *Emperor of Japan: Meiji and His World, 1852-1912*. New York: Columbia University Press, 2002.

Kermode, Frank. "Life and Death of the Novel." In *The New York Review of Books*, October 28, 1965. Accessed May 1, 2023, https://www.nybooks.com/articles/1965/10/28/life-and-death-of-the-novel/.

Kinoshita Mokutarō. *Kinoshita Mokutarō zenshū*, 25 vols. Tokyo: Iwanami shoten, 1981–1983.

Kinoshita Mokutarō et al. "Kōki (*Shinbi kōryō*)." In *Ogai zenshū*, vol. 21, 307. Tokyo: Iwanami shoten, 1973.

Kinoshita Naoyuki. *Bijutsu to iu misemono: Abura-e jaya no jidai*. [1993] Tokyo: Kōdansha, 2010.

Kitazawa Noriaki. *Me no shinden:'bijutsu'juyō shi nōto*. [1989] Tokyo: Buryukke, 2010.

Kobori Kei'ichirō. *Wakaki hi no Mori Ogai*. Tokyo: Tokyo daigaku shuppankai, 1969.

Kojima Kikuo, Yamauchi Hideo, and Shiga Naoya. "Kosumos kaiga gappyō." *Shirakaba*, May 1910, 60.

Komori Yōichi. "3/11 to Natsume Sōseki: 'Gendai Nihon no kaika' kara 100 nen." *Subaru* 33 no. 11 (November 2011): 214–225.

———. *Seikimatsu no yogensha: Natsume Sōseki*. Tokyo: Kōdansha, 1999.

Konno Tsutomu. *Ogai no koibito: hyaku-nijū nen go no shinjitsu*. Tokyo: NHK shuppan, 2010.

Koyama Keita. *Sōseki ga mita butsurigaku: Kubitsuri no rikigaku kara sōtaise riron made*. Tokyo: Chūkō shinsho, 1991.

Kumasaka Atsuko. "Sōseki to 'Asahi bungei ran." In *Meiji han shizen ha bungaku shū*, vol. 2. Ed. Naruse Masakatsu, 362–387. Tokyo: Chikuma shobō, 1968.

Kume Masao. "'Watakushi' shōsetsu to 'shinkyō' shōsetsu." [1925] In *Kindai bungaku hyōron taikei*, vol. 6. Ed. Miyoshi Yukio and Sofue Shōji, 50–57. Tokyo: Kadokawa shoten, 1973.

Kunisue Yasuhira. *Akutagawa Ryunosuke no bungaku*. Tokyo: Izumi shoin, 1997.

Kymlicka, Will. "Citizenship in an Era of Globalization." In *The Cosmopolitanism Reader*. Ed. Garrett Wallace Brown and David Held, 435–443. Malden, MA: Polity Press, 2010.

Latour, Bruno. "Why Has Critique Run Out of Steam? From Matters of Fact to Matters of Concern." *Critical Inquiry* 30, no. 2 (Winter 2004): 225–248.

Lavery, Grace. *Quaint, Exquisite: Victorian Aesthetics and the Idea of Japan*. Princeton, NJ: Princeton University Press, 2019.

Lippit, Akira Mizuta. *Atomic Light (Shadow Optics)*. Minneapolis: University of Minnesota Press, 2005.

Lippit, Miya Elise Mizuta. *Aesthetic Life: Beauty and Art in Modern Japan*. Cambridge, MA: Harvard University Press, 2019.

Lippit, Seiji. *Topographies of Japanese Modernism*. New York: Columbia University Press, 2004.
Loti, Pierre. "Un Bal à Yedo." In *Oeuvres Completes de Pierre Loti*, vol. 6, 471–492. Paris: Calman-Lévy, 1893–1911.
Maruyama Masao. "Nikutai bungaku kara nikutai seiji made." [1949] In *Zōho ban: Gendai seiji no shisō to kōdō*, 375–394. Tokyo: Miraisha, 1964.
Masaoka Shiki. *Shiki zenshū*, 25 vols. Tokyo: Kōdansha, 1975–1978.
Matisse, Henri. "Notes d'un Peintre." [1908] Trans. Alfred H. Barr Jr. [1951]. In *Theories of Modern Art: A Source Book by Artists and Critics*. Ed. Herschel B. Chipp et al., 130–137. Berkeley: University of California Press, 1996.
Miller, David. "Cosmopolitanism." In *The Cosmopolitanism Reader*. Ed. Garrett Wallace Brown and David Held, 155–162. Malden, MA: Polity Press, 2010.
Mitchell, Arthur M. *Disruptions of Daily Life: Japanese Literary Modernism in the World*. Ithaca, NY: Cornell University Press, 2020.
Mitchell, W. J. T. *Picture Theory*. Chicago: University of Chicago Press, 1994.
Miya Yoshihei. *Miya Yoshihei Jiden- Mori Ogai ni aisareta gagakusei M-kun no shōgai*. Ed. Horikiri Masato. Tokyo: Kyūryūdō, 2010.
Miyagi Tatsurō and Hiroshi Sakagami. *Kindai bungaku no chōryū: Shizen shugi to han shizen shugi*. Tokyo: Sōbunsha shuppan, 1977.
Miyamoto Kenji. "'Haiboku' no bungaku: Akutagawa Ryūnosuke no bungaku ni tsuite." [1929] In *Kindai bungaku hyōron taikei*, vol. 6. Ed. Miyoshi Yukio and Sofue Shōji, 225–243. Tokyo: Kadokawa shoten, 1973.
Miyoshi Yukio. "Mushanokōji Saneatsu shi ni kiku." In *Kokubungaku: kaishaku to kanshō* 22, no. 8 (August 1957): 62–75.
———. "Shirakabaha no seishun." *Kokubungaku: kaishaku to kanshō* 22, no. 8 (August 1957): 12–19.
Mizumura Minae. *The Fall of Language in the Age of English*. Trans. Juliet Winters. New York: Columbia University Press, 2017.
Mizusawa Fujio. "Mori Ogai to ken'etsu. (*Tokushū: Mori Ogai no Mondai-kei*.)" In *Kokubungaku: kaishaku to kyōzai no kenkyū* 50 (2), no. 720 (February 2005): 58–63.
Mortimer, Maya. *Meeting the Sensei: The Role of the Master in Shirakaba Writers*. Leiden: Brill, 2000.
Murase Shirō. "'San' to 'Yon' no zushō-gaku: *Sanshirō*, setsudan sareru shōjo tachi." *Sōseki kenkyū* 2 (May 1994): 82–100.
Murck, Alfreda, and Wen C. Fong. *Words and Images: Chinese Poetry, Calligraphy, and Painting*. New York: Metropolitan Museum of Art, 1991.
Murphy, Joseph A. *Metaphorical Circuit: Negotiations Between Literature and Science in 20th-Century Japan*, Ithaca, NY: Cornell University East Asia Program, 2004.
Mushanokōji Saneatsu. "Rodan no chōkoku no kita koto ni tsuite." *Shirakaba*, February 1912, 149–150.
Nakai, Yoshiyuki. "Ogai's Craft: Literary Techniques and Themes in *Vita Sexualis*." *Monumenta Nipponica* 35, no. 2 (Summer 1980): 223–239.
Nakajima, Kunihiko. "Jikkan, bikan, kankyō—Kindai bungaku ni kakareta kanjusei, 18: 'Shōma kyō'to shite no Rodan—Kōtarō to Ogai to no aida." *Waseda bungaku*, no.171 (August 1990): 100–113.

Nakajima, Reiko. "Chūkai (Butōkai)." In *Akutagawa Ryūnosuke zenshū*, 5, 343–347. Tokyo: Iwanami shoten, 1996.
Nakamura Fumio. *Mori Ogai to Meiji kokka*. Tokyo: San ichi shobō, 1992.
Nakamura Fusetsu. "Shinobazu jukkei." In Masaoka Shiki, *Shiki zenshū*, vol. 12, 601–602. Tokyo: Kōdansha, 1975.
Nakamura Giichi. *Nihon bijutsu ronsōshi*. Tokyo: Kyūryūdō, 1981.
———. *Zoku: Nihon kindai bijutsu ronsōshi*. Tokyo: Kyūryū-dō, 1982.
Nakamura Mitsuo. "Fūzoku shōsetsuron." [1950] In *Nakamura Mitsuo zenshū*, vol. 7, 525–618. Tokyo: Chikuma shobō, 1972.
Nakamura Murao. "Honkaku shōsetsu to shinkyō shōsetsu to." [1924] In *Gendai nihon bungaku ronsōshi: jō*. Ed. Hirano Ken et al., 139–145. Tokyo: Miraisha, 2006.
Nakayama Akihiko. "Ratai-ga/ Ratai/ Nihonjin: Meiji-ki 'Rataiga ronsō' dai ichi maku." In *Disukūru no teikoku: Meiji 30 nendai no bunka kenkyū*. Ed. Kaneko Akio et al., 16–55. Tokyo: Shin'yōsha, 2000.
National Student Clearinghouse Research Center. "Spring 2023 Current Enrollment Estimates." Accessed May 25, 2023, https://nscresearchcenter.org/current-term-enrollment-estimates/.
Natsume Sōseki. "One Night." Trans. Alan Turney. *Monumenta Nipponica* 33, no. 3 (Autumn 1978): 289–297.
———. *Sōseki shiryō: Bungakuron nōto*. Ed. Isamu Muraoka. Tokyo: Iwanami shoten, 1976.
———. *Theory of Literature and Other Critical Writings*. Trans. and ed. Michael K. Bourdaghs, Atsuko Ueda, and Joseph A. Murphy. New York: Columbia University Press, 2009.
———. *Tower of London*. Trans. and ed. Damian Flanagan. London: Peter Owen Publishers, 2004.
Ngai, Sianne. *Theory of the Gimmick: Aesthetic Judgment and Capitalist Form*. Cambridge, MA: Harvard University Press, 2020.
Niizeki Kimiko. *Mori Ogai to Harada Naojirō: Myunhen ni mebaeta yūjōno yukue*. Tokyo: Tokyo geijutsu daigaku shuppan kai, 2008.
———. *Sōseki no bijutsu aisuiri nōto*. Tokyo: Heibon-sha, 1998.
Noë, Alva. *The Entanglement: How Art and Philosophy Make Us What We Are*. Princeton, NJ: Princeton University Press, 2023.
Nussbaum, Martha. "Patriotism and Cosmopolitanism." In *The Cosmopolitanism Reader*. Ed. Garrett Wallace Brown and David Held, 27–44. Malden, MA: Polity Press, 2010.
Ochi Haruo. "Sanshirō no seishun." In *Sōseki sakuhinron shūsei*, vol. 5, *Sanshirō*. Ed. Tamai Takayuki and Murata Yoshiya, 24–35. Tokyo: Ofusha, 1991.
Odagiri Hideo. *Kitamura Tōkoku ron*. Tokyo: Yagi shoten, 1970.
Odin, Steve. *Artistic Detachment in Japan and the West: Psychic Distance in Comparative Aesthetics*. Honolulu: University of Hawai'i Press, 2001.
Ogimachi Kinkazu. "Yorozuya." *Shirakaba*, April 1910, appendix, 27–42.
Oishi Naoki. "Ogai no kaiga-ron: Harada Naojirō to no kanren ni furete." *Kokubungaku: kaishaku to kyōzai no kenkyū*, 45 (8), no. 657 (July 2000): 40–44.
Okakura, Kakuzō. *The Ideals of the East, With Special Reference to the Art of Japan*. [1903] New York: Dutton, 1920.

Omuka Toshiharu. *Kanshū no seiritsu: Bijutsu-ten, bijutsu zasshi, bijutsushi*. Tokyo: Tokyo daigaku shuppankai, 2008.
Otsuka Miho. "'Maihime' ga 'kindai-teki jiga' no bungaku ni naru made." In *Mori Ogai ronshū: Kare yori hajimaru*. Ed. Sakai Satoshi and Hara Kunito, 64–106. Tokyo: Shintensha, 2004.
Otsuyama, Kunio. *Mushanokōji Saneatsu kenkyū: Saneatsu to Atarashiki Mura*. Tokyo: Meiji shoin, 1997.
———. *Mushanokōji Saneatsu ron*. Tokyo: Tokyo daigaku shuppan, 1974.
Pincus, Leslie. *Authenticating Culture in Imperial Japan*. Berkeley: University of California Press, 1996.
Reed, Christopher. *Bachelor Japanists: Japanese Aesthetics and Western Masculinity*. New York: Columbia University Press, 2017.
Rickman, Hans Peter. *Philosophy in Literature*. Madison, NJ: Fairleigh Dickinson University Press, 1996.
Rimer, J. Thomas. "Hegel in Tokyo: Ernest Fenollosa and His 1882 Lecture on the Truth of Art." In *Japanese Hermeneutics: Current Debates on Aesthetics and Interpretation*. Ed. Michael F. Marra, 97–108. Honolulu: University of Hawai'i Press, 2002.
———. "Introduction." In Mori Ogai, *Youth and Other Stories*, ed. J Thomas Rimer, ix–xi. Honolulu: University of Hawai'i Press, 1994.
Rokusō Ichika. *Ogai no koibito Erisu no shinjitsu*. Tokyo: Kōdansha, 2011.
———. *Sorekara no Erisu: Ima akiraka ni naru Ogai 'Maihime' no omokage*. Tokyo: Kōdansha, 2013.
Rubin, Jay. *Injurious to Public Morals: Writers and the Meiji State*. Seattle: University of Washington Press, 1984.
Sadoya Shigenobu. *Ogai to seiyō bijutsu*. Tokyo: Bijutsu kōron sha, 1984.
———. *Sōseki to seiki-matsu bijutsu*. Tokyo: Kōdansha, 1994.
Sakai Hiroki. "Chūō Yūrashia to Nihon no minwa denshō no hikaku kenkyū no tame ni." *Wakō daigaku hyōgen-gakubu kiyō* 16 (2015): 41–60.
Sasaki Mitsuru. "Sōseki to Ryūnosuke." In *Kōza Natsume Sōseki*, vol. 1, *Sōseki no hito to shūhen*. Ed. Miyoshi Yukio, 225–252. Tokyo: Yūhikaku, 1981.
Satō Dōshin. *'Nihon bijutsu' tanjō: kindai Nihon 'kotoba' to senryaku*. Tokyo: Kōdansha, 1996.
Satō Haruo. *Shibun han-seiki*. Tokyo: Yomiuri shinbun-sha, 1963.
Satō Yōko. "Chōkoku-ka Rodan to Nihon ni okeru kindai no keisei." *Waseda daigaku kyōiku kenkyū sentā kiyō* 18 (2004): 31–48.
Sawa Hidehiko. *Sōseki to Torahiko*. Tokyo: Chūseki-sha, 2002.
Sawada Suketarō. *Puchito Anako*. Nagoya: Chūnichi shuppansha, 1983.
Scarry, Elaine. *On Beauty and Being Just*. Princeton, NJ: Princeton University Press, 1999.
Sekiguchi Yasuyoshi. *Tokuha'in Akutagawa Ryūnosuke: Chūgoku de nani o mita no ka*. Tokyo: Mainichi shinbunsha, 1997.
———. *Akutagawa Ryūnosuke no rekishi ninshiki*. Tokyo: Shin Nihon shuppansha, 2004.
Sekikawa, Natsuo. *Shirakaba tachi no Taishō*. Tokyo: Bungei shunjū, 2005.
Senuma, Shigeki. *Natsume Sōseki*. Tokyo: Tōdai shuppankai, 1970.
———. *Nihon bundanshi*, vol. 19. In *Shirakaba-ha no wakōdo tachi*. Tokyo: Kōdansha, 1997.
Shiga Naoya, *Shiga Naoya zenshū*, 15 vols. Tokyo: Iwanami shoten, 1973–1974.

Shimizu Shigeru. "Iida hime—'Fumizukai:' 'Hijō' no sentaku to 'ri'in' e no yume. (Mori Ogai no dansō satsuei zō: sakuchū jijbutsu kara mita sakuhin ron)." *Kokubungaku: kaishaku to kanshō* 49, no. 2 (January 1984): 31-36.

Shinbo Kunihiro. "Ogai 'Chinmoku no tō:' ichimei gaisei hika 'Pāshī' sōdō shimatsu ki." *Kōhon kindai bungaku* 25 (December 2000): 1-9.

Shinohara Yoshihiko. "Mori Ogai to Taigyaku jiken: 'Dekigoto chūshin no seken juō ki' no mondai." *Kōchi daigaku gakujutsu kenkyū hōkoku* 40 (1991): 65-81.

Shiozaki, Fumio. "Onna ga otoko wo sasou toki: *Gubijinsō* no chisei gaku (Tokushū *Gubijinsō*; *Gubijinsō* no toporojī)." *Sōseki kenkyū* 16 (October 2003): 24-36.

Smith, Sarah Cox. "The Truth about Japan: Two Articles." In *Not a Song Like Any Other*. Ed. J. Thomas Rimer, 50-73. Honolulu: University of Hawai'i Press, 2004.

Spivak, Gayatri. "Translator's Preface." In Jacques Derrida, *Of Grammatology*, ix-lxxxvii. Baltimore: The Johns Hopkins University Press, 1997.

Suda Kiyoji. "Ogai to Katai: 'Shinbi shin-setsu' wo jiku to shite." In *Kōza Mori Ogai*, vol. 1, *Ogai no hito to shūhen*. Ed. Hirakawa Sukehiro et al., 387-406. Tokyo: Shin'yōsha, 1997.

Suter, Rebecca. *Holy Ghosts: The Christian Century in Modern Japanese Fiction*. Honolulu: University of Hawai'i Press, 2015.

Suzuki Susumu. "Sono kaikō: Ogai to Harada Naojirō." *Mori Ogai no dansō satsuei zō*. *Kokubungaku: kaishaku to kanshō* 49, no. 2 (January 1984): 201-208.

Suzuki, Tomi. *Narrating the Self: Fictions of Japanese Modernity*. Stanford, CA: Stanford University Press, 1996.

Takada Mizuho. *Han shizen shugi bungaku*. Tokyo: Meiji shoin, 1963.

Takamura Kōtarō. *Bōgetsu bōjitsu: zuihitsu*. [1942] Tokyo: Ryūseikaku, 1943.

Takemori Ten'yū. "Jigoku-hen." *Hihyō to kenkyū: Akutagawa Ryūnosuke*. Ed. Inagaki Tatsurō and Itō Sei, 185-199. Tokyo: Haga shoten, 1972.

———. "Ogai sono shuppatsu (122) Horon: Harada Naojirō kara no shōsha: 'Utakata no ki' wo megutte (26)." *Kokubungaku: kaishaku to kanshō* 71, no. 5 (May 2006): 198-206.

Takemura Tamio. "Kagaku to geijutsu no aida: Ikeda Kikunae to Natsume Sōseki no ba'ai." *Natsume Sōseki*, vol. 1, *Sōseki no hito to shūhen*. Ed. Miyoshi Yukio, 265-287. Tokyo: Yūhikaku, 1981.

Taki Kōji. *Tennō no shōzō*. Tokyo: Iwanami shoten, 1988.

Tanaka Yūsuke. "Shikō yōshiki to shite no Taishō kyōyō shugi: Karaki Junzō ni yoru Abe Jirō no hihan no saikentō wo tsūjite." *Ajia bunka kenkyū*, no.30 (2004): 51-69.

Tanizaki Jun'ichirō. "Jōzetsu-roku." (shō) [1927] In *Gendai nihon bungaku ronsōshi: jō*. Ed. Hirano Ken et al., 219-225. Tokyo: Miraisha, 2006.

Tayama Katai. "Rokotsu naru byōsha." [1904] In *Kindai bungaku hyōron taikei*, vol. 2. Ed. Inagaki Tatsurō and Satō Masaru, 360-363. Tokyo: Kadokawa shoten, 1972.

Toyama Masakazu. "Nihon kaiga no mirai." [1890] In *Meiji bungaku shū*, vol. 79, *Meiji geijutsu-bungaku ronshū*, ed. Hijikata Teiichi, 149-164. Tokyo: Chikuma shobō, 1975.

Treat, John Whittier. *The Rise and Fall of Modern Japanese Literature*. Chicago: University of Chicago Press, 2018.

Tsubouchi Shōyō. *The Essence of the Novel*. Trans. Nanette Twine. 1971-1972. Accessed May 1, 2023, https://archive.nyu.edu/html/2451/14945/shoyo.htm#electronic.

———. *Shōsetsu shinzui*. [1885-1886] In *Meiji bungaku zenshū*, vol. 16. *Tsubouchi Shōyō shū*. Ed. Inagaki Tatsurō, 3-58. Tokyo: Chikuma shobō, 1969

———. "Yuriwaka densetsu no hongen." [1906] In *Shōyō senshū*, vol. 11, 824–833. Tokyo: Shun'yōdō, 1927.
Tsuchiya Michio. *Kokugo mondai ronsōshi*. Tokyo: Tamagawa daigaku shuppan-bu, 2005.
Tsuruta, Kin'ya. "Sōseki's *Kusamakura*: A Journey to 'The Other Side.'" *The Journal of the Association of Teachers of Japanese* 22, no. 2 (November 1988): 169–188.
Turney, Alan. "A Feeling of Beauty: Natsume Sōseki's Ichiya." *Monumenta Nipponica* 33, no. 3 (Autumn 1978): 285–288.
Tyler, William. "Anti-Naturalism: Illuminating the Spectacle." In *Modanizumu: Modernist Fiction from Japan, 1913-1918*. Ed. William Tyler, 49–65. Honolulu: University of Hawai'i Press, 2008.
Ueda, Atsuko. "Bungakuron and 'Literature' in the Making." *Japan Forum* 20, no. 1 (2008): 25–46.
———. *Concealment of Politics, Politics of Concealment: The Production of 'Literature' in Meiji Japan*. Princeton, NJ: Princeton University Press, 2005.
Ueda, Makoto. *Modern Japanese Writers*. Stanford, CA: Stanford University Press, 1976.
Ueki Satoshi. *Shin-setsu Ogai no koibito erisu*. Tokyo: Shinchōsha, 2000.
Uno Koji. "'Watakushi shōsetsu' shiken." [1925] In *Kindai bungaku hyōron taikei*, vol. 6. Ed. Miyoshi Yukio and Sofue Shōji, 61–66. Tokyo: Kadokawa shoten, 1973.
Uozumi Setsuro. "Onken-naru jiyū shisōka." [1910] In *Gendai Nihon bungaku taikei*, vol. 40, 9–11. Tokyo: Chikuma shobō, 1973.
Uozumi Takashi. "Kyōyō shugi." In *Nihon shisōshi jiten*. Ed. Koyasu Nobukuni et al., 126–127. Tokyo: Perikansha, 2001.
Usui Yoshimi, ed. *Kindai bungaku ronsō: jō*. Tokyo: Chikuma shobō, 1975.
Viéville, Dominique. *Rodin, le Rêve Japonais*. Paris: Flammarion, 2007.
Wada Toshio. *Meiji bungei'in shimatsu-ki*. Tokyo: Chikuma shobō, 1989.
Walker, Nicholas. "Introduction." In Immanuel Kant, *Critique of Judgement*, vii–xxvii. Oxford: Oxford University Press, 2007.
Wang, W. Michelle. *Eternalized Fragments: Reclaiming Aesthetics in Contemporary World Fiction*. Columbus: The Ohio State University Press, 2020.
Yafen, Qiu. *Akutagawa Ryūnosuke no Chūgoku: shinwa to genjitsu*. Fukuoka-shi: Hana shoin, 2010.
Yamamoto Masahide. *Genbun itchi no rekishi ronkō*. Tokyo: Ofūsha, 1971.
———. *Genbun itchi no rekishi ronkō: zoku-hen*. Tokyo: Ofūsha, 1981.
Yamashita Tsuneo. *Nihonjin no 'kokoro' to shinrigaku no mondai*. Tokyo: Gendai shokan, 2004.
Yanagi Muneyoshi. *Yanagi Muneyoshi zenshū*. 25 vols. Tokyo: Chikuma shobō, 1981–1992.
Yiu, Angela. "Atarashikimura: The Intellectual and Literary Contexts of a Taishō Utopian Village." *Japan Review*, no. 20 (2008): 203–230.
Yoda, Tomiko. "First-Person Narration and Citizen-Subject: The Modernity of Mori Ogai's 'Dancing Girl.'" *The Journal of Asian Studies* 65, no. 2 (May 2006): 277–306.
Yoon Sang In. *Seikimatsu to Sōseki*. Tokyo: Iwanami shoten, 1994.
Yoshida Seiichi. *Yoshida Seiichi chosakushū*, vol. 2, *Akutagawa Ryūnosuke kenkyū II*. Tokyo: Ōfūsha, 1981.
Yoshikawa Yūsuke. "Hanako wo mono ni suruno wa dare?" In *Mori Ogai ronshū: Kare-yori hajimaru*. Ed. Sakai Satoshi and Hara Kunito, 107–139. Tokyo: Shintensha, 2004.

Index

Abe Jirō, 167
Adorno, Theodor, 21–24, 107, 151, 225
Aesthetes (*yuibi-ha* or *tanbi-ha*), 5, 33, 137, 182
Aestheticism (*yuibi shugi*) group, 4–6
aesthetics, 9–10, 21–23, 33, 84, 172, 231; academic works on, 240n35; defined, 10; logical aporia in, 28; Newmann on, 23; Ogai's literary, 131; private vs. shared, 107; Sōseki's commitment to, 31; "unhuman," 58, 62; worldly concerns vs., 34, 66, 112, 151, 185
Ainsworth, William Harrison, 46
Akagi Kōhei, 142
Akutagawa Ryūnosuke, 1–2, 4–6, 25, 33–34, 231–232; "Aru aho no isshō" by, 205–208, 229; *Bungei-teki na* by, 1, 178, 186, 190, 223–226, 237n1; "Butōkai" by, 209–212; in China, 194; compared to previous writers, 177–178; cosmopolitanism of, 25, 33, 206, 209, 216, 219, 225; "Daidōji Shinsuke" by, 203–204, 225; Enlightenment-era stories by, 209–214, 216; on European art or literature, 226–229; "Gesaku zanmai" by, 186–190, 196; "Haguruma" by, 208; inspirations for, 182, 189, 191, 206; on Japanese literary world, 4–6, 33; "Jigoku-hen" by, 191–194, 226; "Kaika no otto" by, 212–215; "Kamigami no bishō" by, 216–217, 219–220, 227; "Kokuhaku" by, 200–201; "Kōsei" by, 187; on language reforms, 179–180; literary anxieties of, 177, 180–181, 186; modernism of, 200; "Mukashi" by, 188; Muromachi-era stories by, 216–217, 219–220; Mushanokōji and, 149, 178, 179; "Nagasaki shōhin" by, 221; on novels, 1–2, 200–201, 223–224; other works by, 199, 222–223, 226, 229; painters or paintings in work by, 189, 191, 193, 199, 205–207, 214, 219, 223; pen names of, 257n8; on "poetic spirit," 34, 223–225; portrait of, 197–198, 201; "Rashōmon" by, 182; "Saigō Takamori" by, 183–184; self-assessments of, 182, 187, 189–190, 199; Shiga and, 178–179, 185–186, 229; "Shūzanzu" by, 194–195; suicide of, 30, 34, 178, 182, 185, 191; Yasukichi stories by, 198, 201–203; "Yume" by, 195, 226

[271]

INDEX

Anker, Elizabeth S., 13–14
Arishima Ikuma, 134, 155, 162, 167, 169, 255n72
Arishima Takeo, 127, 134, 142–143, 175–176
art, 18–24, 131, 229, 240n48; language vs., 55, 67–68, 154–155, 161, 181, 226. *See also* paintings; visual arts
art schools, 18, 89, 93–94, 112, 121
Asahi, Tokyo or *Osaka*, 67, 98, 100, 132, 238n15, 244n56, 245n65; employees of, 66, 141
Asai Chū, 15, 40, 89
Atarashiki Mura, 173–176
Azuma Hiroki, 234

Bansho Shirabe Dokoro, 17
Baudelaire, Charles, 113, 118, 206, 250n74
beauty, 4–5, 30, 34, 234, 254n64; Aesthetes' attraction to, 182; of art, 12, 20, 65, 152, 156, 160, 194, 226–227; comfort provided by, 49–50, 54, 82, 107; external, 104; as goal, 5, 12; "inner flame" of, 113, 114, 223; inspirational, 95, 107, 160; Japanese terms for, 10–11; of literature, 12–14, 35, 185, 226; of objects, 27–29, 106; subjective (or not), 8–10, 51, 152; sublime, 12–13, 20, 227; universality of, 9–10, 28, 51–52, 107, 113, 152, 160
Benjamin, Walter, 167
Bernard, Claude, 86, 246n8
Bowring, Richard, 247n27
Buddhists or Buddhism, 11, 55, 57, 61, 100–102, 217, 222, 227; in Akutagawa story, 191–193

censorship, 124–125, 128–130, 132, 135–136, 152, 250n79, 251n87
Cezanne, Paul, 161, 163–165, 207, 224, 254nn67–68
Cheeke, Stephen, 16–17
Chiossone, Edoardo, 18
China, 26, 91, 138, 185, 194, 217; paintings or *shoga* from, 19, 194; trade with, 221

Chinese: characters or writing, 138, 217; classics in, 37, 52–53, 55, 243n45; poetry in, 16, 52–53, 55, 63; texts in, 182, 208; Taoist lore in, 243n45; vernacular fiction in, 188
Christians, 216–217, 219, 221, 227, 259n59
Chūō kōron magazine, 47, 162, 251n90
cosmopolitanism, 20, 25, 33, 156, 206, 209, 216, 219, 225
Crary, Jonathan, 53–54
criticism, 13–14, 232–233
Cubism, 166, 199

Dadaism, 166, 199, 227
da Vinci, Leonardo, 72, 79
decadence, 4–6, 14, 29, 30, 33, 136
Decadents (*kyōraku-ha*), 137
deconstructivism, 13, 180, 181
Delaroche, Paul, 46
Derrida, Jacques, 96, 114, 180–181
dreams, 50, 75–76, 196, 227; Ogai and, 96–97, 105–106, 110–111

Ebii Eiji, 82, 244n59
Eguchi Kan, 142
ekphrasis, 16–17, 20; Akutagawa's use of, 193–194, 197, 219; Mushanokōji's circumvention of, 161, 164; Ogai's use of, 94, 104, 118–119; Sōseki's allusions to 64, 77
emotions, 50, 55; in Akutagawa's works, 188, 202, 205, 206, 208; distanced, 43, 47, 56, 144, 202; inspired by art, 166; soaring, 12–13; in Ogai's works, 97, 111; in Mushanokōji's works, 178; in Sōseki's works, 37, 41, 63, 67, 76, 201, 223

Felski, Rita, 13–14
feminists, 13, 137
Fenollosa, Ernest, 19–20, 42, 89, 93–94, 240–241n50, 246n16
Foucauldian New Historicism, 13
Freud, Sigmund, 96, 105, 110–111, 249n60

[272]

INDEX

Fujishima Takeji, 16
Fumon Gyō, 199
Futabatei Shimei, 87, 238n8
Futurists, 199–200

Gagaku-kyoku, 17
Gauguin, Paul, 161, 164, 166, 168, 195–196, 254n67, 255n70
gaze, 68, 70, 88, 90, 94, 114, 209
genbun itchi, 4, 8, 91–92, 108, 110, 134, 138, 179–180
gesaku, 186. *See also* Akutagawa Ryūnosuke: "Gesaku zanmai"
Goethe, Johann Wolfgang, 206
Golley, Gregory, 239n28, 250n69
Goseda clan, 214
Goseda Hōryū, 17
Gottschall, Rudolf von, 85, 91, 101, 246n9
Great Treason Incident, 27, 127–128, 130, 133, 135, 136, 137, 152
Greek mythology, 226–227
Greuze, Jean Baptiste, 68–69
Guillory, John, 232–233

Haga Tōru, 101–102
haiku, 39–43, 54, 59, 63
haiku-novels, 35, 45, 50, 54, 64, 66, 76, 205
Hamao Arata, 93
Han Feizi, 208
Hanako (Ota Hisa), 114–115, 250n72
Hara Takashi, 89
Harada Naojirō, 89, 93–94, 97, 108, 109, 123, 247n24, 248n33, 249n49; *Kiryū Kannon* by, 98–103
Harootunian, H. D., 238n9
Hartmann, Eduard von, 83, 84, 97, 103, 108, 129, 248n43, 248n47; terminology of, 100–101
Hasegawa Tenkei, 4, 124–125
Hearn, Lafcadio, 220
Hind, C. Lewis, 164–166, 254nn63–64, 254nn67–68, 255nn69–71
Hiraide Shū, 127–128, 132, 136, 137, 251n87
Hirasawa Chūji, 171, 255n82

Hirayama Mikiko, 90
Hirotsu Kazuo, 175, 182
Honda Shūgo, 140
honkaku shōsetsu, 200
Hori Tatsuo, 182, 257n9
Horikiri Masato, 122
Huang Yifeng, 194–195, 258n29
humanities, 230–232
Hurley, Brian, 8, 239n22

Ibsen, Henrik, 44, 132, 206
Ichijō Narumi, 16
Iida Hatanoki, 210
Ikawa Kyō, 206
Ikeda Kikunae, 78
Ikuta Chōkō, 142
illustrations, 15, 86–88, 108
Imamura Yasutarō, 128–129
Impressionists, 163, 165
Individuation, 53–54
I-novels, 4, 6–7, 200–201, 208, 258n36
interiority, 3, 8–9, 12–13, 19, 114, 163
Ishihara Chiaki, 67
Ishikawa Takuboku, 141
Itō Jakuchū, 55
Iwano Hōmei, 138
Iwaya Sazanami, 128
Izawa Shūji, 89

Japanese, self-images as, 25, 34, 38, 90, 118, 156–157, 171, 217–219, 227

Kagioka Masanori, 249n49
Kaizō magazine, 180, 194, 205, 237n1, 259n62
Kanbayashi Tsunemichi, 19
kanbun, 46, 138
Kandinsky, Wassily, 224
Kaneko Chikusui, 128
Kannon, 98–102, 222
Kant, Immanuel, 10, 11, 21, 28–29, 51, 152
Karaki Junzō, 241n70
Karatani Kōjin, 3, 66, 203, 233–234
Katsushika Hokusai, 58, 171
Kawahigashi Hekigotō, 41
Keene, Donald, 2, 238n8

[273]

INDEX

Kermode, Frank, 24
Kikuchi Kan, 186
Kinoshita Mokutarō, 6, 15, 135, 162–164, 169
Kinoshita Naoyuki, 18
Kinoshita Shūichirō, 199
Kishida Ryūsei, 162, 134, 199
Kitagwa Utamaro, 171
Kitahara Hakushū, 15
Kitamura Tōkoku, 3
Klinger, Paul, 168
Kobori Kei'ichirō, 85
Kōbu Bijutsu Gakkō. *See* art schools
Kojima Kikuo, 162, 168
Kojima Masajirō (Nakatani Chōzō), 191, 257n25
Kokumin no tomo, 86, 245n3, 247n31
Komiya Toyotaka, 47
Komori Yōichi, 80
Konjaku monogatari, 182, 191
Korea or Koreans, 26, 213–214, 221, 234
Kōri Torahiko, 171, 255n82
Kōsen Shōton, 55
Kōtoku Shūsui, 135
Koyama Keita, 78
Koyama Shōtarō, 15
Kume Keiichirō, 16, 112
Kume Masao, 200, 205
Kunikida Doppo, 85, 126, 153, 253n36
Kuroda Seiki, 16, 103
Kyokutei Bakin, 186–190, 196, 257n17

language reforms, 91, 138, 179–180. *See also* genbun itchi
Latour, Bruno, 13–14
Lessing, Gotthold Ephraim, 42, 55, 65, 76
Lippit, Akira Mizuta, 114, 250n69
Lippit, Seiji, 8, 200, 207, 237n4, 241n70
literary criticism, 85, 232–233
literature: aesthetic dimensions of, 2–3, 9, 12–14; anxieties about, 1, 177, 180–181, 232–233; as art, 1–2, 16, 183; binary view of, 13–14; contexts and, 2–3, 9, 12–14, 16, 24; history vs., 184–185; modern, 2, 14, 19, 24, 111, 181; as sanctuary, 3; valued (or not), 233–234
Loti, Pierre, 209–212

Manet, Eduard, 163, 165, 254n68
Maruyama Masao, 6–7
Marxists or Marxism, 13, 30, 37, 182
Masaoka Shiki, 46; literary views of, 39–40; *shasei* concept of, 31, 40–43, 199; Sōseki and, 31, 35–36, 38, 39, 54, 82, 199
Matisse, Henri, 164, 166, 228–229, 255n71
Matsuo Bashō, 59
Matsuoka Eikyū, 55, 243n48
Matsuoka Hisashi, 98
Max, Gabriel von, 101, 102–103
Meiji Bijutsu-kai, 89, 97–98
Merode, Cleo de, 115
Millais, John Everett, 59–61, 68
Mita bungaku magazine, 6, 133, 135, 136, 251n1
Miyamoto Kenji, 182
Miya Yoshihei, 119–120, 122
Miyoshi Yukio, 141
Mizumura Minae, 79, 232
modernism, 8, 55, 200
modernity, 6, 9, 79, 169; individuation and, 53, 65, 82; Japanese, 24–26, 53, 73, 163, 177, 208–210, 212, 216, 220; literary, 15
Mori Junzaburō, 248n34
Mori Ogai, 1, 6, 25, 27, 32, 34, 177, 180, 231–232; art commentaries by, 89–90, 97, 100–104; beauty as theme for, 108, 113, 223; binarism of, 84, 85, 97, 101, 234; as biographer, 84; career phases of, 84–85; censorship and, 128–130, 132–133, 135–136, 250n79; as doctor, 32, 83–84, 108, 162, 233; dreams in works by, 96–97, 105–106, 110–111; ekphrasis used by, 94, 104, 119; "Fumizukai" by, 104–109, 111; German-trilogy stories by, 32, 84, 91–96, 104–108, 111, 248n34; "Hanako" by, 112–115, 117–118, 121, 168; on

[274]

"inner flame," 113–114, 223; on "Kochō" controversy, 86, 88–89; literary ethos of, 110–112, 126–127; "Maihime" by, 91–97, 247n31; "Maihime debates" and, 247n31; Naturalism and, 85, 102, 111–112, 125–126, 131, 135, 238n15; other works by, 110–111; personal life of, 92–93, 108; as philosopher, 32, 83–84, 101, 250n74; *Shigarami zōshi* and, 90–91, 100, 101, 246n4; Shirakaba writers and, 135–137, 152–153; "Shōsetsuron" by, 85–86, 91, 102–103, 126, 246n9; styles used by, 91, 104, 108; "Tenchō" by, 119, 121–124; Toyama Masakazu and, 97–100; as translator, 84, 101, 108, 250n80, 254n56; "Tsuina" by, 110–112; *Vita Sexualis* by, 125–126, 250n79

Morita Sōhei, 142

Mortimer, Maya, 156

Mozume Takami, 91–92

Murphy, Joseph A., 46, 233–234

Mushanokōji Saneatsu, 1–2, 23, 146, 152, 199, 231–232; Akutagawa on, 5, 149, 178, 179, 186; Arishima Takeo and, 142–143, 175–176; artistic ideals of, 164; background or personal life of, 34, 140, 141; commune founded by, 173–176; cosmopolitanism of, 20, 156; criticism of, 142; death of, 176; humanism of, 142–144, 157–161; "indifferent," 144; language or style of, 138–139, 143, 150, 178, 179, 253n50; *Momoiro no heya* by, 149–152; on nation or nationalism, 156–160; on Nogi Maresuke, 156–157; *Omedetaki hito* by, 139–142, 175; self-assessment by, 144, 152, 155, 160; Shiga and, 136, 155, 174–175; as Shirakaba writer, 1, 20, 30, 33, 134, 136–137; Sōseki and, 153–154; Tolstoy and, 143, 151, 252n22; van Gogh poem by, 161; Western artists and, 161, 164, 169–172; Yamawaki Shintoku and, 162–163

Nagahara Shisui, 15

Nagai Kafū, 4, 6, 135, 169

Nagayo Yoshirō, 134, 174

Nakamura Fusetsu, 40

Nakamura Giichi, 163, 248n40

Nakamura Mitsuo, 2, 7

Nakamura Murao, 200

Nakatani Chōzō (Kojima Masajirō), 191, 257n25

Nakayama Akihiko, 88

Natsume Sōseki, 1–2, 6, 27, 31–32, 139, 177, 180, 205, 209, 231–232; Akutagawa and, 179–180, 201, 223, 256n3; authorial codas by, 46, 49; beauty as theme for, 35–36, 47, 49–50, 55–56, 58, 63, 66, 75–76; *Bungakuron* by, 22, 31, 36–38, 41, 45–46, 62, 70, 76–77, 201, 232, 242n2; on Chinese classics, 37, 52, 53, 55; cross-cultural awareness of, 25, 73; early literary thought of, 36, 40; *Eijitsu shōhin* by, 82; in England, 36–39, 59, 73–74, 78; on external motivation, 27; F+f equation of, 37, 41, 63, 77, 221, 223, 234; *Garasudo no naka* by, 82; *Keitō* preface by, 43–44, 243n26; *Kokoro* by, 156–157; *Kusamakura* by, 31, 35–36, 42, 45, 47, 49–58, 63–68, 70, 76–77, 79, 144, 148, 202, 242n1, 243–244n48; Naturalism and, 6, 79, 238n15; pessimism of, 38–39, 73, 153; plots or storylines of, 35, 43, 47, 50, 55, 66, 82; "Rondon tō" by, 36, 45–46, 49, 242n3; *Sanshirō* by, 31, 35–36, 65–68, 70–82, 146, 244n56, 244n59; on scientific thought, 36, 41–42, 77–80; *shasei*-inspired views of, 31, 35, 43, 45, 48–49, 66, 199, 224; Shiki and (*see under* Shiki); Shirakaba writers and, 6, 82, 136, 152–154; *Sorekara* by, 82, 153–154; speeches by, 73, 79–80, 82; trains in works by, 62–63, 65, 70–72, 146; *Wagahai wa neko de aru* by, 39, 43, 47; *Yōkyo shū* by, 45–47

INDEX

Naturalism or Naturalists, 2–3, 12, 32–33, 74, 142, 238nn14–15, 250n80; Akutagawa on, 4–5; autobiographical focus of, 136, 153, 187, 199; censored, 124–125, 128; darker themes of, 137, 142; French, 85, 102; government view of, 125; Japanese, 85, 111, 112, 125, 199, 253n35; Ogai and, 6, 32, 85, 102, 125–127, 131, 135–136, 238n15; reactions to, 5–8, 125, 135–136; realism of, 182, 187; "Romantic," 77, 79
Naumann, Edmund, 90
Neo-Confucianism, 83
New Realism (*shin genjitsu-ha*) group, 5, 33
New Technical Finesse (*shin gikō-ha*) group, 5, 33
Newmann, Barnett, 23
Ngai, Sianne, 149
Nietzsche, Friedrich, 29, 132, 142
Niizeki Kimiko, 93–94, 108
Nogi Maresuke, 156–157
Noh, 59
novels: Akutagawa on, 1–2, 200–201, 223–224; as art, 20; authentic (*honkaku shōsetsu*), 200; experimental, 8; as genre, 24; Kume Masao on, 200; language used in, 110; modern, 3, 4, 56, 238n8; modernist, 8; of *mukōgawa*, 53; Nakamura Murao on, 7, 200; Naturalist, 111; Ogai on, 83, 85–86, 111, 119, 130; popular, 52; reading of, 56; self-confessional (*shishōsetsu*), 238n9; in Shirakaba style, 139; Shōyō on, 20; Sōseki on, 43, 50, 72, 205, 234; storylines of, 43, 82; writing of, 1–2, 185, 190. *See also* haiku-novels; I-novels
nudity, 61, 86–88, 113, 117, 196

Oana Ryūichi, 189, 198, 201, 207
Ochi Haruo, 244n59
Odin, Steve, 10–11, 55, 243–244n48, 244n54
Ogimachi Kinkazu, 136, 147–149
Ogiwara Rokuzan, 112
Okakura Kakuzō, 219
Okakura Tenshin, 89, 93–94, 98
Omuka Toshiharu, 19
Omura Seigai, 101
Orientalism, 113, 209
Ozaki Kōyō, 52, 87

paintings: Chinese, 16, 19, 194; completed (or not), 63–65, 197; discourses of, 68, 89; ink, 55, 61, 89; Japanese, 89–90, 98, 100; in literature, 17, 46, 51, 55, 57, 59, 61, 63–65, 67, 68, 77, 197, 214–215; *nihonga*, 19, 86, 98; novels vs., 190; nude, 61, 196; oil, 17–18, 89, 100; poetry and, 16–17, 20, 40–42, 54, 76, 207; portraits, 17–18, 64–65, 67, 68, 77, 102, 171, 197, 198, 199, 214–215; Post-Impressionist (*see* Post-Impressionists); realist or realistic, 17, 40–41; religious, 98, 102; Romantic, 63; Toyama-Ogai debate on, 98, 100–101, 103; Western, 3, 17–19, 32, 46, 59, 61, 63, 68, 100, 199–200; *yōga* or Western-style, 18–19, 40, 89, 98 (*see also yōga* painters)
Pan no kai salon, 6
Parsis, 129–130
People's Rights Movement, 3, 26
photographs, 17–18, 74, 115, 154, 171, 172, 226
Picasso, Pablo, 228–229
Plato, 16, 17, 20, 29
plays, 59, 83, 91, 111, 119, 221; *Momoiro no heya*, 149–152
poetry, 36, 128; Chinese, 16, 52–53, 55, 63; Goethe's, 206–207; Kakinomoto Hitomaro's, 217; Lessing on, 42; painting and, 16–17, 20, 40–42, 54, 76, 207; Shiki on charm of, 39–40; temporal aspect of, 42, 76; Western, 52, 65
Post-Impressionists, 32, 154, 160, 199, 206, 254n63, 254n67; in Akutagawa's story, 195; Kinoshita Mokutarō on,

[276]

INDEX

162–163, 169; Yanagi Shintoku on, 164–166
psychoanalysis, 13, 96, 114

Qiu Yafen, 258n30

realism, 7, 49, 63, 101–102, 110, 250n69; fantasy and, 102, 188; literary, 178; Maruyama Masao on, 6; modern, 82; Naturalist, 2, 5, 32, 33, 135, 136, 182, 187; psychological, 12, 15, 85; Shiga's, 175, 178; Shōyō's, 12, 15, 42, 85; visual, 17–19, 40–41, 224, 255n71
Redon, Odilon, 227
Renard, Jules, 223–224
Rodin, Auguste, 29, 161, 255n77; bronzes sent by, 171–174, 255n83; influence of, 112; Mushanokōji on, 169–170; in Ogai's "Hanako," 112–118, 168; Shirakaba writers and, 155, 168, 170; Yanagi Muneyoshi on, 171, 255n83. *See also* Shirakaba magazine: Rodin issue
Roka, Tokutomi, 52
Rokumeikan era, 209–211
Romanticists, 3, 135–136
Russian Revolution, 173, 200
Russo-Japanese War, 26, 44, 57, 65, 73, 108

Sada Yakko, 115
Sadoya Shigenobu, 55
Saigō Takamori, 183–184, 257n13
Sakai Hiroki, 259n59
Satō Haruo, 125, 179, 248n34
Satomi Ton, 134
Scarry, Elaine, 11
Schnitzler, Arthur, 111
Schopenhauer, Arthur, 29, 83
Seinan War, 183–184
"self-cultivation," 29–30, 137–138, 167, 241n70
Shakespeare, 46, 60
shasei, 35, 199, 224; Fusetsu on, 40; Harada on, 103; Shiki's concept of, 31, 40–43; Sōseki on, 43, 45, 48–49, 54, 66

Shiba Kōkan, 221, 222
Shiga Naoya, 136, 152, 176, 251n4, 252n14; "Abashiri made" by, 145–148, 252n23; Akutagawa and, 177–179, 185, 224, 229; *An'ya kōro* by, 147; language style of, 138, 179; Mushanokōji and, 174–175; on Nogi Maresuke, 157; introduction of Rodin to his peers by, 168, 255n77; as Shirakaba writer, 33, 134, 145, 167, 175, 177–178
Shima Kakoku, 17
Shimamura Hōgetsu, 112
Shimazaki Tōson, 126, 152–153, 253n35
Shin shōsetsu magazine, 15, 142, 200, 217
Shin-shichō magazine, 135, 251n2
Shinto, 220
Shirai Uzan, 112
Shirakaba group of writers, 9, 14, 16, 32–34, 82, 127, 182, 232; artistic philosophies of, 172–173, 176, 179, 226, 234–235; on the Atarashiki Mura commune, 173–176; backgrounds of, 32, 134, 140–141; cosmopolitanism of, 25; criticism of, 30, 141–143; defined, 134; in early period, 32, 135–137, 152, 166; idealism of, 5, 6, 23; individuality celebrated by, 137, 199; influence of, 137, 142, 178; members of, 134, 255n82; style of, 134, 138–139; Western art and, 30, 32, 112, 154–155, 161–164, 166, 167–172
Shirakaba magazine, 1, 20, 30, 134–135; art or photographs in, 160–161, 166–168, 206; dates of, 134, 137; ethos of, 136–137; geopolitical context for, 137–138; inaugural issue of, 145, 147, 153; Mushanokōji works in, 143, 149, 152–153, 157, 159–160; persona of artists as theme in, 160–161; Rodin issue of, 112, 168–172, 255n77
Shōsetsu shinzui, 3, 12, 15, 19–20, 42, 85, 221, 237nn6-7, 239nn29-31
Sino-Japanese War, 26, 108, 124

[277]

INDEX

socialists, 127–128, 132, 137, 173; censored, 125, 128; executed, 27, 135; ideas of, 30, 124, 128, 176, 175–176, 189, 200; political party of, 124
Sōhei, Morita, 47
soldiers, 57, 157–158
Spivak, Gayatri, 181
Subaru magazine, 6, 128, 135, 136, 248n34, 250n79
subjectivity, 4, 6–9, 12, 84, 181, 207–208; for Akutagawa, 181, 200, 207, 208; for Ogai, 97; for Shirakaba writers, 135, 140, 143–144; for Sōseki, 43, 63
Surrealism, 227
Su Shih, 16
Suzuki Miekichi, 33
Suzuki, Tomi, 4, 238n8, 258n36

Taiwan or Taiwanese, 26, 159–160
Taiyō magazine, 125, 129, 251n87
Takada Mizuho, 6, 238n15
Takahama Kyoshi, 43–44
Takahashi Yuichi, 17–18, 93
Takamura Kōtarō, 112, 169, 199
Takase Toshio, 210
Tanizaki Jun'ichirō, 223
Tayama Katai, 4, 85, 126, 199, 238n14, 250n80
technology, 25, 63, 79–80, 91, 114
Terada Torahiko, 78
Tokuda Shūsei, 152, 253n35
Tokyo Bijutsu Gakkō. *See* art schools
Tolstoy, Leo, 142, 143, 151, 178, 252n22
Tōsei shosei katagi, 15
Toyama Masakazu, 89, 97–98, 100, 248n40
trains, 62–63, 65, 70–72, 145–146, 183–184, 211
Treat, John Whittier, 2, 237n2
truth, 50, 163, 183, 225; of art and literature, 19, 22–23, 63, 195, 225; historical, 185; for Naturalists, 4, 5, 126; scientific, 63, 79, 86, 102
truth content, 22–23, 225
Tsubouchi Shōyō, 3, 12, 15, 19–20, 42, 85, 221

Tsuchida Bakusen, 227
Tsuruta, Kin'ya, 53–54, 60
Turner, J. M. W., 63, 64
Turney, Alan, 47
Tyler, William J., 8

Uchida Kuichi, 17–18
Uchida Roan, 238n8
Ueda, Atsuko, 3
Ueda Bin, 33, 126
Ugolini, Giuseppe, 18
ukiyo-e, 171–172
Umehara Ryūzaburō, 167, 255n72
Uno Kōji, 139, 179
Uozumi Setsuro, 132
Utagawa Hiroshige, 58–59, 171

van Gogh, Vincent, 155, 157, 161–164, 166, 206, 254n67, 255n69; Mushanokōji's poem on, 161
visual arts: Akutagawa's interest in, 177, 189, 223, 225–226, 229; developments in, 14–16, 55, 89–90, 102, 166, 199; literature compared to, 19–20, 40–42, 76–77, 82, 103, 119, 161, 177, 181, 190, 193, 225–226, 229; Ogai's interest in, 89, 126; Shirakaba group's interest in, 154, 160–161; Sōseki's interest in, 46, 59–60, 63, 68
Volkelt, Johannes, 250n80

watakushi shōsetsu, 200. *See also* I-novels
Watanabe Kazan, 189
Watanabe Seitei, 86–88
Watsuji Tetsurō, 138, 142
Watteau, Jean-Antoine, 210
women: in Akutagawa's works, 192–193, 195–197, 210–212, 214–215; depicted in artworks, 68, 86, 102–103, 115, 119, 196, 221–222; femme fatale trope of, 215; in Ogai's works, 95–97, 104–107, 113–118; for Shirakaba writers, 139–140, 145–148; in Sōseki's works, 48–49, 59–60, 65, 68, 70–71, 75–76, 80–81
World War I, 137–138, 158–159, 208

INDEX

Yamada Bimyō, 86–88
Yamagata Aritomo, 124, 128, 132
Yamaji Aizan, 128
Yamamoto Masahide, 108, 110, 138
Yamamoto Take, 102, 249n49
Yamawaki Shintoku, 162–163
Yanagi Muneyoshi, 134, 162, 164–166, 170–172, 174, 255n83
yōga painters, 153, 189; as characters, 50, 54–63, 144, 195, 214; collaborate with writers, 15–16, 108–109; discourse on, 31; Fenollosa on, 19; influence writers, 31, 40, 101, 163, 198–199; organizations for, 89; subjects for, 98
Yomiuri, 43, 85, 88
Yosano Buson, 59
Yosano Hiroshi (Tekkan), 15, 128, 135, 248n34
Yuriwaka, 221, 259n59

Zola, Emile, 85–86, 102, 126

STUDIES OF THE WEATHERHEAD EAST ASIAN INSTITUTE
COLUMBIA UNIVERSITY

The Studies of the Weatherhead East Asian Institute of Columbia University were inaugurated in 1962 to bring to a wider public the results of significant new research on modern and contemporary East Asia.

Selected Titles

(Complete list at: weai.columbia.edu/content/publications)

Building a Republican Nation in Vietnam, 1920-1963, edited by Nu-Anh Tran and Tuong Vu. University of Hawai`i Press, 2022.

China Urbanizing: Impacts and Transitions, edited by Weiping Wu and Qin Gao. University of Pennsylvania Press, 2022.

Common Ground: Tibetan Buddhist Expansion and Qing China's Inner Asia, by Lan Wu. Columbia University Press, 2022.

Narratives of Civic Duty: How National Stories Shape Democracy in Asia, by Aram Hur. Cornell University Press, 2022.

The Concrete Plateau: Urban Tibetans and the Chinese Civilizing Machine, by Andrew Grant. Cornell University Press, 2022.

Confluence and Conflict: Reading Transwar Japanese Literature and Thought, by Brian Hurley. Harvard East Asian Monographs, 2022.

Inglorious, Illegal Bastards: Japan's Self-Defense Force During the Cold War, by Aaron Skabelund. Cornell University Press, 2022.

Madness in the Family: Women Care, and Illness in Japan, by H. Yumi Kim. Oxford University Press, 2022.

Uncertainty in the Empire of Routine: The Administrative Revolution of the Eighteenth-Century Qing State, by Maura Dykstra. Harvard University Press, 2022.

Outsourcing Repression: Everyday State Power in Contemporary China, by Lynette H. Ong. Oxford University Press, 2022.

Diasporic Cold Warriors: Nationalist China, Anticommunism, and the Philippine Chinese, 1930s–1970s, by Chien-Wen Kung. Cornell University Press, 2022.

Dream Super-Express: A Cultural History of the World's First Bullet Train, by Jessamyn Abel. Stanford University Press, 2022.

The Sound of Salvation: Voice, Gender, and the Sufi Mediascape in China, by Guangtian Ha. Columbia University Press, 2022.

Carbon Technocracy: Energy Regimes in Modern East Asia, by Victor Seow. The University of Chicago Press, 2022.

Disunion: Anticommunist Nationalism and the Making of the Republic of Vietnam, by Nu-Anh Tran. University of Hawai`i Press, 2022.

Learning to Rule: Court Education and the Remaking of the Qing State, 1861–1912, by Daniel Barish. Columbia University Press, 2022.

Art Across Borders: Japanese Artists in the United States Before World War II, by Ramona Handel-Bajema. Merwin Asia, 2021.

GPSR Authorized Representative: Easy Access System Europe, Mustamäe tee 50, 10621 Tallinn, Estonia, gpsr.requests@easproject.com

www.ingramcontent.com/pod-product-compliance
Lightning Source LLC
Chambersburg PA
CBHW031235290426
44109CB00012B/302